JUVENILE DELINQUENCY:
CONCEPTS AND CONTROL

JUVENILE

DELINQUENCY

CONCEPTS AND CONTROL

ROBERT C. TROJANOWICZ
School of Criminal Justice
Michigan State University

PRENTICE-HALL, INC., *Englewood Cliffs, New Jersey*

Library of Congress Cataloging in Publication Data

Trojanowicz, Robert C
 Juvenile delinquency, concepts and control.

 Bibliography: p.
 1. Juvenile delinquency.   2. Rehabilitation of
juvenile delinquents.   I. Title.
HV9069.T84   364.36   72-3688
ISBN 0-13-514315-2

Juvenile Delinquency: Concepts and Control

by Robert C. Trojanowicz

10 9 8 7 6 5

Prentice-Hall International, Inc., London
Prentice-Hall of Australia, Pty. Ltd., Sydney
Prentice-Hall of Canada, Ltd., Toronto
Prentice-Hall of India Private Limited, New Delhi
Prentice-Hall of Japan, Inc., Tokyo

Dedicated to my son Eric *and to my daughter* Elise.

CONTENTS

PREFACE

This book describes and discusses the constellation of factors that relate to juvenile delinquency causation, prevention, treatment, and control. A multidisciplinary orientation is utilized to analyze these concepts.

The most popular and prevalent interdisciplinary issues, ideas, principles, and assumptions pertaining to the delinquency phenomenon are presented. The use of numerous examples facilitates the transition from complex theoretical principles to practical application.

Not only does the book provide an overview of the many variables related to delinquency, it points out the duties, responsibilities, and functions of the agencies in the criminal justice system that deal with the juvenile delinquent. The orientation, programs, and procedures utilized by the various criminal justice agencies are discussed to help the reader understand the processes the delinquent goes through from the initial contact with the police to the selection of a dispositional alternative.

The final section of the book delineates a process that can contribute to the mobilization of community resources to combat delinquency and rehabilitate the delinquent.

The strength of the book is that it points out the complexity of the juvenile delinquency phenomenon and the necessity of understanding the many variables related to its causation, prevention, treatment, and control—variables that range all the way from a knowledge of "normal" adolescent behavior to an understanding of organizational principles and dynamics.

The establishment of effective juvenile delinquency prevention, treatment, and control programs can be accomplished only if the many variables identified in the book are understood, assimilated, and then initiated into action.

As with any endeavor, many persons contribute to goal achievement. I received help in completing this book. I would like to extend my appreciation to Ray Valley, Susann Pyzik, Thomas Schooley, and Kathleen Williams for their research assistance; to Edward Francis and Robert Weisman of Prentice-Hall for their encouragement; to Dr. Christopher Sower for his inspiration; and to my wife and family for their support and endurance.

JUVENILE DELINQUENCY: CONCEPTS AND CONTROL

1

INTRODUCTION

The major purpose of this book is to provide the practitioner or the student interested in working with juveniles an overview of the juvenile delinquency phenomenon and the process involved in its causation, prevention, control, and treatment.

The description and discussion of the juvenile delinquency process will facilitate the transition from theory to practice. In addition, the orientation, the programs, the procedures, and the responsibilities of the agencies that comprise the criminal justice system will be emphasized.

Almost everyone, regardless of background or professional training, has his own theories about juvenile delinquency. Many times the logic and insight demonstrated by practitioners or amateur theorists is appropriate and sound, but because they are unaware of popular theoretical assumptions and present programs and practices they are unable to systematically compare their ideas with those of the "experts." This hinders the practitioner or the "amateur" from effectively replicating and refining his own most successful ideas and practices. In other words, the practitioner or the aspiring practitioner "flies by the seat of his pants."

This book provides the reader with an exposure to the thinking of the experts in the field of juvenile delinquency, the process involved in the causation of this phenomenon, and examples of the most successful and effective programs, procedures, and techniques for handling juveniles.

Chapter 2, "Social Deviance," introduces juvenile delinquency as a sub-category of the general concept of deviancy.

Whenever men unite to achieve individual and group goals and to satisfy needs, they must also set limits and make rules to regulate behavior. Where there are rules and regulations, there is the potential for deviance. If the deviant act is committed by a juvenile, it is a delinquent deviant act.

Deviant behavior has existed and will continue to exist as long as man is dependent on his peers for survival. Even though deviancy is usually associated with the social outcast and the criminal offender, at one time or another almost everyone has acted in a deviant manner.

The concept of deviancy is extremely complicated and has to be viewed from many perspectives. Deviant behavior has both positive and negative ramifications. Chapter 2 provides examples of both in an attempt to clarify the concept and illustrate its variability depending on the culture (or subculture), the time in history, and the norms of legal and social jurisdiction.

As Cohen points out, "the study of deviance cannot simply be the study of drunkenness, narcotic drug use, prostitution, etc., for each of these in some society and under some circumstances was socially acceptable."[1] Hence there is the necessity of understanding and recognizing not only the specific deviant act but also the entire concept.

The last part of Chapter 2 traces the history of the development of the delinquent child concept and its changing image.

Just as it is helpful for the reader to understand the complexity and the variability of the concept of deviancy and the ways in which juvenile delinquency is a form of deviant behavior, he should also become acquainted with the most popular theoretical assumptions about the etiology of behavior that manifests itself in a delinquent form.

Chapter 3, "Theories of Delinquency Causation," discusses the many aspects of criminology that are referred to as theories of causation.

Because the study of the delinquent child and of the forces that contribute to his status has taken many avenues and has originated from many disciplines, Chapter 3 uses a multidisciplinary focus and orientation, with major emphasis being placed on the psychological and sociological fields.

It is undoubtedly helpful, regardless of theoretical orientation, to be exposed to many different viewpoints. This not only broadens the reader's outlook but also introduces him to the jargon and tenets of a variety of schools of thought.

To place the most popular theories of juvenile delinquency in perspective, it is necessary to preface the discussion with a description of the two schools of criminological thought that have provided the basis for present-day thinking. Chapter 3 therefore begins with a discussion of the Classical and the Positive schools of criminology.

The chapter concludes by presenting a typology of delinquent behavior and a discussion of descriptive and diagnostic terms.

[1]Albert K. Cohen, *Deviance and Control* (Englewood Cliffs, N.J., Prentice-Hall, Inc., 1966), p. 12.

Chapter 4, "The Family and Juvenile Delinquency," uses the family as a model for incorporating both psychological and sociological theories into a meaningful framework. Regardless of the particular professional or academic discipline or orientation, the family is considered the most significant factor in the development of delinquency because the family is the primary environment of the child. It is the first institution in which the child interacts, and what he learns (or does not learn) in the family is often the model for future behavior. Chapter 4 illustrates psychological and sociological variables interacting within the family. The use of the family as an example of these processes is a logical follow-up to the discussion of theories of causation in Chapter 3.

Chapter 5, "The Adolescent," revolves around the dynamic behavior and development of the youngster during the period of transition between childhood and adulthood. Just as it is important to understand the concept of deviancy and the theories of delinquency causation, it is also important to understand the myriad of factors that accompany adolescence, the period of most juvenile delinquency.

Persons working with juveniles tend to forget that the delinquent is an adolescent first and a delinquent second. They are not familiar with the wide variety of adolescent disruptive behavior that is within the normal range. Often, more is expected of the delinquent than of the normal adolescent. Unfortunately, many prevention, treatment, and control programs are predicated on the "sickness" of the delinquent and not on the "healthiness" of the adolescent. It is important to understand the normal as well as the delinquent adolescent—as much can be learned from normalcy as from deviancy. Chapter 5 also examines the adolescent from many perspectives, including the wide range of his behavior, his relationships with others, his struggle of dependence versus independence, and the most effective methods of relating to him. It also presents relevant examples and a discussion of present-day adolescent problems, such as drug abuse.

To understand the constellation of factors involved in the juvenile delinquency phenomenon, it is necessary to become acquainted with the concept of deviancy, theories of delinquency causation, and adolescent behavior. To further refine one's conception of this phenomenon and its treatment, prevention, and control, it is helpful to understand organization theory and relevant variables because man is a member of many groups, ranging from the family to social, occupational, and political organizations. "Man always exists in groups on which he is dependent and the problems of organization are universal problems."[2]

Not only is juvenile delinquency the result of family and community disorganization—successful prevention, control, and treatment programs are predicated on cooperation, positive interorganizational relationships, and a working knowledge of organization theory.

Chapter 6 "Organization Theory," discusses the most prominent theories of organization, the factors involved when men interact, and specifically the organization variables that are important when planning, initiating, and establishing delinquency prevention, control, and treatment programs within the criminal justice system.

[2]Scott A. Greer, *Social Organization* (New York: Random House, Inc., 1955), p. 5.

Chapter 7, "Handling the Juvenile Delinquent within the Criminal Justice System," discusses concrete methods and techniques and views the delinquent from the perspective, philosophy, and responsibilities of the police, the court, and other agencies.

Relevant Supreme Court decisions are also mentioned and their implications for the handling of the delinquent are discussed. The chapter concludes by presenting a case study of a delinquent and describing the procedure for handling him under recent court decisions and recommended juvenile court rules.

Chapter 8 "Prevention Programs," describes programs that have been established to prevent, control, and treat delinquency. The chapter provides illustrations of how abstract theoretical concepts may be transformed into concrete programs. The problems of transition are most illuminating.

Just as there are many and varied opinions as to how programs should be established and what theory should be transformed into concrete action, there are many views regarding the most effective methods for treatment, prevention, and control.

Chapter 9, "Methods of Treatment," examines the most prevalent, accepted, and thus far successful techniques of treatment. The chapter takes a multidisciplinary orientation and views both individual and group methods, which range from very practical approaches to highly complicated methods that require a great deal of training and skill. Examples are given as to how the various techniques are used, in what types of settings, and under what circumstances, as well as the professional orientation of the persons using them.

Chapter 10, "An Example: Community-Based Treatment Programs," describes a halfway house program and discusses the input necessary for the establishment and operation of such a facility.

Halfway houses are discussed more extensively than other juvenile facilities because (1) other programs, such as probation, institutions, and court services, were discussed in preceding chapters; (2) halfway houses will probably eventually be the most prevalent community-based treatment facilities for juveniles; and (3) a discussion of the halfway house program lends itself to the incorporation of the theories, concepts, programs, and techniques that were discussed in the preceding chapters. The example of a halfway house program illustrates the numerous elements that have to be considered if programs are to achieve their intended goals.

Chapter 11, "A Resolution to Juvenile Delinquency Prevention through Normative Sponsorship," presents an innovative approach to identifying, preventing, and treating delinquent behavior. The chapter examines methods of mobilizing community resources and initiating and establishing effective programs.

Chapter 12 discusses current issues in the criminal justice field, provides recommendations and looks to the future.

SOCIAL DEVIANCE

Deviation is a common feature of society and is implicit in all social organizations.[1]
Deviance is just as much a human characteristic as is *conformity*.

> Every human group no matter how cohesive, stable, and well integrated, must
> somehow respond to such problems as mental illness, violence, theft, sexual
> misconduct, as well as to other similarly difficult behaviors. Problems of
> deviance inevitably are defined as being a real or perceived threat to the basic
> "values" of the society. For whatever reasons, some persons act at times, at
> least, in so bizarre, eccentric, outlandish, abhorrent, dangerous, or merely
> unique and annoying a manner that they cannot readily be tolerated. So
> every society must somehow deal with its saints and its sinners, its kooks and
> clowns, and its dependent, disruptive, inadequate, and aberrant members.
> Understanding deviance involves, at a basic minimum, at least three dimen-
> sions. First, it is apparent that every society *defines* behaviors that are to be
> labeled as deviant and proscribed as undesirable. Second, since deviance may
> be commonplace and even wide-spread, some explanations or *theories* must
> be offered for the existence and persistence of such deviant behavior in the
> face of negative social sanction. Third, there would be little reason to define,
> sanction, and explain deviance without also doing something to, for, or with
> the deviant in order to *correct, deter, prevent,* and/or punish him. Every
> society then defines, explains, and acts with regard to deviance.[2]

[1] David Matza, *Becoming Deviant* (Englewood Cliffs, N.J.: Prentice-Hall, Inc., 1969).

[2] From *Deviance: Studies in the Process of Stigmatization and Societal Reaction* by
Simon Dinitz, Russell R. Dynes, and Alfred C. Clark. Copyright©1969 by Oxford University
Press, Inc. Reprinted by permission.

This book will basically deal with the three issues raised in the above quotation. In this chapter we will discuss the way society *defines* certain types of behavior that it deems unacceptable and in need of sanctions. The line between deviance and conformity is not always clear-cut. Differences exist not only in the earliest cultures but also within cultures, with no common understanding regarding deviant behavior and its treatment. Sanctioning of deviant behavior depends upon not only the act but also the circumstances, the social system, the community, and the prevailing attitudes. Chapter 3 will examine various *theories* of deviant behavior (juvenile delinquency in particular), its causes, and its implications.

Any discussion of the concept of deviancy and the theories of causation should include methods and programs for prevention, treatment, and control. Subsequent chapters will focus on these matters. The construction of the book is such that most issues pertinent to juvenile delinquency will be investigated. They range from understanding the "normal" adolescent to developing effective methods of dealing with delinquency.

SOCIAL INTERACTION

Deviance is a product and process of social interaction.[3] Man's behavior is not simply a result of his motives or other internal psychological dynamics; it is also a product of the social situation in which he finds himself. Behavior that is socially defined as deviant is not a simple phenomenon subject to a simple explanation. Social stratification is linked to deviant behavior through the mechanism of self-esteem. Social stratification, or the way power, wealth, and status are distributed, affects self-esteem by showing the individual how he "stacks up" to the social position, status, and opportunity structure of his peers. When a person's self-esteem is affected by the social institutions in his environment and by his evaluation of how he compares with others in similar or dissimilar situations, deviant behavior may result if he feels he does not compare favorably.[4] Deviant behavior, then, involves at least two basic processes—the way the social system distributes wealth and power, and the way the individual perceives himself in relation to this distribution. As Chapter 3 points out, the distribution of wealth, power, and opportunity can affect the way a person views himself and the way he reacts to strain and frustration. If symbols of success cannot be achieved relatively easily by an individual in a legitimate manner, the method of adaption to his environment may be evaluated as deviant by his community. Juvenile delinquency is a form of deviant adaption.

Deviance, then, which is a relative concept and varies from culture to culture, time to time, and place to place, is often the result of cultural factors.[5]

[3]Earl Rubington and Martin S. Weinberg, *Deviance—The Interactionist Perspective* (New York:The Macmillan Company, 1968).

[4]John P. Hewitt, *Social Stratification and Deviant Behavior* (New York:Random House, Inc., 1970).

[5]Leslie T. Wilkins, *Social Deviance—Social Policy, Action and Research* (London: Tavistock Publications Ltd., 1959).

This means, of course, that the norms which define deviant behavior are not necessarily the same in various cultures nor are they the same in a given culture over a period of time. Homosexual behavior, prostitution, or drunkenness does not constitute deviant behavior in some societies today. Some Scandinavian countries, for example, have such different interpretation of sexual norms that many delinquent and criminal acts in American society would not be regarded as such there. Changed attitudes in the United States over the past 50 years toward tobacco smoking by juveniles and young adults is an indication of how normative standards can be redefined in time. Formerly, there was great preoccupation against smoking among younger groups. Laws were passed forbidding it and often were strictly enforced. Smoking was thought to be related to a variety of other social problems.[6]

Hence the concept of deviance and what is considered deviant by a society, a culture, a state, or even a community varies from time to time. Many great scientists of the past, such as Copernicus and Galileo, were considered deviant during their time, but because of their outstanding contributions, they are revered today.

Labeling

Some deviations are more intense than others and receive much more disapproval from society. Society can react to deviance in a number of ways, ranging from mild disgust to highly legalized and severe punishment. When legal punishment is imposed and social control is manifested, this behavior is usually severe enough to warrant strong societal disapproval. Examples of this type of behavior would be delinquency and criminality. When society does take steps to control deviant behavior, a stigmatization is involved, and the individual committing or perpetrating a particular deviant act is often labeled deviant. This has ramifications as to how he feels about himself and how society reacts to him. He is often considered different and unacceptable, and frequently he is even ostracized by both the formal society and the informal social groups of which he is a part.

When the individual is labeled, stigmatized, and sometimes even ostracized, he often retreats from those conventional groups that can have a positive impact on future behavior and is drawn to those groups where he is readily accepted. Many times these negatively oriented groups have a further contaminating effect on him which, in turn, perpetuates deviancy. This, in turn, perpetuates ostracization and participation in deviant groups. The difficulty that the ex-convict has upon his release to the "free community" is an example of the process of labeling, stigmatization, and his inevitable association with deviant groups that accept his status but may also involve him in future deviant behavior.

Studies have shown that the labeling process and ostracization can have negative effects on the deviant. Freedman and Doob concluded that everyone who is deviant in some way will have feelings of deviancy, and this will affect his

---

[6]Marshall B. Clinard, *Sociology of Deviant Behavior* (New York:Rinehart and Company, Inc., 1957), p. 19.

behavior.[7] Furthermore, deviants will try to conceal their deviancy so that it will not be held against them by nondeviants. Deviants often prefer to associate with other deviants, and, as the authors point out, fear of rejection is a major motivating factor.

THE VARIABLE NATURE OF DELINQUENT BEHAVIOR

Because deviant behavior is not consistent in all cultures, all societies, or even all communities, the question may be asked, What are the reference points for evaluating behavior as deviant or nondeviant, and how can the line between deviance and conformity be drawn more clearly so that the concept can be understood in more concrete terms? The major criteria or reference points utilized to determine if behavior is deviant or not are probably those intangible guides to behavior that we call *norms*. Very simply, norms are the criteria that society utilizes to evaluate behavior.

> They evolve out of the experience of people interacting with society. In turn, they guide, channel, and limit further relationships. So integral a part of human life are norms that many are unaware of their pervasiveness. Most persons are oblivious to the importance of norms in giving substance and meaning to human life. The reason for this lack of awareness is that norms become so internalized as a part of a personality, that people take them for granted. Norms are seldom consciously thought about unless they are challenged by contact with persons conforming to another normative order, perhaps, foreigners, hillbillies or outsiders. This unconscious quality of norms arises from the fact that persons are rewarded for behaving in certain ways and punished for behaving in other ways until behavior according to the norms becomes almost automatic.[8]

As society becomes more complicated, norms become more complicated. Where there is little mobility, little difference in life-style, and where societies are uncomplicated, norms are usually pervasive without even being codified. In complex societies like ours, however, many different styles of behavior have originated from many different cultures. Mobility has also had an effect on norms because there is not the solidified, singular community that exists in many societies. When there is a breakdown of rules or norms that govern behavior, and when the society becomes so complex that communities no longer control their own actions or influence the behavior of their members there is *norm breakdown,* which often results in a high incidence of crime and delinquency. And, in complex societies like ours with different layers of economic prosperity as well as many variations of life-styles resulting from different experiences and cultural backgrounds, there is *norm conflict.*[9] Hence, norm breakdown and norm conflict can contribute to criminality and delinquency.

[7]Jonathan L. Freedman and Anthony N. Doob, *Deviancy—The Psychology of Being Different* (New York:Academic Press, Inc., 1968).

[8]Dinitz, Dynes, and Clarke, *op. cit.,* p. 4.

[9]Ibid., p. 9.

The severity of the norm breakdown or the norm conflict or both would frequently be a determining factor in the seriousness of the ensuing delinquent or deviant behavior. Subsequent penalties for crime and delinquency are determined by community attitudes regarding the seriousness of the offense and the extent to which it threatens and goes contrary to community norms.

> Deviations from norms which are tolerated or which provoke only mild disapproval are obviously of little concern to a society. Only those situations in which behavior is in a disapproved direction and of sufficient degree to exceed the tolerance level of the community constitute deviant behavior—obviously the extent and degree of disapproval in a particular instance are dependent on the nature of the situation and a community's degree of tolerance of the behavior involved.[10]

In regard to crime and delinquency:

> Among the norms whose violation usually exceeds the tolerance limit of the community and even a highly differentiated society are the legal norms. To emphasize their importance and to force compliance with them, a series of penalties has been established by the political state. Enacted laws represent varying degrees of tolerance for the behavior outlawed. Some legal norms forbidding certain behavior are supported by nearly all segments of a society, the behavior in question being regarded as inimical to group welfare, whereas norms embodied in other laws have little support. Deviant behavior such as murder, kidnapping, sexual abuse of young children, or incest, may be overwhelmingly and strongly disapproved. Other behavior, while disapproved legally, may have less public disapproval. Although persons differ about the validity of individual legal norms, there may be agreement that there is need for obedience of the law in general. Most criminal behavior represents a conflict of the norms of particular groups or individuals against those norms which the law represents. Much juvenile delinquency, organized prostitution, gambling, traffic in narcotics, and homosexuality, for example, arise from the growth of subgroups which, although in physical contact with the rest of society, may have different norms. Norms of subgroups which conflict with legal norms may be those of certain age groups, social classes, occupations, neighborhoods, or regions.[11]

Lee has stated that the child learns from many experiences with personal and material carriers of his culture that are dissimilar, unrelated, and confusing; thus, the child's conditioning to a given society may be considerably different from that of the general norm and he may very well become deviant.[12] Chapter 3 points out that conflict between conventional norms and deviant transmissions within the same environment can contribute to delinquent behavior. Furthermore, because all individuals attempt to attain some type of security, recognition, and acceptance within their environment, they are expected to meet group standards of adequacy, worthiness, and security. When an individual fails to obtain satisfaction through socially acceptable channels or when there are conflicting norms, he may obtain

[10]Clinard, *op. cit.,* p. 22.

[11]*Ibid.,* p. 24.

[12]Alfred McClung Lee, *Multivalent Man,* (New York: George Braziller, Inc., 1966).

satisfaction through socially unacceptable channels, experiences that transform individual frustrations into social problems.[13]

Because deviancy is such an elusive concept there is often a very fine line between conformity and deviant behavior, the concept itself cannot simply be correlated with certain social, psychological, or other variables.

> Further confusion arises in the minds of some observers when they perceive that certain factors are associated with the occurrence of deviant behavior. They often jump to the conclusion that two phenomena are related when they may have no connection. When it is noted, for example, that delinquency and bad housing are often associated, the causal relationship may be presumed to exist. Others may perceive that delinquents read comic books so they conclude that comic books can cause delinquency. In both instances, the observer has failed to take in account how set situations may cause delinquency. Most important, however, they may have failed to observe that these same factors, bad housing and comic books, affect a large proportion of our population without necessarily producing deviant behavior. Although most delinquency occurs in so-called slum areas where housing is poor, the relation has little direct connection with any theory of human behavior and must be discounted as an error in perception. Moreover, delinquency does occur in areas of good housing. Hence, if the same logic is used, this situation might be attributed to the adequacy of the housing situation. In studying deviant behavior, it is always necessary to consider whether similar influences are affecting nondeviants. Therefore, some theory of human behavior must be devised which will account for the differential effects if they exist.[14]

Deviance is not always the result of the same processes. The individual can become deviant because of something he is reacting to in his environmental situation or because of conflicts that exist in his psychic mechanism. The labeling as deviant can also be the result of political, economic, and religious factors.

Lofland states that there are two types of deviant acts, *defensive* and *adventurous.* The defensive deviant act is a response to a sense of either perceived or real threat from the environment or individuals in the environment. The deviant act is justified on these grounds. For example, a youngster in the inner city may feel threatened by a group or gang within his environment. He reacts to the threat by "attacking before being attacked," which results in his inflicting bodily injury on his real or imagined attacker. According to Lofland, the adventurous deviant act occurs because all mammals, including human beings, enjoy manageable fear, frustration, and anxiety. The typical and mundane features of human societies are the most important contributors to deviant action.[15] The act is committed to relieve boredom, or in the case of a delinquent it can be a reaction to a "dare" or a desire to impress the group.

All deviant behavior is not necessarily detrimental, however, or should it be

---

[13]Harry C. Bredemier and Jackson Toby, *Social Problems in America—Costs and Casualties in the Acquisitive Society* (New York:John Wiley & Sons, Inc., 1965).

[14]Clinard, *op. cit.,* p. 38.

[15]John Lofland, *Deviance and Identity* (Englewood Cliffs, N.J.:Prentice-Hall, Inc., 1969).

completely expunged by the society, the community, or the organization. Exceptions in social behavior are necessary for social evolution. If some individuals did not take it upon themselves to be different, to develop new ideas, and to persevere in behavior that was not accepted at one particular point in time, social change would not result nor would new modes of behavior that enhance the quality of life.

POSITIVE AND NEGATIVE EFFECTS OF DEVIANT BEHAVIOR

Since all societies, communities, and organizations have rules, they are bound to have rule breakers. Depending on the complexity of the organization and the rule that is broken, the resulting sanctions will vary. If the rule violation is a serious one that will endanger the public order or the life of a citizen, or will affect his possession of his property, then the negative ramifications for the deviant will usually be severe. If, however, the rule violation is within the *limits of tolerance* and is not particularly threatening to the organization—and may in fact be helpful in providing new vitality and insight into organizational operations—the deviant, although he may be reprimanded, will probably not be severely punished. The obvious ways that deviance can be destructive of a society, a community, or an organization and the negative ramifications that can result from deviant behavior will be discussed first.

Negative Effects of Deviance

Deviant behavior in any form can pose a real or potential threat to any society. When deviance is manifested in such *criminal* form as robbery, rape, murder, or grand larceny, it is definitely a threat to both the society and the victim. Every societal organization or complex of organizations (the criminal justice system) develops criteria for identifying deviance and methods for handling it.

Deviance can be viewed on a continuum. Most deviant behavior is not manifested in as extreme a form as criminal activity. A common effect of most, if not all, deviance, however, is that it produces and perpetuates distrust. Both the "manipulator" in a work organization and the criminal are distrusted because of their varying degrees of deviance. The deviant behavior harms not only the victim of the deviant and ultimately the deviant himself (as a result of stigmatization) but societal organizations are also negatively affected. Community organizations feel the impact of criminal and delinquent behavior directly through "victimization and loss" and indirectly through expending resources to control and prevent it—resources that could be utilized in other endeavors.

In work organizations, deviance also has its negative effects. It can destroy morale and trust and hinder organizational operations. If the deviant or the "manipulator" who attempts to bend the rules and goes beyond prescribed limits and is allowed to get away with it, morale will be affected. For example, if a worker in an organization continually, without sufficient reason, utilizes his sick days to avoid going to work or while on the job does not perform his duties adequately, this can negatively affect both the organization and his peers. The organization will be affected because one of its operating components, the worker, is not providing the services he is being paid for. He may affect the morale of his fellow employees to such an extent that they are reluctant to perform adequately, or he may contaminate other workers, influencing them to break the rules because they can get away with it. Also, if the worker who is known as a manipulator or is rewarded by the organization or if he is allowed to function at only a minimal amount of capacity, this not only will affect the organizational process and morale but will neutralize the normative bonds of control which are the cement of an effective organization. If the organization is a public service agency, the public will suffer because services will not be provided in the most efficient manner.

Because of the wide range and varying degrees of deviance, it is difficult to develop specific methods of control and predict when deviance will become devastating to the particular society, community, organization, or individual.

> Indeed, measures to prevent deviance or to reduce its cost after it has occurred—testimonials to distrust—are integral features of almost all organized social action—government, banking, Little League baseball, *ad infinitum.* Just how far the erosion of trust must proceed before it results in the breakdown of organization cannot be stated in general terms. It depends on the organization, on the position within it of those who are the objects of distrust, on the costliness of the anticipated deviance, on the mechanisms available for restoring trust and providing reassurance (e.g., for "turning the rascals out" and replacing them with persons of undoubted integrity) once trust has been shattered.[16]

Positive Effects of Deviance

Some of the obvious negative ramifications of deviant behavior have been mentioned. Now we will examine some of the positive effects to show that the concept has many facets and that the deviant label need not always be feared or viewed negatively. In limited doses, deviance does not usually hinder organizational or societal operation; in fact, it can contribute to increased organizational effectiveness and the development of innovative approaches to problem solving.

Cohen has described some of the positive effects of deviant behavior. His classification follows, and examples relating to each typology will be given.

1. Deviance versus red tape.
2. Deviance as a safety valve.
3. Deviance as an aid in clarifying rules.
4. Deviance uniting the group (against the deviant).
5. Deviance uniting the group (in behalf of the deviant).
6. Deviance functioning as a warning signal.[17]

Deviance versus Red Tape. In any organization the rules that have been

---

[16]Albert K. Cohen, *Deviance and Control* (Englewood Cliffs, N.J.:Prentice-Hall, Inc., 1966), p. 6.

[17]*Ibid.,* pp. 6-10.

established as a means for accomplishing goals can become so cumbersome and complicated that they have the effect of hindering the orderly process of goal achievement. If the rules are followed precisely and mechanically and if red tape becomes prevalent, the rules that were established to increase efficiency will have the effect of decreasing organizational operation. For example, the criminal justice system's organizations, such as the police, courts, correctional facilities, and social work agencies, have been established to protect the community from unlawful behavior, eliminate the causes of delinquency and crime, and treat those individuals who have been engulfed in it. If the organization, whether it be a police department or a social work agency, becomes so large and cumbersome that it has difficulty in responding to the needs of community residents, it will not be fulfilling its major function, namely, serving the community. Large social work agencies often become so bureaucratic and impersonal that the organization manual becomes an end in itself. Service is determined by technicalities rather than by an honest appraisal of the client, his problems, and his requirements. If a worker in this type of organization finds that he is not being responsive to his clients because he spends most of his time making "determinations" by the manual or doing paper work and very little time providing meaningful "direct services," he may decide to innovate by spending less time on red tape and administration and more time on direct services. He would, however, have to develop a priority list of the forms and paper work that were essential and neglect or eliminate whatever he felt was a hindrance to the effective operation of the organization. The worker who altered his duties in this manner could be and probably would be labeled deviant by the organization because he was not functioning according to expectations. If, however, by providing more direct services to his clients it became obvious to the organization that his new orientation and procedures had merit, he might be rewarded and the organization might alter its operations to incorporate his ideas and methods. The organization manual might be consolidated, much red tape eliminated, and the organization's "limits of tolerance" for innovative deviance expanded. Even though many positive changes could result from the initial efforts of an innovative worker who was deviant, he still could have been reprimanded. Not all deviant behavior that attempts to alter organizational operating procedures has the effect of producing positive innovation, however. Individual action that is contrary to operating procedures can also be the result of the individual's desire to circumvent necessary organization rules for his personal benefit. This is why the individual who feels that deviant behavior is required for producing innovation and change will have to be willing to pay the consequences. The consequences will be worth paying, however, if the ultimate results of his actions are beneficial to himself, his organization, and the community.

Deviance as a Safety Valve. Rules, regulations, manuals, and codes are supposed to improve organizational functioning. If workers were robots, they could follow established procedures indefinitely, which would generally insure the smooth operation of the organization. Because workers are social beings and have weaknesses as well as strengths, however, they do not always operate within their environment in a disciplined manner or at a high rate of efficiency. There are lapses in functioning. If parents, within the family organization, expect their children to be "perfect" all the time, or if managers or supervisors expect workers to operate at a high rate of efficiency all the time, it will not be long before the functioning begins to break down and the members begin to react in a hostile and deviant manner because of the resulting frustration and strain. A limited amount of deviance can act as a safety valve by preventing an excessive accumulation of hostility, frustration, and strain, which can be manifested in an extremely deviant form. In police work, many times the spirit of the law rather than the letter of the law is enforced. In certain tense situations, where enforcing the letter of the law could result in more harm than good and increase hostility between the community and the police, the police officer might enforce the spirit of the law even when it would be technically correct to enforce the letter of the law. This could be interpreted as deviance by the organization or, at least, by some members of it. By handling the situation in a judicious manner, however, his "deviance" could act as a safety valve in reducing tensions and might even improve the communication process between the police and the community.

Another example of deviance acting as a safety valve is the use of alcohol by members of the armed forces who are under twenty-one. Drinking alcoholic beverages is not usually normative or legal for persons under the age of twenty-one. However, within the confines of the army, it is accepted as long as the individual soldier does not create difficulty on the post or in the surrounding community. This "deviance" can act as a safety valve by allowing the young soldier to handle some of his frustration and aggression through verbal catharsis as a result of the releasing of tension through the use of alcohol.

A final example of deviance acting as a safety valve is a police organization's chain of command, which a police officer is supposed to use if he has a problem. The problem may revolve around the officer's supervisor, who may not be responsive to problems in general or aware of effective techniques of supervision. The officer may approach his supervisor, using the chain of command, to discuss the problem. If the supervisor refuses to listen, the officer may, without permission, go over his head. In a paramilitary organization this is considered deviant behavior. If the officer contacts higher command officers and complains to them about this and other problems in the department, they may be grateful for the information and may reprimand the supervisor for his inept handling of the men and his failure to deal effectively with departmental problems. If the higher command officers are receptive, in at least some situations, to communication from the men even though it does not always go through the chain of command, this can act as a safety valve. Problems will be discussed and resolved before they become so large that polarization between command and line officers results in difficulties like strikes, mass resignations, or overall organizational subversion. The "deviant" police officer who went over his supervisor's head acted as a safety valve by communicating the frustration that the men were experiencing. His action resulted in the organization's taking positive steps to alleviate the problem, thus avoiding potential long-range difficulties.

Deviance as an Aid in Clarifying Rules. Deviance can have positive results in acting as an aid in clarifying the rules. All persons, whether functioning in the family or operating within an organization, want some type of reference point from which to gauge their behavior. Youngsters want limits set and expectations transmitted so that they will know how far they can go. When this structure and these reference points are not provided, insecurity and anxiety may result. Within the family, if a child does transgress beyond the often ambiguous boundaries that his parents have set for him, he will be reprimanded for his actions. As a result of his transgression, the parents will often outline, in a very specific manner, what is expected of him, how far he can go, and what will happen if he goes beyond the limits established. The child's deviant transgression aided in clarifying the family rules and the expectations that his parents have of him.

In regard to the criminal justice system, deviance can also aid in clarifying the rules. Police officers in many communities often have loosely defined roles. This may be by choice, and not by chance, because a vague role definition facilitates the politician's manipulating the policeman by having him use differential approaches in his police work, depending on the status of the citizen involved. This leaves the policeman in a state of anxiety, and, just like the youngster in the family, he would prefer some reference points or clear-cut and consistent orientation so that he would know how to respond in at least most situations. If administrators are inept and policemen are used as scapegoats by politicians and influential people in the community, then court decisions can be effective in clarifying the policeman's role and the procedures for acceptable police behavior. There has been much discussion about court decisions and their effect on police work. From the positive standpoint, the act of a deviant, in this case the offender who takes his case to court (and possibly all the way to the Supreme Court), can aid in clarifying the rules for the policeman. The court decision will define the limits of the policeman's authority and responsibility and will outline procedures for him to follow. As a result of the establishment of these guidelines, it will be much more difficult for the policeman to be manipulated because of a vague and ambiguous role definition. The "deviant criminal offender" who took his case to court ultimately provided role clarification for policemen and provided them with objective reference points for functioning.

Deviance Uniting the Group—Against the Deviant. Uniting the group against the deviant is also an example of deviant behavior producing positive results. In time of crisis, much energy is mobilized to combat a common threat, such as a foreign enemy or a natural disaster, and divergent groups are pulled together, common interests are identified, and group cooperation is ensured. A deviant who is terrorizing a community through mass murder would undoubtedly have the effect of mobilizing the resources of the community to combat this particular situation. Citizens who had previously been reluctant to cooperate with authorities would become involved by providing information; agencies that had had difficulty working together would cooperate. This crisis would create a cooperative atmosphere of both the agencies and the residents in the community to combat the common enemy.

Another example of uniting a group against a deviant would be World War II and the threat that Hitler posed to the Free World. Most people forgot their petty individual animosities and cooperated as a group to combat the threat of Nazism. In these two examples, then, uniting a group against a deviant has positive results for the individual as well as for other persons and groups.

Uniting a group against a deviant, however, can also have negative ramifications, particularly if a person is evaluated as a deviant by a group merely because he is different. If someone from a minority group moves into a neighborhood that has not previously been inhabited by members of a minority group and he is considered a deviant, which in turn elicits a group effort by his neighbors to antagonize him so that he will be forced to move, group action against a "deviant" will have *negative* results and ramifications. In this example, however, the group reaction itself is the deviant phenomenon.

Deviance Uniting the Group—in Behalf of the Deviant. Uniting a group in behalf of the deviant is also a case where deviant behavior may produce favorable consequences. For example, in an organization a worker may be doing a very effective job, may be very conscientious, and may be highly regarded by his peers. Because of a personality clash with his supervisor, however, the latter may try to antagonize the worker to make him quit. The supervisor may also use his power to the disadvantage of the worker. The actions of the supervisor, if they are successful and the individual does resign or is fired, can have the effect of mobilizing the energy of the worker's peers and having them come to his aid. As a result of their support and the possibility of the problem becoming known to more "powerful" individuals within the organization, the situation will be brought out in the open. The worker will probably be rehired and the authoritarian supervisor reprimanded. Uniting the group in behalf of the deviant therefore produced positive results not only for the individual who was rehired but for the organization by pointing out the inadequacies of the authoritarian supervisor which ultimately could have negatively affected the entire organization.

Deviance Functioning as a Warning Signal. Deviance can have positive ramifications for organizational or societal functioning in that it can act as a warning signal. Regardless of how well an organization's operating procedures seem to be functioning, it is always possible, because of human interaction and personal idiosyncrasies, that dysfunctional aspects of organizational operations will emerge. In organizations where operating procedures are not effective or where employee-employer relationships are not satisfactory, frustration and strain will exist. In a community, if all residents are not afforded equal opportunity, housing, and employment, resulting frustration can ultimately lead to deviant behavior. If an industrial or a public service organization, or a community, is not functioning properly, those persons utilizing the services will usually complain until the situation is improved. In the automobile industry, for example, if a company's sales drop because the automobiles are not being constructed properly, or because of poor quality control, this alerts the organization that investigation and analysis of its procedures and employee functioning is necessary. If a police organization has many resignations, if its employees are not operating effectively or functioning properly, and if the number of citizen complaints is high, the organization obviously has problems that are not being handled properly. If there is also a great deal of employee dissatisfaction and complaining about the organization, both internally and externally, this is deviant behavior when compared with the norm for a police agency. This deviant behavior can be a warning signal to the organization's administrators. An astute administrator would attempt to rectify these problems, determine their cause, and generally improve conditions so that the organization would be more effective. The warning signals can thus be used to the advantage of the organization.

If institutions for juveniles have many AWOLs, this can be an indication of difficulties within the organization. These difficulties could range from poor communication between the boys and the staff to authoritarian measures taken by the staff. The boys might react to these types of situations by going AWOL and trying to flee an unsatisfactory environment. Again, the astute administrator would know that this was only an indication, or warning signal, of some deeper-level organization problem and that measures would have to be taken to rectify the situation. In these examples, the *deviant can act as a warning signal to the administrator* that there are deeper problems within the organization. As a result, new procedures could be established, and ultimately the organization could be much better off than it was before the deviant behavior took place.

In summary, Cohen states that

> deviance if not contained is always a threat to organization. In limited quantities and under certain circumstances however, it may make important contributions to the vitality and efficiency of organized social life and even the conforming members of the group may neither wish to see deviance extirpated nor the deviant members thrust out.[18]

JUVENILE DELINQUENCY AS A FORM OF DEVIANT BEHAVIOR

Thus far we have discussed the concept of deviancy, its variability, and its positive and negative aspects. We will now examine historical data and other perspectives that relate to the juvenile delinquent and his status. Juvenile delinquency is a form of deviant behavior.

History

Cultural factors can play a part in explaining juvenile delinquency and crime because in most instances the culture determines what will be considered crime as well as how the child will be viewed and handled.

[18]*Ibid.,* p. 11.

In developing a definitive concept of juvenile delinquency, Gibbens and Ahrenfeldt cite three stages of cultural change. The first stage is the tribal culture, which has little delinquency. In this setting, crime is defined in terms of adult behavior. The norms of the community control most delinquency. In some cases, such as in Laos where juveniles are treated harshly, adults are reluctant to report delinquent acts for fear of severe punishment of the youngster and therefore much of the difficulty is handled within the local neighborhood. The second stage of cultural change relates to the rapidly developing countries of Africa and the East, where urbanization is disrupting the stability of the family. This also took place in the United States and England when rapid industrialization precipitated the growth of large urban centers. It is during this stage that separate juvenile laws usually originate. In the third stage, a preventive approach becomes more prevalent and the definitions of delinquency become ambiguous. In addition to juvenile law, which originates in the second stage, great emphasis is placed on determining the psychological and sociological factors that contribute to crime causation. The countries of Western Europe and the United States would be considered as being in this stage at present.[19]

Much of American history relating to crime and delinquency is tied to the English judicial system. No distinction was made between adult crime and juvenile delinquency in either early English or American history. If the youngster was involved in the commission of a criminal act, he was tried in an adult court and was usually subjected to the same criteria for processing and determining guilt. There were "young criminals," but no "delinquent children." As a result of greater urbanization and the emerging behavioral sciences, however, the public became increasingly aware that youngsters should not be treated like adult offenders or incarcerated with them, because of the *contamination* effect and the child's lack of life experiences and lack of maturity.[20]

The first juvenile court was established in 1899 in Cook County, Illinois. The social conditions and the social conscience of the people at that time provided a great impetus for the development of the court and the treating of children in a manner different from that of adults.

> The juvenile court, then, was born in an era of reform and it spread with amazing speed. The conception of the delinquent as a "wayward child" first specifically came to life in April 1899 when the Illinois Legislature passed the Juvenile Court Act creating the first state-wide court especially for children. It did not include a new court; it did include most of the features that have since come to distinguish the juvenile court. The original act and amendments to it that shortly followed brought together under one jurisdiction cases of dependency, neglect, and delinquency—the last comprehending incorrigibles

[19]T. C. N. Gibbens and R. H. Ahrenfeldt, *Cultural Factors in Delinquency* (London:J. B. Lippincott Co., 1966), p. 21.

[20]Robert G. Caldwell, "The Juvenile Court: Its Development and Some Major Problems," in *Juvenile Delinquency, A Book of Readings,* ed. Rose Giallombardo (New York:John Wiley & Sons, Inc., 1966), p. 356.

and children threatened by immoral associations as well as criminal law breakers. Hearings were to be informal and nonpublic, records confidential, children detained apart from adults, a probation staff appointed. In short, children were not to be treated as criminals nor dealt with by the process used for criminals. A new vocabulary symbolized the new order: Petition instead of complaint, summons instead of warrant, initial hearing instead of arraignment, finding of involvement instead of conviction, disposition instead of sentence. The physical surroundings were important, too: They should seem less imposing than a courtroom with the judge at a desk or table instead of behind a bench, fatherly and sympathetic while still authoritative and sobering. The goals were to investigate, diagnose, and prescribe treatment, not to adjudicate guilt or fix blame. The individual's background was more important than the facts of a given incident, specific conduct relevant more as symptomatic of a need for the court to bring its helping powers to bear than as prerequisite to exercise of jurisdiction. Lawyers were unnecessary— adversary tactics were out of place for the mutual aim of all was not to contest or object, but to determine the treatment plan best for the child. That plan was to be devised by the increasingly popular psychologists and psychiatrists: delinquency was thought of almost as a disease to be diagnosed by specialists with the patient kindly but firmly diagnosed.[21]

The juvenile court has since become *the* primary judicial agency for dealing with juvenile delinquency. Even though the juvenile court cannot be thought of apart from the rest of the criminal justice system, it nevertheless plays the major role in processing, handling, and treating the juvenile offender. In the spirit of the above quotation, the concept of the juvenile court and the handling of youngsters was taken from the English concept of the role of the king acting as the parent when no parents existed to protect the rights of the child. The concept is better known as *parens patriae.*

As Parens Patriae, the state substituting for the king, invested the juvenile court with the power to act as parent of the child. The judge was to assume the fatherly role, protecting the juvenile in order to cure and save him. The juvenile court withheld from the child a procedure of safeguards granted to adults because it viewed him as having a right to custody rather than a right to liberty and juvenile proceedings were civil not criminal.[22]

Under this spirit, the American courts perpetuated the concept of *parens patriae,* or the court acting in the best interests of the child. Dispositions made are theoretically considered to be in the best interests of the child as well as the community. The child is found delinquent, but not criminal, and is therefore incapable of committing a crime in the conventional sense.

[21] *Task Force Report: Juvenile Delinquency and Youth Crime, Report on Juvenile Justice and Consultants Papers,* The President's Commission on Law Enforcement and Administration of Justice (Washington, D.C.:Government Printing Office, 1967).

[22] C. E. Reasons, "Gault: Procedural Change and Substantive Effort," *Crime and Delinquency,* Vol. 16, No. 2 (April 1970).

The Term *Delinquent* Is Ambiguous

Even though the development of the juvenile court system, which by the year 1941 existed in every state of the Union, did much to protect the rights of the child and extract him from the domain of adult criminality, the term *delinquent* itself still remained ambiguous, with varying connotations and definitions depending upon the legal jurisdiction and the community in which the child lived. There is both a *legal* and a *social* definition of delinquency. To be legally delinquent, the youngster must have violated a statute of some governmental jurisdiction. Many of these statutes, however, involve moral judgments, such as incorrigibility and willful disobedience. Even though there is much more consistency and objectivity today in defining juvenile delinquency, many differences still exist in the way children are handled in various jurisdictions and the way they are treated by the agencies within a community.

As for the social definition of delinquency, the ramifications can be even more devastating than the legal ones. For example, the child may be barred from certain groups, may be labeled delinquent, and may thus be considered un-acceptable in some circles. He may elicit disapproval from the community and be forced to associate with groups and persons who are less conducive to the trans-mitting of socially acceptable norms.

Because of the ambiguousness of the term *delinquent,* it has come to mean all things to all men. A quick perusal of various state statutes shows that delinquency can encompass almost any type of youthful deviant behavior. Even a youngster who has not come in formal contact with courts, the police, or the social agencies, but is merely considered "different" by his community, can also be labeled delin-quent. The economic status of the youngster as well as other factors can affect the way he is handled in the criminal justice system and viewed by the community.

> . . . whether a child becomes a delinquent or not will frequently depend upon the general attitudes of the community toward children and families with certain behavioral problems, upon the character of the social agencies in the community, and more specifically, upon the community's policies of referral for such children. Oftentimes other factors are involved in the handling of delinquents. For example, a child whose deeply disturbed emotional state manifests itself in chronic physical assaults may be taken by his middle-class parents to a child psychiatrist or possibly to a boarding school. The same emotional state in a slum child may result in his being brought summarily to the children's court. While the first child scarcely ever figures as a statistic in our compilation of data on delinquency, the second may account for a prominent part of such data.[23]

Because of such factors as economics and the quantity and quality of

[23]Herbert A. Bloch and Frank T. Flynn, *Delinquency* (New York:Random House, Inc., 1956), p. 42.

community service agencies, some youngsters are stigmatized with the label of delinquency. This of course can have negative ramifications for the youngster.

> The judgment against a youth that he is delinquent has a serious reflection upon his character and habit. The stain against him is not removed merely because the statute says no judgment in this particular proceeding shall be deemed a conviction of crime or so considered. The stigma of conviction will reflect upon him for life. It hurts his self-respect. It may at some inopportune, unfortunate moment rise to destroy his opportunity for advancement and blast his ambition to build up a character and reputation entitling him to the esteem and respect of his fellow men.[24]

Lack of appropriate and adequate community resources and indiscriminate labeling and ensuing stigmatization can be obstacles to effectively treating, preventing, and controlling delinquency.

> While the court may see its intervention as helpful and rehabilitative, prospective employers, for example, tend to view less benignly the fact the youth "has a record." The schools may view with suspicion the youngster who has been pronounced delinquent. Further, it is important to draw the distinction between engaging in one delinquent act and the repetitive commission of delinquent acts. Many young people may engage in one or two delinquent acts as a relatively normal part of their adolescence. Occasional and minor delinquency need not presage a delinquent career. To funnel such youth into the formal juvenile justice and correctional system may have the unfortunate and unnecessary consequence of contributing to the development of a career in delinquency.[25]

The orientation of the agencies of the criminal justice system is also an important factor in effectively dealing with the problem of juvenile delinquency. At present some courts take a social orientation to handling the offender, while other courts are more legalistic in their approach.

The original intent and philosophy of the court was social in nature, that is, the child was to be treated rather than convicted and provided assistance and guidance rather than punished. Many times, however, court personnel as well as other persons within the criminal justice system did not abide by the *spirit* under which the social agency orientation was originally established. They misused their power under the guise of "helping" and made subjective judgments which had little legal basis and often infringed upon the child's civil rights. Because of recent Supreme Court decisions, many courts and agencies are taking a more legal orientation when handling youngsters. The process is becoming more similar to that used with adults.

Even though the social agency orientation and philosophy is idealistically the

[24]Commonwealth v. Fisher, 213 Pa 48 (1905), 85, 87.

[25]*Annual Report of Federal Activities,* (Washington, D. C.: U. S. Department of Health, Education, and Welfare, Social and Rehabilitation Service, Youth Development and Delinquency Prevention Administration, 1971), p. 5.

best method of operation, the abuses that have taken place have precipitated the more legalistic emphasis that exists today. The answer to the dilemma of which orientation the court and related agencies should take is probably somewhere in the middle, with an emphasis on the social "ideal" of treating the delinquent while affording him legal safeguards so that his civil liberties can be guaranteed.[26]

SUMMARY

This chapter has focused on the concept of deviancy. Juvenile delinquency and its many variables were identified as a subcategory of deviant behavior.

The chapter did not discuss the volume and the seriousness of the juvenile delinquency problem. Not only are the *rates* of delinquency increasing, but youth involvement in serious crimes is also increasing. (See Table 1.) The volume of police arrests of persons under eighteen years of age from 1960 through 1969 was four times the percentage rate of increase for the total population. For persons ten to seventeen, there was a 27 percent increase in population during this period. The arrest rate of persons under eighteen, however, doubled.[27]

Similarly, during the same period of time, juvenile arrests for violent crimes increased 148 percent, while arrests for property offenses increased 85 percent. While the total youth population aged 10 to 17 constituted approximately 16 percent of the total population of the United States in 1969, persons under 18 years of age were involved in 32 percent of the Crime Index offenses which were solved.[28]

1969 Arrest Rates for Persons Under Age 18
for Crime Index Offenses

Offense Charged	Percentage of Arrests of Persons Under Age 18	Increase 1960-1969 (percent)
Murder	9.4	151
Aggravated Assault	16.4	123
Forcible Rape	20.1	86
Robbery	33.4	13
Burglary	53.7	72
Larceny-Theft	53.1	100
Auto Theft	58.0	63

Source: *Uniform Crime Reports for 1969* (Federal Bureau of Investigation).

[26]H. Warren Dunham, "The Juvenile Court: Contradictory Orientations in Processing Offenders," in Giallombardo, *op. cit.*, pp. 337-54.

[27]*Annual Report of Federal Activities*, p. 1.

[28]*Ibid.*, p. 1.

Many variables, however, affect the compilation of accurate statistics and influence their reliability. It is difficult to make even historical comparisons of delinquency statistics, mainly because sophisticated statistical evaluation is relatively new and much "hidden delinquency" is never detected or reported.

> The first requirement generally stated for a system of criminal statistics is to know the amount and extent of crime, and the number and kinds of criminals. Crimes can be accounted for only through those special agencies set up to enforce criminal law. Thus has come the general axiom that crimes can be counted best in terms of the known offenses reported to police agencies. Obviously, no one will ever know actually how many criminal offenses are committed. The number and extent of unknown offenses may be a subject of speculation, but not of measurement.[29]

An extensive presentation of elaborate statistics does little to solve the problem of juvenile delinquency. The problem can only be completely understood and dealt with through a knowledge of the many variables that relate to delinquency causation, prevention, control, and treatment. The following chapters address these complex issues.

QUESTIONS AND PROJECTS

Essay Questions

1. How can labeling be avoided when working with juveniles?
2. How much "deviance" should be allowed in an organization?
3. Why do most persons conform even though it is relatively easy to get away with deviant behavior in most organizations?
4. Why is there a need for a juvenile court?
5. Explain why the concept of juvenile delinquency is variable in nature.

Projects

1. Develop a juvenile court model that incorporates both the social and the legal orientation to the delinquent youngster.
2. Develop a plan for realistically and objectively gathering accurate statistics on the amount and kind of juvenile delinquency in your community.
3. Discuss the legal and social criteria that are usually utilized to label a youngster "delinquent."

---

[29]R. H. Beatie, "Problems of Criminal Statistics in the United States," *The Journal of Criminal Law, Criminology, and Police Science*, 46, No. 2 (July 1955), 178.

3

THEORIES
OF DELINQUENCY CAUSATION

This chapter will discuss the many aspects of criminology that are referred to as *theories of causation.* It is sometimes assumed that criminology embodies one specific set of principles and codified knowledge when in fact it includes a wide variety of criminological thought as well as contributing disciplines. Because of the complex nature of the delinquency phenomenon, no single theory exists that can explain all crime and delinquency, nor can one single cause of delinquency be specifically determined and applied in all cases. Because of the varied nature of causation factors and the complexity of the problem, it will be necessary to examine a variety of explanations and schools of thought in relation to delinquency causation. The reader will be exposed to a wide range of views taken mostly from the fields of psychology and sociology.

Before the last half of the nineteenth century, little scientific research was done to investigate the many factors that contribute to delinquency and crime. Most attempts at criminological explanation took the form of moralistic pronouncements or unscientific personal generalizations. Not until the end of the nineteenth century did scientific criminological inquiry begin to emerge in this country. With the onset of the discipline of sociology, academic courses that dealt with crime and criminality began to appear. Even at the present time the major discipline concerned with criminality and delinquency is the field of sociology, although subsequent to the latter part of the nineteenth century, psychology, psychiatry, and to a lesser degree, other related disciplines became more aware of the problem and interested in its causation, control, prevention, and treatment.[1]

Because of the variety of disciplines interested in criminology, there are many different and often opposing philosophies regarding delinquency and crime. To help clarify the different orientations, we shall discuss briefly the two major schools of criminological thought and the orientation that each takes when viewing the criminal offender. These two schools of thought, which give the *Classical* and the *Positive* views of criminology, provide the basis for past and contemporary criminological assumptions and principles of delinquency and criminality.

CLASSICAL AND POSITIVE CRIMINOLOGY

The Positive school of criminology, founded by Cesare Lombroso, uses the criminal actor rather than the criminal law as its major orientation. In other words, motivational, behavioral, and environmental aspects of the offender's situation are the major considerations. The law and its administration is secondary or irrelevant. In addition to the Positive school's emphasis on scientific determinism (both personal and environmental), it rejects the Classical school's belief that man exercises freedom, possesses reason, and is capable of choice and of free will and that the offender is basically no different from the nonoffender. In the Positive school the offender, as Matza points out, is trapped by membership in a family and his environment, while in the Classical school, he is trapped by accident or heredity.[2]

The differences in the theoretical orientation of the two schools have implications for the treatment of the offender. The Classical school states that the offender possesses reason and free will, that the major reason for his negative behavior in the community is that he "willed to commit the crime," and that his punishment should include contemplation and incarceration so that he can "unwill" to commit future crimes. The Positive school states that the offender is sick and that his behavior merely reflects the negative characteristics of his social and personal background. Treatment includes altering the offender's social situation and helping him understand his interpersonal problems and dynamics. Almost all modern theories of crime and delinquency causation have emanated from the Positive school of criminology.

Cesare Beccaria, an eighteenth century criminologist and an influential proponent of the Classical school of thought, felt that because offenders were no different from nonoffenders, punishment for crimes should be the same regardless of the offender, his circumstances, or his mental makeup. Hence, fixed sentences were adopted, utilized, and supported at that time.[3]

[1] Donald R. Cressey, "Crime," in *Contemporary Social Problems,* ed. Robert K. Merton and Robert A. Nisbet (New York: Harcourt, Brace & World, Inc., 1966), p. 160.

[2] David Matza, *Delinquency and Drift* (New York: John Wiley & Sons, Inc., 1964), p. 11.

[3] Martin R. Haskell and Lewis Yablonsky, *Crime and Delinquency* (Chicago: Rand McNally & Co., 1970), p. 344.

In 1789 Jeremy Bentham's great work, *An Introduction to the Principles of Morals and Legislation,* was published. This book contained a prescription for the handing out of punishments as they applied to specific crimes. One of its major assumptions was a discussion of the pleasure-pain principle, which in effect stated that if the punishment for the particular criminal act produced negative consequences that were more severe than were the pleasures derived from committing the act, the potential offender would be discouraged from committing the act.[4]

In addition to the pleasure-pain principle being incorporated into the Classical school of thought, the school was heavily based on *rationalism* and the offender's intellectual ability to enter into certain relationships, both negative and positive, with his peers and his community. He was presumed to have the power to choose right from wrong, since most of his behavior was supposedly guided by his desire to seek pleasure and to avoid pain. Hence, if punishments for criminal offenses acknowledged this assumption and accordingly produced enough pain, the potential pleasure derived from the commission of an offense would be negated and the offender would be deterred from most criminality.

Unlike the adherents of the Classical school of criminology, Lombroso and his followers in the Positive school felt that criminality was determined by factors that the actor or potential criminal could not control and that offenders were different from nonoffenders in more ways than merely "the will to crime." In other words, the Positive school negated the concept of free will. Lombroso's work, however, did not incorporate sociological and psychological considerations as we know them today. His quest for scientific investigation, which did not exist in the Classical school, led him to consider differences in biological characteristics of offenders versus nonoffenders.

Basically, Lombroso felt that (1) criminals were at birth a distinctive type, (2) they could be recognized by certain stigmata, that is, such distinguishing characteristics as "a long, lower jaw," and "a low sensitivity to pain," (3) these stigmata or physical characteristics did not cause crime but enabled identification of criminal types, and (4) only through severe social intervention could born criminals be restrained from criminal behavior.[5] The Lombrosian school of thought relied heavily on *biological determinism*—that is, the biology of the individual offender contributed to his criminality and was used to explain crime causation.

The French social psychologist, Gabriel Tarde, attempted to refute Lombroso's biological determinism concept by emphasizing *social determinism*. He felt that when criminal acts were committed by an offender, it was merely learned behavior that the actor had assumed from persons he had imitated in his environment. It is important to point out that the controversy between biological determinism and social determinism is on the question of the two sets of determinisms, *not* on the question of determinism versus free will, one of the major assumptions of the Classical school.[6]

[4]*Ibid.*
[5]*Ibid.,* p. 345.
[6]Cressey, *op. cit.,* p. 161.

It is interesting to note that one of the major characteristics of the Positive school of criminology was its search for scientific demonstration of causal factors as they contribute to criminality and delinquency. It was through the various efforts of scientific exploration, which Lombroso pioneered, that most of his theories were later refuted. Charles Goring, following a procedure suggested by Lombroso himself, refuted Lombroso's contention that a criminal type could be discerned by a comparison of the physical measurements of criminals and noncriminals. Goring compared thousands of recidivist prisoners with a variety of noncriminal individuals and found that no physical characteristics differentiated the two groups. Goring also refuted Lombroso's contention that criminals could be identified on the basis of physical "stigmata of degeneracy."[7]

The intriguing aspects of some of Lombroso's assumptions about criminality and its biological nature were not, however, forgotten after Goring's scientific investigation. Modern theorists have attempted to further correlate some of Lombroso's earlier assumptions. The physical anthropologist, Ernest Hooton, compared thousands of prisoners with a smaller group of civilians on 107 anthropometric measurements and drew the following conclusions: (1) criminal behavior was a direct result of inherited biological inferiority, (2) particular types of crimes were caused by particular types of biologically inferior persons, as manifested by different patterns of defective autonomical traits, and (3) different races and different nationality groups committed characteristic patterns of offenses. Hooton also felt that environment played a very limited part in criminal behavior when compared with the inherited biological inferiority of "his criminals." He felt that the environment merely accentuated latent biological predispositions.[8]

Hooton's conclusions have, like Lombroso's, been widely rejected by most scientific observers, who not only question his anthropological findings but also his statistical methods and the basis of his reasoning. More recently, however, William H. Sheldon has also attempted to correlate biological inferiority with criminality, but he combines personality traits with the biological emphasis. He has made some interesting assumptions which will be discussed briefly.

Sheldon took the works of Lombroso, Kretschmer, and Hooton and elaborated upon them, combining personality characteristics as they relate to body structure. As a result of his investigations, Sheldon arrived at three body classifications—*endomorph, mesomorph,* and *ectomorph*—which combine certain physical characteristics with temperament characteristics. For example, the endomorph is a rotund person with such temperament characteristics as jovialness and outgoingness. He is considered an extrovert. The mesomorph is muscular, with such temperament characteristics as aggressiveness, competitiveness, and physical drive. The ectomorph is slender and slight. Temperamentally he is aloof and withdrawn, and he is considered an introvert. In evaluating an individual according to these

[7]Charles Goring, *The English Convict* (London: His Majesty's Stationery Office, 1913), p. 175; cited in Richard R. Korn and Lloyd W. McCorkle, *Criminology and Penology* (New York: Holt, Rinehart & Winston, Inc., 1966), p. 215.

[8]Ernest A. Hooton, *Crime and the Man* (Cambridge: Harvard University Press, 1939), p. 130.

characteristics, Sheldon developed a numerical scale. An individual could receive a classification of, for example, 5-3-1, which would indicate that on a 10-point scale, he had a score of 5 for endomorphy, 3 for mesomorphy, and 1 for ectomorphy. Sheldon felt that of the three classifications, delinquents and criminals adhered most closely to his mesomorph classification with the corresponding temperament traits of aggressiveness, competitiveness, and the like.[9]

The biological, or body-type, approach to studying criminality and deviant behavior has been attacked on many grounds. The results at best have been superficial and the theorists themselves have contradicted each other. For example, Hooton felt that criminals and criminal types were inferior physically, whereas Sheldon felt that they were superior. There has been little scientific substantiation of the findings of the relationship of body type to criminality. Most of the studies have been done on institutionalized populations, without the benefit of control groups. Even though Sheldon rekindled some new enthusiasm with his approach, the biological school of crime causation, in general, is not popular at present. Studies have been conducted, however, that some researchers feel point to differences in chromosome makeup between offenders and nonoffenders. The XYY chromosome discussion has received popular attention, although many of the findings are inconclusive.

XYY Man: Recently there has been new emphasis on determining criminality through biological investigation, expecially through investigation of chromosomes. Since the early 1940s it has been recognized that some possible sex chromosome combinations are not normal: XO, XXY, XXX, and XYY and the rare combinations XXXX, XXYY, and XXXXY. All these combinations, except the XYY, had been described and identified prior to 1961. The August 26, 1961, issue of *Lancet* contained a preliminary report of an XYY man being identified, pointing out that this man had two abnormal children, one a mongoloid and one whose internal sex organs had not developed.[10]

After the 1961 discovery of the XYY chromosome abnormality, further studies were conducted. It was not until 1965, however, that a comprehensive report of the incidence of XYY males among mentally subnormal male patients with dangerous violent or criminal propensities, who had been institutionalized, was released. Jacobs, Brienton, and Melville reported that men with an additional Y chromosome presented a rather striking clinical picture. Of 197 patients examined, 12 were found to have chromosomal abnormality. Of this number, 7 were XYY types. One outstanding characteristic of the XYY male was that he was at least six inches taller than the general male population. This was the only unusual feature noted about the XYY man at that time.[11]

[9]Marshall B. Clinard, *Sociology of Deviant Behavior* (New York: Holt, Rinehart & Winston, Inc., 1963), p. 120.

[10]*The Lancet*, August 26, 1961. Note: Much of the research on the XYY man (references 10-14) was done by Roland Burnham, graduate student, School of Criminal Justice, Michigan State University, East Lansing.

[11]Patricia A. Jacobs, M. Brienton, and M. Melville, *Nature,* December 25, 1965, pp. 1351-52.

In 1966 follow-up research was conducted at the same mental hospital, and nine additional cases of the XYY syndrome were identified. Of the nine, eight were considered to be mentally retarded, one was schizophrenic, and all had criminal records. In addition, six of the nine were over six feet tall, although no other physical abnormality was present.[12] Upon additional investigation the researchers found that all nine XYY patients were suffering from a severe degree of personality disorder, though none had a history of any form of brain damage, epilepsy, or psychosis. In general, their personalities showed extreme instability. They had little goal orientation and a low frustration tolerance. The researchers felt that family background was not a significant factor in the XYY man's criminal behavior. In addition, only one of the thirty-one siblings of the nine XYY men had been convicted of a criminal offense. A control group used for comparison showed that XYY males differed in many ways from other incarcerated offenders—they had little skill in crime, their gain from crime was minimal, and they usually came from stable homes.[13]

Since the initial survey in 1965, eighteen other studies have been conducted in the Western world on inmates incarcerated because of criminality, mental illness, and retardation. The various surveys have pointed out that XYY men are much taller than the normal population, as well as having other physical abnormalities. The excessive height has been the one prominent characteristic that has been identified in every study, while other physical abnormalities, such as abnormal genitals, although being identified in most studies, have not shown up in every case.

Research has also indicated that the presence of an extra Y chromosome in any combination appears to greatly increase the probability of psychiatric problems, although an extensive review of available literature revealed no consistent trend toward any one type of psychological disorder in XYY males. No two studies agreed exactly on the psychological profile of the XYY male. The only consistency in the studies was that some type of psychological disorder or personality disturbance was present in all XYY males examined. These findings should be viewed with reservation, however, because of the inaccuracy of much psychological testing. Most testing, regardless of population, will reveal a certain percentage of individuals with some personality abnormality. Even in some studies of the XYY man where control groups have been used, there was little significant difference between the two groups. Research on the XYY man, although interesting, has been sketchy and in many cases inconclusive. Richard G. Fox, in the *Journal of Criminal Law, Criminology, and Police Science,* aptly sums up the present status of the XYY man:

> Although it will be shown that the research findings are less significant than reports first suggested and that there are strong psychological reasons for interest in the topic, the flurry of recent attention has at least provoked criminologists into reexamining the hitherto largely neglected field of

[12]W. W. Price, J. A. Strong, P. B. Whatmore, and W. F. McClemont, *The Lancet,* March 12, 1966, pp. 565-66.

[13]W. W. Price, J. A. Strong, P. B. Whatmore, and W. F. McClemont, *British Medical Journal,* 1 (1968), 533-36.

criminal biology. The new biological research is not simply a revamping of Lombroso or Hooton, but is rather a continuation and extension of the work of Kretschmer, Sheldon, and the Gluecks on the relationship between body type, temperament, and criminality. And in the final analysis its importance lies less in the weight of current findings than in the fact that the attempt to identify the behavioral correlates of particular genetic defects represents one of the important first steps toward the elimination of undesirable traits in human beings by genetic manipulation. The attainment of this goal, however frightening it may appear to be, is no fanciful dream; its realization has been seriously predicted for the first decade of the new century, and with the recently reported isolation of a single gene by a Harvard scientist, this prediction may already require updating.[14]

CONTEMPORARY THEORIES OF CRIMINALITY: AN OVERVIEW

The preceding discussion has attempted to illustrate briefly the transition and the historical development criminology has taken from the older Classical school of thought to the present emphasis on theories whose assumptions are based on the Positive school of criminology. This section will present the views of the major sociological and psychological theorists who have contributed to our present body of criminological knowledge.

Albert Cohen points out that sociological explanations of criminality do not oppose psychological explanations in that they are not rival answers to the same question, but they answer different questions about the same sort of behavior. Psychological theories are concerned mainly with motivation and those factors that contribute to the individual manifesting behavior in either deviance or conformity.

Sociological inquiry or theory is concerned with identifying variables and processes in the larger social system that in turn shape those that are involved in motivation and that determine their distribution within the system.[15]

Cohen further explains that

actions are not only events in the biographies of individuals [psychological theory]—things that people do; they are also events located somewhere in a social system or structure—in a family, a neighborhood, a city, a region, an organization, a country. Different kinds of deviant acts are variously distributed within a given social structure, and these distributions differ from one time to another and from one structure to another. It also makes sense to ask: What is it about social structures—their organization, their cultures, their histories— that accounts for differences within and between them?[16]

To simplify the distinction between psychological and sociological theories, it

[14]Richard G. Fox, The XYY Offender! A Modern Myth? *The Journal of Criminal Law, Criminology and Police Science,* 52, No. 1 March 1971, p. 62.

[15]Albert K. Cohen, *Deviance and Control* (Englewood Cliffs, N.J.: Prentice-Hall, Inc., 1966), p. 47.

[16]*Ibid.,* pp. 45-46.

may help the reader to remember that the psychologist takes a more individualistic, specific view of human behavior and the personal internal factors that contribute to criminality. The sociologist takes a more general view, looking at the external environment in which the individual lives. The sociologist is concerned with the distribution of crime within the environment and the factors in the system that affect the crime rates. The sociologist can usually accurately predict the amount of crime that will be committed in certain areas, but he is unable to pinpoint the specific potential offenders.

MAJOR SOCIOLOGICAL THEORIES

As pointed out earlier, sociology was the first major discipline to study criminology and criminal causation. The sociological approach to crime causation is concerned with the effects the social system or the environment has on the development of attitudes, group patterns of behavior, and other social factors.[17]

Sociologists have been very comfortable and most successful, in dealing with the concept of how society acquires crime and the processes that contribute to crime causation. It becomes more difficult for the sociologist, however, to translate these broad abstract concepts into variables that can give some indication of how the individual acquires criminal behavior—when motivation is discussed, it is usually in the domain of the psychologist.[18] It becomes necessary, however, for theorists to make the connection between abstract general sociological theory and the more specific motivational aspects of psychological theory. In this respect, some theorists are appropriately classified as *social psychologists* because they consider both social and psychological factors in relation to crime and crime causation.

Of all the academic disciplines that have attempted to study crime causation, sociology is probably the most diverse. Many approaches and variations of ideas and assumptions have been incorporated into the field of sociology. For example, social psychologists sometimes use the case history technique of psychiatry. Sociologists sometimes use the interviewing method and the conceptual framework of psycho-analysis, as well as the psychometric methods of psychology if they are statistically sophisticated and trained. Regardless of these variations, however, there is a common emphasis in the field of sociology that the individual's environment is the major contributor to crime causation. For this reason the major emphasis of the theories constructed by sociologists revolves around how the culture, the social system, and the other social processes contribute to crime causation, even though secondary explanations may be borrowed from other disciplines.[19]

Underlying sociological investigation, as it relates to various social processes,

[17]Donald R. Taft, *Criminology* (New York: The Macmillan Company, 1956), p. 84.

[18]Richard R. Korn and Lloyd W. McCorkle, *Criminology and Penology* (New York: Holt, Rinehart & Winston, 1966), pp. 273-74.

[19]Frank E. Hartung, "A Critique of the Sociological Approach to Crime and Correction," *Law and Contemporary Problems,* 23 (Autumn 1958), 703-36.

is the assumption that unfavorable environmental conditions influence an individual's actions and either directly or indirectly force him into delinquency or crime. Emphasis is placed on explaining crime causation by referring to the learning process and the effect the environment has on learning. Some authors point out that the process involved in learning to become a criminal is not much different from the process involved in learning other types of social behavior, such as learning an occupational role, or the role of a teen-ager or a parent.[20] A major criticism of sociological theory is that it does not explain why the majority of people, both juveniles and adults, who live under unfavorable environmental conditions do *not* become delinquent or criminal.[21] Sociological theory obviously does not answer all the questions relating to crime causation.

The way the sociologist views crime causation and the perspectives and assumptions that underly his thinking has been discussed. The following section will present the views of the major theorists within the field of sociology who have contributed to an increased understanding of delinquent behavior and adult criminality. These theorists are by no means the only writers who have had something to say about crime causation. They have mainly been selected because of their specific contribution or because their viewpoints are similar to those of other theorists.

Anomie Theory—Emile Durkheim

Durkheim was one of the earliest theorists to discuss the effect that the social structure and its organization has on rates of deviancy. He specifically studied the way the culture affects suicide rates in different countries, regions within countries, and communities within regions. He felt that because the suicide rate was stable within certain sections of a country, it was typical of the system and the environment. He also felt that the system or environment contributed to other types of deviant behavior that include rates of criminality. He attempted to explain why a lack of social solidarity, with people working at cross-purposes, usually results in confusion, inefficient performance of essential social functions, and a tendency toward social disintegration. This in turn produces unpredictability and uncertainty and causes the regulation of relationships among the various elements of the social system to break down. Durkheim called this condition *anomie,* which, in effect, means normlessness, or a lack of criteria or rules to guide behavior so that it will be somewhat uniform and orderly.[22] Anomie is a state in which social norms no longer control men's actions. Although most of Durkheim's work revolved around his study of the division of labor in organizations and suicide causation, his

[20]Cressey, *op. cit.,* p. 169.

[21]Walter C. Reckless, *The Crime Problem* (New York: Appleton- Century-Crofts, 1967), p. 387.

[22]Emile Durkheim, *Suicide: A Study in Sociology,* trans. by John A. Spaulding and George Simpson (Glencoe, Ill., The Free Press, 1951).

concept of anomie had implications for the study of criminality and crime causation and was developed by Robert Merton in relation to deviant behavior.

Social Structure and Anomie—Robert Merton

The main thrust of Merton's efforts was "in discovering how some social structures exert a definite pressure upon certain persons in a society to engage in nonconformist rather than conformist conduct."[23] He made a threefold distinction in his theory of deviant behavior, which was similar to Durkheim's analysis of suicide causation. There are (1) the cultural goals or aspirations that men learn from their culture, (2) the norms that men employ when attempting to achieve the goals, and (3) the institutionalized means or the facilities that are available for goal achievement.[24]

When there is a discrepancy between the institutionalized means that are available within the environment and the goals that individuals have learned to aspire for in their environment, strain or frustration is produced and norms break down and deviant behavior can result. For example, if a ghetto child is exposed by the mass media to success symbols and a life-style that is difficult for him to achieve because of a lack of such institutionalized means as adequate schools and employment opportunities, this, Merton feels, will create strain and frustration. This strain and frustration can produce behavior that is deviant and contrary to the norms or the rules that generally govern behavior. The delinquency of the ghetto child would be explained by Merton as being the result of a discrepancy between the goals that the child has internalized and the means that were available to achieve these goals in a socially acceptable manner.

All societies differ in the way wealth is distributed and the way opportunities present themselves. Merton saw our society as being extremely productive, but at the same time creating frustration and strain because all groups do not have equal access to institutionalized means to achieve goals legitimately.

In his article, "Social Structure and Anomie," Merton states:

> It is only when a system of cultural values extols, virtually above all else, certain common symbols of success for the population at large while its social structure rigorously restricts or completely eliminates access to approved modes of acquiring these symbols for a considerable part of the same population that anti-social behavior ensues on a considerable scale. The "end justifies the means" doctrine becomes a guiding tenet for action when the cultural structure unduly exalts the end and the social organization unduly limits possible recourse to approved means.[25]

In the same article Merton charts the alternative modes of behavior that may

[23]Robert Merton, "Social Structure and Anomie," *American Sociological Review*, 3 (October 1938), 672.

[24]*Ibid.*, pp. 672-74.

[25]*Ibid.*, p. 679.

result when there is a disjunction between goals, means, and institutionalized norms and when there is an overemphasis on goals or means. For example, when both societal goals and institutionalized means are adhered to, there is *conformity*. If the means are followed but the goal is lost sight of, there will be *ritualism*. The bureaucrat who becomes so engrossed with following the rules that he forgets that the rules are only a means to goal achievement, and not an end in themselves, is an example of ritualistic behavior. Another of Merton's alternatives, *innovation*, is emphasis on the goal and disregard for the institutionalized means. An example of this type of adaptive behavior would be a professional thief who wanted material rewards and success but did not want to follow the prescribed means, namely through legitimate employment, to achieve his goal. Merton discusses two other alternatives: *retreatism*, which is a rejection of both goals and means and can result in drug culture involvement; and *rebellion*, which is a withdrawal of all allegiance to the social system and an attempt to reconstruct a new one. An example of rebellion would be present-day revolutionaries. Merton's approach is essentially sociological because he does not discuss individual motivational factors as they relate to the selection of a particular alternative. His emphasis is on the strain produced by the system and the culture, and the position occupied by individuals, which will depend on the alternative they are forced to select. Merton's theory increases our understanding of the effects of strain produced by the system, but it does little to increase our understanding of why all persons in similar situations do not choose the same alternative, that is, deviance.

Gang Theory—Frederick Thrasher

At about the same time that Merton was positing his views on deviant behavior, Frederick Thrasher was exploring the subject of group delinquency. Many theorists have studied the group and its effect on delinquent behavior. Processes whereby a group takes on certain behavior characteristics and then transmits them to its members are intriguing for both the theorist and the layman. Although other theorists, such as Cohen, Ohlin and Cloward, and Miller, include gang behavior in their studies on delinquency, Thrasher is considered the foremost authority on gang behavior because of his extensive research on the subject.

According to Thrasher, his study

> is not advanced as a thesis that the gang is a cause of crime. It would be more accurate to say that the gang is an important contributing factor facilitating the commission of crime and greatly extending its spread and range. The organization of the gang and the protection which it affords, especially in combination with a ring or a syndicate, makes it a superior instrument for the execution of criminal enterprises. Its demoralizing influence on its members arises through the dissemination of criminal techniques and a propagation through mutual excitation of interests and attitudes which make it easier (less inhibited) and more attractive.[26]

[26]Frederick Thrasher, *The Gang* (Chicago: University of Chicago Press, 1936), p. 381.

Courtesy of Camp Highfields, Onondaga, Michigan

Positive Peer Influence

Thrasher felt that gangs originated naturally during the adolescent years from spontaneous play groups. The major factor that transformed a play group into a gang was conflict with other groups. As a result of the conflict, it became mutually beneficial for individuals to band together in the form of a gang to protect their rights and to satisfy needs which their environment and their family could not provide. By middle adolescence, the gang had distinctive characteristics, such as a name, a particular mode of operation, and usually an ethnic or a racial distinction.

Thrasher is probably best known for the systematic way he analyzed gang activity and gang behavior. His rigorous attempt at analyzing all facets of gang activity has probably never been equaled. He studied the local community to determine what influence it had on gang behavior. He found that the environment was permissive, lacked control, and facilitated gang activity. The presence of adult crime within these communities also influenced gang behavior because many of the adults who had high status in the community were adult criminals. Even though most of the gangs' activities were not illegal, the environment was supportive of gang behavior. Local businessmen would act as fences for stolen goods, and local citizens were readily available customers for the stolen property. Local politics also contributed to gang behavior—political pull was often the only way that benefits could be obtained because of the extreme poverty conditions that existed at this time.

Thrasher also studied gangs at the level of the adolescent and determined what activities were normal for adolescents and what activities were unique to gang members. He showed that gang behavior was enticing, rewarding, and supported within the environment. He emphasized that not all gang activities were necessarily devious and that much of the gang members' time was spent in normal athletic activities as well as in other teen-age endeavors.

Thrasher, like Durkheim and Merton, described how the environment can be conducive to delinquent behavior. The more the environment is supportive of and conducive to delinquency, the more delinquency will exist. Durkheim's example of suicide's being a reaction to the strain produced by the environment, as well as Merton's description of alternatives available to strain, can be correlated with Thrasher's discussion of gang behavior's being a mode of adaption to environmental pressure. The following theorists shed some light on why crime rates and criminal activity are inordinately high in certain environments and sections of the community.

Cultural Transmission: Clifford Shaw and Henry McKay

In attempting to account for the distribution of delinquency in American cities, Shaw and McKay concluded that because the high rate of delinquency that existed in Chicago from 1900 to 1906 had not changed a great deal from 1917 to 1923, even though demographic changes had taken place, delinquency and crime was learned and transmitted from one group to another and from one generation to the next and was fairly stable within the central part of large cities. The core of their theory was that crime was transmitted through personal and group contacts and that lack of effective social control agencies also contributed to the high incidence of crime in these areas.

> In some parts of the city, attitudes which support and sanction delinquency are, it seems, sufficiently extensive and dynamic to become the controlling forces in the development of delinquent careers among a relatively large number of boys and young men. These are the low income areas where delinquency has developed in the form of the social tradition inseparable from the life of the local community.[27]

The authors state that delinquency often becomes enticing because of the contact that the youngster has with persons in his environment. They feel that

> from the point of view of the delinquent's immediate social world he is not necessarily disorganized, maladjusted, or antisocial. Within the limits of his

[27]Clifford R. Shaw and Henry D. McKay, *Juvenile Delinquency and Urban Areas* (Chicago: University of Chicago Press, 1969), p. 316.

social world and in terms of his norms and expectations, he may be a highly organized and well adjusted person.[28]

According to Shaw and McKay, economic status has a great deal to do with the rates of delinquent behavior. The greater the economic deprivation, the greater the delinquency. The less the economic deprivation, the less the delinquency. Like Durkheim and Merton, Shaw and McKay feel that persons living in disadvantaged environments often have the same material aspirations as persons living in areas that have social and economic advantages. Residents in disadvantaged areas soon learn, however, that legitimate access to their goals is difficult. The disparity between their goals and the means available for achieving them in a legitimate manner therefore creates a situation conducive to deviancy, delinquency, and crime in the urban world.

The authors sum up their propositions as follows:

it may be said, therefore, that the existence of a powerful system of criminal values and relationships in low income urban areas is a product of a cumulative process extending back into the history of the community and of the city. It is related both to the general character of the urban world and to the fact that the population in these communities has long occupied a disadvantageous disposition.[29]

Furthermore,

it is the assumption of this volume that many factors are important in determining whether a particular child will become involved in delinquency. Even in those communities in which a system of delinquent and criminal values exist, individual and personality differences as well as differences in family relationships and in contacts with other institutions and groups no doubt influence greatly his acceptance or rejection of opportunities to engage in delinquent activities. It may be said, however, that if the delinquency tradition were not present and the boys were not, thus, exposed to it the preponderance of those who become delinquent in low income areas would find their satisfaction in activities other than delinquency.[30]

Shaw and McKay do acknowledge that other factors may cause certain youngsters to become involved in delinquent activities, but they feel that these individual factors are secondary to the economic and social factors that exist in the community and have little bearing on actual rates of delinquency. The authors' emphasis on crime and delinquency as a learned phenomenon while living in an environment conducive to deviant activity is further defined and elaborated in a theory developed by Edwin Sutherland.

[28]*Ibid.*
[29]*Ibid.*, p. 320.
[30]*Ibid.*, p. 321.

Differential Association—Edwin Sutherland.

Sutherland's theory of differential association is probably one of the most systematic and complete theories of delinquency causation that has yet been constructed. The theory states that (1) criminal behavior is learned; (2) criminal behavior is learned in interaction with other persons in the process of communication; (3) the principal part of learning of criminal behavior occurs within intimate personal groups; (4) when criminal behavior is learned, the learning includes not only techniques for committing the crime, which are sometimes very complicated, sometimes very simple, but also a specific direction of motives, drives, rationalizations, and attitudes; (5) the specific direction of motives and drives is learned from definitions of legal codes as favorable and unfavorable—in American society, these definitions are almost always mixed and consequently there is culture conflict in relation to the legal codes; (6) a person becomes delinquent because of an excess of definitions favorable to violation of law over definitions unfavorable to violation of law; (7) differential association may vary in frequency, duration, priority, and intensity; and (8) the process of learning criminal behavior by association of criminal and anticriminal patterns involves all of the mechanisms that are involved in any other learning.[31]

An important principle of differential association is that delinquent behavior will be predictable if there is an excess of definitions within the environment favorable to the violation of laws versus those definitions that are unfavorable to the violation of laws. When the former set of definitions takes precedence over the latter, the stage is set for the commission of crime. If an individual associates mostly with criminals, chances are that he will become involved in delinquent activity. Conversely, if an individual associates mostly with noncriminals, chances are that he will not become involved in delinquent activity. Sutherland's concepts of *frequency*, *duration*, *priority*, and *intensity* in relation to the quality and quantity of relationships help explain the effects of differential association. If an individual has many contacts with criminals over a long period of time and if they are important to him, as well as intense, he will probably become involved in delinquent activity.

The major criticism of Sutherland's theory is that it is difficult to empirically test the principles and objectively measure "associations" and the priority, intensity, duration, and frequency of relationships. In their book, *Principles of Criminology,* Sutherland and Cressey admit that "the statement of differential association process is not precise enough to stimulate rigorous empirical test, and it therefore has not been proved or disproved. This defect is shared with broader social psychological theory."[32] Even though Sutherland's theory of differential

---

[31]Edwin Sutherland, *The Sutherland Papers,* ed. by Albert K. Cohen, Alfred R. Lindesmith, and Karl F. Schuessler (Bloomington: University of Indiana Press, 1956), pp. 8-10.

[32]Edwin Sutherland and Donald R. Cressey, *Principles of Criminology* (New York: J. B. Lippincott Co., 1966), p. 98.

association is one of the most complete and systematic theories that exists regarding the way criminality is learned and transmitted, he does not adequately handle the problem of why some persons in the same environment incorporate and assume criminality as a mode of behavior while their peers do not. Role theory provides a part of the explanation and adds another piece to the puzzle of crime causation.

Self-Role Theory—George Herbert Mead

Mead lends new insight into why an individual takes on certain types of behavior (roles), becomes comfortable with them, and develops a characteristic life-style.[33] Role theory helps explain why only a limited number of persons assume criminal identities while the majority of people remain law abiding. Cohen adequately sums up the concept of role theory when he states that

> it assumes, like differential association theory, that we do not learn anything without first being exposed to it. It also assumes, however, that whether we take notice of it, remember, and make it our own depends on whether it matters to us. . .from the standpoint of role theory, the central issue in the problem of learning deviant behavior becomes the process of acquiring and becoming committed to roles.[34]

Hence, becoming delinquent and assuming a criminal identity involves more than merely associating with law violators. The associations have to be meaningful to the individual and supportive of a role and self-concept that he wants to become committed to. Durkheim, Merton, Thrasher, and Shaw and McKay all emphasize the effect that the environmental system has on producing strain and, ultimately, deviant behavior. Sutherland explains how criminality is learned and transmitted. Mead tells us why it is incorporated into an identity and perpetuated as a role. The following theorists build upon the contributions of the above-mentioned theorists and blend them with their own.

Working-Class Boy and Middle-Class Measuring Rod—Albert Cohen

Cohen feels that the problem of delinquency is mainly a working-class phenomenon. He states that

> the working class boy, particularly if his training and values be those of the working class, is more likely than his middle class peers to find himself at the bottom of a status hierarchy whenever he moves into the middle class world whether it be of adults or children. To the degree to which he values middle class status either because he values the good opinion of middle class persons

---

[33]George Herbert Mead, "The Psychology of Punitive Justice", *American Journal of Sociology*, 23 (March 1918), 577-602.

[34]Cohen, *op. cit.*, p. 101.

or because he has, to some degree, internalized middle class standards himself, he faces the problem of adjustment and is in the market for a solution.[35]

He further states that

> a delinquent subculture is a way of dealing with the problems of adjustment. . . .These problems are chiefly status problems; certain children are denied the respect of society because they cannot meet the criteria of the respectable status system. A delinquent subculture deals with these problems by providing criteria of status which these children can meet.[36]

In other words, Cohen feels that working-class boys have not been equipped to deal with the competitive struggle that takes place in middle-class institutions. They have not learned the type of behavior that will contribute to their success and therefore are not comfortable when they come in contact with these institutions. As a result of this frustration they react against those institutions that they feel represent an environment that is too demanding, given the preparation they have received. "The hallmark of the delinquent subculture is the explicit and wholesale repudiation of middle class standards and the adoption of their very antithesis."[37]

Group or gang delinquent activity legitimizes and supports aggression against middle-class institutions. The collective support of the group is important to the boy if he persists in delinquent activity, because he is not convinced, at least unconsciously, that his hostile reaction is normal. As long as the group supports his actions he can continue to blame the external middle-class institutions and ward off internal feelings of inadequacy.

Cohen's work, like that of Ohlin and Cloward, the next theorists that will be discussed, combines the work of the sociologists previously mentioned. In addition, Cohen invades the realm of psychology when he talks about the delinquent's having problems of self-esteem and feelings of inadequacy. Cohen can be considered one of the few theorists who attempts to bridge the gap between sociology and psychology.

Success Goals and Opportunity Structures— Lloyd Ohlin and Richard Cloward

To cope with some of the discrepancies presented by anomie theory, role theory, and differential association, Ohlin and Cloward expand upon these precise concepts to give a more comprehensive explanation of the types of alternatives available as a result of strain. They also point out that the environmental system produces strain as a result of a lack of legitimate alternatives to satisfy needs.

[35] Albert Cohen, *Delinquent Boys, The Culture of the Gang* (Glencoe, Ill.: The Free Press, 1955), p. 119.

[36] *Ibid.*, p. 121.

[37] *Ibid.*, p. 130.

The disparity between what lower class youths are led to want and what is actually available to them is a source of a major problem of adjustment. Adolescents who form delinquent subcultures have internalized an emphasis upon conventional goals. Faced with limitations on legitimate avenues of access to these goals and unable to revise their aspirations downward, they experience intense frustrations and exploration of nonconformist alternatives may be the result.[38]

Ohlin and Cloward go on to say that

when pressures from unfulfilled aspirations and blocked opportunity become sufficiently intense, many lower class youth turn away from legitimate channels adopting other means beyond conventional mores, which might offer a possible route to successful goals. . . .Discrepancies between aspirations and legitimate avenues thus produce intense pressures for the use of illegitimate alternatives. Many lower class persons, in short, are the victims of a contradiction between goals toward which they have been led to orient themselves and socially structured means of striving for these goals. Under these conditions, there is an acute pressure to depart from institutional norms and to adopt illegitimate alternatives.[39]

Ohlin and Cloward describe three forms of behavior adaption to environmental strain. First, the criminal subculture, which exists in areas where there is a strong adult criminal culture and where youth groups learn patterns of criminality at an early age and then graduate to adult criminal circles. The illegitimate response to strain in these neighborhoods takes the form of criminal apprenticeship programs. Second, the conflict subculture, which is similar to the criminal subculture in that it offers limited access to goal achievement through legitimate channels; however, no strong ties with the adult criminal subculture exist, resulting in a lack of even illegitimate opportunities for goal achievement. Criminality is more individually oriented in these neighborhoods, and behavior is more violent, and less structured and systematic. Criminal apprenticeships do not generally exist. The third form of behavioral adaption is the retreatist subculture, in which neither avenue of opportunity, legitimate or illegitimate, exists. In addition an individual may also have certain moral inhibitions about becoming involved in a criminal type of behavior. The conflict may be resolved if the person withdraws from his environment and retreats to a drug culture.

Ohlin and Cloward's theories, like most of those that have been discussed, are difficult to test and evaluate empirically. They make assumptions about human behavior and reaction to strain, but there is difficulty in translating the assumptions into practical application. Even though Ohlin and Cloward, unlike the other theorists, give a more definitive description of alternatives to strain, all three forms of reaction and adjustment they described can exist within the same neighborhood.

[38]Lloyd Ohlin and Richard Cloward, *Delinquency and Opportunity, A Theory of Delinquent Gangs* (New York: The Free Press of Glencoe, 1960), p. 86.

[39]*Ibid.*, p. 105.

Their categories are useful for description but are not always reliable for predicting the mode of behavior and subsequent strategies for prevention, control, and treatment.

Ohlin and Cloward, Cohen, Durkheim, Merton, Shaw and McKay, and Thrasher have all either stated or implied that crime is the result of strain produced by a lack of environmental opportunity and is therefore more prevalent among the lower socioeconomic classes. The hostile manifestation of criminal behavior is generally felt to be a reaction to economic and social conditions as well as to those institutions that set normative standards. The next theorist, Walter Miller, proposes that delinquent behavior may not necessarily be a reaction to strain or a rebellion against middle-class institutions, but simply behavior that is contrary to the middle-class standards because of different learned patterns of conduct acquired from their lower-class culture.

Lower-class boy and lower-class structure—Walter Miller

According to Miller,

> in the case of gang delinquency, the cultural system which exerts the most direct influence on behavior is that of the lower class community itself—a long established distinctively patterned tradition with an integrity of its own—rather than a so-called "delinquent subculture" which has arisen through conflict of middle class culture and is oriented to the deliberate violation of the middle class norms.[40]

The lower-class culture that Miller mentions has come about as a result of the processes of immigration, migration, and mobility. Those persons who are left as a result of these processes comprise the lower class and have developed a pattern of behavior which is distinct to that class and is not necessarily reactive against any other class. Miller states that

> expressed awareness by the actor of the element of rebellion often represents only that aspect of motivation of which he is expressively conscious; the deepest and most compelling components of motivation—adherence to highly meaningful group standards of toughness, smartness, excitement, fate, and autonomy are often unconsciously patterned. No cultural pattern as well established as the practice of illegal acts by members of lower class corner groups could persist if buttressed primarily by negative, hostile, or rejective motives; its principal motivational support, as in the case of any persisting cultural tradition, derives from a positive effort to achieve what is valued within that tradition and to conform to its explicit and implicit norms.[41]

Miller also discusses, in addition to distinctive lower-class traits (toughness,

[40]Walter Miller, "Lower Class Culture as a Generating Milieu of Gang Delinquency," *Journal of Social Issues,* 14, No. 3 (1958), 6.

[41]*Ibid.,* p. 19.

autonomy and so on), the effects female-based households in lower-class families have on the adolescent boy's sexual identification. The street group provides him with an opportunity to act tough, become involved in other masculine activities, and reject the female orientation that has been the greater part of his life up to that point. Many of the boy's delinquent activities revolve around his desire to become a "real man." Furthermore, the excitement and free life of the streets and the gratification received from "acting out" by means of the group provide a greater return for the effort expended than can be gained by adopting the more sedentary behavior that is normative to the other socioeconomic classes.

The major criticism of Miller's theory is that today, with mass communication, it is difficult to believe that the distinct lower-class culture Miller describes can exist in such a pure form—Miller's lower class will undoubtedly be influenced by the other classes, and adaption to the environment, whether legitimate or illegitimate, will include influences that extend beyond the immediate community. Miller has presented his ideas on delinquency and its relation to the lower class. Other writers have also correlated delinquency with social class.

Middle-Class Juvenile Delinquency—Edmund Vaz

Much has been written about juvenile delinquency and its prevalence in the lower-class sections of communities. Edmund Vaz is one of the few theorists to focus on middle-class delinquency. He states that

> the apparent inconsistency between the protective upbringing of middle-class children and their delinquencies is a result partly of middle-class delinquency as viewed as a function of conformity to the expectations of the role of adolescent in the middle-class youth culture and to parentally favored activities. Among middle-class teen-agers, sociability is the quickest route to acceptability and status gain. The recluse and the bookworm are seldom admired. Teen-agers expect enthusiastic participation from peers in youth cultured events. But the pursuit of status and the pull of popularity can easily lead to novel kinds of behavior variations on everyday games and practices. Perhaps much middle-class delinquency is precisely these kinds of acts. This suggests that certain kinds of delinquency are an unexpected result of institutionalized patterns of conduct, and that delinquency is spawned among the stable, cherished values, attitudes and activities of the middle class.[42]

Vaz emphasizes the youth culture and particularly the youth culture of late and describes how certain activities are fostered, perpetuated, and supported by adults. Parents consider it important that their children become involved in these activities which are considered normal. At the same time the child feels it is important to gain status with his peers and be an active participant in group activities. It is precisely from these group activities and group involvement that middle-class delinquency evolves. Vaz states that

[42]Edmund Vaz, *Middle-Class Juvenile Delinquency* (New York: Harper & Row, Publishers, 1967), p. 4.

although all behavior is perhaps partly exploratory, stabs at marginal differentiation are likely to be guarded, tentative, and ambiguous and to transpire in a situation characterized by "joint exploration and elaboration" of behavior. Yet extreme conduct of any kind is apt to be strongly disapproved among sophisticated youths, and there exist strong motivations to conform to prevailing norms and patterns. But the boundaries of legitimacy are not impregnable, and it is during these legitimate, fun-ridden activities that boys are encouraged to join in, that unobtrusive acts lead gradually to unanticipated elaboration beyond the precincts of legitimacy. Since adolescent activities occur in a spirit of good-will, creative efforts are applauded, encouraged, and behavioral novelty is seldom considered delinquent.[43]

Vaz, then, is saying that as a result of normal group activities, innovation is tried and deviations that were at first slight and were considered exploratory and adventurous then become normative to the group and are ultimately taken for granted. An example of deviancy that results from normal group association is shoplifting, an activity that has become commonplace among affluent middle-class teen-agers. Youngsters caught shoplifting often explain that their activity originated as a game played for excitement and novelty. The activity, then, is perpetuated for the above factors as well as for other benefits, such as material gain. The important point, however, is that the activity originated from the normal processes of group interaction and involvement. Vaz sums it up very well when he says:

The motives for much middle-class delinquency are learned through sustained participation in everyday respectable adolescent activities. In this manner, delinquency becomes gradually routine in the middle-class youth culture.[44]

All the sociologists discussed thus far have explored the phenomenon of criminality in the tradition of the Positive school of criminology. They emphasize the role of the environment in determining adaptive behavior rather than the free will and rationalism emphasized by the Classical school. The next theorist to be discussed, David Matza, a modern sociologist, combines the most relevant concepts of both the Positive and the Classical schools in an attempt to provide new insights into delinquent and criminal behavior.

Delinquency and Drift—David Matza

Matza attempted to blend the Classical school's concept of "will to crime" with Positive assumptions and methods of scientific investigation. He does not totally agree with the deterministic orientation of the Positive school—that delinquent behavior is caused almost entirely by emotional and environmental factors. Matza acknowledges that environmental and emotional factors can have an effect on the individual's behavior, but he feels that other aspects contribute to making one youngster choose the delinquent route while another youngster in the same

[43]*Ibid.*, p. 135.
[44]*Ibid.*

general environment does not. Matza feels that man is neither totally free, as the Classical school assumes, nor totally constrained or determined, as the Positive school assumes. He feels that everyone is somewhere between being controlled and being free and that everyone drifts between these two states.

> Drift stands midway between freedom and control. Its basis is an area of the social structure in which control has been loosened, coupled with the abortiveness of adolescent endeavor to organize an autonomous subculture, and thus an independent source of control, around illegal action. The delinquent transiently exists in a limbo between convention and crime, responding in turn to the demands of each, flirting now with one, now the other, but postponing commitment, evading decision. Thus, he drifts between criminal and conventional action.[45]
>
> Drift is a gradual process of movement, unperceived by the actor, in which the first stage may be accidental or unpredictable from the point of view of any theoretic frame of reference, and deflection from the delinquent path may be similarly accidental or unpredictable. This does not preclude a general theory of delinquency. However, the major purpose of such a theory is a description of the conditions that make delinquent drift possible and probable and not a specification of invarient conditions of delinquency.[46]

According to Matza, psychological makeup and environmental factors do not destine an individual to become delinquent. There is, however, a movement between convention and crime, and impinging factors, one of them being the individual's "will," can influence which route he ultimately chooses.

Even though most of a youngster's activities are law abiding, he can periodically drift into delinquency because the normal conventional controls that usually inhibit delinquent behavior become neutralized as a result of the drifting process. When the youngster does become involved in difficulty this is not an irreversible process, however, because he can and usually does drift back to conventionality. When the youngster does drift into delinquency and when the moral commitment to conventionality is neutralized, this is when the element of "will to crime" plays an important part. "I wish to suggest that the missing element which provides the thrust or impetus of which the delinquent act is realized is will."[47]

Matza's concept of "will" provides an important element in understanding why some youngsters choose delinquent behavior while most of their peers within the same environment choose socially acceptable modes of adaption. He also explains why delinquency is not an "either-or" proposition. Most youngsters exist somewhere along the continuum between convention and crime. Total commitment to delinquency is uncommon.

Matza's theory also has important implications for fostering cooperation between the professionals who work within the criminal justice system. As will be pointed out in Chapter 6, policemen and social workers, the two largest professional

[45]Matza, *op. cit.*, p. 28.
[46]*Ibid.*, p. 29.
[47]*Ibid.*, p. 181.

groups within the criminal justice system, usually make different assumptions about the etiology, control, treatment, and prevention of juvenile delinquency. Policemen's assumptions are usually derived from the Classical school, whereas social workers' assumptions emanate from the Positive school. Combining the two schools into one comprehensive theory like that of Matza's can provide a new understanding of juvenile delinquency and can foster cooperation between the agencies within the criminal justice system.

CONCLUSIONS FROM SOCIOLOGICAL THEORIES

The preceding section has attempted to give the reader a general view of the major sociological theories of juvenile delinquency. All these theories have their strengths and their weaknesses. Merton and Durkheim have shown how the discrepancy between institutional means available and goals desired can produce strain which can in turn lead to delinquency. Thrasher, in a more general sense, also alludes to strain as a result of poverty and points out that an environment is conducive to delinquent behavior when ineffective social controls and inadequate models for identification exist. Shaw and McKay's and Sutherland's work also stresses the importance of the environment for determining delinquent behavior. They also point out how delinquency and crime are transmitted from one group to another and how stable criminal patterns can result because of this learning process. George Herbert Mead sheds some light on how a delinquent role is incorporated into a life-style. If delinquent behavior is supportive of a person's identity, he will incorporate it and use it. Ohlin and Cloward's and Cohen's work is similar to that of all the above-mentioned theorists in that they too emphasize strain from the social system. However, the delinquent behavior they describe takes on more of a reactive nature against the dominant middle-class system and its social institutions and much of the delinquency is hostile and nonutilitarian and is used solely to vent aggression. Miller and Vaz relate delinquency to class status, with Miller emphasizing the lower class and Vaz the middle class as the major departures for their theorizing. David Matza was important to the discussion because of his attempt to combine the most relevant concepts of both the Classical and the Positive schools of criminology. His realistic description of the "drift" process also helped place the delinquency phenomenon in its proper perspective.

This abbreviated discussion of the major sociological concepts does not of course include all the theorists who have contributed to an understanding of juvenile delinquency. Chapter 4 will examine other concepts as they relate to juvenile delinquency and the family.

Compared with sociological theorists, few psychologists seem to be interested in theorizing about juvenile delinquency and adult crime. Psychologists did not become interested in delinquency and criminality as a unique field of study until fairly recently. Even at the present time the study of delinquency and criminality is often considered only a secondary manifestation of the larger category of behavior termed *mental illness,* and the emphasis has been on studying mental illness in general.

MAJOR PSYCHOLOGICAL THEORIES

Whereas sociologists emphasize the environment of the social structure and its effect on crime rates and crime causation, psychologists take a more specific approach and consider the individual and his motivational patterns in an attempt to describe delinquency and criminality. The present discussion will focus on psychological factors, and the sampling of theorists will range from those who operate under Freudian assumptions to those who use testing as their major method of criminological investigation. Just as all sociologists cannot be grouped into a single category, all psychologists do not, as a group, emphasize the same areas of investigation. Some sociologists are more psychologically oriented than some psychologists, and vice versa. For descriptive purposes, however, it will be assumed that both fields have a distinct body of knowledge and method of investigation and that if a person calls himself either a sociologist or a psychologist certain assumptions can be made about his orientation to delinquency and criminality.

> Although wide-spread disagreement exists about the functioning of organic and environmental factors in the lives of delinquents, there is considerable unanimity on the part of most investigators about the presence of emotionally disturbed states among delinquent offenders, particularly the persistent delinquent. The precise diagnosis of these emotional states, however, is another matter and raises several vital questions—symptomatic states that appear similar need not necessarily be the same and conversely many emotional states that appear different in their manifestations originate from quite similar sources.[48]

At present there is no single psychological theory (just as there is no single sociological theory) that has been tested empirically and totally explains, in all circumstances, juvenile delinquency and criminality. In addition to assumptions not being tested, unsubstantiated overgeneralizations of human behavior have been made.

> This does not mean, however, that the search for valid hypothesis based upon demonstrated proof is not moving forward nor does it mean that the work in the field of delinquency may not be an important step in the development of an adequate personality theory.[49]

Evidence does not support the assumption of Aichhorn and some other

---

[48]Herbert A. Bloch and Frank T. Flynn, *Delinquency,* (New York: Random House, Inc., 1956), p. 153.

[49]*Ibid.,* p. 84.

theorists that all delinquents are emotionally ill. It is generally recognized, however, that many delinquents do have emotional conflicts. The Freudian viewpoint, with which psychoanalysis is most closely identified, is mainly concerned with treating and diagnosing mental illness. Although this approach did not place its major emphasis on investigating crime causation and criminality, attempts have been made, often unsuccessfully, to determine the variables that are related to this phenomenon. Even though psychiatry is not necessarily synonymous with psychoanalysis, some similarities exist, particularly if the psychiatrist does utilize Freudian principles.

One of the basic assumptions of psychiatry is that mental illness (of which delinquency may be a symptom) has its root in early childhood experiences. This approach has had great popularity, especially in the 1960s. Early family training and the supervision of children by their parents is also considered important. It is felt that early deprivation is directly associated with, and related to, later psychological disturbances and emotional problems. The greater the deprivation, the greater the emotional insecurity and the greater the chances for emotional problems.[50]

Psychoanalysis or the psychoanalytic school of thought, which is a particular psychiatric orientation, also makes similar assumptions but in addition uses unique methods of investigation. The psychoanalytic method, which Sigmund Freud, the Viennese psychiatrist, originated, places emphasis on sex, symbolism, and conflicts of the three components of personality—the *id,* the *ego,* and the *superego.* Briefly, the id is the source of all instinctual energy; the ego is the executive of the personality and directs the energy of the id into various channels; and the superego is the conscience, which attempts to satisfy both the needs of the individual and the demands of society.

Psychoanalysts feel that explanations for behavior can be found in analyzing the unconscious and the conflicts that exist. They also assume that childhood experiences take precedence over all social and cultural experiences. Early family relationships and the developing unconscious produce personality types, emotional needs, conflicts, and conforming or deviant behavior in spite of the culture.[51] For present purposes, the assumptions of psychiatry, psychology, and psychoanalysis will be considered as similar, despite the wide variety of behavioral orientation taken by persons identified with the psychological field. Generalizations will be made to facilitate discussion and comparison of psychology and sociology.

Psychiatry, as it became more concerned with the study of criminological behavior, began to examine psychological techniques and assumptions as they relate to crime causation. As pointed out earlier, the study of crime and crime causation had not originally been given priority by psychiatrists because they were more interested in mental illness and the manifestation of neurosis and psychosis.

Many modern concepts regarding criminal behavior are derived from the work

[50]Clinard, *op. cit.,* p. 125.
[51]*Ibid.,* p. 175.

sidered as a dynamic expression; it can be attributed to the innerplay of psychic forces, which have created the distortion which we call dissocial behavior.[60]

Aichhorn felt that reeducation as a result of understanding the delinquent's psychic processes was the way to solve the problem. He believed that help had to be more than just removing the delinquent symptom and that the cause of the problem had to be determined, or else the expression of the symptom would merely take another form.

Because of the conflicts that exist within delinquents, Aichhorn felt that first there had to be an understanding of the three dynamic components of the personality—the id, the ego, and the superego. As a result of understanding the interplay of these three dynamic components, conflicts could be diagnosed and the reasons for dissocial behavior understood. After this had been accomplished, psychoanalytic treatment methods along with the use of the milieu could be used to facilitate recovery. Since dissocial children have inadequate conscience structures, new positive identification models have to be provided so that the child's faulty identification with criminal parents or unacceptable persons in his environment can be altered.[61]

In reference to treatment, Aichhorn states that

re-education, however, is not achieved through words, admonition, scolding or punishment, but through what the child actually experiences. Through the milieu recreated in our institution and through our type of leadership, we had the opportunity every day to give the children experiences, the deep effect of which helped relieve their dissocial behavior.[62]

He goes on to say that

during the course of his training, the delinquent must learn that the amount of pleasure obtained from social conformity is greater than the sum of small pleasures derived from dissocial acts even when the accompanying discomfort of conformity is taken into account.[63]

The following theorists, although they are not considered to be psychoanalysts like Aichhorn, also used individual, psychological principles to study delinquency and crime.

The Individual Approach—W. Healy and A. Bronner

Healy and Bronner did not use the psychoanalytic method as their primary source of investigation and treatment. They state that

[60]*Ibid.*, p. 38.
[61]*Ibid.*, p. 171.
[62]*Ibid.*, p. 126.
[63]*Ibid.*, p. 158.

in terms of a general principle, the origins of delinquency in every case unquestionably represent the expression of desires and urges which are otherwise unsatisfied. For the onlooker, delinquency merely signifies misconduct. For the offender, it is just as much a response to inner drives and outer stimuli as any other kind of conduct. Delinquency is one small part of the total stream of the individual's life activities and in its significance represents, equally with other behavior, a response to inner or outer pressures. In common with all voluntary activities it is one variety of self-expression.[64]

The authors place a heavy emphasis on the child's feeling secure in his family, being accepted by his peers and other groups, and receiving recognition if he is going to make a satisfactory adjustment to his environment. They mention that in relation to their studies there has been

a striking finding ... [regarding] the immense amount of discoverable emotional discomfort that clearly has been part of the story of the origins of delinquency. On the other hand—very few indeed of the nondelinquents in the same families had in their emotional lives any such frustrations—and those few had found channels other than delinquency for modes of compensatory satisfaction.[65]

Furthermore,

when there have been no intense feelings of deprivations, inadequacies or thwartings as related to either ego impulses or desires for affection, the individual has been able to readily find sufficient satisfactions in socially acceptable behavior.[66]

The delinquent, the authors find, has almost universally been one

who at some stage of his development has been blocked in his needs for satisfying relationships in his family circle. On the other hand, the nondelinquent has nearly always been without any such acute frustration. His relationships with those in his immediate social environment had been much more satisfying.[67]

The authors emphasize that the delinquent feels deprived and inadequate and that he has not found socially acceptable channels for satisfying his needs. They explain why this is the case. They state that "the father or mother either had not played a role that was admired by the child or else on account of the lack of a deep love relationship, was not accepted as an ideal."[68] Furthermore,

[64]William Healy and A. Bronner, *New Light on Delinquency and Its Treatment* (New Haven, Conn.: Yale University Press, 1936), p. 3.

[65]*Ibid.*, pp. 6-7.

[66]*Ibid.*, p. 9.

[67]*Ibid.*, p. 201.

[68]*Ibid.*, p. 10.

In the lives of delinquents, the ever flowing stream of urges and wishes which, in general, follow the broader channels of socially acceptable behavior, has met obstructions or frustrations that caused part of the stream to be deflected into currents that sooner or later show the characteristics which we term delinquency. We are convinced that it is possible to discover in nearly every case the nature of these obstructions.[69]

Healy and Bronner go on to say that the nature of these obstructions can generally be discovered through psychological methods and the investigation of individual behavior. Other modern theorists, such as Scarpitti, Murray, Dinitz, and Reckless, have also made reference to psychological factors and their effect on delinquent behavior. They feel that internal factors such as lack of esteem and feelings of inadequacy contribute to delinquent behavior. More specifically, an adequate self-concept (feeling worthwhile) can be an insulating factor in repelling delinquency.

Juvenile Delinquency and Self-Concept— Frank Scarpitti, Ellen Murray, Simon Dinitz, and Walter Reckless

The authors did a longitudinal study comparing delinquent and non-delinquent boys over a four-year period to determine the relationship between a positive self-concept and delinquency.

The follow-up study confirms our 1955 predictions and those of the teachers and mothers of the respondents, as well as of the good boys themselves, that they would remain law-abiding in the future. They continue to isolate themselves from law violating friends and acquaintances; they predict law abiding behavior for themselves and in this respect they reflect their teacher's concepts of them—In sum, they continue to define themselves as good boys and are so defined by others in spite of remaining, for the most part, in high delinquency areas—The results of this investigation may be interpreted to mean that once a favorable self-image has been internalized by preadolescents with respect to friends, parents, school, and the law, there is every reason to believe that it is difficult to alter. ... In view of the relatively stable and cohesive families, the continued interest in and supervision of their activities by their parents, their school aspirations, and isolation from purveyors of delinquent values, it may be predicted that the good boys will persist in their law abiding behavior.[70]

This study indicates that if a youngster feels that he is not going to become delinquent and if he feels that his teachers and parents and other important adults within his environment perceive him as being adequate and not delinquent, then

[69]*Ibid.*, pp. 200-201.

[70]Frank R. Scarpitti, Ellen Murray, Simon Dinitz, and Walter Reckless, "The Good Boy in a High Delinquency Area," in *The Sociology of Crime and Delinquency*, ed. Marvin E. Wolfgang, Leonard Savitz, and Norman Johnston (New York: John Wiley & Sons, Inc., 1962), p. 209.

chances are he will not become delinquent. Conversely, if a child is perceived to be delinquent or predelinquent by his parents, teachers, and others within his environment, this will affect his own concept of himself, producing and perpetuating a negative self-image. A negative self-image or self-concept is conducive to the development of delinquent behavior.

Only a few of the major psychological theories have been examined in this section. Additional related material will be presented in the next chapter. The *multifactor* approach to studying juvenile delinquency will now be briefly examined. It incorporates both psychological and sociological principles. The work of Sheldon and Eleanor Glueck typifies this approach.

Multifactor Approach—Sheldon and Eleanor Glueck

Even though William Healy has been described as a theorist whose work incorporated psychological principles, he like the Gluecks was also influential in contributing to the multifactor approach.[71] In his studies he attempted to select all those factors that he felt explained some part of criminal behavior regardless of whether the principles originated from psychology or sociology.

Although the multifactor approach can make a valuable contribution to the understanding of criminal behavior, it is generally acknowledged that no one body of knowledge can be considered a theoretical base for this approach. Criticisms have been made of the multifactor approach, namely, that it is too loosely defined and that it is no more than a grab bag of superficial generalizations. A brief exposure to the multifactor point of view will be helpful, however, in providing a wider base of understanding of the delinquency phenomenon and how it is viewed by certain theorists.

The Gluecks state that

> persistent delinquency can be the result, not only of one specific combination or pattern of factors that markedly differentiate delinquents from non-delinquents, but of each of several different patterns. The concept of plurality of causal combinations immediately throws light on a host of puzzling problems in the study of crime causation. Just as the fact of a boy's death, although always and everywhere the same terminal event, may nonetheless be the result of various preceding sequences of conditions, so the terminal event of persistent delinquency may have in its causal pedigree and background a variety of different sequences leading to the same ultimate result of habitual antisocial behavior.[72]

In relation to the practitioner,

> many probation and parole officers, teachers, school attendants, officers, and others seem to want specific answers to the "why" of causation; that is, they

[71] Healy, *The Individual Delinquent.*

[72] Sheldon and Eleanor Glueck, *Venture in Criminology* (Cambridge: Harvard University Press, 1967), p. 16.

want to know what the "ultimate cause" of a child's misbehavior is and how it came about. But the ultimate cause is something like a mirage. The more you approach it, the farther it seems to recede.[73]

The Gluecks used the multifactor approach in comparing five hundred delinquents with five hundred nondelinquents. The delinquents were matched by residence in underprivileged areas, age, ethnic origin, and intelligence. The Gluecks considered sociological variables (the environment) and psychological variables (internal dynamic processes). In addition they administered tests. They concluded that the delinquency of the youngsters could not be blamed on any one set of factors. The delinquent behavior was the result of a combination of intellectual, social, temperamental, and physical factors. To pinpoint any particular one would be difficult. They summarized their findings as follows:

> it is particularly in the exciting, stimulating, but little controlled, and culturally inconsistent environment of the urban underprivileged area that such boys readily tend to give expression to their untamed impulses and their self-centered desires by "kicking over the traces" of conventionally dictated behavior. These tendencies are apparently anchored deeply in body and mind and essentially derived from malformations of personality and character during the first few years of life. It will be seen that virtually all the conditions enumerated are of a kind that in all probability preceded the evolution of delinquent careers, and in respect to sequence of events in time may legitimately be regarded as causally connected.[74]

Delinquency, then is the result of an interplay of many different and diverse variables as viewed from the multifactor approach.

CONCLUSIONS FROM PSYCHOLOGICAL THEORIES

Like the sociological theories discussed, the psychological theories add to an understanding and knowledge of deviant behavior, especially of the form that manifests itself in delinquency. As in sociological theory, there should be more scientific substantiation of the principles and assumptions utilized by psychologists and psychiatrists. Psychological theories and especially the psychoanalytic method have assumed certain universal uniformities about human behavior. Generalizations have been made from these assumptions, and hence conclusions are not always applicable to all classes and types of behavior.

There should also be a more precise differentiation of patterns of emotional conflicts and traits of delinquents so that they can be classified more adequately when being compared with both a normal population and a mentally ill population. Even though many delinquents are emotionally disturbed, there are many more

[73]*Ibid.,* p. 17.
[74]*Ibid.,* p. 27.

who are not—and conversely, most children who are emotionally disturbed do not become involved in delinquent behavior. Psychological theories, and especially psychoanalysis and that part of psychiatry that emphasizes unconscious behavior, make subjective judgments about behavior which are difficult to prove or disprove scientifically. Finally, behavior is determined by more than childhood experiences. Environmental factors are also important. Some psychologically oriented theorists fail to take this into consideration, which denies the existence of an entire body of relevant data and variables. The combination and blending of relevant data from many disciplines will contribute to a more thorough understanding of delinquent behavior.

Walter Reckless has been successful in combining psychological and sociological theory in what he calls his "containment theory" to explain both conforming and deviant behavior. He feels that there are two important aspects of control, *inner control* and *outer control,* and that depending upon the balance of these control systems, the individual can take either a deviant or a conformist route. His assumption is that "strong inner and reinforcing outer containment constitutes an isolation against normative deviancy (not constitutional or psychological deviancy). That is, violation of the socio-legal conduct norms."[75]

Some of Reckless's inner containment components consist of self-control, a good self-concept, high frustration tolerance, a well-developed superego, and so on. Outer containment represents factors such as institutional reinforcement of an individual's norms, goals, and expectations and social control factors such as supervision and discipline and limits.

> In a vertical order, the pressures and pulls of the environment are at the top or the side of the containing structure, while the pushes are below the inner containment. If the individual has a weak outer containment, the pressures and pulls will then have to be handled by the inner control system. If the outer buffer of the individual is relatively strong and effective, the individual's inner defense does not have to play such a critical role. Likewise, if the person's inner controls are not equal to the ordinary pushes, effective outer defense may help hold him within bounds. If the inner defenses are of good working order, the outer structure does not have to come to the rescue of the person.[76]

Effective control, then involves both internal factors (the conscience) and external variables (the environment). One compliments the other and often each has to "pick up the slack" and exert influence and control.

The major theoretical assumptions and principles regarding juvenile delinquency causation have been discussed in this part of the chapter. The final section will present some of the most widely used typologies for delinquent behavior.

[75]Walter C. Reckless, "A New Theory of Delinquency and Crime," in *Juvenile Delinquency: A Book of Readings,* ed. Rose Giallombardo (New York: John Wiley & Sons, Inc., 1966), p. 223.

[76]*Ibid.,* p. 229.

POPULAR TERMS FOR CLASSIFYING DELINQUENTS

Many terms and many approaches have been utilized for classifying delinquents. Those presented here will be the ones used most often when referring to categories of delinquent behavior.. There are several classificatory methods, which means that there will be some overlapping.

Classification by Offense. Hirsh, in 1937, delineated the following kinds of offenses: (1) *incorrigibility,* which includes keeping late hours, disobedience, and so on; (2) *truancy,* which can be from home or school, or AWOL from the army; (3) *larceny,* which ranges from petty larceny to armed robbery; (4) *destruction of property,* which includes both public and private property; (5) *violence,* which is perpetrated against the community, by using such means as knives and guns; and (6) *sex offenses,* which can range from homosexual activity to criminal assault and rape.[77]

Eaton and Polk also classify delinquents by the type of offense they have been involved in. They use five categories. (1) *Minor violations,* which includes disorderly conduct and minor traffic violations. Most negative behavior that youngsters are involved in would probably fall into the minor violation category. (2) *Property violations,* which includes all property thefts except automobiles. (3) *Major traffic violations,* which includes automobile theft and drunk driving and any other offense that would involve an automobile. (4) *Human addiction,* which includes sex offenses as well as alcohol and drug addiction. (5) *Bodily harm,* which includes homicide offenses that involve sexual deviation, such as rape, and generally all other acts of violence against a person.[78]

Sellin and Wolfgang also use the type of offense for classifying delinquent behavior. Under Class 1 they list (a) bodily or physical injury; (b) property theft; and (c) property damage. Under Class 2 they list (a) intimidation; (b) property loss with property loss threatened; (c) primary victimization, which is committed against a person; (d) secondary victimization, which is committed against a commercial establishment; (e) tertiary victimization, which includes offenses against the public order and regulatory offenses such as violation of city ordinances; (f) mutual victimization, which includes offenses that involve two individuals, such as adultery or statutory rape; and (g) no victimization, which includes such offenses as truancy from school and incorrigibility.[79]

Kvaraceus classifies youngsters who become delinquent in relation to three

---

[77]Nathaniel Hirsh, *Dynamic Causes of Juvenile Crime* (Cambridge, Mass., Sci-Art publisher, 1937).

[78]Joseph W. Eaton and Kenneth Polk, *Measuring Delinquency* (Pittsburg: University of Pittsburg Press, 1961).

[79]Thorsten Sellin and Marvin Wolfgang, *The Measurement of Delinquency* (New York: John Wiley & Sons, Inc., 1964).

major variables: (1) the extent to which the individual engages in delinquent behavior; (2) the degree of demonstratable emotional pathology; and (3) the individual's social class.[80]

The following classifications do not relate to offense; instead, they describe a behavioral adaption within the environment.

Gang-Organized and Collective Delinquency. Youngsters classified in this category would be those who perpetrate their illegal activities within a group. These children usually come from economically and socially deprived areas of the city and often seek excitement and express themselves through the gang. Much of their delinquent motivation and activity is a result of strain produced by the crowded conditions of their environment in large inner cities where economic opportunities are lacking and where upward mobility is difficult.

Unsocialized Aggressive Boys. Boys classified in this category would have long police records and would probably come from homes where they were rejected or where there was an early identification with a criminal parent—or at least an antisocial type of parent. Families where these children come from are prone to physical violence. There is much hate and aggression within the home, and this hate is often transmitted to the child. His frustration and hatred is then vented on the community, where it becomes very aggressive. This youngster obviously does not learn how to sublimate his impulses in a socially acceptable manner.

Accidental Offender. A youngster classified in this category would be one who is law abiding most of the time, but who has a lapse of judgment. He becomes involved in delinquent activity as a result of unforeseen circumstances. This type of youngster is usually not a problem, and his delinquent behavior ceases when he realizes what he has done or when he has been caught in the delinquent activity.

Occasional Delinquency. In general, the occasional delinquent is similar to the accidental offender in that he also becomes involved in minor offenses, but not on a chronic or regular basis. His delinquency, unlike that of the accidental offender, is planned, and he knows what he is becoming involved in. His family is well integrated and adjusted, and the youngster does not exhibit psychopathic disturbances. He is usually well adjusted, and there is no real pattern to his delinquency.

Professional Delinquency. A youngster classified in this category usually steals for profit. Stealing is for economic gain to satisfy some desire and, in many cases, an extravagant need.

For a detailed discussion of these classifications, see Hewitt and Jenkins, *Fundamental Patterns of Maladjustment: The Dynamics of Their Origin*, and Knulten and Schafer, *Juvenile Delinquency: An Introduction.*[81] The following

---

[80]William C. Kvaraceus, and Walter B. Miller, *Delinquent Behavior: Culture and the Individual* (Washington, National Education Association, 1959).

[81]Lester Hewitt and Richard Jenkins, *Fundamental Patterns of Maladjustment: The Dynamics of Their Origin* (Springfield, Ill.: State Printer, 1946); Richard Knulten and Stephen Schafer, *Juvenile Delinquency: An Introduction* (New York: Random House, Inc., 1970), pp. 109-87.

classifications can be considered psychological typologies because of their emphasis on individual factors and the psychological dynamics of the personality.

Mental Defective. This is an individual who has an organic problem and who has difficulty controlling himself because of it. Offenders who are mental defectives are involved in petty crimes, such as petty theft and petty larceny. This category also includes mentally retarded youngsters. These adolescents do not present a major problem in terms of involvement in serious types of delinquent offenses.

Situational Offender. This type of offender is similar to the accidental offender; however, there are more contributing factors and variables. His delinquency is usually precipitated by a crisis or by some external event that he has difficulty handling. The death of a parent or some other traumatic event in the child's life could present a situation he is incapable of handling and could thus contribute to delinquent behavior. Another example would be a youngster who is confronted with a delinquent opportunity in a unique situation and the temptation displaces his usual good judgment and he becomes involved in difficulty. This type of offender reacts to circumstances that occur in his environment at a particular time. In other words, he does not necessarily go out looking for trouble, but because of tempting circumstances, he does not use good judgment. Because of a series of events over which he initially had little control, he becomes involved in delinquent behavior.

Psychotic Offender. A small number of youngsters do not have contact with reality. They may be classified as schizophrenic or may be given some other psychiatric label. As a result of dysfunctional thought patterns, they may hallucinate, have delusions, or "hear voices" that command them to become involved in certain types of delinquent behavior. The incidence of psychotic-oriented delinquency is minimal in relation to the other forms.

Cultural Offender. A youngster in this category has either emulated faulty identification models or lives in an economically and socially deprived environment. His aggressiveness and delinquent acts may not necessarily be unusual for a youngster with his background. Cultural offenders are considered normal members of a deviant subculture, and their patterns of behavior are often accepted and normative for their environment.

The two major categories of delinquency typologies that are most often used in the psychiatric and psychological literature are (1) neurotic offender and (2) character disorder offender.

Neurotic Offender. This is the youngster whose delinquency is the result of powerful unconscious impulses which often produce guilt which in turn motivates him to act out his delinquency in his community so that he will be caught and punished. Punishment does not totally dissipate the guilt, however, and a vicious cycle develops which involves the manifestation of delinquent behavior. The delinquent act is considered symbolic. For example, if the youngster steals, he is stealing for love and not primarily for material gain. To the neurotic youngster, delinquency is a way of handling his internal conflicts by externalizing the problem within the environment.

Character Disorder Offender. The character disorder offender, unlike the neurotic offender, feels very little remorse when he acts out his delinquency in his community. Because of a lack of positive identification models in his environment, he has failed to develop self-control and does what he wants to do, when he wants to do it, because he wants to do it. He is unable to sublimate his impulses in a socially acceptable manner. He has difficulty postponing gratification, and he is considered irresponsible and emotionally shallow. He has not developed an adequate conscience structure or superego, comes from a disorganized family, and had a very barren environment in his early years. He is self-centered and aloof, and he has difficulty forming meaningful relationships.

The classifications presented are merely general descriptions. They overlap and do not occur in this pure form "in the real world." The major reason for presenting them is that there are different treatment implications for the various categories.[82] These implications will be alluded to in Chapter 9.

SUMMARY

This chapter has presented a sampling of the most prevalent theories of crime and delinquency causation. Because of the complexity of the problem, there is no single answer or "common cure." Many academic disciplines and theoretical approaches can contribute to a better understanding of the delinquency phenomenon and methods for its control, treatment, and prevention. Because a comprehensive knowledge of the problem necessitates an interdisciplinary approach, the next chapter uses the family as a framework for analyzing juvenile delinquency and incorporating psychological and sociological principles.

QUESTIONS AND PROJECTS

Essay Questions

1. What are the major differences between psychological and sociological theories?
2. Which school of criminological thought, the Positive or the Classical, is most appealing to you and why?
3. Is it useful to classify delinquents?
4. Why are biological theories of delinquency and crime causation not generally accepted?
5. Why do some theorists take an individual orientation to studying crime and delinquency causation, while other theorists take an environmental orientation?

[82]Theodore N. Ferdinand, Inc., *Typologies of Delinquency: A Critical Analysis* (New York: Random House, Inc., 1966).

Projects

1. Develop a project that puts into action one or more of the theories discussed.
2. Discuss the ways that your community can benefit from a knowledge of the theories of delinquency and crime causation.
3. Develop a checklist of psychological and sociological factors that have to be considered when trying to determine the causes of crime and delinquency in your community.

4

THE FAMILY
AND JUVENILE DELINQUENCY

This chapter will use the family as a model for integrating various psychological and sociological principles into a meaningful framework and will provide an understanding of both the psychologist's and the sociologist's view of the family's importance and contribution to the phenomenon of delinquency.

Regardless of the particular professional orientation or academic discipline, theorists generally agree that the family plays an important part in the youngster's life. The family institution provides the child with his first experiences in social living, and these experiences have an effect on most of his later development. What happens in the family can have great impact on how the child behaves in other social institutions and on whether he becomes "normal" or delinquent.

Many theorists thus consider the family the most significant factor in the development of juvenile delinquency. A review of the literature reveals that theorists ranging all the way from those oriented to Freudian psychology to those in the sociological field consider the family the most important environment of the child. Socioeconomic status, class status, peer group relations, class mobility, and delinquent subculture are also important, but if analyzed closely, each is either directly or indirectly related to the family environment.

Since no theory has been developed that can adequately account for all forms of delinquent behavior, it will be helpful to isolate those factors that contribute to delinquency. The family is one of the major factors.

Much research has been done by sociologists, psychologists, and psychiatrists concerning the relationship between family and delinquency variables and many theories have been advanced to explain the relationships found. Due to a severe lack of interdisciplinary communication, however, few attempts have been made to consider both the sociological and psychiatric aspects of the family's role in delinquency.[1]

An interdisciplinary effort, viewing the family's role in delinquent behavior as a model, can therefore be helpful in examining the delinquency phenomenon. The family can provide a basis for incorporating concepts and variables from both the psychological and the sociological disciplines to give a more insightful understanding of delinquency and a comprehensive approach to the problem.

Using the family as a model for examining the delinquency phenomenon can account for delinquency in all socioeconomic classes, since unhappy home situations and resulting problems cut across class lines and economic strata.

If class were the major determinant of delinquent behavior, the great majority of urban slum children would be delinquent. The great majority of urban slum children, despite their deprived environment and lack of adequate opportunity, do not become involved in delinquent behavior. As Gold points out, child-rearing variables that effect delinquent behavior regardless of class are found to be similar in delinquent families regardless of class.[2]

Delinquency cuts across all class lines, and a great deal of hidden delinquency never comes to official attention. There are indications that delinquency is more evenly distributed throughout the classes than most official records indicate.[3]

Official records deal only with those juveniles who have come into formal contact with the criminal justice system. It is difficult to determine the number of youngsters who have been reprimanded, taken to their parents, or released as the result of some other informal disposition. Even the determining factors related to formal disposition are often correlated with the economic status of the family, the location of the child's home, and other similar variables.

> Police dispositions tend to be related to demographic characteristics of offenders, thus, males, Negroes, lower income youths, and older boys are more frequently dealt with formally by court referral.[4]

Studies that are based on data from the records of officially adjudicated delinquents may lead to a theory of causation that is almost entirely related to socioeconomics (as were some of the theories discussed in Chapter 3). It is there-

---

[1]Hyman Rodman and Paul Grams, "Juvenile Delinquency and the Family; A Review and Discussion," *Task Force Report: Juvenile Delinquency and Youth Crime*, p. 195.

[2]Martin Gold, "Status Forces in Delinquency Boys," in Rodman and Grams, *ibid.*

[3]F. Ivan Nye, *Family Relationships and Delinquent Behavior* (John Wiley and Sons, New York, 1958), p. 23.

[4]Don C. Gibbons, *Delinquent Behavior* (Prentice-Hall, Inc., Englewood Cliffs, New Jersey, 1970), p. 45.

fore preferable to seek explanations that are not linked to class. Utilizing the family as a model for examining juvenile delinquency causative factors is a more logical approach.

PSYCHOLOGY AND THE FAMILY

Chapter 3 pointed out that psychological theories are mainly concerned with variables that relate to early childhood experiences which influence the formation of the personality. Psychologists feel that much early emotional deprivation is directly associated with, and related to, later psychological disturbances and emotional problems. The greater the deprivation, the greater the emotional insecurity, and therefore the greater the chance for emotional problems or deviant behavior.

August Aichhorn, a psychologically oriented theorist, stresses the importance of the family in shaping the children. He feels that the family should provide the child love and security and at the same time be a haven of relief from outside pressures.[5]

Sidney Berman believes that delinquent children have often had difficulty in their early relationships with their parents.

> This implies that these children have reacted adversely to certain early life experiences which other children have been guided through more adequately. The concern, therefore, is with the psychological factors which structure this morbid behavior.[6]

The early life experiences of the child in the family lay the groundwork for the type of future behavior and the development of attitudes, values, and a life-style. Parental hostility, rejection, and inconsistency can all contribute to delinquent behavior.[7] The family is the backdrop in which the child learns to deal with his emotions and drives and handle his problems in a socially acceptable manner. When the family does not help the youngster to adjust to his environment, he loses the most important means of psychological support and the most effective agent for socialization. Aichhorn states that so strong is the influence of the family in shaping behavior that pathology undoubtedly exists in all families where there is a delinquent youngster—even though families of delinquents may appear to be at least superficially normal and well adjusted, further investigation will identify some type of pathology or sickness. In addition to open hostility, there will often be shallow relationships between family members, little concern felt by parents for their children, and absence of a role model with whom the youngster can identify.[8]

[5] August Aichhorn, *Delinquency and Child Guidance* (International Universities Press, New York, 1969), p. 16.

[6] Sidney Berman, "Antisocial Character Disorder," in *Readings in Juvenile Delinquency*, ed. Ruth S. Cavan (J. B. Lippincott Co., Philadelphia, 1964), p. 142.

[7] *Ibid.*, pp. 142-43.

[8] *Ibid.*, p. 132.

When parents identify with and support positive community norms and values, they will be effective socializing agents for their children. If, however, parents do not transmit positive community norms and values to their children and fail as positive identification models, the children will often come in conflict with community institutions.[9]

There is widespread consensus, then, that early family training is important in influencing future behavior. Early childhood experiences, especially those experiences within the family, determine in great part how the youngster will be molded and how he will eventually adapt to the external environment.[10] Delinquency signifies more than merely misconduct—it is the expression of desires, drives, urges, and motivations which have been greatly influenced by the youngster's early experiences in his family. If early family experiences have been positive, the youngster will be able to handle the pressures and responsibilities he will meet in adjusting to the community because his parents will have assisted him in developing problem-solving capabilities.

Psychologically oriented theories that emphasize the importance of early parent-child relationships can be helpful in identifying those factors that most directly affect the child-rearing process. The identification of these variables is important in pinpointing reasons for the abnormal expression of behavior. When the behavior is expressed in an antisocial form, juvenile delinquency is the result.

SOCIOLOGY AND THE FAMILY

Whereas the psychologist is concerned with the identification of individual variables, such as motivation, drives, values, and needs, the sociologist is concerned more with the general environment as it relates to the distribution of crime, the factors in the system that affect crime rates, and the functioning of the institutions of control that have been commissioned to deal with the offender. In other words, sociology attempts to explain the manner in which society acquires crime, the processes that contribute to crime causation, and the mechanisms developed to deal with it.

Underlying sociological investigation is the assumption that unfavorable environmental conditions in the social system influence an individual's actions and, in fact, can force him into delinquency or crime. Even though sociology and psychology deal with different aspects of the crime problem (sociology stresses the system, psychology stresses the offender), both disciplines look at "control." Psychology emphasizes the process of personal or internal control that is represented by the superego (conscience). Sociology emphasizes the institutions in the community that directly influence the external social control processes. Reiss views delinquency as being the result of the failure of both personal and social controls to

[9]*Ibid.*, p. 232.

[10]Beatrice Simcox Reiner and Irving Kaufman, *Character Disorders in Parents of Delinquents* (Family Service Association of America, New York, 1959), p. 15.

produce behavior that conforms to social norms and is acceptable to the community.[11]

> Delinquency results when there is a relative absence of internalized norms and rules governing behavior in conformity with the norms of the social system to which legal penalties are attached, a breakdown in previously established controls, and/or a relative absence of a conflict in social rules or institutions of which the person is a member. Hence, delinquency may be seen as a function or consequence of the relationship established among the personal and social controls.[12]

The chance of delinquency becomes greater when both personal controls and social controls break down. In Chapter 3 we saw that when such community institutions of social control as the courts and the police are ineffective, delinquency and crime are more prevalent. Similarly, when the individual does not have an adequate conscience structure, internal personal control is ineffective. When there is a combined lack of *personal* and *social* control, delinquency and crime are often the result.

The family is extremely important because it can both influence the development of the internal control structure (conscience) and have an effect on the external control social process by its methods of direct control and discipline.[13] If the parents are not adequate models of identification, so that a positive conscience can develop, and if their methods of discipline are not effective, community social control institutions usually have to intervene.[14] Thus, if the youngster is going to refrain from delinquent behavior, he has to be guided by both internal and external control structures.[15] The family plays the greatest role in both these processes. Community institutions of control intervene only after the family has been unsuccessful.

THE ENVIRONMENT OF THE FAMILY

As Chapter 3 pointed out, sociological explanations of criminality and delinquency do not oppose psychological explanations because they are not rival answers to the same question but they answer different questions about the same sort of behavior.[16] The environment of the family can be appropriate for answering the "different" questions posed by both psychology and sociology. This section will

[11] Albert J. Reiss, Jr., "Delinquency as the Failure of Personal and Social Controls," *American Sociological Review,* 1951, pp. 196-207.

[12]*Ibid.,* p. 196.

[13]Nye, *op. cit.,* p. 72.

[14]*Ibid.,* p. 23.

[15]Gold, *op. cit.*

[16]Albert K. Cohen, *Deviance and Control* (Englewood Cliffs, N.J.: Prentice-Hall, Inc., 1966), p. 47.

discuss family environmental factors that can have an impact on producing delinquent behavior—broken home, family tension, parental rejection, methods of parental control, parental emotional stability, and family economics.

Broken Homes

Sheldon and Eleanor Glueck define a stable family as one in which at least one parent has a continuous physical and affectional relationship with the children.[17] They found that a much higher proportion of nondelinquents were exposed to households where there were minimal disruptions rather than those typified by parental separation, divorce, death, or parental absence. In a substantial number of the broken homes, the youngster was under five years of age at the time of the break.

> It is probable that the first definitive breach in the organic structure of the family is crucial because it is likely to deal the greatest blow to a child's conception of the solidarity and reliability of the parental team and to disrupt his general sense of security as well as of family stability.[18]

Over half of the delinquents studied were reared by one parent, whereas only 10 percent of the nondelinquents were reared by one parent.

Toby feels that the American family has its greatest influence over the younger children in the family, and hence it is most devastating to these children when the family becomes disrupted for whatever reason.[19] The older children in the family, because they have more autonomy and have developed various patterns for coping with problems, are not as adversely affected. This view corresponds with some psychologists' contention that a child's behavior patterns and psychic structure are almost completely formed by the time he is five and that instability and physical and psychological deprivation at a very early age can be devastating to the youngster. Monahan[20] found that delinquents from broken homes were more likely to be recidivists than those from unbroken homes; Browning,[21] Gold,[22] Slocum and Stone,[23] and Peterson and Becker,[24] like the Gluecks, found that a

[17]Sheldon and Eleanor Glueck, *Delinquents and Nondelinquents in Perspective* (Harvard University Press, Cambridge, Mass., 1968), p. 12.

[18]*Ibid.*, p. 12.

[19]Rodman and Grams, *op. cit.*, p. 196.

[20]Thomas P. Monahan, "Family Status and the Delinquent Child," *Social Forces,* 1957, pp. 250-58.

[21]Charles J. Browning, "Differential Impact of Family Disorganization on Male Adolescents," *Social Problems,* 1960, pp. 37-44.

[22]Gold, *op. cit.*

[23]Walter Slocum and Carol L. Stone, "Family Interaction and Delinquency," in *Juvenile Delinquency,* ed. Herbert C. Quay (D. Van Nostrand Co., Inc., Princeton, New Jersey), 1965.

[24]Donald R. Peterson and Wesley C. Becker, "Family Interaction and Delinquency," in *Juvenile Delinquency,* ed. Herbert C. Quay.

significantly greater number of delinquents than nondelinquents were from broken or disorganized homes.

Although Sterne agrees on the fundamental importance of the family in shaping behavior, he does not believe that a broken home is a major cause of delinquency.[25] He explains that the actual breaking up of the home is preceded by much disruption, disorganization, and tension. Therefore, because negative factors existed before the formal separation, the broken home in itself was not the major contributing factor to delinquent behavior. The tensions and problems that created and contributed to the actual breakup are the real causative factors, with the eventual breakup being only the final link in a long line of disruptive activity.[26]

Family Tension

Sterne's statement that the cluster of events preceding the formal breakup is the major contributing factor to delinquent behavior is most illuminating because this is often overlooked in studies of broken homes.[27]

Abrahamsen believes that family tension greatly contributes to delinquent behavior.[28] The tension that exists in many "intact" families of delinquents results from hostility, hatred, bickering, and the like. This type of tension-filled family environment is obviously not conducive to making the youngster feel secure and content. Long-term tension reduces family cohesiveness and affects the parents' ability to provide an atmosphere conducive to satisfactory child rearing and family problem solving.[29]

Andry found that tension in homes of delinquents is also manifested through intersibling quarrels.[30] Aichhorn states that

> the relationship [of children] to the parents has somehow become abnormal and the original relations of the children to one another, stressed as they are by competition, have not developed into a normal brotherly bond as they should have if they had been submitted to the influence of an equally divided affection toward the parents.[31]

In regard to family cohesiveness, the McCords and Zola agree that cohesive homes produce few delinquents, whereas homes where tension and hostility exist are good

---

[25]Richard S. Sterne, *Delinquent Conduct and Broken Homes* (College and University Press, New Haven, Conn., 1964), p. 21.

[26]*Ibid.*, p. 28.

[27]Glueck, *op. cit.*, p. 12.

[28]David Abrahamsen, *The Psychology of Crime* (Columbia University Press, New York, 1960), p. 43.

[29]*Ibid.*, p. 46.

[30]R. G. Andry, *Delinquency and Parental Pathology* (Metheun, London, 1960), p. 64.

[31]Aichhorn, *op. cit.*, p. 154.

breeding grounds for future delinquents.[32] When a great deal of tension and hostility exists in the home, the youngster is often forced to find "peace of mind" in groups outside the family environment. When the youngster seeks relief from the constant bickering and quarrels within his family, he often flees and "takes refuge in the street."[33]

According to the McCords and Zola:

> Quarrelsome, neglecting families actually had a higher crime rate than homes in which a permanent separation had disrupted the family—conflict and neglect within the home predisposes a child to crime (even more so than broken homes).[34]

Nye shows a relationship between quarreling and delinquent behavior for girls, but not for boys.[35] He explains this by pointing out that the family is more of a focal point for girls than for boys and that the boy can often retreat to the streets or to other groups more readily than can his female counterpart.

Disruptive, quarrelsome, and tension-producing relationships between parents not only affect the marital relationship but disrupt the entire family.[36] This total family disruption can often contribute to and even produce delinquent behavior. The Gluecks found that one in three delinquent families, as compared with one in seven nondelinquent families, were disrupted when one of the parents left the family because of a tension-filled and quarrelsome relationship.[37] Aichhorn found that in all the families that he worked with that had a delinquent youngster, some kind of conflict or disturbance was present in the family relationships.[38] Slocum and Stone noted that 52 percent of delinquents studied, compared with 16 percent of nondelinquents, considered their families uncooperative—which can be another indication of conflict or tension.[39]

If, then, the family environment is unstable and if the parents quarrel most of the time and have difficulty getting along together, they will be unable to exert a positive influence on their children. When there is a great deal of conflict within the household, the child often bears the brunt of much of his parents' hostility. The youngster can get caught up in parental quarrels and be negatively affected by family disruption. The Gluecks point out that

> there is already evidence that the forces of disruption found excessively in the families of the delinquents were greater and stronger than those making for

[32]William and Joan McCord and Irving Zola, *Origins of Crime* (Columbia University Press, New York, 1959).

[33]Aichhorn, *op. cit.,* p. 164.

[34]McCord and Zola, *op. cit.,* p. 83.

[35]Nye, *op. cit.,* p. 48.

[36]Rodman and Grams, *op. cit.,* p. 198.

[37]Glueck, *op. cit.,* p. 8.

[38]Aichhorn, *op. cit.,* p. 33.

[39]Slocum and Stone, *op. cit.*

cohesiveness. In addition, it should be pointed out that less than two in ten in the families of the delinquents, compared to six in ten families of the control group, evidenced strong and steady affectional ties among the members, shared joint interests, took pride in their homes, and felt themselves to be "one for all and all for one." Thus, a highly important quality that is both expressive of loyalty to the blood group and supportive of the individual in his sense of security and in devotion to others, the delinquents were far more deprived than nondelinquents.[40]

Even though some disagreement may exist as to the amount of influence that the divorced versus the hostile but nondivorced family has upon delinquent behavior, it is evident that marital adjustment, family cohesiveness, and the amount of tension existing in the family are directly related to juvenile delinquency.[41]

Parental Rejection

From the psychological standpoint, emotional deprivation as the result of lack of parental love has much to do with juvenile delinquency. If a rejected or neglected child does not find love and affection, as well as support and supervision, at home, he will often resort to groups outside the family; frequently these groups are of a deviant nature. The hostile or rejecting parent is usually not concerned about the youngster's emotional welfare, nor is he concerned about providing the necessary support and guidance. In many cases, parents only become concerned about their child's activities outside the home when he becomes involved in difficulty and embarrasses them. After the youngster has been apprehended, the parent or parents often react in a pseudo-concerned manner. The hostility and the open rejection characteristic of many parents of delinquents are replaced by an appearance of concern.[42]

Nye points out that many studies have been made of parents' attitudes toward their children, but almost no research has been done to find out what children think of their parents. Youngsters' perceptions of their parents can lend insight into the behavior of rejecting or hostile parents and can contribute to a better understanding of this negative dynamic. Studies have found that mutual rejection of parent and child markedly affects positive relationships and can ultimately result in delinquent behavior. When there is mutual animosity and rejection, the chance of maladaptive behavior within the community can become commonplace.[43]

Jenkins found that parental rejection had a direct effect on the child's ultimate development and growth of a conscience.[44] He stated that the lack of an

[40]Glueck, *op. cit.*, pp. 9-10.

[41]Rodman and Grams, *op. cit.*, p. 198.

[42]Nye, *op. cit.*, p. 73.

[43]*Ibid.*, pp. 74-75.

[44]Richard L. Jenkins, "Motivation and Frustration in Delinquency," *American Journal of Orthopsychiatry*, 1957, pp. 528-37.

adequate conscience structure, combined with feelings of hostility for being rejected, led to general unsocialized aggression. On the other hand, socialized delinquent behavior would result when there was parental indifference rather than outright rejection. In other words, the form of aggression was less serious in those youngsters whose parents showed indifference than in those youngsters whose parents showed outright rejection.

According to Andry, delinquents were the recipients of less parental love both in quantity and in quality than were nondelinquents.[45] There was also less adequate communication between child and parent in homes of delinquents. If a strong positive emotional tie does not exist between parents and children, this can produce problems. A positive atmosphere in the home is conducive to effective modeling by the parents and also increases the amount of influence that parents exert over their children. The Gluecks found that in twice as many nondelinquent homes the father showed a great deal of warmth and affection than in delinquent homes. In nondelinquent homes mothers also were much more affectionate than in delinquent homes.

> The extent to which the boy's father was acceptable as a figure with whom to identify is revealed in a finding that fewer than two out of ten of the delinquents, as contrasted with more than half of the nondelinquents, considered their father to be the kind of man that the boy himself would like to be and had respect for the father's vocational and social standing as well as having some sort of common understanding with him.[46]

Bandura and Walters, like the Gluecks, found a direct correlation between rejecting, hostile fathers and delinquent behavior.[47] Fathers of delinquents spent far less time with their sons than did the fathers of nondelinquents. Their rejection and hostility can take both direct and indirect forms. The direct forms are obvious. Indirectly, however, the parents may reject the youngsters by becoming so involved in other activities that they substitute the giving of material awards for emotional affection and security. In addition, if parents are away from the home most of the time, either because of an occupation or because of outside activities, their exposure to their children is limited.

When parents spend a great deal of time away from home, they are often tired when they get home and apathetic about their children. They can be more concerned about achieving financial or social success than about providing their children with love, affection, understanding, and realistic discipline; elements that children interpret as love and concern. The father can often be the greater abuser. In many families the father's main role is being the provider and nothing more. He may "put bread on the table," but he plays little part in providing emotional warmth and security by paying attention to his children and becoming actively

[45] Andry, *op. cit.*
[46] Glueck, *op. cit.*, p. 14.
[47] Abrahamsen, *op. cit.*, p. 62.

involved in their lives. In addition, he is often not an adequate identification model. It then becomes more difficult for the youngster to assume a socialized internal control structure (conscience).[48]

Although somewhat skeptical of delinquency theories based solely on family relationships, Gibbons believes that "scientific candor compels us to conclude that the link between parental rejection and aggressive conduct is one of the more firmly established generalizations concerning delinquency."[49]

Many professionals in the fields of both psychology and sociology agree that open rejection and hostility can directly affect youngsters and ultimately produce delinquency and that the family institution has the greatest influence on the youngster's behavior in the community. Parental control is both direct and indirect. Parents indirectly control their children through the identification process, which ultimately results in the development of an adequate conscience structure. Parents exert direct control by developing a system of rewards and punishments. The method of parental control is an important aspect of child rearing.

Methods of Parental Control

Just as tension, rejection, and a broken home can affect the stability of the family structure, methods of control or processes and forms of discipline can play a part in the development of delinquent behavior.

Every parent uses some type of discipline in rearing children, even though it may differ from situation to situation and from child to child, as well as in content and form. Nye discusses discipline and its effects on child rearing and says that an authoritarian approach to discipline may affect the adolescent in his peer group relationships. The child will not be able to interact freely with his peers if his mobility is hindered by extremely strict parents. Conversely, a too permissive type of discipline will not provide the child with the necessary controls and limits so that reference points can be established to guide behavior.

> Unfair or partial discipline may be associated with an ambivalent or negative attitude toward the parent which reduces the indirect control that can be exerted by the parent. An attitude of this type toward parents is thought to make it difficult for the parents to act as an agent in the formation of an adequate conscience in the child, prevents the adults from serving as a model to be imitated by the child, and reduces the wish of the adolescent to conform to please the parent and to avoid delinquent behavior or avoid hurting the parent.[50]

The Gluecks identified differences in disciplining patterns in parents of delinquents. They found that the parents of delinquents used physical punishment more than verbal discussion. Mothers were much more permissive and less strict

[48]*Ibid.*

[49]Gibbons, *op. cit.*, p. 202.

[50]Nye, *op. cit.*, pp. 79-80.

than fathers. Both parents were less consistent in their disciplinary measures than were the parents of nondelinquents.[51]

Because of this inconsistent discipline and lack of cooperation between parents, an adequate control structure does not exist within the home. The child then often rejects the entire sphere of parental influence because he loses respect for the process of control utilized by his parents.[52] Parents cannot present a united front if inconsistency and disagreement exist, and therefore the youngster will not be influenced by his parents, will often belittle their efforts, and will not develop an adequate superego (conscience). The youngster can also manipulate the inconsistent pattern of control to turn one parent against the other. The ultimate effect is that the youngster does not have benefit of consistent guidelines and limits to assist him in behaving in a socially acceptable manner.[53] The attitude of "nothing can happen to me" will develop because the youngster learns that his parents' inconsistent discipline and demands are seldom translated into coordinated action.

Nye, interestingly enough, found that unfair punishment, although not having a direct effect upon delinquency when administered by the mother, did have a marked effect when administered by the father.[54] It can be assumed that the more severe discipline is usually administered by the father and thus makes a greater impact. The McCords and Zola classified methods of disciplining youngsters under six types: (1) *love-oriented discipline,* in which reasoning is used with the child and punishment involves withholding rewards or privileges; (2) *punitive discipline,* in which a great deal of physical violence is used and there is a great deal of anger, aggression, and threat; (3) *lax discipline,* in which neither parent exerts much control; (4) *erratic discipline,* in which one parent uses love-oriented methods and the other is lax or wavers between the two types; (5) *erratic discipline* (love oriented, lax, and punitive), in which both parents waver in using the three methods, so that all three are combined; and (6) *erratic discipline* (punitive and lax), in which one parent is punitive and one parent is lax, or both parents waver between the methods.[55]

The McCords and Zola found that lax or erratic discipline involving punitive methods was strongly related to delinquency, whereas consistent discipline, either by punitive or love-oriented methods, was significantly related to nondelinquency. The erratic nature of the discipline, not the amount involved, was the major variable in producing the delinquent behavior.

> Contrary to our expectations (and to the findings of previous studies) we found no evidence that consistently punitive discipline leads to delinquency. In fact, we were surprised to discover that the 14 children who had been severely but consistently treated had the lowest rate of crime. Consistent use of love-oriented techniques also seems to produce noncriminality. These

[51]Glueck, *op. cit.,* pp. 15-16.

[52]Nye, *op. cit.,* p. 48.

[53]Aichhorn, *op. cit.,* p. 233.

[54]Nye, *op. cit.,* p. 80.

[55]McCord and Zola, *op. cit.,* p. 76.

figures indicate that the consistency of parental behavior is more important than the methods parents use for enforcing their demands.[56]

Discipline and the way in which it is administered can have a marked effect on delinquent and adolescent behavior. Consistency is extremely important, and a united approach by parents is desirable—but difficult to present if there is a broken home, a great deal of tension in the home, or parental rejection. All these factors can be important negative contributory variables in the delinquent's home. Another important aspect of the environment of the family, which can have a marked effect on how the child ultimately reacts in the community, is the emotional stability of his parents.

Parental Emotional Stability

Delinquent behavior can often be directly traced to behavioral disturbances and emotional instability in one or both of the parents. Parents who have their own emotional sickness frequently "act out" the sickness or transmit it to their children. Freeman and Savastano found that although some mothers of delinquents wanted to give their sons "adequate mothering," their own personality problems interfered with their effectiveness as mothers. If the only time the mother shows a great deal of tenderness is after she punishes the boy, he will often deliberately misbehave for the express purpose of receiving the tenderness, even though it is not under the most optimal conditions. The erratic and misdirected tenderness is an important motivating factor in his negative behavior.

Children can also be the recipients of much hostility and jealousy from emotionally unstable parents.

> Mothers who are jealous of their growing daughters, cannot reconcile them-selves with the loss of their own femininity; they cling abnormally to their husbands; they try exaggeratedly to limit his freedom of action and often rob him of the opportunity to exchange a few loving words with his own child; they observe suspiciously every gesture made by husband and daughter and then discharge their dissatisfaction upon the daughter alone. Consequently, the daughter feels still drawn more toward her father or step-father. Family life becomes impossible, the more so because the girl is intolerant of her mother and uses every opportunity to withdraw from the domestic environ-ment; a reaction which exposes her to the dangers of waywardness.[57]

Conversely, if there is little love between the parents, the youngster can become the "love object" of one or the other. The inordinate amount of attention the young-ster receives because he is being used as a substitute for the rejected marital partner can greatly confuse him. Freeman and Savastano reported that marital conflict was

[56]*Ibid.*, pp. 77-78.

[57]Beatrice Freeman and George Savastano, "The Affluent Youthful Offender," *Crime and Delinquency*, 1970, pp. 264-72.

frequently expressed in the parent-child relationship. The mother gives the child a great deal of love and affection, worries about the child constantly, and does not let him have much freedom. The child can often exploit this situation by being disruptive. He knows he can get away with a great deal of misbehavior. He does not receive control from his mother because he has become a substitute love object in an entangled relationship. In addition, the lack of control creates uneasiness for the youngster because no limits are established for him, nor reference points to guide his behavior. As a reaction to this type of situation, he may "act out" further so that controls will be imposed and some type of structure developed for him. A negative cycle develops. The more "acting out" the child does, the more the mother hovers over him with her permissiveness, and then the greater the "acting out" in the hope that controls will be imposed. This type of abnormal relationship is not conducive to effective child rearing and can ultimately contribute to delinquent behavior. When the marital relationship between parents is not positive and the child is the recipient of inappropriate and exaggerated emotions, he soon learns that he is not loved for himself but is being used as an object by one or both parents to vent their hostility on each other.[58]

The type of role that the parent plays within the family can also affect the youngster's perception of his parents and ultimately his perception of himself. If the mother is domineering and aggressive and the father is weak, the modeling process of father to son is complicated and the formation of an adequate conscience is affected.[59]

In households where parents do have behavioral disturbances and manifestations of emotional immaturity, instability, or insecurity, there is frequent loss of temper and the direction of inappropriate emotions to children. Where tension, hostility, and displaced emotions exist, the family environment will not be conducive to producing children who are themselves stable and who can function effectively. In families where one or both parents have emotional disturbances—or a disease such as alcoholism—the youngster runs a much greater risk of developing problems that often manifest themselves in a delinquent activity. The Gluecks found that a significantly large number of parents of delinquents had problems themselves and came from homes that had an alcoholic in the family, mental retardation, or emotional disturbances. And mothers of delinquents, as well as fathers, were often inferior physically, intellectually, and emotionally.[60] Aichhorn also associated behavioral disturbances of parents with delinquent behavior of their children and pointed out the negative family environments that parents of delinquents often come from.

> More significantly, however, such severe emotional abnormalities as psychosis, psychoneurosis, epilepsy, sex inversions, marked emotional instability and pronounced temperamental deviation existed in one or more members of

[58]*Ibid.*
[59]*Ibid.,* p. 170.
[60]Glueck, *op. cit.,* p. 5.

at least one-fourth of the families from which the delinquent father sprang, compared to but one-sixth of nondelinquents' paternal families. The maternal families of delinquents were also found to be far more pathological emotionally than those of nondelinquents.[61]

Reiner and Kaufman noted that parents of antisocial character disorder children often acted out their own unconscious parental wishes through other children.[62]

> Often a parent engages in overt delinquency or shows deviant attitudes that are a counterpart to the child's behavior. But even in such cases when the child gets in conflict with the law, the parent is enraged at the child's behavior. He does not condone the delinquency in the child or really condone it in himself. In some instances, one form of delinquency may be acceptable to the parent while another form is not acceptable. In these cases, we find that the parent has led the child in a particular direction by his prohibitions. The parent is afraid that his own impulses, against which he has built a rigid reaction formation, will break through, and he projects this danger onto the child.[63]

Other theorists, such as Aldrich,[64] generally agree with Reiner and Kaufman's statement that many parents receive vicarious satisfaction when their children act out unacceptable impulses. These parents have emotional disturbances themselves and have never really worked out their internal conflicts. The major energy release for their own instability comes through their children's delinquent activities.

Practitioners in the field of criminal justice can give many examples of parents who, either directly or indirectly, condone the delinquent activities of their children. In some cases, parents even encourage this negativism because they themselves harbor pent-up hostility and resentment.

The unconscious transmission of negative attitudes of parents to their children has been a subject of much discussion. Even though theorists disagree as to the amount and form that these transmissions take, they believe that much, if not most, delinquent behavior is spawned in the family. Even though Bandura and Walters in their study of adolescent aggression found no evidence that parents had displayed "consistently blatant anti-social behavior," they did find that many of the fathers of the boys had provided aggressive models for imitation.[65] Parental emotional instability can take many forms, but regardless of the form of expression, the effect on youngsters can apparently be devastating.

[61] Aichhorn, *op. cit.*, p. 146.

[62] Reiner and Kaufman, *op. cit.*

[63] *Ibid.*, pp. 15-16.

[64] C. Knight Aldrich, "Thief," *Psychology Today,* March 1971, pp. 67-68.

[65] Albert Bandura and Richard H. Walters, *Adolescent Aggression* (Ronald Press, New York, 1959), p. 355.

Family Economics

Families of delinquents, regardless of socioeconomic status, usually have certain characteristics that are different from those of families of nondelinquents— disruptive homes with a great deal of tension and rejection, ineffective methods of parental control, and parental emotional instability.

Even though these conditions can exist in all homes regardless of economic status, family economics can be a contributing variable to delinquency. Reiss, for example, concluded that there is an association between a family's economic dependence and a son's success on probation.[66] A family's inability to provide for the material needs of the youngster can create insecurity and affect the amount of control that the family exerts over the youngster because he often seeks material support and security outside the home.[67] Other theorists have pointed out that the homes of delinquents are often physically deteriorated, which can affect the boy's perception of himself and the attitude of the community toward his family.

According to Peterson and Becker:

> The homes in which delinquents live tend to be dirty and rundown—the homes of delinquents are often disorderly and cluttered, present routines are weakly fixed, physical space is at a premium and privacy can best be had by leaving the house—there is little order in the model delinquent home. As a physical social stimulus the typical delinquent home acts mainly as a repellent, driving people away.[68]

It should, however, be pointed out that many delinquents come from homes that do not typify the above description. Economic status and material possessions might be directly correlated with delinquent activity in some cases, but they do not explain middle- and upper-class delinquency. The economic condition of the family can be one of many contributing factors in a multiproblem family.

Barker and Adams find that almost without exception delinquents come from multiproblem homes where other siblings are in trouble and where there is a great deal of personal and family disorganization as well as some economic handicap.[69] "Too often their parents are 'losers,' unable to make a marriage go, unsuccessful in business or alcoholics, emotionally unstable, or have other problems."[70]

[66]Reiss, *op. cit.,* p. 198.

[67]*Ibid.*

[68]Peterson and Becker, *op. cit.,* p. 67.

[69]Gordon H. Barker and W. Thomas Adams, "Glue Sniffers," *Sociology and Social Research,* 1963, pp. 298-310.

[70]Howard James, *Children in Trouble,* (David McKay Co., Inc., New York, 1969), p. 196.

Tait and Hodges feel that the typical delinquent family is working under many more handicaps than the average family, thus making it difficult for the child to be integrated into the family in a meaningful manner. In healthy families the youngster has a secure atmosphere and can learn socially acceptable modes of behavior and a life-style that will help him adjust effectively in the community. Conversely, in homes of delinquents, the family fails both the youngster and ultimately the community because it does not provide the proper atmosphere for helping the youngster to develop into a productive citizen.[71]

Family economics is probably one of the least meaningful variables that is directly related to delinquent behavior, although it can play a part when combined with other factors. We now examine the contemporary family and some of the problems associated with present-day child rearing.

THE CONTEMPORARY FAMILY

Adolescents present peculiar problems to their families and their communities. Because this is a topic of great interest and importance, Chapter 5 will focus on the physical, psychological, and social problems that accompany adolescence. When these problems become acute, patterns of delinquent behavior often emerge. The major purpose of discussing the adolescent in this section is to point out the gap that often exists between the generations and the effect this has on effective problem solving within the family structure.

Caplan and Lebovici postulate that whenever social and technological change accelerates, the gap between the generations increases and each succeeding generation has to deal with the accumulation of problems that develop. And because adults often have to work out methods of coping with environmental challenges without benefit of youthful input, problems between generations arise. Although parents transmit to their children both directly through communication and indirectly through modeling various patterns of behavior for coping with problems, historical and technological change often leaves the patterns that have been transmitted inadequate to solve a totally new range of problems.[72]

The Group for the Advancement of Psychiatry suggests that because of adult resistance to change and interest in maintaining the status quo, many adolescent problems are created which contribute to stressful relations between generations.[73] In complex societies such as ours where major transitions are taking place daily, the gap between the younger and the older generations increases because of a lack of meaningful communication and the inability of both genera-

[71] Downing Tait, Jr., and Emory F. Hodges, Jr., *Delinquents, Their Families and the Community* (Charles C. Thomas, Springfield, Ill., 1962), p. 90.

[72] Gerald Caplan and Serge Lebovici, *Adolescence: Psychosocial Perspectives* (New York and London: Basic Books Inc., 1969), p. xi.

[73] Group for the Advancement of Psychiatry, *Normal Adolescence: Its Dynamics and Impact* (New York: Charles Scribner's Sons, 1968), pp. 95-96.

tions to identify with each other's problems and problem-solving processes. The conflict and the gap between the generations seem to be increasing. Adults and youth have difficulty not only adjusting to the changes but also developing patterns of behavior that can be both meaningful and compatible. Adolescents feel that many of the changes that are occurring are the result of adult decision making in which they have not been involved, and they therefore have difficulty committing themselves to a style of life and a problem-solving process of which they do not feel a part. Often, because adults have no clear answers to their own problems in our complex society and because the experiences of their own adolescent years are far removed, they lack empathy or understanding and are unable to provide guidelines and dependable role models for youngsters. Garrison comments that tension between the generations is an inevitable consequence of the rapid rate of social change that is taking place in our society. "Since western society is above all a society of change, conflict between our society and the growing child is inherent in the development of personality."[74]

Caplan and Lebovici sum up the conflict that exists between generations and the reasons for its development as follows:

> this situation is complicated by the fact that as participants in an evolving culture, we adults have continually been adjusting to a succession of changes. We have developed selective perceptual distortions and ways of reconciling ourselves to discrepancies between feasible "reality" and our basic theories and stated values, which allow us to pursue our paths in life with relative equanimity, even though it may well be that these paths turn out to be unsuccessful. We communicate only our abstract concepts and values to our adolescents. And since they have not shared in the process whereby we insensibly adjusted these to our experience of reality, when they come relatively suddenly onto the adult scene, with open eyes, they correctly perceive the discrepancies between our precepts and our practice. Moreover, they do not have our commitment to the ways of life we have worked out or need to rely on them because of personal investment. Since adolescence is a developmental period marked by a rapid increase in the capacity for abstract conceptualization and an interest in active exploration and analysis of the world, adolescents often confront us with fundamental questions about our adult ways. Their lack of adult bias and stereotyped thinking frequently results in their seeing a situation more clearly and truly than we do. They propose valuable and innovative approaches precisely because they are not aware of those "facts of life" to which we possibly ill-advisedly have accommodated ourselves.[75]

Adolescent questioning of adult values and refusal to accept societal institutions on faith create unpleasant feelings of doubt and anxiety in adults and renew the awareness of their own shortcomings. Outmoded approaches to life may be exposed by adolescent skepticism. For example, parents may have evolved a

[74]Karl C. Garrison, *Psychology of Adolescence* (Englewood Cliffs, New Jersey: Prentice-Hall, Inc., 1965), p. 18.

[75]Caplan and Lebovici, pp. xi-xii.

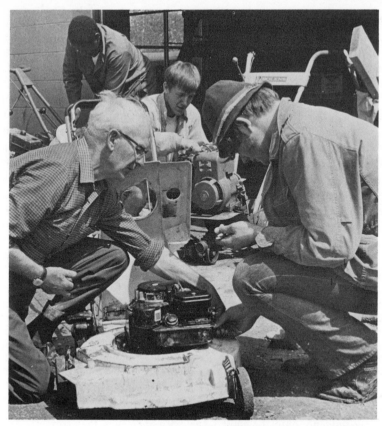

Courtesy of Camp Highfields, Onondaga, Michigan

Figure 2
There is No Generation Gap When There is a Common Focus

precarious balance between the strict moral teachings of their youth and their own personal immoral behavior, but exposed to blunt challenges the balance may be upset. "The painful exposure and self-reappraisal caused by the 'show me,' 'prove it' attitude of the adolescent and his behaving in ways that adults may envy, but no longer allow themselves are difficult to experience with equanimity."[76]

The Group for the Advancement of Psychiatry contends that because adults have repressed conflicts and anxieties during their own adolescent years, they are unable to share the adolescent's dilemma sufficiently to be able to empathize and help him. The attitude and rebelliousness of the adolescent often generates consternation in alarmed parents. Their attempts to reason with the adolescent in order to solve conflicts may be met with hostility. Parents often react by giving up in despair or reverting to the authority that they believe they still possess. Results

[76]Group for the Advancement of Psychiatry, p. 98.

of such confrontations are often alienation of the adolescent and the adult from each other. The adolescent feels he is being "managed" rather than receiving the respect due him as an individual in his own right.[77]

These findings lend new insight into the problems that parents have in influencing their youngsters in socially acceptable ways so that the conflicts that inevitably exist between the community and its residents can be minimized. The importance of the family in shaping the youngster's attitudes and behavior cannot be overemphasized. The contemporary family is faced with problems that have no historical precedent. The gap that naturally exists between parents and youngsters because of our highly complex technical society and the vast amount of change that has taken place lends itself to further difficulty and problem situations within the family constellation. We will now focus on the contemporary family and some of the problems that exist between parents and youngsters that can ultimately contribute to delinquent behavior. Many of the problem areas to be discussed are not peculiar to any socioeconomic class or ethnic group but seem to be symptoms of our present complex society.

Many people consider today's social problems an enigma because many of the communities experiencing the greatest difficulty do not have problems emanating from poverty, unemployment, or lack of education. Paradoxically, these communities seem to have problems that result from affluence, overcompetitiveness, and—in some cases—too much reliance on formal education. Contemporary parents have become so involved in daily competition for material success and rewards that they do not take time to reflect on their goals in life or evaluate the process of achieving them. Jobs and social activities become ends in themselves and not means to self and family fulfillment, and life goals become slowly and unintentionally altered because of the emphasis on material success. The result is that children often become "caught up" in this competitive process.[78]

Formal education has sometimes become an end in itself and not a means for improving the individual, the family, and the community. Education without practical application is like a servant without a master. Parents have lost their ability to intuitively perceive the problems of their youngsters and to effectively communicate with them. Many contemporary parents have tried to obtain the answers to their questions in textbooks or from professionals, forgetting that the cornerstone of any strong unit, and especially a family unit, is the ability of its members to be sensitive to the needs of each other. Even though material possessions and status have been achieved by many parents, their ability to relate to their children has taken a secondary position in their lives.[79]

Use of External Resources. The reliance on technical assistance from professionals and "outsiders" has become commonplace. Textbook knowledge and professional assistance is necessary, but any honest professional would be the first

[77]*Ibid.*, p. 95.
[78]Caplan and Lebovici, *op. cit.*, p. xi.
[79]Abrahamsen, *op. cit.*, p. 43.

to point out that outside assistance should only be used to supplement the intuitive sensitivities, feelings, and judgments of parents. If parents depend exclusively on outside resources, they lose their ability to empathize and to communicate effectively with their children.

After reviewing the literature, it becomes evident that although much has been written about preadolescent child care and development, comparatively little has been written about the way parents should relate to their teen-age children. Many specialists are willing to work with preadolescents, but few of them want to work with adolescents. This is unfortunate because the teen-age years, the period of most juvenile delinquency, is a time of turbulence and the youngster is attempting to determine who he is and what his goals in life should be. He is developing a self-concept and attempting to cope with the struggle of dependence versus independence. If parents have depended exclusively on child-rearing manuals during their children's early years, they have not learned to handle their children's problems through an honest direct relationship. Instead of communicating directly in accordance with the emotion that accompanies the particular confrontation or event, the communication process becomes tempered and complicated with jargon and popular theoretical cliches. Parents often deny and repress the acceptable and common human emotions of anger and ambivalence. When these emotions are not expressed directly and honestly, they are often manifested in subtle forms that are difficult for the child to understand and accept.[80]

For example, a parent may be irritated at his child's behavior in a particular situation, but because the parent believes that the emotion of anger is abnormal, he does not express his feelings or set limits on the child's behavior. Instead, he may deny that the emotion exists. Denial is not totally effective, however, because invariably the feelings are expressed in some form which if not expressed directly, usually takes a passive-aggressive (indirect) channel. The result is that the parents may "pick at" the child for such insignificant matters as haircuts, dress, and taste in music. The child then, because he cannot understand why his parent is "bugging" him, overreacts by going to extremes. Problems such as this can be avoided if parents can learn to handle the situation and their emotions on the spot. The child, if dealt with directly, can much more readily accept his parents' anger and understand the need for imposing limits and the rationale for the particular restriction. Expression of displaced emotions is not effective in problem solving. It only contributes to a denial of the problem and further widens the gap between generations.[81]

Parents are able to "get away with" their dependence on outside resources during the early years of the child's life because children are fairly predictable at this time and most of their difficulties revolve around physical rather than emotional problems. When the child reaches adolescence, however, there are not only limited outside resources (psychiatrists, reading material, etc.) but the child is

[80]Group for the Advancement of Psychiatry, p. 98.

[81]Nye, *op. cit.*, p. 73.

no longer as predictable. If parents have not learned to use their intuitive feelings and good judgment to react spontaneously in a sensitive manner, they will be at a loss during the teen-age period. The problem becomes increasingly severe as a result of their increased frustration and need for help during the teen-age years. Parents who have not learned to relate to their child become even more amenable to popular cliches and shallow jargon, and their effectiveness in preparing the youngster for interactions in the community becomes neutralized.[82]

Decision Making. Parents find that one of their most difficult tasks is decision making. Parents avoid making important decisions for their children in many ways. They can relegate their decision-making responsibility to others (outside resources), or they can simply avoid making them. Because an efficient and non-anxiety-provoking decision-making process is sought, simple answers to complicated child-rearing problems are often forthcoming. (See Chapter 5.)

Because parents do not know how to react to the adolescent struggle of dependence versus independence and are not confident of their own decision-making ability to take the adolescent problem as it comes on a case-by-case basis, they often tend to oversimplify the process by subscribing to either an extremely permissive or an extremely disciplinarian philosophy and approach to child rearing. Both extremes can have disastrous results. The strictly disciplined child rebels against the stringent demands of his parents, while the "free-floating" child does not know where he is going and may react in a delinquent manner because he fears the extensive freedom given to him so readily. Many practitioners have had delinquent adolescents tell them that they wished their parents had exerted more controls and set limits because they interpreted limits and controls as being an expression of love and concern. Extreme permissiveness can be harmful to, and misunderstood by, the child, and the family therefore becomes an ineffective agent of socialization for him. Extreme permissiveness and extreme discipline are merely different sides of the same coin. They are symptoms of the same problem—inadequate parenting. Excessive discussion and rationalizing of these symptoms may often only be a diversionary tactic that parents find useful when they do not want to examine their own motives for taking extremes rather than considering the youngster's individual situation, circumstances, and personality. Of course, when parents do take all these factors into consideration, the decision-making process becomes much more difficult than it would have been if they had merely adhered to either the permissive or the disciplinarian philosophy. It is much easier to say yes or no to the child than to analyze each situation for its merits and disadvantages.[83]

Unrecognized Immaturity. Technological advances and rapid social change have led many parents to believe that because their youngsters seem more sophisticated intellectually and socially, they are also better equipped emotionally to

[82]Clyde E. Vedder and Dora B. Summerville, *The Delinquent Girl,* Springfield: Charles C. Thomas, 1970.

[83]John and Valerie Cowie, and Eliot Slater, *Delinquency in Girls.* London: Heinemann Educational Books, 1968.

handle complex problems. When parents assume this, problem situations arise and the generation gap broadens. Parents often accept totally whatever their youngster says, but are not sensitive to his feelings and nonverbal communication. The youngster may say he is grown up, may sound as if he is grown up, and may look as if he is grown up, but he still vacillates between wanting to be a child and wanting to be an adult. He still seeks assistance from his parents in planning and guiding his life, but because his parents believe that what he says and what he looks like indicate his true personality, they react by giving the youngster more freedom than he is capable of handling. In other words, many youngsters grow physically and intellectually, but not emotionally. They believe that their parents want them to be sophisticated, and the parents believe that their youngsters want to be treated as sophisticated adults. This faulty communication process exists because parents have not relied on honest communication in respect to feelings, nor have they been sensitive to their children's needs and nonverbal communication. Too often parents give their children decision-making power under the guise of the children's right to individual freedom, self-destiny, and self-expression when, in fact, they want to reduce their own anxiety and indecisiveness. They therefore relinquish their own decision-making responsibility and force it on their children. This again is an undesirable assumption and process because only with the guidance of parents within a cohesive family unit can youngsters become astute decision makers.[84]

A Matter of Priorities. Parents can also lose sight of priorities in their relationship with their children. Listing priorities is a facet related to decision making and a process followed whether it is in the workaday world or within the family constellation. Just as sometimes a priority of means rather than ends takes precedence in our daily struggle for material prosperity, so can secondary child-rearing priorities take precedence over primary priorities. For example, even though the giving of material rewards to children is a part of the natural child-rearing process, this should not become an end in itself, nor a substitute for the giving of emotional security, guidance, and support. Or a parent may be a heavy smoker or drinker, but because he feels it will be harmful for his child, lies to him and tells him that he does not smoke or drink. The child may later see his parent slightly intoxicated or surreptitiously smoking. The child has caught his parent lying. The priority of not lying to the child should have taken precedence over the child's not knowing that his parent smokes or drinks. Lying can have far-reaching negative consequences. It can affect the basic relationship between parent and child, further increase the gap between generations, and neutralize the effectiveness of the family as a socializing agent.[85]

Unconscious Parental Transmissions. The subtle negative ways in which parents can influence their children's behavior can also contribute to delinquent behavior, and they are often the result of the parents' own emotional instability

[84]McCord, McCord and Zola, *op. cit.*
[85]Aichhorn, *op. cit.*, p. 233.

and neurotic method of problem solving. As was pointed out earlier, these undesirable transmissions from parents to children can be a contributing factor in the youngster's "acting out" his parents' feeling in an antiauthority, antisocial manner. When parents transmit only negative feelings or attitudes without assisting their youngsters in developing the accompanying frustration tolerance and self-control, problem situations can occur. Youngsters cannot usually handle these transmissions without support. They have not learned the accompanying controls because they have not been exposed to the necessary life experiences and are not familiar with the decision-making processes that can assist them in analyzing the total situation. Most human behavior is the result of an "attitude set," plus an evaluative process and then a decision as to what mode of behavior will be appropriate. Children who pick up negative transmissions from their parents without the accompanying controls only have the benefit of one of the variables in the decision-making process—an attitude.[86]

Parents can also transmit to children the attitude of individual rights and freedom of expression, two highly valued norms in a democratic society, without emphasizing personal responsibility and social consciousness. The use of drugs, a contemporary social problem, is an example of how children pick up their parents' transmissions without accompanying controls (see Chapter 5). Although most parents will subscribe to, and transmit to their children, the values of individual freedom of expression, most parents will not condone drug use by their children. Parents do not realistically discuss the constellation of factors involved in using drugs and may only transmit an attitude or feeling of individual freedom of expression. Youngsters can therefore logically conclude that individual rights and freedom of expression can be extended to the individual's right to use drugs and become involved in other self-gratifying behavior. The parents' transmission of feelings and attitudes without communicating the ramifications of these feelings and attitudes and the spectrum of their life experiences gives the child only half the picture.

Persons working with juvenile delinquents can also be guilty of the same phenomenon. For example, a probation officer may personally feel that drug laws should be liberalized. He may either consciously or unconsciously transmit this to the child. The youngster, not having the accompanying controls, "acts out" the probation officer's feelings, uses drugs, is apprehended, and is convicted. The probation officer can receive vicarious satisfaction from the child's acting out against the establishment that has imposed the legal restrictions against the use of drugs. The probation officer, however, does not have to pay the penalty for the use of drugs. The delinquent youngster "pays the price"; the probation officer receives the satisfaction. If the probation officer in this example found it necessary to transmit the attitude, he should also have discussed the ramifications regarding the use of drugs, the logic behind the law, and the process for changing it. Again, as in the example of the parents and the child, the delinquent has been given only half

[86]Reiner and Kaufman, *op. cit.,* p. 15.

the picture. The mere transmission of an attitude without accompanying explanations can initiate or perpetuate antisocial behavior.[87]

CONCLUSION

The complexities of the family environment and the way they contribute to the "gap" between youngsters and parents and delinquent behavior have been discussed. Specific problem areas that exist in the contemporary family were also delineated because they can affect the family environment, and the family is obviously the major agent in influencing the youngster's future behavior. Many contemporary parents have substituted cliches for feelings and have transmitted attitudes to their youngsters without accompanying explanations of the total picture. Parents often tell their children that when they were their age, they solved complicated problems very easily. This is not realistic. The problem-solving and decision-making processes, whether in the workaday world or in the family, are difficult processes at any age. A transmission to children that decision making is difficult and that only through mutual assistance can the process be effective will be helpful in presenting a realistic picture of the life process and in establishing an effective communication process between the generations. The generation gap between young and old is somewhat inevitable because of present rapid change and technological advancements. The negative effects of the generation gap can be reduced, however, if parents will take the time to pay attention to their youngsters and help them adjust to complex problems. A realistic and empathetic approach to child rearing that includes assistance and guidance in daily decision making to prepare youngsters for future roles in their communities is much more effective than a superficial or mechanical approach that substitutes material rewards for emotional security and support.[88]

If *generation gap* means inability of adults to relate to youth and meaningfully communicate both verbally and nonverbally with the younger generation, then the gap is indeed a real problem and a cause for concern. The generation gap is not necessarily detrimental if meaningful communication does exist. A gap between the generations can have positive secondary effects. It is important that the younger generation learn from the life experiences of their elders so that they can avoid the mistakes their elders made by the trial-and-error method. Conversely, the older generation needs the vitality and idealism of the young so that social institutions can change and be responsive to the needs of all community members. Cooperative involvement between generations is the most effective approach to problem solving and self-fulfillment. The family and the total environment of the family can be much more effective in handling youngsters' problems if mutual understanding and support exist. Even though totally free communication between the generations is an idealistic goal, "peaceful coexistence" is possible and, furthermore, necessary if the many social problems that exist are to be solved.[89]

[87]Caplan and Lebovici, pp. xi-xii.

[88]Reiner and Kaufman, *op. cit.,* p. 15.

[89]Group for the Advancement of Psychiatry, *op. cit.,* p. 95-96., Garrison, *op. cit.,* p. 18.

SUMMARY

This chapter has attempted to use the family as a model not only to incorporate both sociological and psychological principles but also to point out the usefulness of blending the two disciplines for a more comprehensive understanding of the delinquency phenomenon. The sampling of material presented illustrates the factors in the family environment that contribute to delinquency and the importance of a healthy family atmosphere in influencing youngsters in socially acceptable ways.

Practical suggestions have been made for increasing the effectiveness of the family in the contemporary community so that the gap between the generations can be understood and the problems contributing to hostility and resentment can be reduced. There are numerous other ideas, theories, and assumptions about the influence of the family on delinquent behavior. Gibbons points out that a typology of delinquency has to be developed that incorporates what is known about delinquent behavior into some kind of meaningful framework. At present, a "smorgasbord" approach exists. "Instead, some way must be found to judiciously put these influences into some kind of coherent order and to assign different weights to them depending on the contribution they make to delinquent conduct."[90] Even though all delinquent behavior cannot be explained by studying the family, the importance of the family in regard to this phenomenon cannot be denied. It is probably the single most relevant variable that consistently plays a part in the causation of delinquent behavior. The following chapters will reemphasize this point. The next chapter focuses on adolescence and the peculiar problems that accompany this stage of development.

QUESTIONS AND PROJECTS

Essay Questions

1. Why is the family so important in the youngster's life?
2. Are economic conditions of the family directly related to delinquency causation?
3. Are teen-agers more mature or less mature today? Explain.
4. Is some form of discipline necessary in each family?
5. Will early parent-child relationships predestine the child's behavior?

Projects

1. Develop a community program that can help strengthen the families of delinquents.

[90]Gibbons, *op. cit.*, p. 93.

2. Develop guidelines for parents to use in rearing their children.

3. State the major reasons why the older and the younger generations have difficulty communicating. How can they better understand each other?

5

THE ADOLESCENT

Because most juvenile delinquency occurs during the adolescent stage of development, it is important to understand the dynamics of the phenomenon of adolescence. Even though all adolescents are not delinquents, all juvenile delinquents are adolescents. Therefore, to understand the juvenile delinquent it is necessary to understand the adolescent stage of development.

> Adolescence encompasses an extensive period of accelerated physical and psychological growth. Its onset can be determined by observation of physical changes—change usually begins at about the age of ten in girls and the age of twelve in boys. Clinical evidence shows that modifications of the psychological structure take place at approximately the same time as the physical change occurs.[1]

It is easier to determine the physical changes of adolescence than the psychological changes for obvious reasons. The psychological changes and difficulties that occur during adolescence have particular ramifications regarding whether the youngster satisfactorily adjusts to his environment or reacts in a delinquent manner.

Adolescence is a phase of development that cannot be totally explained by one academic discipline.

[1]Irene M. Josselyn, *The Adolescent and His World* (New York: The Family Service Association of America, 1952), p. 5.

Marked social, psychological, and physical changes are characteristic of this age span and they do not occur unrelated to each other. The physical changes have definite effect on the social and psychological adjustments of the individual; social factors influence the psychological and physical changes. The psychological factors have reprecussions both socially and physiologically.[2]

Much has been written concerning the so-called period of adolescence, it often being described as a very turbulent phase of development in which many problems occur and many conflicts exist. Even though it is recognized that social, psychological, and physiological changes take place, the assumptions regarding the most predominant determining variables that affect the adolescent have been many and varied. For example, Margaret Mead, in her famous study, *Coming of Age in Samoa,* concluded that adolescence and the characteristics peculiar to it are culturally determined—depending on the culture, the adolescent will be happy or unhappy, constrained or uninhibited, and his state as an adolescent will be almost solely determined by the culture in which he lives.

Mead felt that the Samoan culture, unlike the culture in our country, was much more conducive to the adolescent youngster's experiencing less turmoil and adjusting satisfactorily to his environment. Other writers have pointed out that American adolescents have a distinct system of shared values which are very different from the values of their parents.

Our society has within its midst a set of small teen-age societies which focus teen-age interest and attitudes on things far removed from adult responsibilities and which may develop standards that lead away from those goals established by the larger society.[3]

Even though there is much conjecture, discussion, and theorizing from many different disciplines regarding the adolescent phase of development, it will be helpful to present some of the most prevalent ideas and views of the adolescent phenomenon. A more thorough knowledge of the characteristics and behavior of the adolescent will lend insight into the behavior of the delinquent adolescent.

A CULTURAL PERSPECTIVE OF ADOLESCENCE

The adolescent phenomenon is not the same in all cultures. The Cavans point out that a shortening or even an omission of adolescence occurs in societies where there is a well-organized family controlled by family elders. In some cultures the child's entire behavior revolves around the family, and little outside assistance supplements the material and psychological support that the child receives from his family. The

---

[2]*Ibid.,* p. 10.
[3]T. Coleman, *The Adolescent Society* (Glencoe, Ill.: The Free Press, 1961).

particular role that the youngster occupies in the family or in his community is well established, with little room for experimentation or mobility. When the youngster becomes physically mature, he is considered an adult and is given the privileges of adulthood as well as its responsibilities.

> In contrast is a situation in western industrialized societies where both the period of adolescence and a concept of juvenile delinquency exist. The family does not operate as a social, economic, or political unit. A child at an early age enters specialized agencies that compete for his loyalty and open many choices to him for present or future aspirations and goals. The passage from childhood to adulthood is not clearly and almost inevitably channeled toward a specific adult role. In the transition from early childhood in his family to later childhood in organized agencies, the child may escape incorporation into any conventional organized group and become a kind of "free lance" in his behavior lacking in self-discipline or clear orientation toward a goal.[4]

Also, in industrialized and technologically advanced countries like the United States, the period of adolescence is much longer than it is in underdeveloped countries mainly because of the need for increased training and specialization and less dependence on the family as a total unit. Education of the adolescent is extended beyond the secondary grades and even well into the college years, which means that the period of adolescence is often prolonged and the dependence on the family, at least financially, becomes even more accentuated and the transition from adolescence to adulthood is delayed. During the nineteenth century, education was not greatly emphasized in the United States, and the period of adolescence was not as extended as it is today.

In addition, in less-industrialized cultures and in primitive societies the treatment of adolescents and the transition from childhood to adulthood was much different.

> The younger teen-agers were sequestered from the community, starved for prolonged periods, then circumcised en masse. These ritualistic practices supervised and executed by the constituted authority of the gens or clan were probable assertions that the youth was not an independent entity, an island to itself, but belonged to his society (gens or clan). After the contemplation of these sadistic, humiliating, and impotenizing (castrating) rituals, the youngster was fully accepted into the fraternity of the males in his community. He had equal status with his elders in the men's house and participated on an equal basis with them in hunts and wars.[5]

In situations like the above where "rites of passage" from childhood to adulthood exist, the transition to adult status and delineation of role requirements are facilitated.[6]

---

[4]Ruth S. Cavan and Jordan T. Cavan, *Delinquency and Crime: Cross Cultural Perspectives* (Philadelphia: J.B. Lippincott Co., 1968), p. 8.

[5]S. L. Slavson, *Reclaiming the Delinquent* (New York: The Free Press, 1965), p. 7.

[6]Walter C. Reckless, *The Crime Problem* (New York: Appleton-Century-Crofts, 1967), p. 175.

Reckless cites Bloch and Niederhoffer on the adolescent gang in our society and its having rituals similar to rites of passage.

> The puberty rites of tribal societies not only prepared youth for adult status, but also satisfied the concealed needs of youth (such as the need to overcome anxiety and doubt). In the absence of such rites and ceremonies in modern society, spontaneous gang patterns develop which satisfy the needs and yearnings of youth. Hence, informal rituals of modern American gangs are quite similar to the puberty rites of tribes.[7]

Because of the extended period of adolescence, the youngster often looks to the group or the gang for the security and at least some definition of a role and expected behavior. This is even more accentuated if the family does not provide the needed structure and guidance.

The gang, which is often negatively oriented, provides the youngster with at least an orientation and often a role. This can be a substitute for his need for identification during the turbulent and nebulous adolescent period.

If the adolescent cannot obtain satisfaction from his home or from socially acceptable groups, he may be attracted to individuals who have similar problems and needs, and many times this takes the form of a gang. If the gang exerts a great deal of influence over him, he will begin to utilize their standards and value system. This value system is often in contrast to that of his parents and community. If the value systems greatly vary, serious delinquent behavior may result.

Research has shown that almost all youthful delinquent acts are committed by groups rather than by individuals. If a youngster is looking for some type of structure and guidance and support that he cannot find in his family, but can find in the group or gang, he will evidently take on the characteristics of the group, identify with it, and abide by its codes.

> Among the rites of contemporary gangs of modern America may be found: decoration which includes tattooing, scarification, wearing distinctive apparel; the acquisition of a nickname and gang jargon; the seclusion from women in hangouts "like the bachelor huts of some tribes," and the development of age gradations (the kids, the midgets, the juniors, the seniors); hazing and ordeal as tests of fitness to belong, etc. The ganging together in all levels of modern society alleviates the storm and stress of adolescence.[8]

Even though gang activity is not normative for most children, involvement with the group and the dynamic processes that take place are very much a part of the adolescent's adjustment phase and a very real exposure to his world.

> The freedom offered adolescents by the peer group does not come without a price. Often the peer group exercises a dictatorship over the attitudes and behavior of its members that is more tyrannical than anything ever devised by

[7]*Ibid.*, p. 422.
[8]Reckless, *op. cit.*, p. 9.

the adult world. Nevertheless a great many children evidently have to go through the process of submitting to group domination before they are ready to stand on their own feet and make their own decisions. It is hard for adults to understand the why's and the wherefore's of adolescent behavior. When we see an adolescent engaging in behavior which seems silly or illogical but which conforms to the standards or norms of his group, we forget that he may not be psychologically free to behave differently. He is in effect a prisoner of the norm.[9]

Many persons do not have the strength to resist the pressures of the gang or group, not only during the adolescent period but even in later years. The maturity level of these individuals is retarded, and they often have difficulty adjusting to the adult world of expectations, demands, and responsibilities.

The group, then, can exert a great deal of influence on the youngster, and group involvement can be normal and beneficial. The group experience can be devastating, however, if the group is negatively oriented and contributes to the youngster's becoming a delinquent.

Just as the majority of adolescents do not spend most of their time in negatively oriented groups, the period of adolescence is not a common phenomenon in all cultures. The state of the adolescent depends upon how he is perceived and what place there is in the society for him. Coleman states that

adolescence is not a time of stress and turmoil in all cultures. Where the adolescent has a well-structured role, contributes to the social group and has assured status, he does not suffer the insecurities and fears of our adolescents or exhibit the extreme behavior many of our adolescents manifest in their attempt to feel important and worthwhile. In proportion then, as we encourage and plan for a useful part for our adolescents to play in their community, and insofar as we are able to solve our own uncertainties and provide a stable social and economic setting in which they can see a meaningful place as they reach adulthood, we shall be fostering mental health and preventing abnormal behavior.[10]

Like most technically advanced societies, ours keeps adolescents out of the labor market for as long as possible, thus extending and accentuating the adolescent period. As mentioned earlier, increased training and specialization are the main reason for this delay; however, an individual's job or vocational skill is one of the major factors in his achieving adult status and the rewards that go with it. If the youngster is kept out of the labor market because of the real or imagined need for educational diplomas and degrees, this has the effect of not only prolonging adolescence, but if the youngster quits school and cannot find a job, it can contribute to delinquent behavior.

[9]Henry Clay Lindgren, *Educational Psychology in the Classroom* (New York: John Wiley & Sons, Inc., 1967), p. 140.

[10]James C. Coleman, *Abnormal Psychology and Modern Life* (Glenwood, Ill.: Scott Foresman & Company, 1956), p. 596.

The Cavans point out that the traditional Eskimo society lacked both adolescence and delinquency.

> The child and youth was never physically separated from his family, either on a daily basis for education, employment or recreation, or on a yearly basis at college or for a prolonged journey. There were no hangouts or lighted street corners were youth might gather. As adult skills were learned, the child's status increased and in some groups special recognition was given as each new stage was reached. A special step toward adulthood was reached when a boy was given his own kayak, usually about the age eight or nine, or when inland he brought down his first carabao at about age eleven or twelve. In some groups a killing of the first major meat animal called for a special celebration. As soon as the youth had killed at least one of each such animal he was considered ready for marriage. Thus, step-by-step the boy made his way from childhood to adulthood always living and participating in the activities of family and community.[11]

Even the Eskimo community, however, has been affected by technology and change, and at present, as the Cavans point out, there are increasing signs of youthful male delinquency. The delinquency occurs in the towns and not in the rural settings that once typified Eskimo life. Eskimos in towns have more difficulty conforming to the traditional Eskimo behavior, and the function of the family is changed. Because many of the Eskimo youngsters want steady jobs so that they can earn money and have the same luxuries as other local ethnic groups, there is an increased "breaking of the bonds" between the youth and their families. The result is that the extended family exerts less control and has less influence over the youngster's behavior and actions, which in turn affects the delinquency rates.

Adolescence has to be viewed both historically and culturally. We have seen that technological advancements and the resulting industrialization contribute to a prolongation of the adolescent period, which can have a great affect on delinquency rates. The following section will examine the normal adolescent in greater detail so that a more realistic and insightful picture can be obtained of the delinquent adolescent.

THE NORMAL ADOLESCENT

The combined physical and psychological changes that take place during the adolescent period affect the adolescent's conception of himself, the way he feels, and the way the environment often reacts to him. In the child's early development there is not the turmoil or negative behavioral manifestation that exists during adolescence. Even in the early stages of adolescence problems do not emerge. Josselyn describes the initial stages of adolescence as being generally free of anxiety and conflict. The youngster participates in his groups and associates with his peers

[11]Cavan and Cavan, *op. cit.,* p. 23.

Courtesy of Camp Highfields, Onondaga, Michigan

Figure 3
Adolescence—A Time to Grow

in a very adaptable manner. His protests against his parents are minor and sporadic. The youngster handles problems with surprising facility and can even adequately adapt to tragedy, such as the loss of his parents. However, as Josselyn points out, this period does not last long, and the transition from the early period of adolescence to the next phase is anything but smooth. The transition takes place when physical maturity begins and when reproductive organs become developed.

> The youngster at this time may seem fatigued and often depressed—she may be sensitive, easily hurt and perhaps quarrelsome—teachers may observe the sensitivity and irritability. They may notice that she is not so reliable or conscientious as in the past. Concurrently she may make increased demands for greater independence and privileges . . .[12]

In addition, there are often other expressions of erratic and hostile behavior.

> During adolescence, anxiety, emotional confusion, erratic social behavior, shifting concepts of self in the outer world, weakness of reality perception, vacillating moral standards, instability and irregularity of impulse control, and

[12]Josselyn, *op. cit.,* p. 21.

fickle ambivalent interpersonal relations may all be part of a normal transitional adaption. Transitory mild disturbances of these types may not constitute clinical pathology. Clinical diagnoses can in no way be based on intrinsic adolescent phenomena.[13]

Redl describes the different developmental clusters of behavior that exist during adolescence and are part of the normal teen-ager's behavioral constellation:

1. Conflict of double standards: individual child still parent loyal, peer group code basically "anti-adult." Result: new waves of guilt and shame in both directions.
2. Embarrassment about open submission to adult politeness and good manner codes.
3. Shamelessness in language and behavior bravado through flaunting of health and safety rules, special joy in risk taking.
4. Avoidance of too open acceptance of adults in official roles even of those very much liked (teachers and parents, for example).
5. Loyalty to peers and risk taking in their favor even when they are personally despised or feared.
6. Openly displayed freshness against authority figures.
7. Deep-seated revulsion toward any form of praise or punishment which seems to be perceived as "infantilizing."
8. Safety in homosexual groupings; view of the other sex as "hunter's trophy" rather than in terms of interpersonal relationships.
9. Negative loading of any form of official acceptance of help from adults; pride in "taking it bravely" at any price.
10. No prestige of verbal communication with a trusted adult; hesitation about communicating about feelings and emotions.
11. Apathy toward adult as partner in play life unless it is a group game situation.[14]

These comments about the normal adolescent are important for those persons working with the juvenile delinquent. It is often easy to forget that the youngster is an adolescent first and a delinquent second and that much of the behavior he manifests is normal for his particular age group. When working with delinquents, much of the behavior that is well within the range of "normal" limits for an adolescent may be interpreted as inappropriate and "abnormal." If the person working with the delinquent adolescent is too quick in shutting off the normal adolescent expression of verbalizations and behavior, this can compound the problems for the delinquent youngster. The delinquent youngster should have at least the same amount of leeway as his nondelinquent counterpart and should receive the same consideration. If the practitioner who is working with the

[13]Nathan W. Ackerman, *The Psychodynamics of Family Life* (New York: Basic Books, Inc., Publishers, 1958), p. 231.

[14]Fritz Redl, "Adolescents—Just How Do They React?" in *Adolescence: Psychosocial Perspectives,* Gerald Caplan and Serge Lebovici (New York: Basic Books, Inc., Publishers, 1969), p. 82.

delinquent does not understand the normal clusters of behavior typical of "normal" adolescents, he will have difficulty working effectively because he will often overreact to normal behavioral manifestations. This overreaction will affect his relationship with his client by constraining the youngster's normal actions and activities. This puts pressure on the youngster to act in a manner that is abnormal for teenagers in general (quiet, sedentary, etc.). When the youngster is unable to handle this pressure, he often releases his energy in an exaggerated manner. The exaggerated behavior is often in the form of juvenile delinquency.

In many respects it is much more difficult for the practitioner today to work with the youngster who has been labeled delinquent than it was in the past. The styles of hair and dress and behavior of youngsters today are much different from those of even a few years ago. Therefore, it becomes much easier to stereotype and label youngsters, even when this is inappropriate and overgeneralized. Extensive overgeneralizations and labeling can hinder the helping process and create imaginary boundaries that do not have to be constructed.

> There certainly is a general trend toward longer hair, sideburns, beards, mustaches and so on, among young men in our society just as there is a general trend toward fewer and more flimsy clothes, more casual clothes, longer, less constricted hair styles and so on, among young women. But today, none of this can be taken to be symbolic of a growing youth rebellion or any such thing. For the older members of our society these personal styles are still very much a subject of great concern—a symbol of revolt—because they have some effect on what the older members of our society think about the young and what they do. These personal styles are of significance, but they are not significant as symbols of a general youth culture. In general there are still far too many differences among young people in our society, especially class differences and so on, and these are still far too important to the young people themselves in many different specific ways, for a general youth culture in the sense of a distinct set of values, beliefs, commitments and everyday patterns of activity to have developed.[15]

The point is that although many adults feel that young people are a threat to the adult way of life, most youngsters are closely aligned with many adult values. Just as there is not the great schism of viewpoints between youngsters and adults that is often imagined, much of the behavior of the delinquent adolescent is well within the range of normal acceptance. It is not the purpose of the person working with the juvenile delinquent to change the youngster's entire personality and orientation, for much of his orientation, feelings, and expectations are the same as those of the normal adolescent. What does have to be altered are those aspects of his behavior that go beyond the limits of acceptability. This can best be accomplished by perceiving and treating him as an adolescent first and a delinquent second.

[15]Jack D. Douglas, *Youth in Turmoil, America's Changing Youth Cultures and Student Protest Movements,* Crime and Delinquency Issues: A Monograph Series, National Institute of Mental Health Center for Studies of Crime and Delinquency, Public Health Services, Publication No. 2058, p. 30.

CHILDHOOD DEVELOPMENT

During the period of adolescence—especially in a highly industrialized culture like ours—not only are physical and psychological changes taking place, but the youngster is attempting to develop a self-concept. This is a difficult process; therefore, much of his behavior is contradictory and he often vacillates from one mood to another.

> Today he may idealize a certain philosophy of life only to express tomorrow slavelike devotion to a completely contrasting approach to the problems of living. At one time he follows too rigidly an idealized code of conduct, the demands of which if he really met, would deny him all human gratification. As if by a sudden metamorphosis of character he then violates—or more often talks of violating—even acceptable "behavior."[16]

The youngster's change in mood from day to day causes his parents much concern. The contradictions in his verbalizations or in his behavior or the contradictions in both his verbalizations and in his behavior are, as Josselyn feels, the result of an attempt to find clear-cut answers to internal conflicts.

> He is attempting to avoid discord by choosing a variety of notes to play singularly. He does not know how to play several notes in harmony.[17]

This has important implications in working with the youngster. Adults often find it frustrating that the youngster fluctuates in moods and in behavior so readily and so easily. This frustration can be transmitted to the youngster and can contribute to his insecure feelings. If the adult merely takes much of the youngster's erratic behavior in stride, the "testing" he is doing on his environment and his parents will subside. With the guidance and support of the adult, more consistent orientations to problem solving can occur.

Coleman discusses the conflicts or problem areas that adolescent youngsters have to deal with during adolescence.[18] He points out the main areas of adaption that have to take place during this period if the youngster is going to handle his problems with some semblance of order and ultimately be a productive citizen. First, the youngster struggles with the phenomenon of dependence versus independence. Up to the point of adolescence, he has generally been dependent on his parents for the satisfying of both his emotional and his physical needs. As he proceeds through the adolescent period he becomes more independent, possibly by

[16]Josselyn, *op. cit.,* p. 10.

[17]*Ibid.*

[18]Coleman, *op. cit.,* p. 65.

having a part-time job or by being able to spend his allowance with more flexibility. (Because the dependence-independence conflict is important, it will be elaborated upon later.)

Second, Coleman points out that the adolescent period is a transition also from pure pleasure to reality. Before the adolescent period and in the infant stages, the youngster did not usually have to be concerned about "basics" such as food, clothing, and shelter. As he progresses through adolescence, there is much pressure on him to start thinking about a vocation and a role in life. The reality of the future and how he is going to provide for himself becomes manifest.

Third, Coleman describes the problem the youngster has transcending from incompetence to competence. Before the adolescent period, the youngster did not have to have specific skills either educationally or vocationally to survive. With the onset of adolescence, however, he has to become competent so that he can support himself in the future. In addition to this, the adolescent youngster has to consider what Coleman identifies as extending beyond himself to "other-centered activity" rather than merely self-centered activities. As he goes through the adolescent period and starts thinking about an adult role and vocation, he has to extend beyond his own self-centeredness and egocentricity and learn to give as well as take. When he eventually prepares to raise his own family, this will necessitate that he become involved in "other-centered" projects so that he can provide for their support.

Finally, Coleman mentions that the adolescent youngster develops from a nonproductive to a more productive orientation. Before adolescence and, ultimately, adulthood, the youngster did not have to be productive and contribute to the social group as a whole. His family made a major investment in him and provided for his physical and emotional needs. As he proceeds through the adolescent period and begins thinking about his adult obligations and responsibilities, however, he has to learn how to become productive. This is usually realized through a vocational or professional role which he attempts to prepare for. Obviously, not all these areas of adjustment that Coleman discusses are adequately handled by all adolescents.

> Although these pathways toward maturity characterize normal development, it is possible for development to be arrested or fixated at different points along the continuum from infancy to maturity. This might be the case with the middle-aged Don Juan whose sexual behavior resembles that of an adolescent or the developmental sequence may be reversed as in regression where the individual reverts to behavior which once brought satisfaction.[19]

Ackerman feels that one of the greatest struggles for the adolescent is to resolve his identification with his parents and to build an identification and self-concept that is uniquely his own.

> Adolescence is a groping, questioning stage, a phase in which the adolescent condenses the values that will guide his social perspective for the major part

[19]*Ibid.*, p. 66.

of his life. It is exactly here that he confronts the challenge of bringing into harmony his view of self and his view of the world. He must now link his life-striving with a personal philosophy. The adolescent asks: What is life? Who am I? What am I good for? Where do I fit? Who are my real friends? Who are my enemies? What must I fight, with whom, against whom, for what life goals? And finally: Is life really worth the struggle? The kind of feverish, anxious, searching for identity, values and social orientation is paralleled by an expanding interest in social and economic conflicts, in religion and philosophy. In the service of this search the adolescent mobilizes his intellect and exploits it as a defense against his anxiety. Such struggle deeply affects the adolescent's choice of group association, in the time of testing of parental images and temporary dissolution of self, the adolescent seeks to identify with something larger than himself. His urge is to ally with a cause greater than his own.[20]

There is a push-and-pull phenomenon which creates many difficulties and conflicts for the adolescent. On the one hand, his parents and their expectations have been with him his entire life; on the other hand, the peer group begins to become much more important to him. The peer group often has a life-style and a value system that are much different from those of his family. Because in our society there is not the control of the extended family that existed in the past, the peer group takes on much more importance and therefore exerts much more influence. If the influence and the life-style of the peer group are greatly different from those of the family, problems can arise.

The adolescent who loves his parents but who also wants to be accepted by his peers, may have a problem in deciding which standard will govern. Usually he makes some kind of compromise, letting parental standards govern some aspects of his behavior, and peer standards other aspects. But the peer group often has the edge in such contest partly because of the generally outward direction of social development, and partly because our culture places so much value on getting along with one's peers. This is less of a problem in other cultures. Young people in Germany, for example, are more concerned about maintaining good relations with their parents, whereas American youth tend to be more interested in getting others to like them—adolescents today, thanks to the general availability of part-time jobs and the generosity of their parents, are relatively free to do as they will, buy what they want and use time as they think best—all without being responsible to anyone.[21]

The increased freedom and material possessions, however, are often not much help when the youngster needs the guidance and assistance of mature adults and concerned parents. Wolfgang aptly points out that

many youth feel forced into detachment and premature cynicism because society seems to offer youth today so little that is stable, relevant and meaningful. They often look in vain for values, goals, means and institutions

[20]Ackerman, *op. cit.,* p. 215.

[21]Lindgren, *op. cit.,* p. 140.

to which they can be committed because their thrust for commitment is strong. . . . The social isolation, social distance, alienation and retreat from the adult world are increased by many social and technological mechanisms operating to encourage a youth subculture. As the numbers and intensity of value sharing in the youth subculture increase, the process of intergenerational alienation also escalates. Parents have almost always been accused of not understanding their children. What may be new is that more parents either do not care that they do not understand or that it is increasingly impossible for them to understand. Perhaps then it is not that the parents are poor models for the kinds of lives that their youths will lead in their own mature years; parents may simply be increasingly irrelevant models for their children. So rapid is current social change that the youth of today have difficulty projecting a concept of themselves as adults.[22]

Furthermore, the general status of the adolescent in our society is very tenuous, and in many respects he is the forgotten segment of the community.

While young children occupy a special protected status and adults an authority status, adolescents have no defined position in current society.[23]

In effect, then, adolescents do not have the protection that is given to younger children, not do they have the rights and privileges that accompany adult status. This is one of the main reasons that youngsters often retreat to the group or the gang. It has been suggested that the only way to rectify this lack of status is to involve adolescents in the decision-making processes of their community. The recent passing of voting rights bills and the granting of other privileges to youngsters are an attempt to involve the adolescent, at least the late adolescent, in these processes. This should resolve one of the problems of status affirmation which is often lacking in Western society and makes it difficult for the adolescent to find his rightful place as a contributing member of his community.[24] Much of the futility and frustration that exists among teen-agers can be reduced if they are involved in community problem solving and decision making. This not only will be a wise use of human resources but also will contribute to a more definite role definition for young people and possibly reduce many of the problems associated with the transition from adolescence to adulthood.

THE STRUGGLE OF DEPENDENCE VERSUS INDEPENDENCE

The prolongation of dependency relationships between parents and youngsters can have many negative ramifications. It is mandatory that parents understand the

[22]Marvin E. Wolfgang, "The Culture of Youth," *Task Force Report: Juvenile Delinquency and Youth Crime,* U.S. Department of Health, Education, and Welfare, p. 148.

[23]Slavson, *op. cit.,* p. 8.

[24]*Ibid.*

adolescent's conflict of wanting to be independent but becoming frightened when parental guidance and support are withdrawn too soon. (Chapter 4 discussed this aspect of child rearing.)

Parents often, either consciously or unconsciously, perpetuate the dependency relationship by never helping their child to become independent and self-sufficient through a mutual process of cooperation, communication, and assistance.

> Many parents while they consciously wish their child to grow up actually are resistant to this process. Perhaps they cannot face the vacuum that will exist when the child is no longer dependent on them. Sometimes they are jealous of the child entering early adulthood with all its apparent glamour when their own adulthood seems tarnished.[25]

Often parents live and relive their own childhood experiences and problems through their children. The child is not viewed as a unique individual but is used as a pawn to be manipulated for selfish parental interests.

If the child is forced into prolonged dependence or if his parents do not allow him to develop into an eventual productive citizen, he will often rebel through delinquent activity. Once delinquent behavior has become manifest and the child has come in contact with the criminal justice system, it becomes much more difficult to bridge the communication gap between the youngster and his parents. When communication between them breaks down, the adolescent's perception of all adults can become negative.

> He perceives adults as agents bent on denying pleasures and frustrating consummation of sexual urges which are now at their height. He views adults as determined to restrict his awakening striving for self-direction and autonomy. While the adolescent attempts to defend himself against infantile strivings, he also feels with increasing anxiety, the strain of pressures of making his way into the wider world of which he knows he must become a part.[26]

In its extreme form, when problems snowball and when communication lines are broken between parents and the youngster, the situation becomes so severe that the youngster may completely disassociate himself from his family and make his own way in the community or in the delinquent group. Parents are then viewed as a necessary evil to provide the "basics" and material satisfaction.[27]

The precipitating factor that often directly contributes to faulty communication between the youngster and his parents is the youngster's attempt to achieve some independent status within his community and within the family constellation. Parents do not realize that the search for an independent identity is

[25]Josselyn, *op. cit.,* p. 29.

[26]Slavson, *op. cit.,* p. 11.

[27]Lindgren, *op. cit.,* p. 141.

normal, as is the vacillation between dependency and independency. As Chapter 4 pointed out, when parents react in an extreme manner, such as overpermissiveness or authoritarianism, this does not solve the adolescent's struggle. It only accentuates it.

> As a result [of the struggle of dependence versus independence] he is apt to make demands for dependence which he has not made since he was a small child. At the same time, he wants advice about what clothes to wear, what hours to keep, what food to eat, what political party to respect, or what ethical or moral formula to embrace.[28]

When the adolescent finds himself slipping into dependency on his parents, he often overreacts by exerting his personality in a very independent manner. At this point his parents cannot be winners, only losers, and no matter what type of advice they give the youngster it will not be satisfactory because he himself does not know what route to take. At this point it is helpful if parents at least understand the dependent-independent dilemma. The mere understanding and awareness of this dynamic situation will prevent overreactions and will transmit to the youngster that his parents have the situation under control. When overreaction occurs, the youngster often retreats to his peer group for support and guidance.[29] The peer group may be negatively oriented and may therefore contribute to delinquent behavior.

THE DELINQUENT ADOLESCENT

The number of delinquent youngsters appearing before juvenile courts has become a serious problem.

> Youth crime seems to be predominantly a phenomenon of urban adolescents giving each other social support in the promotion of delinquency. Eighty to 90 per cent of offenses referred to juvenile courts involved two or more juveniles as associates in the offense. Similarly the proportion of inmates having co-defendants or rap partners in their offense is also regularly higher in youth prisons and reformatories than in penitentiaries for adult offenders. Each involvement in crime and each experience of arrest and correction or confinement increases a youth's estrangement from home and school, at the same time that it enhances his prestige and self-esteem in delinquent social circles.[30]

Again it should be emphasized that the delinquent adolescent is an adolescent first and a delinquent second. When this is forgotten, the practitioner in the

[28]Josselyn, *op. cit.*, p. 38.
[29]Coleman, *op. cit.*, p. 595.
[30]Douglas, *op. cit.*, p. 21.

criminal justice system may have difficulty relating to the youngster as a teen-ager and be guilty of perpetuating the labeling process and viewing the delinquent as "extremely different." (See Chapter 3, "Theories of Delinquency Causation.")

WORKING WITH THE ADOLESCENT

Lubell points out that the existence of a youth subculture diametrically opposed to adult life-styles, ideals, and values is probably exaggerated and that there are many more youngsters who share the viewpoints of their parents than those who do not.

> The dominant impression left by the term generation gap is that of a unified younger generation that is breaking drastically from both its elders and society in almost every conceivable way. Actually through my interviewing over the last four years on how young people differ in their thinking from their parents suggests that: (1) Much more continuity than gap exists between the two generations; (2) Parents have not been rendered obsolete but continue to exert an almost ineradicable influence on their children . . .[31]

Even though the differences between generations may not be as great as is popularly portrayed, there are at least some differences, especially between delinquent youngsters and law-abiding adults. The practitioner in the criminal justice system not only has to be aware of these differences but has to be willing to communicate honestly with these youngsters so that problem solving can be facilitated.

Adolescents in general are very difficult to work with, and delinquent adolescents present an even greater challenge. Slavson states that during the adolescent period

> there is doubt about sexual and social adequacy and self-regard is at a low ebb. To a large extent the adolescent adopts as a defense against these self-doubts a stance of self-maximization and employs antiphobic attitudes of omnipotence so that he may maintain an image of strength. He thus wards off hopelessness and depression. To admit to doubts, vacillation, conflicts and especially inability to deal with problems on his own and to have to seek help, constitutes a source of severe narcissistic injury against which the adolescent defends himself. This complex of feelings constitutes one of the main sources of resistance to therapy, only second in intensity to the rise of awareness of inadequacy.[32]

The major purpose of this section has been to point out the dynamics and conflicts that exist in the developmental period called adolescence. Even if the

---

[31]Samuel Lubell, "That Generation Gap," in *Confrontation,* ed. Daniel Bell and Irving Kristil (New York: Basic Books, Inc., Publishers, 1968), p. 58.

[32]Slavson, *op. cit.,* p. 11.

youngster does not become involved in delinquent activity, there are still many problems and conflicts. It is necessary that the practitioner understand the dynamic processes and conflicts of adolescence if he is to be successful in his delinquency prevention and rehabilitation efforts. The practitioner should remember that he himself was an adolescent at one time and that during his teen-age years conflicts and frustrations (such as the struggle for independence) also existed. The conflicts and frustrations may take a different form of expression today, but the basic need to develop an adequate self-concept, feel worthwhile, and be accepted by the group is not much different from that of past generations. To be effective in working with young people, Anthony states that

> adults need to recognize that adolescents are people, and particular people at that. It is important to remember that the stereotypes that have been cultivated are not necessarily even true of a minority of adolescents and that adolescents are not all delinquent, irresponsible, hypersexual or simpleminded creatures in pursuit solely of a good time. As long as these stereotypes persist, adolescents will respond by setting up barriers to communication, excluding the adult by the conspiracy of silence or by a language and culture of their own. The adults are then narcissistically affronted that the youth want to act and look and talk differently from them and then interpret this as rebellion, overlooking the fact that the adolescents want to act and look and talk differently from the children and are deeply engaged in delineating their identities as in revolting against authority. The principle of secrecy and silence adopted by the adolescent culture toward the adult is a universal phenomenon appearing in all cultures and can be understood as a counter-response to the secrets and silences that adults have preserved in the face of consistent childhood curiosities and interests.[33]

The concept that adolescents are people with feelings and problems, as well as with a unique status in life, must also be extended to the delinquent youngster, who in addition to having the normal problems of adolescence often has severe economic, social, and psychological problems.

What Socrates said about adolescents approximately twenty-five hundred years ago still applies today, even though the behavior of adolescents and the "symptoms" take a different form:

> Our adolescents now seem to love luxury, they have bad manners and contempt for authority. They show disrespect for adults and spend their time hanging around and gossiping with one another—they are ready to contradict their parents, monopolize the conversation in company, eat gluttonously and tyrannize their teachers.

Caplan aptly points out that parents should look at their teen-agers in the context of total development:

[33]James Anthony, "The Reactions of Adults to Adolescents and Their Behavior," in *Adolescence: Psychosocial Perspectives*, Gerald Caplan and Serge Lebovici (New York: Basic Books, Inc., Publishers, 1969), p. 82.

> If the adult remembers how much of himself has gone into the making of the adolescent he would be able to sympathize and empathize to an extent that should make for a partnership based on mutual respect and affection.[34]

The practitioner in the criminal justice system dealing with the juvenile delinquent should also understand the adolescent and his problems and dynamics. This chapter will conclude with a discussion of a pertinent, contemporary adolescent problem—the use of drugs.

ADOLESCENT DRUG ABUSE

The adolescent drug problem today is so widespread that it can no longer be considered a phenomenon solely of urban centers. The adolescent drug user comes from all socioeconomic levels and all environments, and he cannot be associated with any particular racial, ethnic, or religious group. Not all drug users are dope fiends. Many respectable citizens and youngsters have been "hooked" on drugs, but regardless of socioeconomic class, the results of drug abuse are often devastating. Drug use has become so prevalent and drugs so widely available that the problem among adolescents has reached epidemic proportions. As pointed out previously, the youngster encounters many problems, both physical and psychological, during the adolescent stage of development. Often, without proper guidance and support, deviant and delinquent behavioral adaption to the environment become common-place. For the teen-ager who has difficulty in developing meaningful relationships with parents, adults, and peers and has problems adjusting to the environment, the use of drugs may become an expedient means of temporarily relieving frustration and strain.

The use of drugs has often been compared with the use of alcohol. Regardless of the similarities or dissimilarities, much more research needs to be done to determine the potential effects of both "hard" and "soft" drug use by teen-agers. The lack of scientific information regarding the effects of drugs should be reason enough to discourage its use. This section will discuss the drug phenomenon because it is a contemporary problem and prevalent among adolescents. Reasons for drug abuse, the abuser, drug control, types of drugs, and methods of treatment will be examined.

Amount of Drug Abuse

The Bureau of Narcotics and Dangerous Drugs reports that although no one really knows how many drug addicts there are in the country, at the close of 1968 some 64,011 active narcotic addicts were recorded. Even though these statistics may not be totally reliable, they are the only ones available. There is approximately

[34]*Ibid.*, p. 77.

one addict for every 3,157 persons, and most of the addicts are from four states. New York alone accounts for 50 percent of the addicts, while nearly 78 percent are from California, Illinois, New Jersey, and New York. Nearly 47 percent of the addicts are between the ages of twenty-one and thirty.

> As opposed to the majority of the "hard" narcotic users who are reported by law enforcement agencies or private agencies, the users of marihuana, hallucinogens, stimulants and depressants are seldom discovered unless they are involved in a criminal action and arrested. Estimates of their numbers can be gained only through well-designed representative surveys of the populations. Therefore, there is no way at the present time to document the number of abusers of these drugs. There have, however, been estimates and controlled surveys which indicate that there may be as many as 20 million users of marihuana in the country, although this figure can be accepted only as an estimate. One thing is a fact—any individual who is dependent on a drug for any reason other than one established by the person's physician is an abuser of drugs.[35]

Recent statistics on the extent of illicit drug use among students indicate varying rates of usage. Surveys show that the proportions of high school and college students who have ever used drugs are surprisingly similar. Twenty-one percent of the students participating in a referendum at a West Coast university in 1967 reported that they had used marihuana one or more times. During the same year 31 percent of the students at a high school farther up the coast indicated that they had tried marihuana at least once. School authorities in Grosse Pointe, Michigan, estimated that 50 percent of their high school students were experimenting in some way with drugs, while in Montclair, New Jersey, authorities estimated that around 33 1/3 percent of the high school population were using drugs. Other high schools and colleges report much lower rates of marihuana use. Surveys similarly indicate varying rates of use of LSD, the amphetamines, and the barbiturates.[36]

In addition to the personal tragedy drug abuse causes for the user, there is also a great loss to the community. Not only are productive and potentially productive citizens affected because of the use of drugs, many crimes are committed by users so that they can support their habit.

The Bureau of Narcotics and Dangerous Drugs reports that narcotic addicts drain millions of dollars from society because the very cost of the drugs themselves on the illicit market is exorbitant. The average addict spends approximately fifteen dollars a day for drugs, although some of the hard narcotic users require one hundred dollars a day.

> Because most addicts cannot obtain the cash to buy their drugs legally, they turn to crime. Most convert stolen merchandise into cash. It takes about

---

[35]*Fact Sheets,* Bureau of Narcotics and Dangerous Drugs (Washington, D.C.: Government Printing Office) p. 5-1.

[36]George S. Larimer, Alvin H. Tucker, and Ellen F. Brown, "Drugs and Youth," *Pennsylvania Health,* 31, No. 4 (Winter 1970), 3.

$3-$5 in stolen goods to get $1 cash. So to support a $15 a day habit, the addict has to steal $50 worth of property a day or $18,250 a year. Assuming all addicts in the country use this method—and they don't (some rely on prostitution, shoplifting, burglary, forgery, theft of legitimate drugs or illegal production of drugs)—more than one billion dollars worth of merchandise must be stolen to provide narcotics for this country's addict population each year.[37]

The economic, social, and personal loss as a result of the use of drugs is therefore immeasurable. Furthermore, because of inadequate statistics and identification methods, only the tip of the drug iceberg is exposed. Many more persons who have developed a physical or a psychological dependence on drugs represent the submerged portion of the iceberg which often does not become exposed until tragedy such as suicide, serious crime, or family disruption occurs.

Reasons for Drug Abuse

Some of the basic reasons why persons choose a deviant method of adaption to the environment, whether it be delinquency, drug abuse, or both, were discussed in earlier chapters. Contributing factors can include lack of opportunity in the environment, poor relationships with parents and peers, and inability to adjust satisfactorily in the community. Even though it is difficult to generalize the reasons for drug abuse, one of the most prevalent explanations is that youngsters use drugs because they feel alienated from their environment and the adult world. There is often a great deal of peer influence in the use of drugs, and it can be considered the "in" thing to do. Even though there are many deeper explanations for the use of drugs, many young people look for kicks and "this is one way to obtain kicks."[38]

Because there are many reasons for taking drugs and variations of each reason, it is not particularly important to dwell on individual cases or individual rationalizations for the use of drugs. The point to be made is that the totality of the problem has to be understood, recognizing that, unfortunately, the use of drugs is seen as a viable alternative by many youngsters.

The use of drugs or the motivation for their use does not suddenly emerge. Many experts feel that youngsters today are exposed to the drug culture long before actual usage. For example, youngsters see their parents often rely on barbiturates to help them go to sleep, stimulants and amphetamines to pep them up, and tranquilizers to calm them down. Many youngsters justify their use of drugs by rationalizing that their parents use them, although in different forms. Television has also transmitted through advertisements and popular programming the ready accessibility of legitimate drugs and the "magical" way that they can solve problems and contribute to happiness in our fast-paced world.

[37]*Fact Sheets,* Bureau of Narcotics and Dangerous Drugs, p. 5-2.

[38]Clifford Denton, "The Growing Drug Menace," *Pennsylvania Education,* 2, No. 1 (January-February 1970), 18.

The lack of a cohesive family structure can also be a contributing factor to increased drug use. Today the family no longer exerts as much influence on the child as it did in the past. The family has become restructured. The extended family, which consists of parents, children, grandparents, uncles, aunts, and cousins, no longer is a cohesive unit that can exert influence and on which the child can depend for support and guidance. Only the nuclear family, which consists of parents and a small number of children, is prevalent today.[39]

The family, however, still has a vital role to play today even though it has been restructured. It has to help the youngster make the link between adolescence and adulthood in an orderly manner so that the youngster can become a productive citizen.[40] Through the family and the initial relationships that the youngster has with his parents, he learns how to effectively relate to his environment and handle its pressures and responsibilities. If parents relinquish their rightful roles of guiding, supporting, and teaching their youngsters, the peer group will become the primary source of influence. The peer group is usually not equipped to handle the youngster's problems or satisfy his needs in a socially acceptable manner.

It is unfortunate that some parents have by accident or design provided their children with material possessions but have failed to provide an emotional environment that is conducive to fostering future emotional stability and positive behavioral adaption in the community. When this emotional support is not provided, the youngster often sees drug abuse as an alternative.

Because many of today's parents were materially deprived in their youth, they overreact by providing their children with material possessions, often at the expense of providing emotional support and guidance while the youngster is progressing to adulthood.

> After listening to a tape recording on "Marcy," a drug addict and fugitive from home, one teenage boy commented, "It is beautiful. Why don't they explain the causes of what went wrong with Marcy. My father belonged to the depression generation, he suffered so much from lack of material things that he spent his whole life making sure we had the things that warm us outside, but he never had time to give us things that warm us inside."[41]

The Drug Abuser

There is much conjecture concerning the type of person who abuses drugs as well as his reasons for using them. Even though many persons are exposed to drugs, both legitimately and illegitimately, only a relatively few when compared with the total population become drug abusers.

---

[39]Urie Bronfenbrenner, "Parents Bring Up Your Children!," *Look*, January 26, 1971, pp. 45-46.

[40]The President's Commission: *Task Force Report: Juvenile Delinquency and Youth Crime* (Washington, D.C.: Government Printing Office, 1967), p. 41.

[41]"From a Hippie Soul," *Saturday Review*, December 16, 1967, p. 46.

Although much is known about the effects of drugs, with abuse potential, the user himself remains the enigma. Slum conditions, easy access to drugs, peddlers and organized crime have all been blamed for the problem. While any of these factors may contribute, no single cause, nor single set of conditions clearly leads to drug dependency, for it occurs in all social and economic classes. The key to the riddle may well lay within the abuser in any one of many sets or conditions. True, drug dependency cannot develop without a chemical agent. Yet, while millions are exposed to drugs by reason of medical need, relatively few of these people turn to a life of drugs. It is true that in metropolitan areas there are invariably found groups of "hard-core" users and a large proportion of the young persons who use drugs in the ghetto areas. Even though drugs may be available on street corners, in metropolitan areas, only a small percentage of the individuals exposed join the ranks of abusers.[42]

Many assumptions have been made about the drug abuser. Some say he is emotionally unstable; others say that he has difficulty developing interpersonal relationships. His withdrawal from society seems to indicate that he cannot accept the responsibilities and pressures of society, and therefore he turns to a life of drugs as a way of avoiding reality. The teen-age years (when many addicts have their first drug experience) are very difficult, and the transition to adulthood is seldom smooth.

The early and middle teens bring a loosing of family ties, a diminution of parental authority, increasing responsibility and sexual maturing beset with anxiety, frustration, fear of failure, interconflicts and doubts. The adolescent may find that amphetamines and marihuana promote conversation and sociability, barbiturates relieve anxiety, hallucinogens heighten sensations and narcotics provide relief and escape. Drug abuse may provide the entree into an "in group" or be a way of affirming independence by defying authority and convention.[43]

The Federal Bureau of Narcotics and Dangerous Drugs typology divides drug abuse into four categories: situational, spree, hard-core, and hippie. The first type of abuser employs drugs for a specific or *situational* purpose. Users in this category could be students who use amphetamines to keep awake at examination time or housewives who use diet pills. The drug in these and similar cases provides an immediate function or "solution" for the user. This type of user does not usually become dependent on the drug, although he may manifest psychological difficulties and use drugs in particularly anxious situations.

The second type of drug user defined by the bureau is the *spree* user. Drugs are used usually by college or high school students for "kicks" or to be exposed to a new experience. Even though there may be little physical dependence, because of the sporadic nature of the involvement, psychological dependence can develop.

[42]*Fact Sheet,* Bureau of Narcotics and Dangerous Drugs, p. 4-1.
[43]*Ibid.*

Some "spree" users may only try drugs once or twice and decide there are better things in life. Drug sprees constitute a defiance of convention, an adventurous daring experience or a means of having fun. Unlike "hard-core" abusers, who often pursue their habits alone or in pairs, spree users usually take drugs only in groups or at social functions.[44]

The third type of user is the *hard-core* addict. He often lives in a slum area of the city, and his life revolves around the use of hard drugs. He exhibits strong psychological dependence on the drug, often reinforced by physical dependence when certain drugs are being used. He feels he cannot function without the use of drugs and his drug abuse often started on a spree basis. His drug abuse is more than a passing fancy.

The fourth type of drug user is the *hippie.* Hippies react to the system, or the "establishment." They believe the system is antiquated and wrong and that the use of drugs can provide a new experience and add new meaning to their lives. Even though drugs are an integral part of the hippie life-style and many hippies may be considered hard-core users at times, they are different from the typical hard-core type because most hippies do not come from slum areas. They come from middle- or upper-class families, and their educational level is much higher than that of the hard-core inner-city drug user.[45]

There can be much overlapping of the four types, and the spree user or the situational user may become a hard-core user if drug use is continued.

Slum sections of large metropolitan areas still account for the largest number of known heroin abusers. But frustration, immaturity and the emotional deprivation are not peculiar to depressed neighborhoods, and the misuse of drugs by middle and upper economic class individuals is being recognized with increasing frequency. Drug dependence is not discriminating. A drug, an individual, an environment which predisposes use, and a personality deficiency are the key factors in its development.[46]

Drug Control

Because the misuse of drugs is illegal in the United States, many persons feel that the drug control answer can be found in more stringent laws and that drug use can only be prevented through legal enforcement and penal sanctions. The result of this assumption in many cases has been mandatory prison terms and increased punishment for repeated offenses. In many cases, however, severe punishment has not deterred drug use and thus other methods are being considered.[47]

[44]*Ibid.*, pp. 4-1, 4-2.

[45]*Ibid.*, p. 4-2.

[46]*Ibid.*

[47]The President's Commission: *Task Force Report: Narcotics and Drug Abuse* (Washington, D.C.: Government Printing Office, 1967), p. 7.

In addition to rehabilitative efforts, numerous enforcement agencies have attempted to both detect persons using drugs and prevent the flow of drugs into the country. The Bureau of Narcotics and Dangerous Drugs maintains units in various overseas districts to locate and seize illicit opium and heroin supplies before they appear in the United States. The Federal Bureau of Customs maintains a force at ports and along land borders to prevent the smuggling of contraband, which often includes drugs. The Customs Agency Service, which is composed of custom port investigators and enforcement officers, conducts vessel and aircraft searches and keeps airports, piers, and border-crossing points under surveillance. Customs Agency Service also investigates and disseminates intelligence information. Once the drug has been transported to the United States, the efforts of the Bureau of Narcotics and Dangerous Drugs are coordinated with state and local law enforcement agencies to identify users and pushers and to prevent the dispersion of drugs.[48]

Even though there is a coordinated effort between federal, state, and local agencies to prevent drugs from coming into this country and to detect suppliers and users once they have arrived, many difficulties are involved in the control of illicit drugs and enforcement in itself is not the total answer.

Types of Drugs

The Bureau of Narcotics and Dangerous Drugs reports that there are two main currents of illicit traffic in opium and the opiates. One begins in the Middle East and ends in North America. The other pattern is from Southeast Asia directly to Hong Kong, Japan, China (Taiwan), and the West Coast of America. Secondary flows include routes from Mexico to the United States. The greatest proportion of the heroin drug is produced from opium poppies grown in Turkey and eventually diverted to the North American continent, the principal target of illicit heroin traffic. After the raw opium is converted into a morphine base in clandestine laboratories, it is most often shipped through Istanbul and Beirut and smuggled into France to be processed into heroin.

> At this point, the heroin may be smuggled directly into the United States or transported through Italy, Canada or Mexico. It is, nevertheless, destined for the U.S. market. Underground heroin trade from France generally involves large quantities of heroin smuggled by well-organized international traffickers who have contrived all types of devious methods and devices to conceal the contraband.[49]

The Turkish farmer gets less than one thousand dollars a year for his poppy crop, but when opium is converted into morphine, ten pounds of opium produces one pound of morphine worth one thousand dollars. In Marseilles, France, where

---

[48]*Ibid.*

[49]*Fact Sheets*, Bureau of Narcotics and Dangerous Drugs, p. 3.

many clandestine laboratories exist for converting morphine into heroin, one thousand dollars worth of morphine becomes heroin worth twenty-five hundred dollars a pound. By the time it reaches New York it is worth up to five thousand dollars a pound, while the wholesale price on the street goes to one hundred thousand dollars a pound. The plant, which originates in Turkey, many times finds its mark by a needle in a youngster's arm in the United States.[50]

In regard to other types of drugs, marihuana, although grown heavily in the Near East and Middle East, is also produced in Mexico, the United States' largest supplier. A great majority of amphetamines and barbiturates that are diverted to illicit use most often come from legal channels, although a small proportion of illicit amphetamines and barbiturates are smuggled into the United States from Mexico.

> Other portions of the illegal supply originate through theft and by production in clandestine laboratories, operating illegally in garages, basements and warehouses—even in trucks. Some registered manufacturers, under the cloak of legality, make quantities of dangerous drugs unlawfully and dispose of them through the black market trade. The illegal "bulk peddler," who deals in hundreds of thousands of capsules and tablets, is an important link in the traffic in dangerous drugs. Since there is no legal production of hallucinogenic drugs in the United States, the illicit traffic depends on production from illicit laboratories or smuggled drugs from Europe, Mexico, Canada and Australia.[51]

Most of the narcotics and dangerous drugs (excluding heroin, marihuana and hallucinogens) are used for medicinal purposes and are dispensed by pharmacies and prescribed by physicians. Because of the ready availability of legal drugs, the drug abuser has much latitude in his methods for obtaining drugs, which may range all the way from altering a legitimate prescription to stealing them. The problems of control are obviously immense.

Drugs can be classified into five main types: (1) narcotics, (2) hallucinogens, (3) stimulants, (4) depressants, and (5) marihuana. A description of each will follow.

Narcotics. The term *narcotic* refers to opium and to pain-relieving drugs made from opium, such as morphine, paregoric, and codeine.[52] Synthetic drugs such as demerol and methadone are also classified as narcotics. Narcotics are used in medicine mainly to relieve pain and induce sleep. The narcotic abuser develops a physical addiction to the drug, and as the body develops a tolerance, larger dosages are needed to satisfy the craving. When the narcotic is withheld or when use has ceased, there are withdrawal symptoms and physical trauma such as sweating,

---

[50]Horace Sutton, "Drugs: Ten Years to Doomsday," *Saturday Review*, November 14, 1970, p. 19.

[51]*Fact Sheets*, Bureau of Narcotics and Dangerous Drugs, p. 2.

[52]Most of the descriptive information relating to the different types of drugs has been taken from documents provided by the U.S. Department of Health, Education, and Welfare.

shaking, nausea, and even abdominal pains and leg cramps. In addition to the physical dependence, however, psychological dependence results, and the individual who uses narcotics and becomes addicted attempts to handle his problems by using the narcotic drug.

> Narcotic use can become even more of an escape than expected. Contaminated injections or unexpectedly high dosages caused over 900 deaths in New York City alone during 1969; over 200 of these were among teenagers.[53]

Heroin, the most prevalent narcotic taken by drug addicts, is usually adulterated and mixed with other substances, such as milk sugar or quinine. The drug makes the person believe that his problems have been eliminated or that he can deal with life more adequately. Once the drug has worn off, however, the reality of daily responsibilities and pressures becomes even more acute, and as a result increased dosage is usually needed to "feed the habit."

Because of the cost of the drug and the fact that it often reduces hunger and thirst, addicts often become malnourished and physically emaciated. They then become more susceptible to diseases like tuberculosis and pneumonia. Negative side effects, such as hepatitis (from unsterile needles) and blood infections, are common. Even though narcotic addiction is still more prevalent among minority groups in the large inner-city areas, it has spread to persons of all backgrounds regardless of race, sex or national origin. Cases have been cited where professionals such as doctors and pharmacists use drugs not only because of their ready accessibility but because they are a short-term method of dealing with pressure.

In addition to the stringent penalties established under the Narcotic Control Act of 1956 and revised under the Comprehensive Drug Abuse Prevention and Control Act of 1970, treatment for the narcotic addict is often complicated and is generally a long-term process. One of the greatest difficulties is that when the individual has been released from the hospital (after going through withdrawal symptoms and the psychological problems associated with withdrawal), he often finds it impossible to remain off drugs and pursue a "conventional" existence in the community. Rehabilitation is complicated because not all addicts have the same problems, and therefore it is difficult to focus on specific methods of treatment. Also, many communities do not have facilities to help the addict once he has been released from the protection of the hospital.

The Narcotic Addict Rehabilitation Act of 1966 (NARA) gives certain addicts a choice of treatment instead of prosecution or imprisonment. If addicts are not charged with a crime, they have the right to ask for treatment on their own initiative or it may be requested by a relative. Federal legislation also provides for a complete range of rehabilitation services to be made available to addicts in their own communities. The act states the following:

---

[53]*Narcotics, Some Questions and Answers,* U.S. Department of Health, Education, and Welfare, Public Health Service Publication, No. 1827 (Washington, D.C.: Government Printing Office, 1970).

1. An addict charged with a non-violent Federal offense who elects to be committed for treatment instead of prosecuted for his crime, can be committed to the Secretary of Health, Education and Welfare for examination, treatment and rehabilitation.
2. An addict after conviction of a Federal offense can be committed to the Attorney General for a treatment period of no more than ten years or for the maximum period of sentence that could be imposed for his conviction.
3. An addict not charged with an offense can be civilly committed to the Secretary of Health, Education and Welfare for treatment upon his own application or that of a relative or another "related individual."[54]

Care of the addict after his release from the hospital is a key aspect of his treatment. Aftercare programs can provide continuing treatment for up to three years in the addict's own community. These programs are individually designed to meet the user's special needs. NARA is administered by the National Institute of Mental Health, Department of Health, Education and Welfare and by the Department of Justice.

Hallucinogens. Hallucinogens are drugs that can have unpredictable effects on the mind. They include such drugs as peyote and mescaline, as well as lysergic acid diethylamide, or LSD which is the best-known hallucinogen and will be the focus of our discussion. LSD is most known for the bizarre mental reactions it causes and the distortions in the physical senses of touch, smell, and hearing.

The reasons for experimenting with and using LSD vary with the individual's motivations. It may be taken because of curiosity, because of peer pressure, or because of claims that it can expand the mind and increase the physical sensitivities.

LSD can be taken in the form of a capsule or it can be placed in other substances. It can have both physical and psychological effects. Enlarged pupils, flushed face, and rise in temperature and heart beat are some of the common physical effects. Even though LSD is not a physically addictive drug, it can have psychological ramifications.

Illusions and hallucinations can occur, and delusional thoughts are sometimes expressed. The sense of time and of self are strangely altered. Emotional variations are marked, ranging from bliss to horror, sometimes within a single experience. Because of the impaired time sense—a few minutes may seem like hours—such an experience can assume the proportions of a terrible nightmare from which one cannot easily awaken.[55]

The National Institute of Mental Health is attempting to determine the biological, psychological, and genetic effects of LSD on animals and humans. Research will continue until many of the questions about this drug have been

[54]*Ibid.*

[55]*LSD, Some Questions and Answers,* U.S. Department of Health, Education, and Welfare, Public Health Service Publication, No. 1828 (Washington, D.C.: Government Printing Office, 1970).

answered. Many medical authorities believe that the chronic or continued use of LSD changes values and impairs the user's power of concentration and ability to think rationally. As of now, it has not been proven, as some proponents claim, that LSD can increase creativity. In fact, because of lack of research the actual workings of LSD in the body are not yet known.

> The strange sensations in clash of moods the drug causes can be frightening, even for a mature person. For young people who are still undergoing the process of emotional development, and who may lack the resilience to maintain the mental equilibrium under LSD, the effects can be even more frightening and confusing. The young, growing brain is more vulnerable to all mind-altering drugs than a brain in which metabolic activity is stabilized.[56]

Although LSD has not been used extensively for medical purposes, available evidence suggests that it may be useful, under controlled conditions, for neurotics and alcoholics. Although the drug may be a valuable tool in biomedical research, present indications are that its therapeutic value is limited. The penalty structure for illegal possession and distribution of LSD is delineated in the Comprehensive Drug Abuse Prevention and Control Act of 1970.

Stimulants. Stimulants are drugs, usually amphetamines, that stimulate the central nervous system. They can increase alertness and are often used to combat fatigue, reduce depression, and control appetite. In addition to amphetamines, stimulants include cocaine, dextroamphetamine, and methamphetamine ("speed"). Stimulants are also known as pep pills. Coffee, tea, and caffeine are considered mild stimulants.

Abuse of amphetamines and stimulants can begin in the doctor's office as a result of a prescribed dosage which becomes abused and overextended. In some cases, over half of the legally manufactured supply of amphetamines finds its way into illegal channels for nonprescriptive use. In regard to the effects of amphetamine use:

> in ordinary amounts the amphetamines provide a transient sense of alertness, wakefulness, well-being and mental clarity. Hunger is diminished, and short term performance may be enhanced in the fatigued person. The drugs may increase the heart rate, raise the blood pressure, produce palpitation and rapid breathing, dilate the pupils, and cause dry mouth, sweating and headache—if use continues, however, a person can become psychologically dependent on the drug in a few weeks. The sense of power, self-confidence, and exhilaration artificially created by amphetamine use is so pleasant, and the fatigue and depression that follow discontinuance are so severe, that the user is heavily tempted to revert to the drug.[57]

[56]*Ibid.*

[57]*Stimulants, Some Questions and Answers,* U.S. Department of Health, Education, and Welfare, Public Health Service Publication, No. 2097 (U.S. Government Printing Office, Washington, D.C. 1970).

Amphetamines can be taken intravenously to produce a quicker and more pronounced "high." Prolonged use of "speed" has many negative ramifications, including psychological disturbances and the impairment of physical health as a result of body abuse and poor nutrition. Because the use and abuse of amphetamines is fairly recent, especially intravenous injections, few specific rehabilitation and treatment services exist. Most formal drug treatment programs in the United States are designed primarily for narcotic addicts. Information services, however, are being developed daily to alert communities to the negative effects of the inappropriate use of stimulants, pointing out that housewives and businessmen can become dependent on these drugs even though they begin taking them for "legitimate" reasons. Research on stimulants such as amphetamines and cocaine is at present being undertaken by the National Institute of Mental Health. As is the case with other dangerous drugs, not enough is known about the effects of stimulants so that suitable treatment approaches can be initiated. A number of surveys supported by the institute are being undertaken to determine both the extent of the use of these drugs and the methods for combating their abuse.

Depressants. Depressants are sedative drugs that are manufactured for medical purposes to reduce tension and anxiety, as well as to treat epilepsy. Barbiturates are the largest group of sedatives, or depressants, and without medical supervision to avoid habituation, the ultimate effects can be very destructive.

Because barbiturates depress the brain function and the central nervous system, they create a very powerful depressant. Continued use can produce tolerance and create a desire for taking them on a long-term basis. When barbiturates are combined and used with amphetamines, a chemical imbalance can result and can create a pleasant mood-elevating effect which entices a user to take increased amounts.

The majority of these drugs are used legally for tranquilizing purposes. Many of the drugs fall into illegal hands, however, and like the stimulant drugs, abuse can often start in the doctor's office as a result of a legitimate prescription.

Barbiturates can be dangerous when not taken under medical supervision, and death may result from an overdose. Withdrawal from the drug can cause many unpleasant physical symptoms—the withdrawal resembles delirium tremens. Like the stimulant drugs, sedative drugs are available only on prescription and are controlled by the Comprehensive Drug Abuse Prevention and Control Act of 1970.

> Tighter regulations and enforcement of law on the legitimate manufacture and distribution of barbiturates and tranquilizers are part of the answer. Because barbiturates and tranquilizers have sound medical usefulness, physicians must be wary of yielding to the demand of patients for increased amounts when, in fact, they may be manifesting tolerance. Widespread dissemination of information about the dangers of overusing these addictive drugs is essential.[58]

[58]*Sedatives, Some Questions and Answers,* U.S. Department of Health, Education, and Welfare, Public Health Service Publication, No. 2098 (U.S. Government Printing Office, Washington, D.C. 1970).

Like the other drugs mentioned, a great deal more has to be learned about the effects of sedatives on the body, brain, and nervous system. Consequently, research programs are under way to determine the entire scope of the use of sedatives, in both their positive and their negative aspects.

Marihuana. Marihuana is derived from the Indian hemp plant, *Cannabis sativa,* and grows wild in many parts of the world, including the United States. It can be used commercially in the production of fiber for ropes and birdseed. It can vary greatly in strength, depending upon where it is grown and whether it has been specifically cultivated for smoking or eating.

When smoked, marihuana enters the bloodstream and within a very short time can affect the mood and the thinking of the user. The specific reactions that the drug has on the mind are not completely understood, and therefore a great deal of research is being conducted to determine the many effects of the drug. Some of the specific physical effects, however, are reddening of the whites of the eyes, increased heart beat, and sometimes coughing due to the irritating effect of the smoke on the lungs. The psychological effects of the drug can vary markedly, depending upon the user and the strength and quality of the drug. Terms such as suspiciousness, exuberance, sleepiness, loss of recall, inability to make decisions that require logical thinking, and euphoria have all been used to describe the effects of marihuana.

As for comparing marihuana with alcohol:

> we know that alcohol is a dangerous drug physically, psychologically or socially for millions of people whose drinking is out of control. There is no firm evidence that marihuana would be less harmful if used consistently. American experience to date has largely been limited to marihuana of low potency, infrequently used over a relatively short period of time. In countries where the use of marihuana and related drugs has been widespread, "skid rows" based on marihuana use exist. At present the research evidence is insufficient to answer this question of certainty. It should, however, be remembered that it frequently requires extensive use over a long period of time by large numbers of people before the public health implications of a drug are clearly understood.[59]

Marihuana, which is not a narcotic, does not cause physical dependence as do heroin and other narcotics. Therefore, the body does not develop a tolerance to the drug, and withdrawal from marihuana does not usually produce physical sickness. Many scientists believe, however, that psychological dependence can develop. As to whether it leads to harder narcotics:

> A 1967 study of narcotic addicts from city areas showed that more than 80 percent had previously used marihuana. Of the much larger number of persons who used marihuana, scientists agree that few go on to use morphine and heroin. No direct cause and effect link between the use of marihuana and

---

[59]*Marihuana, Some Questions and Answers,* U.S. Department of Health, Education, and Welfare, Public Health Service Publication, No. 1829 (U.S. Government Printing Office, Washington, D.C. 1970).

narcotics has been found. Researchers point out, however, that a person predisposed to abuse a drug may be likely to abuse other, stronger drugs.[60]

The one general conclusion that can be drawn from the above discussion is that more research needs to be undertaken to determine the effects of all types of drugs so that a comprehensive program of education can be developed for the public, and especially for youngsters. The potential long-range problems will have to be identified. A knowledge of the different types of drugs and their effects, however, does not in itself solve the drug problem. It is only through effective prevention, rehabilitation, and education that the drug problem can be understood and adolescents can be saved the grief that predictably follows the abuse of drugs.

Drug Prevention and Rehabilitation Programs

According to the Bureau of Narcotics and Dangerous Drugs:

> Until recently, the public has regarded addicts as incurable. Once "hooked" there was no road back. This idea arose from the fact that so many opiate addicts relapsed to drug use, even after long periods of hospitalization. Not long ago, treatment for addiction consisted of little more than withdrawal from the drug and detoxification. When more ambitious programs were attempted, they had only limited success in terms of "cured" addicts, but each contributed to knowledge about the addict, the drugs he uses and the ways to effect his rehabilitation.[61]

Drug rehabilitation and prevention programs today encompass much more than withdrawal and detoxification. With the support of the federal government, communities are attempting to develop services that can help the addict once he is released from the hospital. It is only through an intensive program that the drug addict can be "cured" and provided with new alternatives for functioning within the community. Such community services as mental health clinics, educational facilities, employment programs, and other methods of supporting the ex-addict will help solve the addiction problem.

Federal Efforts. In addition to the voluminous amount of drug education material it distributes, the federal government has two hospitals for drug addicts, one at Lexington, Kentucky, and the other at Fort Worth, Texas. Addicts can voluntarily commit themselves to treatment or be committed by the court. Many times the positive gains that were made at these hospitals could not be maintained because of a lack of viable community programs to assist the addict once he was released back to the community. When specific community services are not provided, the chance for the addict to become a productive citizen is very limited. The Narcotic Addict Rehabilitation Act of 1966 has been very effective in helping to combat addiction. It specifies that federal support can be given to states and

[60]*Ibid.*

[61]*Fact Sheets,* Bureau of Narcotics and Dangerous Drugs, p. 12.

communities for training programs and for the construction, staffing, and operation of new addiction treatment facilities on a joint federal-state basis. Because of the increased resources provided by the federal government, many states are now developing facilities that can more adequately deal with the addict. In addition, private facilities have been established in many communities. Private hospitals, halfway houses, service organizations, religious groups, and other community-based organizations have become more active in assisting the addict.

If drug addicton is to be conquered and drug use prevented, the community must become involved in programs of assistance, education, and prevention.

> If criminals are to change, they must be assimilated into groups which emphasize values conducive to law-abiding behavior and alienated from groups emphasizing values conducive to criminality—the community should restore a former addict to his proper place in society and help him avoid associations that will influence him to return to the use of drugs.[62]

Synanon. Synanon is a private organization which focuses on rehabilitating the narcotic addict. The Synanon program, initiated by Chuck Dederich, began in 1958 as an experimental project in response to the drug problem. The program is mainly funded by contributions from private citizens and businesses. The residents live, work, and interact in the "therapeutic community" of the Synanon program. The use of both individual and group counseling has proved successful in helping the addict adjust to his community without the use of drugs.

The criticism has been made, however, that the Synanon program does not solve the problem because it makes the addict dependent on the program rather than on drugs. This is a minor criticism. Dependence on the program is a much more acceptable alternative than dependence on drugs. Synanon is one of the very few programs that has given some indication of success in treating and rehabilitating the drug addict.[63]

Methadone Maintenance Programs. In 1963 Vincent P. Doyle, a physician at Rockefeller University, and Marie Nyswander initiated a treatment program for narcotic addicts which revolved around the drug methadone, a synthetic pain killer. Methadone blocks the euphoric high and the physical cravings for heroin. The exponents of the drug feel that when given under controlled conditions by a qualified person, the addict can live a normal life in the community. Even though methadone itself is a narcotic, it is felt that it can be a less harmful substitute for heroin and opium and a realistic partial solution to the hard addiction problem. Methadone programs, which can operate on both an in- and an out-patient basis, are felt to work best in the initial treatment stages of narcotic addiction. Methadone

---

[62]Donald Cressey and Rita Volkman, "Differential Association and Rehabilitation of Drug Addicts," *American Journal of Sociology,* 69 (September 1963), 129-31.

[63]Alison Wyrley Birch, "Where Addicts Become Adults," *The Reader's Digest,* December 1970, pp. 92-96.

can best be used to help the addict through the withdrawal period rather than as a permanent substitute for heroin or opium use.[64]

There has been some controversy over the merits of a methadone program and its use in the community. A major criticism is that methadone only replaces one drug habit with another and that its use does not offer a cure, only a less expensive substitute. Some law enforcement personnel feel that if methadone is made too readily available, new addicts will be exposed to drug addiction and will become dependent on the methadone drug. Many questions still have to be answered about the use of methadone. Only through research can objective conclusions be drawn and the true merits of the treatment approach be evaluated.

Psychotherapy, Group Therapy, and Counseling. Psychotherapy, group therapy, and counseling have been utilized in some cases to treat and rehabilitate the drug user (see Chapter 9). These methods are often used to supplement many methadone programs and other community programs such as Synanon. Like other approaches discussed, these methods are not the total answer. They are only supplemental resources which have to be coupled with client motivation and the use of total community resources.

Drug Abuse Prevention Education. There is increased awareness that a primary method of preventing drug use is to provide a comprehensive education program for both youngsters and adults. Because the drug problem has become so .immense in the last few years, it is difficult to change the attitudes of many present users. Therefore the education program has to be extensive and vigorous, and it has to reach young children.

In addition, adults have to be made aware of the contradictory picture that they present to youngsters. It is difficult to convince youngsters that drug use is harmful when they see their parents constantly using tobacco, alcohol, tranquilizers, and amphetamines.

Because the attitudes and values of youngsters will only be changed gradually, a total education program has to be initiated early in the youngster's training. Children are exposed at a very early age to drug abuse by not only their parents but also the mass media. "Television conditions the children from the age of two to wake up, slow down, be happy and relieve tension with pills."[65]

The schools can be an important vehicle for making children aware of the dangers of drug use. "It is the schools and the teachers that are capable of providing the best opportunity for instilling permanently an understanding of the dangers of drug abuse in our young people."[66]

The child spends more time in school than in any other institution except the

[64]"Methadone and Heroin Addiction: Rehabilitation without a Cure," *Science,* May 8, 1970. Reprint.

[65]"Does TV Make Drug Addicts?," *Listen,* 33 No. 10 (October 1970), 19.

[66]Clifford Denton, "Crusade in the Classroom," *Pennsylvania Education,* 2 (January-February 1970), 23.

family. Therefore, the schools are the most logical choice for drug education. The presentation of drug education material should be honest and factual so that the teacher will gain credibility and the student will not feel that he is being "conned." Adult misuse of alcohol and other synthetic substances should not be condoned, and the dangers of the misuse should be pointed out. This transmits to the youngster that a double standard should not exist for adults and youngsters. The misuse of any synthetic substance, whether alcohol or drugs, is detrimental.

Clifford Denton gives the following criteria for coordinating and presenting a drug education program:

1. Organize an all-out drug prevention campaign with promotion being handled by radio, newspapers, and television.
2. Provide postgraduate seminar study for teachers so that they can review the range of the drug abuse program within their schools, check the quality of the program, and evaluate the need for its expansion.
3. Encourage students to arrange "rap" sessions for their own examination of drug use.
4. Make stronger efforts to see that drug education, which is geared to the younger child whose attitudes are still being formulated, is in effect.
5. Encourage colleges to include drug education in their curriculum for student teachers, especially those in physical education. Provide workshops for teachers already in the classrooms.
6. Encourage programs on drug abuse in schools providing training for the medical professions.
7. Arrange seminars for clergy and community leaders to gather support for community programs.
8. Establish "Dial-a-Junky" drug information centers, staffed by professionals and ex-addicts.
9. Tape dramatic one-spot television messages.
10. Mobilize ex-addicts to travel to schools to speak about their own first-hand experiences with drugs.
11. Increase the supply of drug literature available in school libraries and encourage its use.[67]

Even though the school will be the major vehicle for transmitting this educational information, the entire community should be involved in drug control, identification, prevention, and rehabilitation. Community agencies both internal and external to the criminal justice system have to cooperatively become involved in this endeavor. Without total involvement and commitment by both the citizens and their service agencies, the problem will not be solved.

SUMMARY

This chapter has discussed the period of development termed *adolescence*. When the youngster does not adequately handle the pressures and areas of adjustment

[67]*Ibid.*

during the teen-age years, juvenile delinquency is often the symptomatic result and takes the specific form of drug abuse. The constellation of factors surrounding adolescence, the delinquent adolescent, and the drug user were mentioned. The next chapter discusses organization theory. A knowledge of principles of organization is helpful when establishing and operating drug prevention facilities as well as other types of delinquency prevention programs.

QUESTIONS AND PROJECTS

Essay Questions

1. Is the adolescent period similar in all cultures?
2. Why is it important for the person working with delinquents to understand "normal" adolescent behavior?
3. Why is adolescence a difficult period of development?
4. Is adolescence more difficult for a youngster today than it was in the past?
5. Why is drug use so prevalent today?

Projects

1. Develop a realistic and workable drug education program for your community.
2. Establish guidelines to differentiate the delinquent adolescent from the "normal" adolescent.
3. Develop a process for involving teen-agers in community problem-solving and community development activities.

6

ORGANIZATION THEORY

We are all members of many organizations, ranging from the very simple form found in the family to the very complex form found in the work environment. Because men constantly interact in all kind of groups and group situations and in all types of organizations, it is important to understand organization components and variables and the dynamics that are present in *intraorganizational* and *interorganizational* relationships. Furthermore, because the subject of this book is juvenile delinquency prevention and its concepts and control, it is important to understand those organizational variables that exist when men and organizations interact, because these variables ultimately affect the planning, initiating, and establishing of programs that prevent, control, and treat the delinquent within the criminal justice system.

THE CONCEPT OF ORGANIZATION

Because we are members of many organizations, we are usually dependent on others for fulfilling our individual and group needs and goals. Hence problems that each individual encounters are in most cases common with problems encountered by others. Therefore, common problems exist in all organizations, regardless of complexity, and have common elements which need to be identified for a more comprehensive understanding of the composition and functioning of organizations. Organizations do not remain static. They have to be constantly evaluated and analyzed to determine their effectiveness or reasons why they are operating dysfunctionally. An understanding of organizational components and dynamics will facilitate this evaluation and analysis.

Being members of many organizations, we have had to learn how to operate within them. This involves either conscious or unconscious analysis and organizational manipulation. We take these acquired abilities for granted and often do not give ourselves credit for being organizational "experts." Combining these natural abilities learned in our daily organizational life with a formal knowledge of organizational elements and dynamics will facilitate even greater operating effectiveness and enable us to replicate and improve the most successful aspects of the personal and professional organizations to which we belong. Furthermore, if we are members of the criminal justice system, this increased awareness and understanding of organizational functioning and operation will contribute to a more effective system of juvenile delinquency prevention, control, and treatment.

THE ELEMENTS OF ORGANIZATION

Greer states that the necessary condition for social organization is "the integration of behavior of two or more persons for social ends."[1] Therefore, we will assume that for a social organization to exist, two or more people have to be operating in at least some loosely defined interdependent relationship. The integration of behavior and interdependent relationships have their roots in the family organization. The pattern established in the family is often carried over into other organizations long after we leave the household. The point being made here is that understanding the organizational process, even of very complex work organizations, is not complicated if we remember that the basic elements in these complex organizations are generally the same as those we have lived with in the family organization.

Division of Labor

Whether the social organization is the family, the work organization, or a social group, there needs to be, to varying degrees, an integration of behavior in the form of division of labor so that the organization can operate smoothly and achieve its goals.[2] Division of labor is merely the breaking up into parts of those functions that are similar or the allocation of like functions which contribute to goal achievement and work performance. Depending on the complexity of the social

[1] Scott A. Greer, *Social Organization* (New York: Random House, Inc., 1955), p. 5.

[2] Edgar H. Schein, *Organizational Psychology* (Englewood Cliffs, N.J.: Prentice-Hall, Inc., 1965), pp. 6-7.

organization, the grouping of duties may be very broad, as in a family, or they may be very specific, as in a police department crime laboratory, a highly specialized unit. After the division of labor has been completed, and when functions have been assigned, members usually become identified with their particular functions and duties. In the larger and more complicated social organizations, when the functions and the duties become clustered or standardized and when expectations become solidified and predictable, we say that a role has been established.[3]

Roles

According to Greer, a role is "a clearly defined complex of rights and duties assigned to the person occupying a certain position in a group. It encompasses what is expected of him and what he has the right to expect of others."[4] Roles exist in very simple organizations such as families when we consider that the father usually has a prescribed set of duties and functions, as do the mother and even the children in a less well defined manner. Roles certainly exist in more complicated organizations, such as work groups and social clubs. The more standardized the roles become, the more clearly the expectations become defined. It is possible to both *underplay* and *overplay* a role. When someone is said to be really "playing the role," it implies that the actions of the participant are either overdetermined or so obvious that the naturalness and the spontaneity of the role is strained.

Roles of individual members, of course, do not operate in isolation from each other, especially in more complicated organizations. If a person has certain rights and duties that are ascribed to his role and a certain set of expectations, there will have to be mutual dependence between the various role relationships. This will necessitate a coordination of roles and a realistic and periodic appraisal and evaluation of expectations and duties. For example, in a police department a juvenile officer has a role different from that of a traffic officer or an administrator. Each of these roles has different expectations, rights, and duties. However, they should not operate in isolation from one another, and all roles combined contribute to the fulfillment of the police department's organizational goal. If any one of these sets of roles begins to operate independently of the other sets of roles, coordination will be ineffective and the completion of the goal will be hindered. A standardization of roles also contributes to goal achievement and the integration of members within the organization because each member knows what slot he fits in and what the expectations are. He is aware that if he performs within the limits of the role, most of his relationships will be predictable, his duties delineated, and the overall goal of the organization achieved.

It is important then for the member of an organization to be able to coordinate his efforts with those of other members for organizational goal achieve-

---

[3]Amitai Etzioni, *Complex Organizations* (New York: The Free Press, 1961) p. 17.
[4]Greer, *op. cit.*, p. 22.

ment and attainment while at the same time receiving enough personal benefit so that he will be motivated to become involved in this coordinated effort. The forces that cement the bond between organizational role systems and units are called norms. (Norms are also discussed in Chapter 2.)

Norms

The common bond or the integrative relationships that develop within an organization above and beyond the particular rewards achieved, both material and nonmaterial, are referred to as *norms*.[5] Norms are values that are shared by all members of the group and form a bond between members so that common efforts can be coordinated. Norms provide the basis for agreement among members regarding the orientation of the organization, the performance of its duties and functions, and the evaluation and achievement of its goals. Although norms are not tangible, they are a powerful force which not only solidifies the group but provides an orientation and focus for goal achievement. For example, in a police organization, certain guidelines have been established to regulate a policeman's role and behavior as well as the performance of his duties. It is normative for a policeman to protect the rights and property of citizens within his community, and it is normative for him to perform his duties in an equitable manner. In most police departments, these norms would be explained, codified, and transmitted to their members. A member who deviated from these expectations would not be operating according to the normative guidelines established by his department. His behavior could result in formal or informal sanctioning, a concept we will discuss shortly.

Norms not only help give the group direction through certain sets of expectations, they provide a reference point for evaluating behavior. We have all heard the terms *ingroup* and *outgroup,* which refer to the normative process that we utilize to make evaluations about personal or group behavior. A policeman in his daily duties may use, either wisely or unwisely, certain clues or indicators to evaluate persons with whom he comes in contact. These persons can be perceived many ways, such as deviant or conforming individuals of an ingroup or an outgroup. For example, a policeman may consider "longhairs" as members of an outgroup in relation to his own reference groups. He makes this evaluation because the appearance of the person he has contacted is not normative to his behavioral orientation. Furthermore, his normative orientation is often reinforced and supported by his police peer group, just as the normative orientation of the "longhair" is supported and reinforced by his peer group.

The norm is thus a product of an interaction with the person's group. The norm could be brought to the organization and then supported, or it could be developed within a particular organization and then perpetuated.

Greer states that a norm

[5]Walter C. Reckless, *The Crime Problem* (New York: Appleton-Century-Crofts, 1967), pp. 37-38.

is a product of interaction in a group. With the norm once established, it increases the power of the group as a motivator and controller of the individual members. Here is the familiar vicious cycle model which is so important in the study of social behavior. A given group may begin with only rudimentary norms brought from the outside to the group's situation. Once the members interact, other norms have generated and the group's moral density increases far beyond the minimum necessary for the physical job to be done. Norms integrate the various specialized roles with the behavior of the group, as a whole, and they may also strengthen the motivation of the members to conform. They increase the moral similarity of the members and the greater their moral similarity, the greater the potential solidarity of the group.[6]

Solidarity of a group, of course, is very beneficial in terms of group identification, development of an *esprit de corps*, and fulfillment of goals. Group solidarity within units of an organization or within agencies of the criminal justice system can be dysfunctional if, for example, the various agency personnel overidentify with their own group or profession and have difficulty extending beyond their limited orientation to cooperate in overall goal achievement. In this case it will be difficult to initiate viable delinquency prevention, treatment, and control programs because this necessitates interagency cooperation—a topic that will be discussed later in the chapter.

Sanctions

Thus far we have talked about division of labor, roles, and norms. The next logical question to ask is, Even though workers are divided into work groups and certain functions and duties are assigned to them (roles), and there are guiding expectations called norms which regulate behavior and transmit to the individual what is expected of him, why do people conform? The answers to this question are numerous and complicated. There are as many reasons why people conform as there are individuals working on the job. For example, an individual may conform because he wants the paycheck. He may conform because he wants to please his boss. He may enjoy the informal rewards that are gained through group membership, group support, and group identification, or he may conform for all these reasons as well as many more. Regardless of the reasons, some system of reward and punishment is necessary if the organization wants to make certain that the worker will carry out his duties. The method used for distributing rewards and punishments and regulating behavior is called sanctioning.[7] The major purpose of sanctions is to reduce unpredictable variables in the organization and to assure patterns of behavior that will facilitate goal achievement. Formal and informal sanctions exist in all organizations.

[6]Greer, *op. cit.*, p. 25.

[7]Don C. Gibbons, *Society, Crime and Criminal Careers* (Englewood Cliffs, N.J.: Prentice-Hall, Inc., 1968), p. 18.

The direct rewards (or punishments) received by the member of an organization in the form of monetary remuneration, vacation days, use of the family car, and so on, are called *formal* sanctions. In addition to formal sanctions, however, the member of an organization receives certain rewards that are not tangible and do not necessarily operate on a systematic basis. These rewards (or punishments) are called informal sanctions. When there is subtle, or not so subtle, rejection by peers in the organization, and when there is hostility or scapegoating, this type of behavior is considered informal sanctioning. For example, a policeman who does not perform according to the normative expectations of his organization may receive both formal and informal sanctioning. His department may formally sanction him through firing, demotion, layoff, pay decrease, or formal reprimand. His work group may informally sanction him through rejection, by ostracizing him from the group and not involving him in social or work activities. The isolation that results from the informal sanctioning process of peers can often be more devastating than the formal sanctioning process of the organization. The organization administrators can not only administer formal sanctions, they can also be a part of the informal sanctioning process. An example would be an administrator who has a party and invites only certain members of his staff. Negative sanctioning results when members of an organization extend beyond the limits of acceptability and are evaluated as deviant.

Deviation

The concept of deviancy, its ramifications, and its implications for organizational functioning and social control is one of the important elements of organization.[8] (See Chapter 2.) Even though in most organizations there are work assignments (division of labor), roles, norms, and sanctions, there is always going to be a certain amount of deviation. Deviation within acceptable limits is healthy for an organization and contributes to its growth, as well as to organizational renewal and updating. Deviance, however, that extends beyond the boundaries of tolerance can be destructive and threatening to the organization. Most deviation can be controlled through normative influence and the sanctioning process. Deviation on an extensive scale is an indication that the sanctioning process, influence, and role functioning are breaking down, which will contribute to dysfunctional organizational processes.

Summary

This discussion has attempted to describe important organizational elements that exist in both simple and complex organizations. Many other factors and

[8]Amitai Etzioni, *Modern Organizations* (Englewood Cliffs, N.J.: Prentice-Hall, Inc., 1964).

processes are a part of organizational dynamics and will be examined in the next section. The important point to remember, however, is that all the elements discussed contribute to goal achievement only if there is effective communication, interdependence, integration, and cooperation. If these processes do not exist and individuals operate independently, organizational behavior will be overindividualized, coordination will be lacking, and goal achievement will be hindered.

Workers in organizations are dependent upon one another, and it is mutually advantageous to cooperate and carry out roles systematically. This will be elucidated in the last section of this chapter when we discuss the criminal justice system, its component parts, its varying philosophies, and the difficulties that exist in coordination. Relationships among roles within and without organizations have to be connected in some manner so that there is a semblance of order and a blending of cooperation and understanding. For example, the police department is only one component of the criminal justice system, but if it is to operate effectively and achieve its long-range goals of preserving peace and controlling crime, cooperation from the other criminal justice agencies will be necessary. If this blending of cooperation does not exist, goal achievement will become fragmented, and the prevention process stymied.

THREE THEORETICAL VIEWS OF ORGANIZATION

The preceding section discussed the major elements common to all organizations.[9] We will now examine the three most prevalent theoretical orientations to organizational functioning. An analysis of these theoretical views will be helpful in determining the organizational orientation of the criminal justice system and the implications the particular orientation has for delinquency prevention, treatment, and control. In the final section of the chapter it will become obvious that the agencies within the criminal justice system do not have a common organizational structure or operating philosophy. This does create some problems for interagency cooperation. An understanding of the different organizational viewpoints is important also because each theory and ensuing operational philosophy makes certain assumptions about the organizational structure, how the worker should relate to it, and how goals should be achieved. The discussion of the three views is by no means all-inclusive. Volumes have been written on each school of thought. The highlights of each theory will be presented, and the differences between the· theories will be explained.

An Overview. The three major theories of organization are known as the *Classical* view, the *Human Relations* view, and the *Structuralist,* or *Integrated,* view. Classical theorists attempted to state very concisely the principles that should guide the manager in the execution of his functions and in the operation of his organi-

---

[9]Greer, *op. cit.,* p. 20.

Courtesy of the Michigan State Police

Figure 4
A Cooperative Case Conference Involving the Judge,
a Policeman and a Social Worker

zation. The identification of these principles and functions is considered basic and essential. The major emphasis of the Classical view is on the formal structure of the organization and on the way things "ought to be." In other words, they assume that the organization will operate according to the formal blueprint. The approach does not consider such informal organizational influences as social interaction, social rewards, and other intangible aspects that affect organizational operation.

As a reaction to this type of approach the Human Relations school of thought evolved, which in contrast to Classical theory emphasized the nonrational, emotional, and more informal or social aspect or organizational operation. In sharp contrast to Classical theory, which considers the organization of primary importance and the workers of secondary importance, the Human Relations approach reverses priorities and considers the workers the most important variables. The organization takes a secondary position, with the assumption that most of the time the organization can be made adjustable to fit the workers.

The Structuralist, or Integrated, approach, attempted to extract from the Classical and the Human Relations schools the best principles and integrate them into a more comprehensive theory of organization.

Not only do these three schools differ in their views of the organization, but they suggest quite different conceptions of man and society—classical approach recognized no conflict between man and organization. Their view of the organization was from a highly managerial standpoint, assumed that what was good for management was good for the worker. The classical school argued that highly efficient labor will in the end pay off for both groups by increasing the effectiveness of the organization. High productivity leads to higher profits which, in turn, leads to higher pay and greater work satisfaction. The human relations group pointed out that the workers had many needs other than purely economic ones and that the classical approach benefits neither management nor the workers. If management paid attention to the noneconomic, social, and cultural needs of the workers, their satisfaction would increase as well as their productivity. The structuralist school, unlike both the classical and human relations schools, viewed conflict and strain between man and organization as inevitable and by no means always undesirable.[10]

The Classical View

The Classical view of organization has sometimes been known as administrative management theory, scientific management theory, or traditional theory of organization. It came into vogue around 1900 when Frederick W. Taylor attempted to develop a concept of how organizations could be more efficient and organization participants more effective on their jobs.[11] Taylor's approach to management and organization became known as the school of scientific management. He was mainly concerned with an economic approach to motivation, feeling that the economic motive and the desire for preservation of self and the family was the greatest factor in motivating individual workers. Because of this, he believed that it was possible to determine routine tasks, which if defined and codified, could assist the worker in performing his job in a uniform, predictable, and efficient manner. For example, he considered fatigue merely a muscular or physical matter which had no implications or basis in the psychological makeup of the worker or social factors within his work environment. If economic rewards for the job were commensurate with the worker's output and if the worker was shown the proper procedure for conserving energy and making his movements count in a very smooth process and to his maximum capability, he would be effective and efficient on his job, the goals of the organization would be accomplished, and the worker would be satisfied.

Many important theorists followed Taylor's lead in analyzing organizations with Classical principles. Although agreeing with many of his basic assumptions, they altered their orientation and added new meaning to his approach. Some of the most important contributions to the development of Classical theory were made by Gulick and Urwick.[12] They, like Taylor, believed that an efficient organization was one that was well organized, where there were specific functions detailed to the members of the organization, and where the more skilled the worker, the more efficient he would be in performing on his job. Some of the most prominent Classical concepts developed were the following.

Scaler Principle. The scaler principle states that in any organization there

[10]Etzioni, *Modern Organizations*, p. 21.

[11]Frederick W. Taylor, *Scientific Management* (New York: Harper & Bros., 1911).

[12]Luther Gulick and Lyndall Urwick, eds., *Papers on the Science of Administration* (New York: Columbia University, Institute of Public Administration, 1937).

should be a hierarchy of authority with an even flow of responsibility throughout the organization. This is what is meant by *chain of command* and the relationship of the superior to the subordinate. The organization is depicted in a vertical manner, and relationships between superiors and subordinates and the chain of command become very apparent through the use of boxes on an organizational chart showing the various positions of the organizational members. The organizational chart is considered an essential tool in describing authority relationships in a functional arrangement.[13] A police organization with its layers of ranks would be an example of the scaler principle. On the organizational chart the captain would be placed above the lieutenant, the lieutenant above the sergeant, and so on. Authority and responsibility would be commensurate with the rank of the person in the organization as represented by the organizational box on the chart. The higher the person in the organization, the more authority and responsibility he would have.

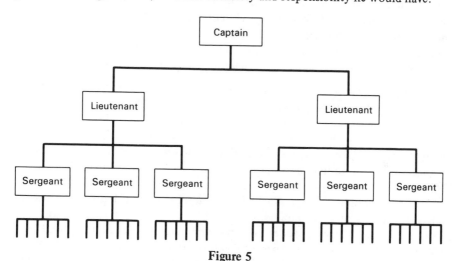

Figure 5

Unity of Command Principle. The major tenet of the unity of command principle is that an employee should not receive commands from more than one supervisor. This will contribute to an even flow of communication and the delineation of responsibility in the carrying out of functions. Supposedly, no problems will be encountered if the relationship between superior and subordinate is maintained in a formal line of authority between the various levels of supervision and line activity. Human factors, such as personality clashes, are not taken into consideration or felt to affect the formal relationships between superior and subordinate.[14] Commands and directives within the organization are provided by

[13]Joseph L. Massie, "Management Theory," in *Handbook of Organizations, ed.* James G. March ed. (Chicago: Rand McNally & Co., 1965), p. 396.

[14]H. Fayal, *General and Industrial Management,* trans. Constance Stours (London: Sir Isaac Pitman & Sons Ltd., 1949), p. 24.

the worker's immediate supervisor. The captain, for example, would issue the command through the lieutenant, the lieutenant through the sergeant(s), and so on. Direct lines of authority would never be circumvented, such as orders from the captain to the sergeant, nor would the communication process be routed in a direction other than the formal chain of command.[15]

Span of Control. The span of control concept refers to the supervisor's having only a limited number of supervisees. This enables the supervisor to provide close guidance and maintain quality control. The number of employees that should be under one person's command ranges from two or three to about six or seven, and sometimes more. This will depend on the complexity of the organization, its orientation, the education level of its employees, and its managers' preference for either a "tall" or a "flat" organizational chart and levels of supervision.[16] The organization chart illustrates not only the levels of ranks but also the number of workers at each rank. Effective supervision depends on the supervisor's ability to control his men. This ability is considered to be incorporated into the rank or position, and not with the man himself. For example, each captain would usually command the same number of men as determined by an efficiency study.

The Principle of Organizational Specialization. The Classical view holds that for the most efficient output of work, employees should be placed in units where they can concentrate on their particular specialization and where their unit, in coordination with the other units of the organization, can be integrated and systematized for more effective operation. It is assumed that the organization manager is able to outline in detail all the tasks and operations that are needed to achieve the goal and that these tasks can be compartmentalized into very uniform and predictable units.[17] For example, because physical capabilities and physical energy management is so important in the Classical school, it is assumed that a worker can learn to master fewer tasks much more quickly and efficiently. If he is taught routine tasks that are repeated many times a day (or many times an hour), he will learn to use his physical capabilities to their fullest extent. Working in a unit that performs the same functions constantly will increase the worker's ability to be more efficient. If, for example, a police officer's total working time is spent in traffic investigation, he will master his job and do it more efficiently than an officer who is involved in traffic only part time.

Gulick and Urwick also described four main criteria that could be used when grouping work activities: (1) the major purpose to be served, (2) the process to be used, (3) the clientele to be served, and (4) the place where the activities would

[15]V. A. Leonard, *Police Organization and Management* (Brooklyn: The Foundation Press, 1951).

[16]E. Dale, *Planning and Developing the Company Organization Structure* (New York: American Management Association, 1952), p. 57.

[17]E. Petersen, E. G. Plowman, and J. M. Trickett, *Business Organization and Management* (Homewood, Ill.: Richard D. Irwin, Inc., 1962), pp. 165-80.

take place.[18] The basic idea was that although functions that were similar should be based in one unit and those that were not similar in a separate unit, other considerations could also contribute to organization effectiveness. A police department, for example, could conceivably utilize all four methods of grouping. All juvenile work would be grouped together, while patrol activities would be in another unit. This would be grouping the work by *purpose*. As for *process* used, the crime laboratory processes information and evidence given to it by both the juvenile and the patrol units. (It can be seen that in this case there is a blending of both process and purpose within the crime lab unit.) In regard to *clientele*, the juvenile unit serves juveniles and their parents, whereas the patrol division serves the general population. The last grouping technique, by *place*, would be the department divided into precincts and serving a particular geographical location. When all four grouping techniques exist in the same organization, overlapping usually occurs.

Line and Staff. Classical theorists use two terms that relate to organizational structure—*line* and *staff.* Line activities are the major functions that form the essential skeleton of the organizational structure. In a police organization these functions would be carried out by those officers providing direct service. Staff refers to those organizational components that exist primarily for providing advice, support, and consultation to line units. In a police organization this would refer to the personnel division or the executive division. This was a very important concept for Classical theorists because of their emphasis on specialization, division of labor, unity of command, and formal relationships between organizational workers and units.

Efficiency. The Classical view considers efficiency to be the major activity that contributes to production and goal achievement. In other words, efficiency is directly related to output—the greater the productivity of the organization, the more efficient it is. In the criminal justice system it is difficult to measure efficiency by the Classical method because statistics are inadequate and because the majority of services cannot be measured in an objective tangible manner.

Rationality. According to Classical theory, the organizational process is considered rational and predictable if the principles are followed. In other words, if a supervisor were to tell his subordinate to do something, he would not only do it but he would do it well. Directives would not be questioned and the worker, in cooperation with his supervisor, would always try to improve his performance and complete his tasks in the most logical and efficient manner.

Supervision and Direction. Workers in an organization need close guidance and supervision if the worker and the organization are to operate in the most efficient manner. It is also assumed that workers want little freedom in determining their own approaches to problem solving and that they prefer to be closely

[18]Gulick and Urwick, *op. cit.,* pp. 15-30.

directed. They want clear and precise limits established. If limits and areas of responsibility are not clearly defined, the worker will probably not perform efficiently or extend beyond his limits of responsibility and authority. Workers will not cooperate unless there is a formally planned pattern of functions, authority, responsibility, and work relationships.

Motivation. A worker's activities and the rewards given to him should be viewed on an objective basis without regard to personal problems or individual idiosyncrasies, keeping in mind that workers are motivated by economic rewards and physical needs. Therefore, incentive should be gauged to satisfy the worker's materialistic drives and physical capabilities.

Authority. Authority has its source at the top of the organization hierarchy and is delegated downward. The supervisor gives the command, and the worker is expected to carry it out in the most efficient manner possible. Communication is essentially a one-way process from the top down. Authority is never questioned, and informal influence is not recognized.

Environment. Simple tasks are easier to master than more complicated tasks, and hence there will be higher productivity by concentrating on a narrow scope of activity. These activities have universal characteristics and can be performed in a given manner regardless of environment and the qualities of the personnel involved.[19]

Criticisms of Classical Theory. Classical theorists and their assumptions about organization structure and functioning have been criticized in many areas. Classical thought has been criticized because it considers organizational operation to be rational, precise, and predictable. The approach is oversimplistic and does not consider human factors. It is more a commonsense approach than a theory that has resulted from carefully constructed and scientifically proved assumptions and propositions. Many writers feel that Classical theory is based on false premises—for example, the premise that economic considerations are the major, if not the only, considerations for employee motivation. Furthermore, they feel that many of the Classical principles of management are pure conjecture, that they are generalized solely from experience, and that no real scientific substantiation or investigation has ever been made to prove or disprove their credibility.

William C. Scott states that

> it would not be fair to say that the classical school was unaware of the human problems which affect organization. They simply do not treat in any systematic way the interplay of individual personality in formal groups, interorganization conflict, and the decision process in their conception of the formal structure. Additionally the classical school has failed to incorporate into its theory contributions of the behavioral sciences as part of the

[19]James G. March, ed., *Handbook of Organization* (Chicago: Rand McNally & Co., 1965).

comprehensive explanation of human behavior in the organization. Classical theory, however, has relevant insights into the nature of the organization which should not be discounted, but the value of this theory is limited by narrow concentration in the formal anatomy of organization.[20]

Pffifner and Sherwood feel that

to recapitulate, traditional organizational theory tended to "dehumanize" the individual by assuming that one man is pretty much the same as another. Any minor differences would cancel themselves out. Secondly, it leaned heavily on the marketplace theory that man would rationally pursue his own self-interest. Thus, to get more production was to boost the payoff. Thirdly, a single standard of value, variously known as efficiency or productivity, pervaded the literature . . . A tremendous number of variables which serve to complicate organization behavior were thereby removed from concentration by the traditionalists, in whose picture there was also implicit the expectation that anyone who deviated from the simplified picture established should be dealt with summarily. This was the heart of managerial prerogative.[21]

This is a sampling of the type of criticism that has been leveled at Classical theory, although as pointed out by Scott, there are some principles that can be useful when trying to understand how organizations operate and how they are viewed by some theorists and organization managers.

The Human Relations View

The Hawthorne experiment of the 1930s and 1940s provided some interesting results.[22] This experiment, along with a challenge by behavioral scientists of the Classical school for more empirical scientific substantiation of Classical assumptions, provided the impetus for a vigorous investigation of organizational dynamics. As a result of these and other factors, advances were made toward the understanding of human behavior and organizational operation.

The Human Relations approach, unlike the Classical approach, makes different assumptions about the worker and his work environment. The Human Relations school states that work output is determined by social capacity—not physical capacity, as stated by the Classical school. According to the Human Relations school, extreme specialization is not necessarily the most efficient form of division of labor because overspecialization can produce monotony and affect socialization which is a contributing factor to goal achievement. Effective socialization contributes to more effective organizational operation because workers react

[20]William C. Scott, *Human Relations in Management* (Homewood, Ill.: Richard D. Irwin, Inc., 1962), p. 121.

[21]John M. Pfiffner and Frank P. Sherwood, *Administrative Organization* (Englewood Cliffs, N.J.: Prentice-Hall, Inc., 1960), p. 109.

[22]F. J. Roethlisberger and W. J. Dickson, *Management and the Worker* (Cambridge: Harvard University Press, 1939).

as members of groups, not just as individuals, and they receive intangible satisfaction from group participation and interaction.[23] These now famous Hawthorne studies looked at the effect that increasing the illumination in the workroom had on worker productivity. The assumption was that the greater the illumination, the greater the workers' output because of the direct relationship of physical capacity and physical environment to output. Greater illumination would facilitate seeing, which would in turn increase the workers' physical capacity. The interesting result was that even though increased illumination increased productivity, decreased illumination also increased productivity. Additional studies were performed and the conclusion was that

> increased production was the result of a change in the social situation of the workers. There was a modification of their level of psychological satisfaction and new patterns of social interaction brought about by putting them in experiment rooms with the special attention involved. The discovery of significance in social factors was to become the major find of the Hawthorne study.[24]

This study and further studies refuted the rational, logical approach that was proposed by the Classical school, and they showed that economic rewards were not the sole criteria for motivation and that the group and the group process had a great deal to do with whether the individual worker was happy and satisfied. Worker contentment would contribute to increased productivity.

The Human Relations school held that the greatest motivation came from the group and from social rewards and psychological factors, not from physiological capacities and economic remuneration.

The Human Relations school also altered some assumptions about group participation in decision making. It was learned that the group could influence individual members by pressure exerted through social relationships—the organization's goals could be subverted, new standards set by the group, and production levels altered. And if there was group support and group acquiescence, the group could, in fact, control managerial functions. It was also assumed that if the workers were involved in participatory processes, if they were given some decision-making power, and if benefits were increased (and not necessarily tangible monetary benefits), this would increase happiness which would in turn contribute to greater worker satisfaction and greater productivity. It was also found that many of the assumptions of the Classical school about authority were faulty and that authority was not necessarily from the "top down." There could be influence from the "bottom up" exerted through the informal structure of the organization. The worker could subvert the formal authority of the organization by using informal channels of communication and the group processes and relationships that existed

[23]Kurt Lewin, "Group Decision and Social Change," in *Readings in Social Psychology*, ed. G. E. Swanson, T. M. Newcomb, and E. L. Hartley (New York: Henry Holt and Co., 1952).

[24]Etzioni, *Modern Organizations, op. cit.,* p. 33.

within the organization. Persons who have had experience in organizations, especially in complicated organizations like public service agencies or industrial corporations, know that supervisors within the organization, merely because they have a higher rank than subordinates, do not always necessarily exert the most power or influence. Social factors and social relationships do dictate what types of policies are adhered to, carried out, and, in fact, even initiated. For example, according to the Classical school, it would be assumed that a lieutenant or a captain would have much more decision-making power and influence in the department than would a sergeant. If a sergeant in the organization socialized with the chief or happened to live in the same neighborhood as the chief, however, many decisions could be made on the golf course or at a social event before the formal discussion and decision making which would ultimately take place within the organization.

The Human Relations school also held that reciprocal communication was an important factor in organizational effectiveness. Employees should not merely be directed to perform a particular task in a routine, mundane manner, but the task and the way it fit into overall organizational functioning should be explained. Management should also be open to workers' suggestions for improving operating procedures.

Because the Classical school and the Human Relations school took a very different approach to viewing, analyzing, and making assumptions about organizations, one could almost take the basic principles outlined in the preceding discussion of the Classical school and conclude that the Human Relations school would either state that the principles were insignificant or take the opposite viewpoint.

Whereas the Classical school held that the most rational, efficient, and economically oriented organization would be the most productive and most satisfying for the workers, the Human Relations school held that worker satisfaction was directly related to social rewards. Economic rewards were secondary. Just as the Classical school may overstate the rational and economic approach, however, the Human Relations school's overemphasis on the satisfaction of human social needs and their one-big-happy-family emphasis was an oversimplification in the other direction.

An important distinction between the Classical and the Human Relations schools of thought is their view of organizational structure. The formal structure is synonymous with the Classical view, and the informal structure with the Human Relations view. Formal relationships are the basis for an effective organization, according to Classical assumptions. All authority is carried out through the formal structure, relationships between employers are formal, and productivity is the direct result of this formal emphasis. In the Human Relations school, social factors are considered paramount, and the formal structure is at best a necessary evil. Informal relationships and processes are considered the main force behind organizational productivity and employee satisfaction.

The Structuralist, or Integrated, View. The Integrated approach to organizations is basically a synthesis of the Classical, or formal, view and the Human Relations, or informal, view.[25] The Integrated approach takes a much more realistic view of organizations and organization behavior. It reacted to the concept of both the Classical and the Human Relations views that with certain variables held constant there would be harmony between management and the workers. In the Classical view, if physical movements could be determined so that the worker could conserve his energy and perform the task in the most efficient manner and if he was subsequently rewarded for this activity, he would be satisfied and the organization's goals would be achieved. In the Human Relations view, with its emphasis on the informal group and social interaction, if the worker received rewards in the form of social interaction, and intangibles such as prestige and status as well as participation in decision making, this would make him happy, he would become more productive, and the organization would achieve its goals.

The Integrated approach reacted against both naive extremes, stating that disharmony in an organization was inevitable. There was no way that the perfect formula of economic reward correlated with physical capacity and output could ever be determined or that social rewards, prestige, status, group participation in decision making, and the like, could be correlated with production. It was felt that the Classical school was unrealistic, dogmatic, and too formal in orientation, whereas the Human Relations school was manipulative and naive, with an overemphasis on the positive effects that informal rewards could produce.

The Integrated school adherents took a more general approach in their analysis of organizations, not only extracting what they felt was most relevant from the other two schools of thought but extending their studies beyond industrial organizations. The other two schools concentrated on studying industrial organizations, often overemphasizing and generalizing those aspects that they considered relevant and eliminating those aspects that they considered irrelevant. The Integrated school adherents went into their studies with an open mind, looking at hospitals, social work agencies, police organizations, churches, and many more. In these studies, it was found that although the other two approaches did have merit, and did make some contributions in terms of understanding organizations and organization behavior, their cases were overstated and their findings were frequently no more than assumptions generalized from limited observation.

The Classical approach and its orientation is more typical and operates fairly effectively in large industrial organizations where the educational level is low, the tasks are routine, and the giving of status symbols is difficult. Police organizations for some of the same reasons, in addition to being paramilitary oriented, could also fit the Classical structure. In organizations where there is a high percentage of college graduates, which facilitates group decision making, the Human Relations approach can be successful. Status symbols do play an important part in these organizations, such as titles, office space, and community acknowledgement. Even though these two approaches do have merit in certain organizations as an orientation to human behavior, in most organizations they still cannot be applied without

[25]*Ibid.,* pp. 41-44.

major alterations. Police organizations and other agencies of the criminal justice system, for example, cannot be pinpointed to operate totally within any theoretical framework. Even in a police department, where the organization is usually classically structured, the tasks performed are not necessarily routine because of dealing with the public, nor is the major aspect of the rewards gained always monetary remuneration. The Integrated approach can lend new insight and contribute to increased cooperation in the criminal justice system. As this approach points out, some conflict will always exist both intraorganizationally and interorganizationally. A certain amount of conflict can be functional if it facilitates getting problems out in the open. This can make communication more direct, which can result in compromises that will facilitate satisfaction and goal achievement of all parties involved. If conflict is not identified, if hostility is not aired, and if compromises are not made, the aggression can be turned inward, which can become subversive and dysfunctional for the organization. Furthermore, as a result of conflict and the airing of viewpoints, all concerned parties can learn from each other. New methods of operation can be developed, updating and innovation can take place, and better services can be provided to the community.

Summary

Even though the Classical approach and the Human Relations approach can increase organizational understanding and can, taken in their proper perspective, contribute to a more well rounded knowledge of organizational behavior, they nevertheless are not as realistic as the Integrated approach. The Classical approach has tinges of authoritarianism, which can cause problems, while the Human Relations approach is manipulative. It can manipulate by providing status symbols such as titles instead of monetary rewards. It can also manipulate by making the employee believe he is being involved in decision making when in fact it is only a gesture because major policy matters are decided in closed circles. The Integrated approach is more honest, deals with employees in a direct manner, and tries to avoid manipulation and authoritarianism. Furthermore, studies have disproved many of the Classical and Human Relations assumptions.[26]

The Integrated approach, then, has led to new realistic insights into organizational dynamics by pointing out that both social and material rewards are important; that both formal and informal groups exist to varying degrees, depending on the organization and its functions; that no happy balance is totally possible in an organization; and that disharmony can produce positive results. All three approaches, however, will be helpful to the reader in understanding the operation of all the components of the criminal justice system and the ramifications that exist when the components have "mixed" orientations to organizational operation and functioning.

[26]Robert Dubin, "Industrial Workers' Worlds: A Study Of the 'Central Life Interests' of Industrial Workers," *Social Problems* (1956), p. 136.

THE SOCIAL ORGANIZATION
OF THE CRIMINAL JUSTICE SYSTEM

Chapter 3 discussed how the agencies of the criminal justice system have different philosophical orientations to criminal behavior. It was pointed out that the police are oriented to the Classical school of criminology, while social workers adhere to the Positive school.

It is understandable why policemen subscribe to the Classical school philosophy. Their profession is commissioned with dealing with the delinquent in a practical, legalistic, objective, and expedient manner. The policeman does not have the luxury of spending a great deal of time with the offender to talk about his psychological dynamics and his environmental background. He has to be practical because of the demands of his job. Many policemen have only a high school education and therefore have not been exposed to the popular psychological and sociological theories of juvenile delinquency, most of which have emerged from the Positive school of criminology. As a result of these factors, the Classical school of criminology is most appealing to policemen.

Those professionals oriented to the Positive school are usually in social work and social service professions. They feel that the offender is sick and needs social and personal treatment. Social agency professionals subscribe to the Positive school of criminology for many reasons. They do not have to deal with the immediate problems of arresting, processing, and responding to the actual delinquent act within a community. They have more time to probe into the environmental and personal background of the offender to determine why his behavior took an antisocial channel. Also, social workers are more thoroughly grounded in the social sciences than are policemen. They have been exposed to the popular theoretical assumptions that have emerged from the Positive school of criminology. As a result of these factors, most social workers quite naturally subscribe to the Positive school.

The preceding analysis illustrates that the different criminological orientation of social workers and policemen does have a sound and logical basis, just as differences in organizational orientation also have a basis. These different theoretical orientations, both criminologically and organizationally, have implications for the cooperative establishment of delinquency prevention, treatment, and control programs.

The orientation of the additional community agencies in the criminal justice system in regard to criminological and organizational base vary somewhere along the continuum between the Classical and Positive schools of criminology and the Classical and Human Relations schools organizationally. Our emphasis will not, however, be focused as heavily on these agencies because their orientation is not reflected in as extreme a manner as police and social work agencies. Also policemen and social workers are the professionals who most directly come in contact with the delinquent offender, and it is their handling of the offender that can have the most long-lasting effect on future behavior.

As for differences in criminological philosophy, David Matza has given us some important insights in how to combine the two schools of criminology to make it more realistic and more acceptable to both policemen and social workers. In revising and combining the two schools of thought, Matza fits

> many of the empirical observations of positive criminology into a framework more consistent with classical assumptions and teachings. The classical conception of a "will to crime" is utilized in order to maintain the ineradicable element of choice and freedom inherent in the condition of delinquency.[27]

Chapter 11 will discuss the method of increasing interagency coordination and cooperation which can facilitate more effective delinquency prevention, control, and treatment. It should be mentioned here, however, that the establishment of training programs that are responsive to the feelings, orientation, and needs of both professions would be helpful in creating a more cooperative attitude between them. Each profession needs greater insight into the other's profession. New models for training would be conducive to developing joint efforts toward this understanding in order to produce more effective and coordinated programs.

Differences in Organizational Perspective. The existence of conflict between criminal justice agencies is a readily accepted fact. The interesting point, however, is that even though interagency conflict is sometimes a result of power building, boundary maintenance, and professional jealousy, it also occurs somewhat unknowingly because of the different professional and theoretical organizational orientations. Differences in criminological orientation have already been discussed. In addition to the difference in criminological philosophy between the components of the criminal justice system—police and social work agencies—there is also generally a difference in organizational structure, philosophy, and orientation. The first section of this chapter discussed the three major organizational schools of thought, namely, the Classical, the Human Relations, and the Integrated. It was pointed out that most organizations do not fit one of the typologies in its purest form, although there is usually a major emphasis on one of the schools. When analyzing agencies within the criminal justice system it becomes obvious that police organizations, because they are paramilitary and because their functioning often necessitates discipline and order as well as immediate response to command, are established according to Classical organization theory. They have an emphasis on ranks, a specific authority structure, a close adherence to the unity of command and span of control principles, and a delineation of functions by specialization.

Social work or social service agencies are closer to the Human Relations approach because of the more casual atmosphere in which they operate. They also have more specialized and advanced training and greater latitude in job functioning. Furthermore, the theoretical base upon which their profession is oriented, namely, psychological and sociological theory, presupposes that they will naturally be more

[27]David Matza, *Delinquency and Drift*, (New York: John Wiley & Sons, Inc., 1964).

concerned about interpersonal relations, participation in decision making, and emphasis on social interaction.

Developing Coordination. In a large bureaucratic organization, it is difficult to develop coordination between subunits. Hence, it is even more difficult to develop a coordinated effort between many bureaucratic organizations within the same system, such as in the criminal justice system. Within all agencies of the criminal justice system, however, there are, of course, different roles and norms that are followed and different penalties for deviation. These roles and norms have been established, standardized, codified, and carried out over a long period of time and through a long process of development. Therefore, they can be very difficult to change.

Social work agencies do not have as stringent a division of labor as exists in police organizations and do not need the same kind of discipline and order. Even though there is a similar normative orientation within social work agencies, there is a great deal more latitude for role playing than exists in police organizations. The greater degree of formal education is a major contributing factor.

Authority. Another important difference when comparing police and social work organizations is that there usually exists, at least on the surface, a different method of influence and authority. It is widely recognized that if direction is to be given, guidelines presented, and quality control preserved, there has to be a system of influence or authority. All organizations develop some type of contract between employer and employee so that the functions can be carried out systematically, the organization can achieve its goals, and the employee will be rewarded for his efforts. Regardless of whether the agreement is codified, some type of psychological contract exists between employer and employee.[28] Management expects employees to perform certain tasks that will contribute to organizational output and goal achievement, but on the other hand, the employee expects certain rewards from the management for performing these tasks. The authority system utilizes the formal structure to provide the tangible rewards. Another aspect of organization that plays an important part in employee functioning and goal achievement and producing rewards, the informal structure, has already been pointed out. Even though organizational roles demand only certain limited activity from each person, it is the whole person who functions on the job. He brings with him many attitudes, feelings, and perceptions which are not necessarily anticipated, nor can they be controlled by the organization. They do not clearly fit into a blueprint or a plan. When he works with others on the job, he develops relationships with them, informal agreements, and patterns of behavior, all of which go beyond specified formal relationships outlined by the organization. Many times these informal patterns develop as a result of the formal structure's inability to cope with such aspects of organizational functioning as decision making and formal authority. Many organizational problems develop because of a lack of integration of the

[28] Schein, *op. cit.*

formal and informal structures or a lack of awareness by the administrator that an informal organization exists and exerts influence. In a traditional police organization, if the manager does not understand this informal process and assumes that his authority will always be accepted without question, he will have difficulty relating to his workers and this will ultimately affect organizational functioning. In other words, a great deal of subversion of formal authority will exist. Social work agencies, operating on Human Relations principles, understand and recognize the power of the informal structure but can disregard the necessity or legitimacy of the formal structure.

Achieving greater integration, therefore, involves not only a rational design of the formal organization but also informal understanding and procedures that improve communication among subgroups within the organization. This is also true for a system of organizations (criminal justice system). Even though formal procedures are established to increase organizational operations and functioning, if they are unrealistic and unacceptable by the employees, they can be subverted by the informal processes. In a police organization, an officer can circumvent the directives of an authoritarian supervisor by utilizing his individual discretion in the field because of his great amount of latitude. The point to be made is that both structures, the formal and the informal, exist in organizations. A recognition of them is not only helpful but mandatory if the organization is going to achieve its goals. It is even more important in the criminal justice system because the organizations within it often emphasize and operate under different organizational premises. Police departments emphasize the formal structure but must also recognize informal processes. Conversely, social work agencies are more oriented to the informal organization but nevertheless must also utilize the formal structure. When attempting to coordinate the efforts of these two groups, it is important to understand their emphasis so that cooperative procedures can be developed that foster consensus and support of all concerned components. (Chapter 11 will elaborate on these procedures, and Chapter 7 will present more information on the structure and organization of agencies within the criminal justice system.)

The last section of this chapter will view the contrasting occupational cultures of policemen and social workers in an attempt to give the reader an idea of the different personal and organizational orientations that the two professions take to problem solving. This will make the reader aware of the reasons why problems exist in the cirminal justice system and provide a basis for suggestions for solving them.

THE CONTRASTING OCCUPATIONAL CULTURES OF POLICEMEN AND SOCIAL WORKERS

Studies have shown that different occupations produce different occupational personalities. Occupational personalities tend to be most sharply differentiated in the professions; and over a period of time every profession develops a common set of beliefs, values, attitudes, and working styles which tend to characterize members of that profession. The specific mechanisms that establish the professional sub-culture include the attraction of particular types of personalities, the informal and formal selection processes for admittance, the formal professional training, and the reinforcement of desired characteristics and behavior. The process referred to as "socialization of the professional" is based on shared assumptions within the profession regarding the ideal philosophy, the ideal set of behavior, and the ideal person for the profession. The resultant personality structure consists of those interests, attitudes, values, modes of relating to others, and other characteristics that make the individual maximally receptive to the cultural ways and ideologies of his profession and enable him to achieve adequate gratification and security.

In a dynamic society, professions tend to differentiate into fields of specialization, making it necessary to include in studies of professions both the common cultural characteristics and the subspecialty configurations. The pragmatic test for subspecialities is the degree to which the members of a profession are interchangeable with a reasonable amount of training. Lack of inter-changeability points to the existence of subspecialities.

Kelly and Goldberg,[29] Terman,[30] Strong,[31] and Rosenberg[32] have provided evidence of the existence of occupational personality patterns, and their results suggest that cognitions, wants, interpersonal response traits, values, interests, and attitudes of individual members help define these patterns.

A report of an exploratory study of the measured behavioral styles of persons in the police and social work professions follows. *Measured behavioral styles* refer to the consistent ways an individual organizes his physical, emotional, and energy resources. They are those characteristics that are hypothesized to be relevant to job functioning, and the formulation and measurement of these styles is obtained through the use of the Job Analysis and Interest Measurement (JAIM), a self-report testing instrument.[33]

A sample of one hundred social workers with master's degrees in social work, from the Lansing, Michigan, area was compared with a sample of one hundred

[29] E. L. Kelly and L. R. Goldberg, "Correlates of Later Performance and Specializations in Psychology," *Psychological Monographs,* 73, No. 12 (1959), 22-23.

[30] L. Terman, *et al., Genetic Studies of Genius*, Vol. I: *Mental and Physical Traits of a Thousand Gifted Children* (Stanford: Stanford University Press, 1925).

[31] E. K. Strong, *Vocational Interests 18 Years After College* (Minneapolis: University of Minnesota Press, 1955).

[32] M. Rosenberg, *Occupations and Values* (Glencoe, Ill.: The Free Press, 1957).

[33] The instrument was developed by R. H. Walther, *Job Analyses and Interest Measurement* (Princeton, N.J.: Educational Testing Service, 1964). The following studies have used the J.A.I.M.: R. H. Walther, *The Psychological Dimensions of Work: An Experimental Taxonomy of Occupation* (The George Washington University, 1964); R. H. Walther and S. D. McCune, *Socialization Principles and Work Styles of the Juvenile Court* (The George Washington Center for Behavioral Sciences, 1965); R. H. Walther, S. D. McCune, and R. C. Trojanowicz, *The Contrasting Occupational Cultures of Policemen and Social Workers* (Experimental Publications System, December 1970); Robert C. Trojanowicz, "The Policeman's Working Personality," *The Journal of Criminal Law, Criminology and Police Science*, December 1971; Robert C. Trojanowicz, "The Contrasting Behavioral Styles of Policemen and Social Workers," *Public Personnel Review*, October 1971.

policemen from a large Michigan police department (see Table 2). A gross comparison was made between social workers and policemen, as well as intraorganizational subspecialty and rank comparisons.

Results of the rank, subspecialty, and gross comparison and discussion of their ramifications and their implications for the criminal justice system will be discussed.

Origin of the Study. Policemen and social workers are often stereotyped and perceived to have different behavioral orientations. They are in fact often in disagreement regarding how social problems should be solved and crime controlled and prevented. Clark states that

> a significant portion of the police and other agency personnel manage to curtail interaction in official matters and therefore mutually isolate each other within the social control system. This phenomenon is particularly noticeable between the police and social workers which may reflect the presence of conflicting operating ideologies, lack of professional respect and ignorance of the other's operations.[34]

Because of the stereotyping of the two professions and their interorganizational conflict, the assumption was made that if social workers were compared with policemen their occupational systems and resulting behavioral styles would be different because of their different orientations to social control. A further assumption was that there would also be varying behavioral styles within the two professions in accordance with the particular area of specialization and rank.

Other writers have also researched the two professions, and their work has provided the basis for assumptions made in the present study. Some of the major findings of other studies will be reported briefly.

The Police Profession. Law enforcement functions have not always been delegated to men working in a formalized structure like a police department. The professional policeman is a product of the nineteenth century. Before that time law enforcement was usually a private matter and amounted to a self-protection of property and rights. With the establishment of police forces, the public, in effect, delegated its law enforcement power to a relative handful of professional guardians. For the most part these guardians were given a low status by the general public. A study by Hatt and North in 1947 sought to determine the prestige of ninety occupations.[35] The results showed that policemen ranked fifty-fifth. A replication of this study by Hodge, Siegel, and Rossi (1964) showed that the police still ranked low—forty-seventh.[36]

[34]John P. Clark, "Isolation of the Police: A Comparison of the British and American Situations," *Journal of Criminal Law, Criminology and Police Science,* September 1956, p. 313.

[35]P. K. Hatt and C. C. North, "Prestige Ratings of Occupations," in *Man, Work and Society,* ed. S. Nasow and W. Form (New York: Basic Books, Inc., Publishers, 1962), pp. 277-83.

[36]R. W. Hodge, P. M. Siegel, and P. H. Rossi, "Occupational Prestige in the United States, 1925-1963," *American Journal of Sociology* 70 (1964), 287-94.

Other studies have attempted to describe the policeman's personal characteristics and his working milieu. From a survey of backgrounds of more than twelve hundred recruits who graduated from the New York Police Academy from 1952 to 1967, it was found that most of the candidates were from the upper-lower class. Only a few were above that class. About 95 percent had no college training. The typical characteristics of recruits include a cautious personality, a working-class background, a high school education or less, and average intelligence.[37]

Sheldon has extensively studied body types and has tried to correlate temperament factors with various body classifications.[38] Niederhoffer feels that the policeman's physique fits Sheldon's mesomorph category perfectly.[39] Temperament characteristics associated with the mesomorph category include the need to dominate, assertiveness, competitive aggressiveness, ruthlessness, and other traits associated with authoritarianism.

The supposed authoritarian orientation of policemen was not supported in a study using the well-known F-scale (Adorno et al., 1950).[40] The mean score on the F-scale was 4.15 as compared with a score of 4.19 for the working class. Niederhoffer concludes that police candidates are generally no higher in authoritarianism than the rest of the working class and also suggests that there is no self-selection among authoritarian personalities before appointment.[41]

Niederhoffer believes that the police system is the major factor in transforming a man into a special type of authoritarian personality required by the police role. As a result of the socialization process in the police system, the officer feels justified and many times righteous in using power and toughness to perform his duties.[42]

In terms of the specific role and working milieu of the policeman, Skolnick believes that the two principal variables involved in police work, danger and authority, operate in an atmosphere of a constant pressure to appear efficient. Danger in his work requires that the policeman be especially attentive to situations that have a potential for violence and law breaking. Thus, danger, as an integral part of police work, generally contributes to the policeman's being a "suspicious" person.[43]

The above, of course, is only a brief description of the policeman's personal characteristics and his working milieu. These same general characteristics will be discussed in relation to the social work profession.

---

[37] A. Niederhoffer, *Behind the Shield* (New York: Doubleday and Company, Inc., 1967).

[38] W. H. Sheldon, *The Varieties of Temperament: A Psychology of Constitutional Differences* (New York: Harper & Bros., 1942).

[39] Niederhoffer, *op. cit.*

[40] T. W. Adorno, E. Frenkel-Brunswick, D. S. Levinson, and R. N. Sanford, *The Authoritarian Personality* (New York: Harper & Bros., 1950).

[41] Niederhoffer, *op. cit.*

[42] *Ibid.*

[43] S. H. Skolnick, *Justice without Trial* (New York: John Wiley & Sons, Inc., 1966).

The Social Work Profession. Although there has been comparatively little research relating to the social workers' occupational milieu, there have been several reports relating to the personal characteristics of those persons who choose a social work career. Kadushin, for example, comments that there is a pattern that applies to social work and that certain types of persons are likely to be attracted to it. A profile of such a person, as reflected from Kadushin's research, would be a female who was of above-average intelligence, had professional middle-class parents, lived in a northern city, and had occupational interests and values revolving around a desire to work with people in an effort to help them through the use of verbal skills.[44] Pins does not agree with Kadushin's findings. He says that social work is attractive to people who are in their early twenties, come from lower-middle-class homes in large cities, majored in social science, achieved average college academic records, had previous experience in social work, and enjoy people.[45] Gockel adds to the picture by stating that social workers place high value on jobs or careers that give them an opportunity to be of service, are relatively uninterested in jobs that contain an intellectual component, and are relatively uninterested in monetary rewards and the opportunity to operate independently on the job. In summary, he says that rates of recruitment in social work are relatively low among students who endorse the following values: freedom from supervision, a chance to exercise leadership, and opportunities to be original and creative, living and working in the "world of ideas" and making a lot of money.[46]

Kidneigh and Lundberg, in comparing social work students with those of six other professional schools, found that social work students were more liberal in their thinking.[47]

In a later report McCormack and Kidneigh utilized the Strong Vocational Interest Blank in studying a sample of members of the American Association of Social Workers. After computing the results there was an indication, as would be expected, that social workers liked those activities that involved working with people. They also enjoyed verbal activities and indicated a dislike for "conservative" people. It was also found that male social workers disliked physical sciences and athletic men, while women social workers disliked athletic women as well as scientific, selling, and clerical activities.[48] The results of the present police and social work study substantiated some of these findings but also refuted some important misconceptions.

[44]A. Kadushin, "Determinants of Career Choice and Their Implication for Social Work," *Social Work Education,* April 1958, pp. 37-43.

[45]A. M. Pins, *Who Chooses Social Work, When and Why? An Exploratory Study of Factors Influencing Career Choices in Social Work* (New York: Council on Social Work Education, 1963).

[46]G. Gockel, *Silk Stockings and Blue Collar: Social Work as a Career Choice of America's 1961 College Graduates* (University of Chicago: National Opinion Research Center, 1966).

[47]J. Kidneigh and H. W. Lundberg, "Are Social Work Students Different?," *Social Work,* 3 (May 1958), 57-61.

[48]R. McCormack and J. Kidneigh, "The Vocational Interest Patterns of Social Workers, *Social Work Journal,* 35, No. 4 (October 1959), 161-63.

Table 2
Comparison of Policemen and Social Workers on Standard
Scores on the JAIM Scales (N = 197)

JAIM Scales	Police N = 99	Social Work N = 98	Total N = 197	F-Ratio	CL	
01 OPTIMISM	-18	3	-7	2.495	n.s.[a]	
02 SELF CONFIDENCE	-57	19	-19	25.209	.01	X[b]
03 PERSEVERANCE	45	-21	12	23.392	.01	O[c]
04 ORDERLINESS	42	-53	-5	64.923	.01	O
05 PLAN AHEAD	-59	-9	-34	12.527	.01	X
06 MORAL ABSOLUTES	69	-29	20	44.767	.01	O
07 SLOW CHANGE	50	-5	23	18.793	.01	O
08 PERSUASIVE LEADERSHIP	14	-7	3	2.642	n.s.	-
09 SELF ASSERTIVENESS	71	-31	20	44.368	.01	O
10 MOVE TOWARD AGGRESSOR	-32	17	-7	11.908	.01	X
11 MOVE AWAY FROM AGGRESSOR	-11	-26	-19	1.407	n.s.	-
12 MOVE AGAINST AGGRESSOR	2	26	14	2.589	n.s.	-
13 PREFER ROUTINES	46	-32	6	39.709	.01	O
14 AUTHORITY IDENTIFICATION	-23	-17	-20	0.294	n.s.	-
15 INDEPENDENCE	-42	32	-5	33.760	.01	X
16 DIRECTIVE LEADERSHIP	44	-56	-5	53.090	.01	O
17 PARTICIPATIVE LEADERSHIP	-26	13	-6	8.168	.01	X
18 DELEGATIVE LEADERSHIP	-9	45	18	15.121	.01	X
19 KNOWLEDGE OF RESULTS	-34	3	-15	6.695	.01	X
20 EXTERNAL CONTROLS	70	-46	11	65.314	.01	O
21 SYSTEMATICAL-METHODICAL	8	-64	-28	28.166	.01	O
22 PROBLEM ANALYSIS	0	-18	-8	2.338	n.s.	-
23 SOCIAL INTERACTION	-36	37	0	42.033	.01	X
24 MECHANICAL ACTIVITIES	93	-25	34	79.458	.01	O
25 SUPERVISORY ACTIVITIES	24	-14	4	9.166	.01	O
26 ACTIVITY-FREQUENT CHANGE	0	-16	-7	1.215	n.s.	-
27 GROUP PARTICIPATION	31	43	37	0.768	n.s.	-
28 STATUS ATTAINMENT	-21	-48	-34	2.934	n.s.	-
29 SOCIAL SERVICE	-22	87	32	52.955	.01	X
30 APPROVAL FROM OTHERS	-55	2	-26	20.045	.01	X
31 INTELLECTUAL ACHIEVEMENT	-56	-11	-34	12.244	.01	X
32 MAINTAIN SOCIETAL STANDARDS	8	47	28	7.154	.01	X
33 ROLE CONFORMITY	101	-12	44	75.203	.01	O
34 ACADEMIC ACHIEVEMENT	-81	-10	-46	24.157	.01	X

Note: Three answer sheets (two social work and one police) were eliminated because of coding problems.
$P < .05$ with R = 3.84
$P < .01$ with R = 6.63
[a]n.s. = not significant.
[b]X = Social Worker higher.
[c]O = Police higher.

The Police and Social Work Comparison. Table 2 illustrates the F-ratio results when the one hundred policemen and the one hundred social workers were compared on standard scores on the thirty-four JAIM scales. The standard scores are based on the average of forty-two occupational groups, including foreign service officers, lawyers, secretaries, business executives, ambassadors, engineers, physicists, army officers, and judges. The mean is equated to zero and the standard deviation to 100. The analysis of variance technique was utilized, and the F-ratio in the case of the one degree of freedom is the square of the T-value. Any scale over 3.84 is significant at the .05 level of confidence (the criterion for acceptance or rejection of a relationship), and any scale over 6.63 is significant at the .01 level of confidence. Twenty-five scales were significant.

The table demonstrates that all twenty-five scales were significant at the .01 level of confidence. None of the nine remaining scales were even close to the minimum .05 level of confidence. In other words, each scale either was extremely significant or showed very little difference between the two professions. A profile as a result of the comparison will be given.

The Police Profile

The police profile suggests that the policeman prefers to work in a structured setting (Prefer Routines, Orderliness) and to use the structure for guiding the behavior of others (External Controls). He is guided by internal standards, and he believes that moral principles come from a power higher than man and that it is important to have faith in something (Moral Absolutes). As for leadership style, he prefers a direct approach through the use of external controls (Directive Leadership).

He knows what he wants and is willing to strive to reach some goal that he has established for himself (Perseverance, Supervisory Activities). He pursues his goals and performs his duties even though he may not receive the approval of others. He values himself according to how successfully he has conformed to the role requirements and duties of society (Role Conformity). He is cautious concerning abrupt changes and feels that change should be initiated in a conventional manner (Slow Change).

He uses systematic methods for processing information and reaching decisions (Systematical-Methodical). He likes mechanical and outdoor activities (Mechanical Activities), does well under stress and competition, and is proficient in athletic endeavors (Self-assertiveness).

The Social Work Profile

The social work profile suggests that the social worker has a preference for working independently (Independence, Delegative Leadership), directing his own activity toward goal achievement (Plan Ahead), and utilizing groups for decision making (Participative Leadership). He believes that people are motivated best by intrinsic motivation and proof (Knowledge of Results).

He prefers a job that involves working with other people (Social Interaction). He wishes to be considered understanding and charitable and prefers work that permits him to be helpful to others (Social Service). He also likes congenial co-workers, and he wants to be well-liked and please others through his work (Approval from Others).

He feels he can influence future events by his own action (Self-confidence) and values himself by his contribution to social improvement (Social Service). He also values himself for his intellectual achievement, and he does well in academic situations (Academic Achievement).

Subspecialty and Rank Comparisons. Intraorganization subspecialty and rank comparisons were also significant, although the number of scales and their level of significance was not as pronounced. In addition, the rank comparisons, which included command officers and troopers for the police, and consultants, supervisors, and caseworkers for social work, were not as pronounced as the subspecialty comparisons. The subspecialty comparisons in the social work profession included mental health, social service, schools, and private agencies. In the police profession, the subspecialty comparisons include police training, crime lab, patrol, and juvenile.

In the one comparison between police ranks, command officers and troopers, six scales were significant at (at least) the .05 level of confidence. Command officers prefer directive measures of leadership, enjoy supervising others, and are guided by internal standards. They also prefer to try to "win the person over" when they are treated in an aggressive manner. Troopers, on the other hand, scored higher only on the scale that measures the desire for independence.

In the social work rank comparisons, consultants when compared with supervisors produced the most significant differences (nine significant scales). Consultants scored higher on items that indicated a preference for moral absolutes and a method of reacting to aggression by withdrawing. They prefer routines, conform to the role requirements of society, and more readily identify with authority. Supervisors are more self-confident, prefer to plan ahead, desire independence, and use intellectual achievement as a measure of success. When consultants were compared with caseworkers and when supervisors were compared with caseworkers only four scales were significant in each instance, which would indicate that behavioral style differences between these groups is minimal.

The subspecialty comparisons showed a much greater variation in behavior style differences within the social work profession than within the police profession. Two of the six relationships for the social work sample (private agency workers versus school workers and social service workers versus school workers) were not significant, while four of the six subspecialty comparisons within the police sample were not significant. Only the comparisons of police patrol versus police crime lab and police training versus police crime lab were significant. These comparisons show that crime lab officers possess behavioral styles that reflect their different functions and work environment.

In regard to the significant relationships between social work subspecialties, school social workers and social service social workers are most alike and as mentioned previously, there was not a significant difference when the two were compared. They are generally more structured, enjoy mechanical activities, and believe in moral absolutes, which overall reflects a more conservative profile.

Mental health workers are the most dissimilar of the four subspecialties. Their most distinguishing characteristic is their desire for independence. Although private agency workers are more aligned with mental health workers, they do not present as many distinguishing behavioral style characteristics as do the workers in the other three subspecialties.

Summary

It can be concluded that there are not only differences between policemen and social workers but also differences within the two professions, depending on rank and subspecialty; these differences are significantly less, however, than the differences between the two professions.

An important issue is the cause-and-effect relationship. To what extent does the policeman or the social worker develop these characteristics because of the demands of his job and to what extent was he that way to begin with? Furthermore, what implications does this have for personnel selection, training, and management within the criminal justice system? While only comprehensive longitudinal studies can answer these kinds of questions, some information bearing on these issues and its implications will be discussed as a result of this study.

The markedly different profiles of policemen and social workers suggest why the members of these professions may have great difficulty communicating with each other and why, as Wilensky and Lebeaux have pointed out, schools of social work have exhibited only minor interest in working with criminal offenders. Successful work with many offenders may require greater use of external controls than social workers believe desirable.[49]

This has interesting implications because the contemporary emphasis is on a systemic approach to social control. This is reflected by reference to crime prevention and the social control process as being accomplished within the criminal justice system. Organizations included in the system are the police (which does not employ social workers), the courts, social work agencies, and correctional facilities. An important variable for the success of this systemic approach, however, is that the professionals within the system, such as policemen and social workers, have to support this approach if it is to exist in more than name only. A systemic approach to social control has implications for personnel selection, training, and management.

Even though this study did not attempt to correlate success on the job with

[49]H. Wilensky and C. Lebeaux, *Industrial Society and Social Welfare* (New York: Russell Sage Foundation, 1958).

behavioral style, it can reasonably be assumed that it is not necessary, realistic, or even desirable that all the various professional groups within the criminal justice system have the same behavioral style. The breadth and the flexibility of most professions permit different types of individuals to succeed for different reasons. As this study shows, differences in behavioral styles can be expected to develop within the larger professional culture, based on the different tasks to be performed. A wide variety and diversity of tasks need to be completed if the criminal justice system is to operate effectively. Both engineering psychology (fitting the task to the man) and personnel psychology (fitting the man to the task) can be utilized, depending on the task to be performed and its relationship to goal achievement.

For example, the profile studies show that social service and school social workers when compared with mental health social workers are almost identical to policemen when compared with social workers. Social service and school social workers have behavioral styles that would probably be more conducive to cooperating with other "line" professionals, such as policemen, in processing and treating offenders. Selective "matching" between professionals in the criminal justice system would allow the professionals to utilize their unique areas of expertise. Generalized conclusions about professionals and their inability to perform some functions and work in a certain environment would then be reduced.

In addition to effective task selection, training can also contribute to better performance. Areas of concensus and disagreement between the professions can be identified. As a result of this identification process, more areas of consensus may emerge between the professions than were originally believed to exist. The present study points out that two important styles of behavior affecting the social control process, thought to be different for policemen and social workers, proved to be very similar. Two of the scales (Authority Identification and Move against Aggressor) suggest that policemen do not, as popularly believed, more often counterattack than do social workers when treated in an aggressive or a belligerent manner. Nor are policemen overidentified or underidentified with authority when compared with social workers.

Determining similarities such as these is important because it eliminates undue stereotyping which can perpetuate interagency conflict.

CONCLUSION

That juvenile delinquency is a serious problem today is a readily accepted fact. That the problem is getting worse instead of better is, however, an enigma because extensive resources, both material and human, are being devoted to the juvenile delinquency problem. In addition, numerous theories of causation, treatment, control, and prevention from many different academic disciplines and fields of practice are being utilized. We have discussed these theories and the differences in criminological and organizational philosophies of persons in the criminal justice system.

Let us look at some of the additional reasons why, despite extensive resources and theoretical knowledge, the problem of juvenile delinquency is becoming increasingly severe.

It cannot be assumed that merely because an agency has as a part of its function the prevention, control, and treatment of delinquency, the goal will necessarily follow the good intentions of the initiators of the particular program. All agencies that deal, either directly or indirectly, with delinquents have the *potential* for perpetuating and, in fact, sometimes producing delinquency as well as reducing it.[50]

The School. Dinitz, Reckless, and Murray and others have shown that in addition to being a vehicle for directing the student's energy into positive channels, the school can also contribute to the student's developing a negative self-concept which can have implications for his future behavior both in the school and in the community.[51] Many students, particularly those from disadvantaged groups, have difficulty competing in the classroom in accordance with the criteria that have been established by the particular school system. As a result, some students are handicapped because of a lack of competitive and social skills. They retreat from the academic competition, which is subsequently interpreted as their not being interested or capable of producing within that system. When a child retreats in this manner and is labeled as a failure or a potential failure by his teachers, this can affect his self-concept not only in the school but outside the school and help create and perpetuate the child's feeling that he is less than capable when compared with his peers. Albert Cohen pointed out the negative ramifications of an unequal competitive system and its relation to the delinquent phenomenon (see Chapter 3).[52] When children are unable to compete in the "system" and do not learn to sublimate their energies in a socially acceptable manner, a delinquent solution to problem solving is often the result. School programs and teachers have to be responsive to the needs and abilities of all students. Flexible and innovative programming and curriculum development accompanied by sensitive classroom behavior by teachers is mandatory.

The Juvenile Court. The juvenile court also has the potential for producing and perpetuating delinquency. If the court is not responsive to the needs of the total community and, in fact, indiscriminately prosecutes and processes children from limited segments of the community, the indiscriminate labeling can affect

[50]Walter Miller, "Inter-Institutional Conflict as a Major Impediment to Delinquency Prevention," *Human Organization* 17 (Fall 1958).

[51]Simon Dinitz, Walter Reckless, and Ellen Murray, "Self-Concept as an Insulator against Delinquency," *American Sociological Review*, 21 (December 1956).

[52]Albert Cohen, *Delinquent Boys* (Glencoe, Ill.: The Free Press, 1955).

both the child's attitude toward himself and the community's attitude toward him. The social ostracism and the negative self-concept can contribute to his antisocial behavior in the community. Court procedures should be equitable and sensitive to the possible negative ramifications of h. jty labeling. Realistic, humane, and appropriate methods of processing and treating juveniles are necessary if the court is to be an effective component in the criminal justice system.

The Police. Police agencies can also contribute to the perpetuation of delinquent behavior. Many times the first contact that a child has with the criminal justice system is with a police officer. Many young people, delinquents in particular, have problems with authority because of poor authority relationships in their past. If a child'd first contact with a police officer is negative and the police officer exerts his authority in an arrogant manner, this can support the child's already negative concept of authority and contribute to his futher acting out against authority within the community. However, an officer who impresses the child as being an understanding but firm adult who will treat him fairly can have a positive impact and can be one of the major factors in influencing the boy to alter his behavior and divert his energy into socially acceptable channels.

Social Work Agencies. Social work agencies can also contribute to delinquent behavior by perpetuating the delinquent's irresponsible behavior. Too often social workers, in an attempt to help the delinquent or the predelinquent, readily give him excuses for his behavior and transmit to him either overtly or covertly that because of his past and present circumstances, he does have an excuse for committing delinquent acts. Social workers should remember that it is possible to accept the delinquent's negative feelings toward authority and the community but at the same time not transmit to him that he has a "right" to act out against the community. It is possible to accept the child's feelings, but not his negative behavior. A more responsible attitude on the part of some social workers can help in reducing the acting out of negative impulses within the community.

All agencies that deal with the juvenile delinquent have to be constantly aware of their presence in his life and not take for granted that merely because they were established to prevent and treat juvenile delinquency, their programs and polices always forster this end. Many times these same "helping" agencies produce, foster, and perpetuate the very phenomenon that they are trying to eliminate.

Because there is a need for the policeman and the social worker to have greater insight into each other's profession, new models for training may have to be developed for both professions. Joint training efforts could produce a more effective and coordinated treatment and prevention process.

It would be helpful if the police were to absorb some of the social workers' general theories and concepts which would aid them in understanding social problems and people who were inflicted. On the other hand, it would be helpful if social workers were to absorb some of the policemen's "reality therapy" and appreciate some of the problems he encounters in his face-to-face confrontation with the social deviant.

SUMMARY

This chapter has discussed the major elements of social organization and the most prevalent theories of organizational structure. In addition, the social organization of the criminal justice system was described and relevant examples were presented. A knowledge of organizational theory is important in understanding the many factors that have to be considered when delinquency prevention, treatment, and control programs are initiated and operated.

The chapter also identified the differences in theoretical orientation (both criminological and organizational) between policemen and social workers, the two main professional groups that work in the criminal justice system. The understanding of the different orientation of these two professions, and Matza's attempt to reconcile these differences through a new theoretical model, will be helpful in creating a normative approach to juvenile delinquency prevention, control, and treatment that will be acceptable and successful.[53]

The next chapter discusses the processing of the delinquent in the criminal justice system. A knowledge of organization theory is helpful not only in understanding the process but also in analyzing the components of the criminal justice system that do the processing.

QUESTIONS AND PROJECTS

Essay Questions

1. Explain why regardless of their size and complexity, all organizations have common components.
2. Which theory of organization appeals to you most and why?
3. Why do most police organizations subscribe to the Classical theory of organization?
4. How is a knowledge of organization theory relevant to juvenile delinquency prevention?
5. Why do policemen and social workers have different behavioral styles?

Projects

1. Develop a plan for coordinating the efforts of all the components of the criminal justice system within your community.
2. Develop an organizational scheme that will incorporate the most effective aspects of both the Classical and the Human Relations schools.
3. Develop a quality control mechanism for the components of the criminal justice system so that they do not perpetuate—or produce—juvenile delinquency.

[53]Matza, *op. cit.*

7

HANDLING THE JUVENILE DELINQUENT WITHIN THE CRIMINAL JUSTICE SYSTEM

In Chapter 6 we discussed the social organization of the criminal justice system, namely, those components charged with handling, controlling, and preventing delinquency most directly. We saw that social workers and police are the two most involved professional groups and that their handling of the delinquent can greatly affect his future behavior. This chapter will emphasize the major components of the criminal justice system—the police department, the probation department and the court,—and will focus on the juvenile bureau of the police department, where the delinquent first comes in contact with the system and is either released or processed forward; the intake division of the probation department, where, again, the delinquent is either released or processed to the juvenile court; and the juvenile court, whose options range from outright release to incarceration. We will examine their philosophy, their duties, and the processes they use, individually and jointly, when handling the delinquent.

Other agencies can also be considered a part of the criminal justice system, such as schools and related social work agencies. However, they do not usually deal with serious delinquent activity directly. They function mostly as a referral source for the police juvenile bureau, the probation department, or the court.

In Chapter 6 we also discussed the roles of the main components of the criminal justice system, pointing out that natural conflict can exist because of different professional training, organizational and criminological philosophy, and overall general perception of how things should be done when handling the delinquent. The police do not have the amount of formal education that the judge or the social workers have. The social workers are more behavioral science oriented than either the police or the judge and, many times, more transient because of job mobility. Many judges, because they are elected, often have political aspirations and therefore consider the juvenile court position only a stepping stone to higher office. Thus the police in many respects are the most "stable" component of the criminal justice system, whereas the judges, social workers, and lawyers come and go.

In terms of role definition for the three occupational groups, the police have the major role of maintaining public order and safety, as well as enforcing laws. They do this by collecting facts and processing those persons who have transgressed. Social workers, whether in the probation department, the court, or a mental health agency, have the major role of utilizing social science principles to develop treatment programs and to provide insight into human dynamics.

The judge makes a case determination by referring to the "facts" gathered by the police and the social science principles interpreted by social workers. The judge, then, with the assistance of police and social workers, has the major role of being the objective decision maker who supposedly weighs the facts, evaluates the situation and the circumstances, and decides what alternatives should be used in the particular case. The major components of the criminal justice system must work with resource services and referral sources if a meaningful determination is to be made and the process of handling the juvenile is to be beneficial for both the community and the child. Each major component will be discussed separately.

THE POLICE

The police are commissioned with preserving the peace, maintaining order, enforcing laws, and preventing and detecting crime. Because of specialization and because much of the work load of the police involves youngsters under eighteen years of age, much of the processing and handling that the police do is with juveniles. Current statistics show that contact with juveniles is important and that a large percentage of crime and even serious offenses are committed by juveniles.[1] The police also handle many non-delinquent juvenile matters. For example, a great many neglect cases as well as minor infractions, are handled by the police juvenile bureau or some other designated unit. Depending upon the community, its orientation to youth, and the size of the police department, there will be a juvenile division, a juvenile unit, a youth bureau, or some other designated unit to handle juveniles. The specialized unit for the juvenile has become much more prevalent in the past few years as witnessed by the new emphasis on training juvenile officers and the new awareness by the public that because of the increased volume of crime

[1] Richard W. Kobetz, *The Police Role and Juvenile Delinquency,* International Association of Chiefs of Police, Inc., 1971, pp. 33-34.

Courtesy of the Michigan State Police

Figure 6   Positive Police—Juvenile Relations Begins Early

by juveniles, there is a need for greater focus on children and their behavior and on methods for controlling and treating them.

The complexity of our communities and the impersonality of many of the organizations that serve community residents have also contributed to the greater need for juvenile bureaus. In the past the policeman usually lived in his district, and therefore he knew the community, knew its residents, and understood its problems. Many problems were handled informally because the policeman's constant interaction with the community was conducive to maintaining interpersonal communication. The increased problems of urbanization, however, and the impersonality of present-day communities have not only forced police work in general to become more routinized and impersonal but have made it necessary to focus attention on cases involving juveniles. Because of the volume of youthful crime, but also because juveniles are sometimes the victims of circumstances, intervention by the court, such as in neglect cases, is necessary for their protection.

The juvenile unit will vary in size, depending upon the type of police department and community. In some departments where there is a low volume of juvenile crime or where a full-time juvenile unit is not deemed necessary, certain officers may be assigned to part-time work with juveniles. In middle-sized departments, there will be full-time officers, but not many. In larger departments, the juvenile bureau can be a very large unit with the necessary resources and personnel. Depending on the size of the department, then, the juvenile officer's responsibilities will vary; however, some common functions will exist in most departments. The juvenile officer will usually deal with all offenses that involve juveniles as well as family cases that involve neglect and abuse. The juvenile officer's duties will include processing juveniles, talking to their parents, determining circumstances surrounding the offense, and maintaining juvenile records. In more sophisticated departments, the juvenile officer is also involved in preventive-type activities, such as giving speeches to schools and coordinating programs with other agencies in the community. The juvenile officer may also attempt to influence the members of his department by making them aware of the special problems that exist when dealing with juveniles and the appropriate methods for processing them.

The police have a great amount of discretionary power, ranging all the way from releasing the juvenile at initial contact in an unofficial manner to referring him to the juvenile court, which may result in detention. The officer can also refer the youngster to a community agency, such as a Big Brother organization or a mental health clinic. He can also apprehend the youngster and take him to the police department. In almost all cases the officer will contact the parents. The only exception would be when the incident was minor and a verbal warning was sufficient.

> In sum, the range of police dispositions is considerable, and the criteria for selection of disposition are seldom set forth explicitly, ordered in priority, or regularly reviewed for administrative purposes. Inservice training designed to assist police in exercising their discretionary functions is unusual; . . . further investigation for improvement of the police discretionary process holds promise of more discriminating judgments between offenders who should be retained in the system and those who need, if anything, service rather than adjudication.[2]

Figure 7 illustrates the steps followed when the police officer comes upon an "event" or receives a complaint. This is the beginning of the process that ultimately determines whether the youngster will come in contact with the court or whether he will be released. At the time of the event or the complaint, the officer may decide that the offense is minor and does not necessitate further investigation, and therefore the child can be released on the spot. If the officer feels that additional information is necessary, he can briefly interview the youngster and then decide that the situation does not warrant further discussion and release him to his parents. If the officer feels that the offense or the complaint is serious enough to warrant further investigation and discussion, he can refer the case to the police department's juvenile bureau. The options of the juvenile bureau are illustrated in Figure 7. A juvenile bureau officer can interview the child and then release him with an informal reprimand or with a formal, or official, reprimand. Another option is to release him with police supervision. In all these cases, the child is released to the community, which usually means to his parents. The process in these cases would end with the juvenile bureau of the police department. If, however, the juvenile bureau officer feels that the situation warrants further attention, the child can be referred to the juvenile court for a determination. Before a determination, however, the youngster can be delivered to a juvenile home or a

[2]*Task Force Report: Juvenile Delinquency and Youth Crime,* The President's Commission on Law Enforcement and Administration of Justice (Washington, D.C.: Government Printing Office, 1967), p. 14.

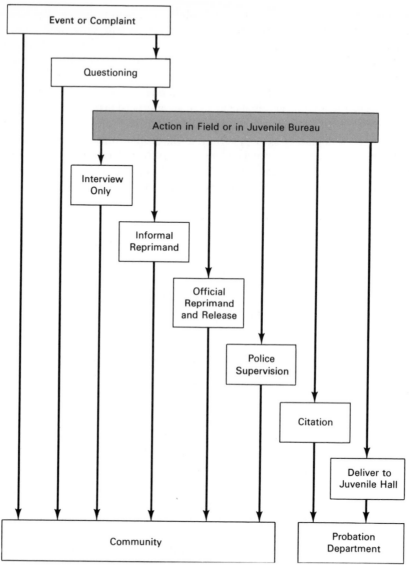

From James T. Carey, Joel Goldfarb, Michael J. Rowe, and Joseph D. Lohman, *The Handling of Juveniles from Offense to Disposition*, U.S. Department of Health, Education, and Welfare (Washington, D.C.: Government Printing Office, 1967), p. 26.

Figure 7   Decision Points in Police Handling of Juveniles

detention facility. The intake unit of the probation department will then make a determination as to whether the process should end at intake or continue to juvenile court proceedings.

Because of the great number of delinquent offenses as well as the wide range of discretionary powers held by the police, procedures will vary from community to community. Other factors also enter into the decision-making process:

> Decisions are generally based on the nature of the offense, the *appraised character* of the youth, which in turn is based on such facts as his prior police record, age, association, attitude, family situation, the conduct of his parents, and the attitude of other community institutions such as his school. The external community may exert pressure on the police department which may affect the disposition of any case. Here attitudes of the press and the public, the status of the complainant or victim, the status of the offender, and the conditions which prevail in the available referral agencies (the length of the waiting list, the willingness of social agencies to accept police referrals) are all of consequence. Internal police department pressure such as attitudes of co-workers and supervisors and the personal experience of the officer may also play an important part in determining the outcome of any officially detected delinquent offense. These factors also indirectly determine the officially recorded police and court delinquency incidence rates.[3] (Italics added.)

Many factors, therefore, determine whether a youth is to be processed or not and whether he may eventually end up in the formal criminal justice system.

THE INTAKE DIVISION OF THE PROBATION DEPARTMENT

Probation services are often administratively a part of the juvenile court; however, all cases that come in contact with the intake division of the probation department are not necessarily processed through the court. If the child is ultimately processed through the court, he can then receive the probation services of the probation department. Intake is only one division of an entire probation department.

Probation is one of the services that developed out of the nineteenth century awareness that children should be treated differently from adults. Its main emphasis is on diagnosis and treatment, and it provides services for the youngster when he does not receive the proper support and guidance from his parents or from institutions within the community. The probation officer is a necessary element in the criminal justice system because he is supposed to gather and furnish the necessary information and social-psychological history so that the judge can make a determination and select an alternative appropriate to the individual child. The duties of the probation officer will depend on the size of the department and the community. In large departments, there will be a separate intake unit from the direct probation services that result after a court determination. In small departments, the intake officer may also be the supervising probation officer when the child has been adjudicated. Juvenile probation exists by statute in every state.

[3]*Ibid.,* p. 419.

Regardless of their organizational niche, juvenile court probation officers serve two major functions: making social studies of cases referred to the court and supervising juveniles placed on probation. Their duties may, in addition, entail intake functions such as screening cases referred to the court and determining the necessity for detention, administering the juvenile detention facility, and managing the court's probation department and court attached diagnostic and treatment services (clinics, camps, halfway houses, community residential facilities).[4]

The intake process of the probation department may, in turn, be a subunit of the juvenile court, but intake is

essentially a screening process to determine whether the court should take action and, if so, what action or whether the matter should be referred elsewhere. Intake is set apart from the screening process used in adult criminal courts by the pervasive attempt to individualize each case and the nature of the personnel administering the discretionary process. In adult criminal proceedings at the postarrest stage, decisions to screen out are entrusted to the grand jury, the judge, or usually to the prosecutor. The objective is screening as an end in itself: attempts to deliver service to those screened out are rare. . . . At intake in the juvenile courts, screening is an important objective, but referral to if not insistence upon service and imposition of controls are additional goals. Thus, the expressed function of intake is likely to be more ambitious than that of its criminal law counterpart and the function is performed chiefly by persons who are neither legally trained or significantly restricted in the exercise of ·their discretionary authority by procedure requirements comparable to those of the criminal law.[5]

Figure 8 illustrates the process and alternatives that exist at the intake phase. After the intake process there can be outright dismissal; admonishment and dismissal; informal supervision by the probation staff; or referral to a community agency for mental health services, Big Brother programs, and so on. The child can also be placed in detention if he is not already there, and a petition can be filed for a court hearing. "Unless a prima facie case of jurisdiction is established, the only defensible recourses at intake are immediate dismissal or voluntary referral to a social agency or other sources of assistance."[6]

At the intake phase a great deal of juvenile misbehavior can be handled through alternatives other than adjudication. Community agencies and organizations such as social work agencies, Big Brother, employment facilities, school programs, and other viable resources can help the child rectify his problem and alleviate his negative situation. One of the primary considerations at intake should be the effect that labeling and the formal adjudication process will have on the youngster. Even though juvenile records are not public records, it would be naive to

[4]*Ibid.,* p. 6.
[5]*Ibid.,* pp. 14-15.
[6]*Ibid.,* p. 15.

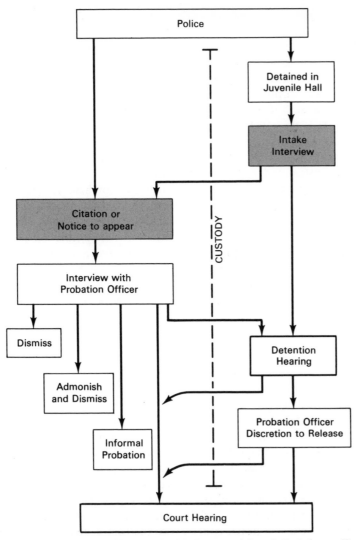

From James T. Carey, Joel Goldfarb, Michael J. Rowe, and Joseph D. Lohman, *The Handling of Juveniles from Offense to Disposition*, U.S. Department of Health, Education, and Welfare (Washington, D.C.: Government Printing Office, 1967), p. 26.

Figure 8   Decision Points in Probation Handling of Juveniles

assume that there would not be a contaminating effect as a result of formal adjudication. Hence, the reason for attempting to make a referral other than formal adjudication in the court.

The intake and screening process is an important aspect of the criminal justice system. When used properly, it can effectively curtail or interrupt much delinquent behavior before it becomes serious. The intake process can also involve community agencies in helping the parents to understand their child's behavior and measures needed to prevent future delinquent acts.

If, however, the intake process is used by the court as a means of indiscriminately screening out youngsters merely because of cost factors, this can have a detrimental effect on the youngster as well as on the entire criminal justice system. Resources should be provided by the community so that the intake and screening process can be utilized to its fullest extent. When sufficient resources are not provided, both in the initial contact stage where the police officer makes his screening and determination and in the intake process at the probation department, there will be negative ramifications. Screening will be little more than filtering youngsters through the system and making hasty decisions and determinations about their cases. When the police department and the intake unit have adequate resources, dispositions should be much more closely thought out and the processes used to their fullest extent rather than just as methodical operations and necessary functions. Ideally, there should be a follow-up, after referral, by either the police or the intake deparment. Follow-up will facilitate not only services to the child but closer cooperation between the agencies involved. Again it should be emphasized that one of the major problems of effective prevention, treatment, and control programs is lack of cooperation and meaningful interaction between the criminal justice agencies.

THE JUVENILE COURT

In handling the delinquent, processing in the juvenile court is the third major phase of the criminal justice system. Because the police come in contact with the juvenile first, the police officer can utilize his wide discretionary power to select one of several alternatives. If the youngster is not released immediately, the officer, if he is not a part of the juvenile bureau, can refer him to the juvenile bureau at which time other decision-making processes go into effect. If the youngster continues through the criminal justice system process, he then comes in contact with the intake unit of the probation department. One of the alternatives as a result of intake is further processing in the criminal justice system, with the next contact being made at the juvenile court.

Today there is a juvenile court in every state of the Union. It is usually a specialized unit in the state judicial system and is based in the local community. The legislature determines its proceedings; higher courts can supervise its actions; and various state agencies, such as state welfare departments, influence its fiscal policies. The court is usually financed by the local government, the judge is elected, and the police, schools, and other agencies make referrals to it.

Because the court is dependent on local resources and because it does not always have high status within the community or among other courts, organizational difficulties may exist. The court often operates under unsatisfactory monetary conditions, which is not conducive to an orderly operation or the providing of services to the client and the community.

> The court's dilemma in coping with such critical pressures is sharpened by its dependence on local agencies or publics for support and cooperation. Many local units must be relied upon to provide assistance in case handling and service. The resources of police departments, schools, social agencies, welfare bureaus, the bar association, and the medical societies are needed to supplement those of the court. The dilemma also has more general terms of reference. The election of the judge and the basic operating budget necessitate maintenance and good will from a broad range of local units and interest groups. Certain organizations, furthermore, play crucial roles in validating court performance among the general public. Police judgments, in particular, but also those of schools, welfare agencies, and professional associations are taken as more or less authoritative evaluations of juvenile court activity and the risk of public challenge from these units must be taken into account as the court deals with individual cases.[7]

The organizational pattern of the juvenile court varies from state to state, and few juvenile courts are independent courts. Most of them are a part of the circuit, district, superior, county, common pleas, probate, or municipal courts. Regardless of the administrative and organizational pattern of the court, its jurisdiction generally includes delinquency, neglect, and dependency cases; however, adoption, appointment of guardians for minors, determination of custody, and termination of parental rights are also included in the juvenile court process. The age of the juvenile who is processed by the court also varies. The upper limit is usually eighteen, even though jurisdiction can extend all the way to age twenty-one under special statutes.

The juvenile court is greatly misunderstood by not only the general public but also the various components within a criminal justice system, including the police. Because of this misunderstanding and lack of procedural knowledge, the child often gets the worst of two worlds, which means that he does not receive the procedural safeguards guaranteed in adult criminal courts nor is he given the individualized treatment that was the original intent of the juvenile court movement.[8]

Chapter 2 mentioned the basis on which the court is established, the concept of *parens patriae*, which makes the state responsible for the welfare of the child. Because the court is generally a part of a larger court system, such as a probate court, the amount of time that the judge spends on juvenile matters will be determined by the caseload of the court and his other duties and priorities. For example, if the juvenile court is a part of the probate court, the judge may spend the major part of his time on probate cases and a minimum amount of time on juvenile matters.

[7]Robert D. Vinter, "The Juvenile Court as an Institution," *Task Force Report: Juvenile Delinquency and Youth Crime*, pp. 86-87.

[8]Kent v. United States, 383 U.S. 541 (1966).

The juvenile court, besides having a judge, usually has at least one probation officer, who may be either full time or part time depending upon the resources of the community. In large cities, the court will employ many probation officers. Qualifications of court personnel, including both the judge and the probation officers, vary from jurisdiction to jurisdiction. Some judges have few qualifications for handling juvenile delinquents and little training in the behavioral sciences. Other judges will be very sophisticated in both the law and the behavioral sciences. Preferably, the judge should be a lawyer so that he can understand judicial process, and he should also have training in the behavioral sciences. Qualifications and training of probation officers also vary, with many jurisdictions not having a probation officer with a college degree.

Even though the juvenile court's original intent was to rehabilitate rather than to punish, the lack of resources, lack of cooperation, and lack of insight have often turned it into a second-rate agency for processing and treating juveniles. Decisions made in a methodical, routine, quick manner do not facilitate the child's receiving all his legal safeguards. An ideal situation would be to have the court guarantee the child's legal rights through procedural safeguards yet not lose the individualized treatment approach that has been the stated philosophy of the court.

RELATED CRIMINAL JUSTICE AGENCIES

Thus far the focus has been on the three main components of the criminal justice system most directly concerned with handling juveniles—the police, the intake division of the probation department, and the juvenile court. Most of the other agencies involved either directly or indirectly in the criminal justice process provide auxiliary services for the three main components and include mental health agencies, social agencies, school programs, private agencies, Big Brother services, employment services, and any other services that may be effective in providing support to the child who finds it lacking in his home or in his community. Just as there is a lack of coordination between those agencies directly involved in the criminal justice process, there is often a lack of coordination between the auxiliary agencies, and police officers, court workers, and even judges are not aware of the facilities for juveniles that exist within their communities. Even though most communities have a directory listing their services, professionals within the system often neglect to orient themselves to the agencies and the services provided. The reasons for this are many, but regardless of the reasons the end result is a lack of cooperation which affects the establishment of effective delinquency treatment, prevention, and control programs. It is to everyone's advantage to utilize all available community resources. It makes the professional's job easier, it helps the delinquent, and most of all it eliminates the stigma of the child's being processed through the official criminal justice system.

POLICE PROCEDURE FOR HANDLING JUVENILES

The police procedure for handling juveniles from initial contact to disposition involves many important elements. Because the police make the first contact with the juvenile and because they have wide discretionary powers, they can have a great influence on the child's future behavior within the community. The police must always remember that juveniles should be handled differently from adults, even though there are legal safeguards that apply to both. It is interesting to note that even now the juvenile court process is taking on some of the aspects of criminal proceedings. Even though the juvenile court philosophy proposes that the handling of juveniles is not a criminal proceeding, the use of district attorneys, direct examination, cross-examination of witnesses, and review of the officer's handling of juveniles is becoming much more common. The day may come when these processes become even less informal and take on the adversary characteristics that now exist in criminal court. It should be kept in mind that all the procedures of lawful arrest, search and seizure, and court rulings on advising a person of his rights before taking statements apply to juveniles as well as to adults. If evidence is unlawfully seized and confessions are taken in violation of a youngster's constitutional rights while he is under juvenile court jurisdiction, they cannot be admitted as evidence against him in future proceedings if he is waived to circuit court.

Neglect Cases

Contact of the police officer with youngsters is not always for delinquent offenses; many times it will be of a noncriminal nature, such as with the dependent neglected child. The officer should investigate whether the neglect case is only one of many instances of parental abuse or whether it is an isolated situation. Usually individuals other than parents make the complaint, and therefore it is sometimes difficult to get the cooperation of the parents, especially in prolonged cases of neglect. The officer first has to make sure that neglect does exist and that the methods he uses in gathering evidence are similar to those he would use in any other situation, such as taking statements from witnesses and complainants, interviewing the parents and the children, and observing and evaluating the general situation. It is often helpful to use photographs in these cases, since they can sometimes vividly substantiate the circumstances that existed at the time of contact.

The officer will have to determine the seriousness of the situation and whether immediate action needs to be taken for the child's well-being. Many cases can be disposed of by a warning or a reprimand, with the officer informing the parents that any further complaints regarding their handling of their children may necessitate court action. The officer may also decide, because of circumstances involved and his belief that the parents will cooperate, to refer the family to a social agency for further help. Thus, it is important that the police officer know his community, the services available, and the agencies that can be utilized in all juvenile matters.

In circumstances where the officer determines that it is not a minor case of neglect or, while not necessarily serious, the parents are unwilling to cooperate and seek assistance from some other social agency, the officer may make a recommendation for a formal disposition. If informative records have been kept by his department, this will help him in determining the seriousness of the present occurrence and whether it is part of a pattern of neglect and abuse. The formal disposition (as well as informal referrals) should be a cooperative arrangement between all concerned agencies.

Taking Custody of Juvenile Offenders

Because the police have a wide range of discretionary powers, the officer does not necessarily have to take a child into custody but may immediately release the child, admonish the child, or do both, and allow the parents to take the child home. When taking a child into custody the officer has to use good judgment, paying particular attention to the youngster, his home conditions, his intent in the violation of the law, and the seriousness of the offense. Whether a child is taken into custody or whether some other alternative is utilized often depends upon the state or local statutes, the policies of the department, and the attitude of the community. For example, the authority by which a police officer can take a juvenile into custody, Section 712-A.14 of the compiled Michigan laws of 1948, as amended by Act 133 of the Public Laws of 1952, states that

> any municipal police officer, sheriff, or deputy sheriff, state police officer, county agent, or probationary officer of any court of record may without the order of the court immediately take into custody any child violating any law or ordinance, or whose surroundings are such as to endanger his health, morals, or welfare. Whenever any such officer or county agent takes a child coming within the provisions of this statute into custody he shall forthwith notify the parent or parents, guardian or custodian, if they can be found within the county. Unless the child requires immediate detention as here and after provided, the arresting officer shall accept the written promise of said parent or parents, guardian or custodian, to bring the child to the court at the time fixed therein. Thereupon such child shall be released to the custody of said parent or parents, guardian or custodian. If not so released, such child and his parents, guardian, or custodian, if they can be located, shall forthwith be brought before the court for preliminary hearing on his status and an order signed by the judge of probate authorizing the filing of a complaint shall be entered or the child shall be released to his parents, guardian, or custodian.

(Examples of Michigan laws will be given because they are representative of the statutes in most states and because Michigan juvenile laws were established according to guidelines provided by the federal government.)

The law of arrest without a warrant does not make any special provisions for the juvenile offender because of his age. Therefore, when the officer does take the child into custody, the child should be afforded the same rights as an adult, with age not being a consideration. It is in the police officer's and the child's best interests that when a juvenile is taken into custody without a warrant, the same safeguards be given to him as will be given to an adult who is arrested. If the child has committed a felony or a misdemeanor, but not in the presence of the officer, and the conditions present are detrimental to the child's welfare, the officer can provide the court with the necessary information to obtain a preliminary hearing. It would then be up to the court to decide whether the child and the parents should be ordered into court.

After the juvenile has been taken into custody, certain procedural rights and safeguards have to be considered before his parents are notified. As a result of the 1964 *Escobedo* v. *Illinois* decision, police officers are required to notify suspects of their right to legal counsel at the time of arrest.[9] This also applies to juveniles. The 1966 *Miranda* v. *Arizona* decision requires that suspects be advised of their rights before interrogation, or their confessions cannot be used in court.[10] The officer must advise the suspect of his right to remain silent and of his right to speak to an attorney and must inform him that if he wishes an attorney but cannot afford one the state will provide him with one. Finally, he is told that anything he says may be held against him. Even though the suspect may be an immature youth, the same safeguards have to be adhered to. The court has the jurisdiction to determine whether the youth, if he waived his rights, knew what he was doing and understood the circumstances. If the juvenile is processed further through the criminal justice system and comes in contact with an intake probation officer, the intake officer should also read the *Miranda* warnings to him. This will be double assurance then that the child's legal safeguards have been protected.

Notification of Parents

The officer who takes the child into custody is also responsible for notifying the child's parents. For example, Michigan juvenile court rules of 1969 not only require the notification of parents or guardians but also specify that a written record must be prepared and filed with the court indicating the names of persons notified, the time of notification, or what attempts were made to notify. Rule 2, Section 2, of the Michigan juvenile court rules defines the conditions under which an officer may take a juvenile into custody without a court order:

1. When a child is found violating any law or ordinance.
2. Conditions exist which make the arrest lawful if the child were an adult.

[9]Escobedo v. Illinois, 378 U.S. 478 (1964).
[10]Miranda v. Arizona, 384 U.S. 436 (1966).

3. The officer reasonably believes the child is evading the person or proper authority having legal custody.
4. Conditions or surroundings under which the child is found are such as to endanger his health, morals, or welfare.
5. The officer continues a lawful arrest made by a private citizen.

After parents have been notified, the juvenile still has the same constitutional right as an adult—he has the right to contact an attorney or have anyone of his choosing present during an interview. The basis for this is the 1963 Supreme Court decision which ruled on an appeal case of *Gideon v. Wainwright* that new trials could be demanded by anyone convicted of a crime without legal counsel.[11] The *Gideon* decision, the *Escobedo* decision,[12] and the *Miranda* decision[13] all apply to both adults and juveniles.

Interviewing the Juvenile Offender

Because the officer can have a great deal of influence, both positive and negative, he should be concerned about the methods he uses in discussing the situation with the juvenile. Many favorable as well as unfavorable impressions have been transmitted as a result of this first contact.

Once a juvenile has been taken into custody, he should be afforded all his rights. The officer should make at least a preliminary determination regarding the juvenile's participation in the immediate offense as well as the physical, psychological, and social condition of his environment. Interviewing techniques will vary from officer to officer, and as long as the child's rights have been transmitted to him, any reasonable interviewing method will usually be acceptable. Physical abuse, vulgarity, obscenity, profanity, or derogatory remarks cannot be tolerated while interviewing a juvenile. The reasons for this are obvious.

The officer is the symbol of authority, and because persons of authority in a child's past have often been negative authority figures and have abused him, he has every reason to impute the most negative aspects to the officer. The officer can change the child's negative perception if he treats the child fairly, but firmly. If the officer treats the child with respect, he can have a long-lasting impact on his future behavior and attitude toward other adults.

Fingerprinting and Photographing

Fingerprinting and photographing juveniles, as well as keeping records, often creates controversy. Even though these may be important tools for the police in detecting crime and preventing delinquency, they nevertheless have to be used with

[11]Gideon v. Wainwright, 372 U.S. 335 (1963).
[12]Escobedo, *idem.*
[13]Miranda, *idem.*

discretion. Records can be an important help not only to the police but to the community in preventing and treating juvenile delinquency. They are useful for providing background information on offenders who have had many contacts with the department as well as providing the community with data that can be helpful in establishing prevention programs.

The controversy about records revolves around the question of who is to see them and what data should be recorded. The officer has to use good judgment, but generally records should be kept in any case where a formal disposition is going to be necessary. There is some confusion over utilizing the records in other cases, and the specific procedure will vary from community to community.

Some states forbid both fingerprinting and photographing of children except when a special court order is issued. Different policies exist in different jurisdictions, and of course the officer working within the jurisdiction will have to know the policy of his area. Rule 10 of the Michigan juvenile court rules of 1969 states:

> Fingerprinting or photographing of children may be permitted by the court when the child is in custody or under investigation. Fingerprints and photographs shall be filed in a separate confidential file subject to being located and destroyed upon order of the judge. The child and his parent, parents, guardian, custodian, or duly appointed guardian shall be first advised of the right to counsel and shall have opportunity to consult with counsel before the child shall be required to appear in a show-up. All show-ups shall be conducted in the presence of counsel, either retained or appointed by the court to observe the show-up except in cases where an immediate show-up is necessary.

This rule also covers the procedure to be followed in placing the juvenile offender in a lineup. The rule is an outgrowth of *United States v. Wade*, which requires the presence of counsel at a lineup for adult prisoners.[14] This same constitutional safeguard also applies to juveniles.

There are many pros and cons for utilizing photographs, lineups, and fingerprints. The greatest objection is the association of these techniques with criminality and their closeness to criminal proceedings. These tools can be utilized very effectively, however, in making positive identification of youngsters in cases of runaway and can assist authorities in identifying a youngster when he does not give his name. Most juvenile court rules do make provisions enabling the police to obtain the authorization of the court to fingerprint and photograph when the youth is in custody or under investigation. There is usually no prohibition against fingerprinting and photographing upon consent of the parents, child, or attorney.

Fingerprints and photographs and records can undoubtedly be important aids in police work. If the overriding consideration is protecting the child, however, and at the same time protecting the community, fingerprints, photographs, and records will only be used when necessary.

[14]United States v. Wade, 338 U.S. 218.

Disposition of Juvenile Offender Taken into Custody

After taking a juvenile into custody and abiding by the legal safeguards and procedures that were outlined, the officer must again decide whether the child should return to his parents without a court referral or whether court action is necessary. This decision will be the result of investigating the situation, checking out the home conditions, and determining the juvenile's reasons for committing the offense, the parents' attitude, and the need for additional correctional treatment. The juvenile will generally be released to his parents if the offense is minor and there is no habitual delinquency pattern. If the relationship between the child and his parents is good and if there is not a pattern, the parents will usually be able to handle the situation.

The juvenile court judge is the final authority in determining whether the juvenile will be held in custody, and when the hearing will be. In regard to detention, Section 712A.15 of the compiled laws of Michigan, 1948, states:

Detention pending hearing shall be limited to the following children:
A. Those whose home conditions make immediate removal necessary.
B. Those who have run away from home.
C. Those whose offenses are so serious that release would endanger public safety.

The judge will make this determination upon request by the officer if the officer feels that immediate detention is warranted. If immediate detention is not warranted, the child will be released to his parents. The parents will provide a written promise to produce the child in court.

If a referral is made to the court, sufficient information should be provided by the officer. Even though the juvenile court conducts its own investigation, it revolves more around determining social and psychological factors, and hence the police report can help the judge make a meaningful determination. Some of the data that may be useful to the juvenile court from police reports are the name, address, birth date, race, religion, school, and grade of the offender, the name and address of both parents or guardian, a copy of the investigation report, which will include the facts of the offense, dates and nature of previous contacts with the juvenile, and the attitude of the juvenile, his parents, and the complainant.

Waiver of Juvenile to Adult Court

Some youngsters who, according to the statutory age limit imposed by the state, are close to adulthood may have been involved in repeated offenses and difficulties within the community. Because they have already been through the juvenile court and have utilized all community services, they sometimes cannot be helped under juvenile jurisdiction. A youngster may have reached the point where he is a detriment to himself and the community and where he will contaminate other youngsters incarcerated with him in juvenile facilities. The investigating officer provides the prosecuting attorney and the probate court judge with such information, which determines the severity of the offense so that a decision can be made regarding whether the offender should be prosecuted in adult court.

The legal procedure under the Michigan adult statutes can be found in Section 712A.4 of the compiled laws of 1948:

> In any case where a child over the age of 15 is accused of any act the nature of which constitutes a felony, the judge of probate of the county where the offense is alleged to have been committed may, after investigation and examination including notice to the prosecuting attorney and parents or guardians, if addresses are known, and upon the court's own motion or motion of the prosecuting attorney, waive jurisdiction. Thereupon it shall be lawful to try such child in the court having general criminal jurisdiction over such offense.

The flow chart in Figure 9 describes the general procedure for police handling of juveniles. Upon coming in contact with the juvenile the officer has the option to release him immediately or, in the case of a more serious infraction, release him to his parents. If the offense is so serious or the circumstances surrounding it are such that further action needs to be taken, the officer, upon releasing the youngster to his parents, receives a written agreement stating that they will produce the youngster. If the youngster is considered a threat to the community or to himself or if he has committed such a serious offense that it is deemed necessary that he be incarcerated, the officer can attempt to get a detention agreement. Under Michigan juvenile court rules this can be obtained for one of four reasons:

1. The child has run away.
2. The child has committed a serious offense that endangers the community.
3. The child is imperiled by his surroundings.
4. The child needs observation, study, and treatment.

During court hours the officer takes the child forthwith for a preliminary hearing. If it is outside court hours, the officer contacts a court official. Usually, in all jurisdictions, a court official is assigned to handle these matters on a twenty-four-hour basis. The court official can deny detention and then the officer releases the youngster, usually to his parents. The court official can also agree to detention pending the preliminary hearing, which has to take place within forty-eight hours. The youngster is given the Miranda warnings, and the decision is made to either authorize a petition or detain the child further pending hearing. If a petition is not authorized, the child is released to his parents. If a petition is authorized, the child then continues his processing through the juvenile court.

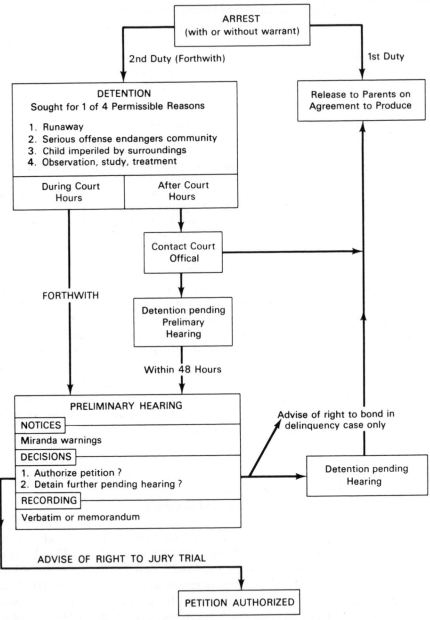

Prepared by Judge Robert L. Drake, Deputy Court Administrator, Michigan Supreme Court.

Figure 9   Flow Chart—Juvenile Court Under Michigan Juvenile Court Rules 1969

JUVENILE COURT PROCESSING AND PROCEDURE

A special study commission on juvenile justice in the state of California points out that all juvenile courts do not operate in the same manner and that their structure, philosophy, and activities are not uniform:

> There is considerable diversity in practice among the 58 counties of this state in terms of law enforcement procedures, probation functions, and juvenile court processes and decisions. As a result, whether or not a juvenile is arrested, placed in detention, or referred to the probation department, and whether or not the petition is dismissed, probation is granted, or a youth authority commitment is ordered by the juvenile court, seems to depend upon the community in which the offense is committed and upon the intrinsic merits of the individual case—there are not only variations in practices among the 58 counties, but equally varied is the nature and extent of services provided to juveniles by probation, law enforcement, and juvenile court judges.[15]

The procedure of the juvenile court begins with a complaint against the child which usually originates from a law enforcement agency, although it can originate from other sources. For example, school authorities can refer cases that are related to truancy, vandalism, and so on. Other agencies may also refer a child to the court, but generally the police are the major referral source.

Intake

Although the intake unit of the probation department is a screening process to determine the proper alternative and disposition for the youngster, it should be remembered that up to this point many youngsters have already been through the police screening process. Some of them have been released, while others may have been placed under voluntary supervision of the police. Police voluntary supervision does not take place in every jurisdiction, and it is probably not a common policy for most departments; mainly because of legal technicalities. The intake unit of the probation department, if it is a large department, will assign an intake worker to screen the incoming cases referred by the various agencies within the community. When the referral is made, the intake worker will review the case and the circumstances, verify the facts, and generally prepare a brief social history for the court. The case often goes no further than this, and the determination is made to release the child to his home or possibly to put the child under informal probation supervision by one of the probation officers. Many courts have the philosophy that it is

[15]*Special Study Commission on Juvenile Justice,* State of California, February 2, 1959.

far better to handle the youngster, if he needs supervision, in this informal manner without having him come in contact with the formal criminal justice court processes. As pointed out earlier, the further the child extends through the criminal justice system, the greater the chances are that he will be labeled delinquent, which has negative ramifications for him both in the immediate situation and in the future. Ideally, the records that are kept on juveniles are not supposed to be public, but in many cases certain data are released for various reasons, military induction being one.

If the youngster on informal probation has difficulty and it is deemed necessary that further action be taken, the probation officer who is supervising him can initiate a petition. Also, for those cases coming to the intake unit where further action is deemed immediately necessary, a petition will be originated right there without first putting the child on informal probation. The petition, which states the circumstances of the child's situation, precedes the *preliminary hearing,* which is set before a judge. The reason for the preliminary hearing is to decide if there are enough facts to warrant court action. The petition that originates this action can be a petition for a delinquent, a dependent, a neglect, or any other type of juvenile case. The petition can be signed by any authorized person—a police officer, the probation officer who was supervising the child if he was on informal probation or a citizen. The parents are notified of this action. If the youngster is going to be waived to circuit court, he has to be provided the legal safeguards stated in the *Kent* case: a hearing, counsel, the right of counsel to see the court reports, and a statement by the judge in writing as to his reasons for the waiver.[16]

The *Gault* decision states that there has to be adequate notice in writing of the charge, and verification of the child's right to counsel at the hearing has to be made unless it was intelligently waived. There is also a privilege against self-incrimination unless intelligently waived, and in the absence of a valid admission, determination of delinquency rests upon sworn testimony in open court.[17]

Adjudication Hearing

At the adjudication hearing the youth is questioned about the offense, the circumstances, and the facts that have been presented. The petition may be dismissed at this hearing if there is not enough evidence. If there is a finding of delinquency (or neglect, etc.), a new court date is set for the disposition hearing. The lapse between the adjudication hearing and the disposition allows the court to assign a probation officer to make a report called the *social investigation.*

Disposition Hearing

There is supposed to be enough time between the adjudication hearing and the disposition hearing to allow the probation officer to make a social investigation.

[16]Kent, *idem.*
[17]In re Gault, 387 U.S. 1 (1967).

At the disposition hearing the judge uses this investigation to decide what alternatives will be most appropriate for the child. The social investigation includes an evaluation of the child's environment, the interrelationships of the child and his family, the child's attitude and behavior in his neighborhood, his community, and his school, the amount of supervision he gets at home, the circumstances regarding his difficulty, and the ability of the parents to provide supervision and guidance at home. The probation officer can consult neighbors, school counselors, teachers, and any other persons who may know the youngster. After the judge has the social investigation, he may also question the parents or the probation officer to elaborate upon material that may or may not be a part of the social investigation. After considering all the relevant factors in the case, the judge will make a disposition. He can:

1. Release the child to his parents.
2. Place the child on probation.
3. Commit the child to an institution.
4. Utilize a foster home placement.
5. Make the child a ward of the court so that he can receive necessary medical services or other supervision, especially in cases of neglect.

In severe cases of neglect, the court can also sever some parental rights. This option is not often used because taking children away from their natural parents is a very difficult decision to make.

The determining factor in the disposition should not be what is convenient for the state or economically feasible for the court. The overriding consideration should be selecting the alternative that is best for the child.

Additional Legal Safeguards

It should also be remembered that the child is entitled to the same legal safeguards that are given to the adult. This is even more relevant today with the recent Supreme Court decisions. Some of the other legal safeguards that are provided to juveniles will be briefly highlighted.

Whether the juvenile proceeding is civil or criminal, the *Winship* case stated that

> in effect the court of appeals distinguished the proceedings in question here from a criminal prosecution by use of what Gault called a civil label of convenience, which has been attached to juvenile court proceedings—we made clear in that decision that civil labels and good intentions do not themselves obviate the need for criminal due process safeguards in juvenile courts.[18]

In regard to self-incrimination, the same legal safeguards apply to juveniles that apply to adults. Even when confessions are obtained after advising the child of

[18]In re Winship, 38 L. W. 4253 (1970).

his rights, there can be questions of whether the child was intelligent enough to understand the warnings and whether the waiver was given voluntarily. The *Gallegos* case stated:

> The youth of the petitioner, the long detention, the failure to send for his parents, the failure immediately to bring him before the judge of the juvenile court, the failure to see to it that he had advice of a lawyer or friend—all these combined to make us conclude that the formal confession on which this conviction may have rested was obtained in violation of due process.[19]

The *Gault* decision also made reference to this subject:

> It would be entirely unrealistic to carve out of the Fifth Amendment all statements by juveniles on the grounds that these cannot lead to criminal involvement. In the first place, juvenile proceedings to determine delinquency, which may lead to commitment to a state institution, must be regarded as criminal for the purpose of the privilege against self-incrimination. We conclude that the constitutional privilege against self-incrimination is applicable in the case of juveniles as it is with respect to adults.[20]

Finally, in a recent landmark Supreme Court decision regarding juveniles, the *Winship* case also commented on evidence beyond a reasonable doubt in juvenile cases:

> We therefore hold in agreement with Chief Judge Fuld in dissent in the Court of Appeals that when a 12-year-old is charged with an act of stealing which renders him liable to confinement for as long as six years and as a matter of due process—the case against him must be proved beyond a reasonable doubt.[21]

Dispositional Alternatives

Of the dispositional alternatives that the judge has, the alternative of sending the child back to his home is of course self-explanatory. The second alternative, probation, is a service provided by the court which compels the child to meet certain requirements established by the court and carried out under the supervision of a probation officer. The major requirement is that the youngster meet with the probation officer during a specified period of time. Probation is a trial period during which the youngster attempts to mobilize his own resources as well as those of the community and, under the supervision of the probation officer, become rehabilitated. The length of probation can range from a few months to a few years. While the youngster is on probation, it is expected that the resources presented to him will be utilized and that the supervision and guidance which he did not get in

[19]Gallegos v. Colorado, 370 U.S. 49 (1962).
[20]Gault, *idem.*
[21]Winship, *idem.*

his home will help him to succeed not only on probation but also in the community when he is released from probation.

If the probationer abides by the rules set by the court, under the supervision of the probation officer, and satisfactorily completes the requirements, he is then released from probation and expected to make a successful adjustment in the community. If he is not successful on probation and becomes involved in recurring difficulties, another plan may be made for him. This plan could include incarceration in a training school or placement in a setting that would provide more stringent supervision and guidance, such as a halfway house.

Chapter 8, "Prevention Programs," will discuss institutional facilities, another alternative available to the judge. Chapter 10, "An Example: Community-Based Treatment Programs," will discuss such services as halfway houses. Upon release from the training school or another residential facility, the child is often supervised by an aftercare worker, a parole officer, or some person with a similar title. The supervision is similar to what the child would have received had he not been incarcerated and had he been placed on probation.

In some states the court has jurisdiction over aftercare services, while in other states they are the responsibility of such departments as the Department of Social Welfare or Social Services. Regardless of the administrative structure, the basic concept is to provide supervision and guidance because the youngster is not ready to experience total freedom in his community.

Conclusion

This section has discussed the procedure that policemen, court personnel, and other relevant community agencies should follow when handling the juvenile delinquent. It should again be emphasized that the successful handling of the delinquent can only take place in an atmosphere of cooperation between all agencies involved. Effective utilization of the resources available within the community is also necessary to insure the successful treatment and rehabilitation of the juvenile.

A CASE STUDY

The process of handling the juvenile from the first contact with the police to a disposition by the court can be illustrated by the following case study.[22]

The case involves a youngster whom we will call John Smith. John is fifteen years of age and lives in Marquette, Michigan. The contact John has with the Lansing, Michigan, police is the result of his being stopped for a traffic infraction. John is unable to produce a driver's license or a registration for his vehicle. The

[22]Developed and coordinated by Sgt. Ray C. Valley, Michigan State Police, East Lansing, Michigan.

officers, because they are suspicious, make a quick radio check with their head-quarters and determine that the car was stolen in John's hometown. John is apprehended for unlawfully driving away an automobile (felony), for failing to stop at a red light, and for not having an operator's license or a vehicle registration on his person.

After a short conversation John tells the officers that he stole the car in Marquette and that he would like to talk about the incident.[23] At this point the officers are obliged to (1) advise John of his constitutional rights, (2) determine his age, which in this case is easily learned through other identification that John has on him, (3) obtain the address of John's mother and father because it is necessary to contact them immediately and notify them of the detention of their child, who is four hundred miles away from home. A record of the notification is also made.[24]

The officers make contact with John's parents, and the parents give a verbal waiver which allows the officers to interview John. The local probate court is contacted, and the judge gives his verbal agreement that custody and detainment is advisable in this case and that a petition will be signed later in the morning.[25]

The vehicle John is driving has the original license plates on it, as determined by a check of the owner, who lives in Marquette. The owner is advised that the vehicle is being held in Lansing. The owner states that John has taken the auto-mobile without permission, hence verifying that the vehicle was stolen.

The officers take John to the juvenile home where he is lodged, and a custody statement is filed.[26]

John, acting somewhat remorseful, states again that he would like to talk about the circumstances under which he stole the automobile. The officers again advise him of his constitutional rights before interviewing him and request that he sign a waiver. The officers make the determination that he is sophisticated and intelligent enough to make this waiver.[27]

The next morning a probation officer is assigned by the local judge to act as John's guardian until he is returned to his home community.[28] The probation officer decides to advise John against further interviews by the police officers, and all interviews are terminated.[29]

[23]Gallegos, *idem* (limitation re interrogation of minors); Miranda, *idem* (interrogation of suspects).

[24]Officer's custody statement and record of notification to parent, guardian, or cus-todian (the specific form used in this case and following examples will depend on the state).

[25]People v. Roberts, 364 Mich. 60 (duty to take before court, 1961); in re Mathers 371 Mich. 516 (adequacy of petition, 1964).

[26]Obinetz v. Buddo, 315 Mich. 512 (statement of custody).

[27]Hailing v. U.S., 295 Fed. 161 (use of admissions following waiver, 1961); Reddick v. U.S., 326 Fed. 650 (admissibility of conversations with police, 1964); Gault, *idem*.

[28]Michigan juvenile code, 12A, 14 (juvenile in custody; detention areas. ". . . child to be completely isolated so as to prevent any verbal, visual or physical contact with any adult prisoner.").

[29]Kent, *idem*.; Gallegos, *idem*.

Arrangements are made to have John meet with the probate judge that morning at 10:00 A.M., at which time the officers request an authorization for a petition. The petition is authorized, it is signed by the officers, and the following charges are made before the judge: (1) unlawful driving away of an automobile, (2) no operator's license, (3) no vehicle registration, (4) failure to stop for a red light. The petition must allege the facts with particularity.[30]

The preliminary inquiry is held before the judge. John, the officers, the probation officer, and John's parents are present. At this time the judge decides that since the automobile was stolen in another community, John should be tried and a disposition should be made in that community. John is then returned to Marquette by juvenile authorities of that community.[31]

If the judge had determined that John could return with his parents, a bond might have been required to assure that John would appear before his home court.[32]

It is determined before John's leaving for home that fingerprints and a photograph will be helpful, and permission is granted by the court.[33]

Summary of procedures thus far:

1. Custody was taken when subject was apprehended for a felony and misdemeanors.
2. Juvenile was advised of his constitutional rights.
3. Parents were contacted and notified of apprehension, and the time was recorded.
4. Probate court was contacted: detention was requested and was granted by the court.
5. Waiver was obtained before interviewing the juvenile.
6. Request for a petition was made and granted.
7. Petition was signed, and alleged facts were set forth with particularity.
8. After the judge had considered all the facts, John was transferred to the jurisdiction of his home community.
9. Petitions for fingerprinting and photographing were approved by the court.
10. John was returned to his home community.

In Marquette the juvenile authorities are presented with the information that has been compiled thus far by the Ingham County Probate Court. After reviewing the information and again being advised of his constitutional rights, John is released to his parents. The parents sign a written release assuring the court that John will be present when a time is designated.[34]

[30]Gault, *idem.*

[31]State statutes relating to the transfer of juveniles.

[32]State statutes relating to the right to bond.

[33]State statutes relating to fingerprinting and photographing juveniles.

[34]State statutes relating to duty to release the juvenile upon assurance of parents that he will appear before court when requested.

The preceding steps taken in court are part of the preliminary hearing, which must be held forty-eight hours from the time the juvenile is taken into custody. Since the purpose of the hearing is to determine if there are enough facts to support court action and if protection or supervision of the court is necessary, in most cases the hearing is informal and a lawyer is not required. Where a felony has been committed, however, such as in the present case, an attorney can and probably will be called.[35] There are two more phases of court hearings, an adjudication hearing and a disposition hearing.[36]

The adjudication hearing is considered a part of the preliminary hearing, and both this hearing and the disposition hearing usually have stenographic equipment to record what takes place. States differ in their requirements, but if no specific law exists, there is usually a probate rule or a written memorandum referring to the use of stenographic or mechanical equipment.

The adjudication hearing determines whether the child will come under the jurisdiction of the court. The child and his parents or a guardian ad litem are present. All witnesses and evidence or facts are now brought before the court. The juvenile has the right to waive his right to counsel or to retain counsel at this time. If the juvenile does not understand his constitutional rights, the judge appoints counsel for him. The judge does this if he feels that the child will not adequately be represented by the parents. The request for an attorney is made in writing, stating the names of the parties represented. The attorney is furnished copies of all pleadings.[37]

In regard to the hearing being held before a jury, there is some confusion over this matter and most states do not allow jury trial for juveniles.

At the adjudication hearing for John, the facts presented are sufficient and a disposition hearing date is set. The probation department is requested to do a social investigation of John to provide the judge with adequate information so that a meaningful disposition can be made. If a youngster pleads guilty to an offense and if his parents and his attorney consent, the disposition phase can sometimes be held immediately.

The plea of guilty has much more significance in adult court. In juvenile cases the emphasis is not on guilt or innocence, but on individualized justice. There is concern not only with the incident but with the future welfare of the child as well. The social investigation is important in contributing to this end.

In the case of John, a probation officer conducts a social investigation including the factors that were mentioned earlier.

The dispositional hearing determines what measures the court will take in selecting an alternative that will be most beneficial to John. The allegations are read and presented, and John and his parents are again advised of their right to counsel.

[35]Escobedo, *idem* (right to counsel); Gault, *idem* (right of child and parent to be notified).

[36]Gault, *idem*.; in re Mathers, 371 Mich. 516 (1964).

[37]Gault, *idem.*

John is also advised of his right to remain silent and his right to cross-examination. A record of the proceedings is also made.[38]

After all the facts are considered, the judge makes a determination as to the disposition of the case. The alternatives open to the judge were mentioned earlier.

Probation is usually the alternative selected, and in the present case, John is placed on probation. It is determined that his offense is not an indication of a pattern of delinquent or criminal behavior and that he can be helped at home and can be guided and supervised by a probation officer. In John's case, it is determined that he stole the car upon a dare from friends after they had been involved in "drinking." John and his friends were only going to take the car for a short ride, but they were having so much fun driving the automobile that they impulsively decided to take it out of town. John is to report to a probation officer for two years, and he cannot apply for a driver's license until he is released from probation.

SUMMARY

This chapter has focused on the processing and handling of juveniles through the various components of the criminal justice system. The three major components discussed were the police, the intake division of the probation department, and the juvenile court. A case study was utilized to illustrate the procedure involved. The next chapter will discuss prevention programs. Effective prevention would of course reduce or even eliminate the need for processing juveniles through the criminal justice system.

QUESTIONS AND PROJECTS

Essay Questions

1. Should the police be given more discretion or less discretion in their handling of juveniles?
2. With all the recent Supreme Court rulings, has the handling of juveniles become too legalistic?
3. How can a community guard against "assembly line" justice within its criminal justice system?
4. Why do some communities have much more effective procedures for handling youngsters than other communities?
5. Why are some juvenile cases handled informally by the court while others are processed through formal channels?

[38]Gault, *idem.*

Projects

1. Develop the ideal criteria that should be applied when selecting a juvenile court judge.
2. Develop a list of alternatives that the community can use in place of formally exposing the youngster to the juvenile court.
3. Develop an information services program that alerts the community to the needs of its youngsters and keeps the community abreast of new developments.

8

PREVENTION PROGRAMS

Juvenile delinquency prevention is one of the most elusive concepts now existing in criminological theory, thought, and literature. Many contemporary prevention programs and treatment approaches make assumptions about human behavior which often do not have a firm basis in either science or causal relationships. Furthermore, there is not a great deal of evidence that either proves or disproves the effectiveness of the many treatment approaches, programs, and strategies.

Early efforts at delinquency prevention and the establishment of programs and strategies were usually local endeavors initiated by privately supported family-centered agencies and groups. Urbanization necessitated that both private and public agencies become involved in delinquency prevention because of the immensity of the problem and the complexities of the urban society.

In recent years a wide variety of community, state, and national agencies have become involved in delinquency prevention, control, and treatment. Most of these efforts, however, have been independent and uncoordinated.

By the mid-1950's the delinquency prevention effort in virtually every large city was like a jigsaw puzzle of services involving important government departments which had heretofore operated with relative independence. The agencies concerned with delinquency prevention included the schools, recreation departments, public housing authorities, public welfare departments giving family service and administering child welfare, private social agencies and health departments and other medical facilities (including psychiatric hospitals and clinics). The size, shape, and strength and position (role in the community) of the various pieces of the delinquency prevention picture varied greatly from one city to another—the format for delinquency prevention services varied from city to city partly because the coordinating agency in each city is the one which happened to be the strongest.[1]

Many other problems also hinder delinquency prevention efforts, and often a coordinated endeavor by the community does not exist.

A general lack of communication between agencies and between disciplines was increasingly evident and variations in policies between agencies often made it impossible for them to function effectively together for the benefit of the child.[2]

The absence of rigorous evaluation has been criticized in relation to most delinquency prevention and treatment programs, and the importance of proper evaluation cannot be overstressed. Both the lay public and the criminal justice practitioner have particular methods for addressing the problems of delinquency. In the competitive marketplace, however, evaluation is absolutely essential when making judgments about alternative strategies for delinquency prevention, control, and treatment. The social policy implications are obvious.

Wilkins points out that

the best research in the fields of criminology and penology seldom seems to do more than clarify the unknown. It is doubtful whether even the most enthusiastic research worker in these fields could sustain a claim to having added significantly to knowledge. Myths and beliefs of the past have little or no support when subjected to rigorous examination, but in their place only the most tentative suggestions can be brought forward. This is perhaps to be expected and hardly to be regretted. More regrettable is the fact that all too often research ends by noting nothing more significant than that the questions with which the project began were inappropriate. But these types of research are in the main the most satisfactory studies. Most research projects make larger or more practical claims and usually lack validity when subjected to critical assessment.[3]

Two types of delinquency prevention will be discussed in this chapter: *pure prevention*, or primary prevention, which attempts to inhibit delinquency before it takes place; and *rehabilitative prevention*, or secondary prevention, which treats the youngster once he has come in contact with the formal criminal justice system. Rehabilitative prevention, if effective, can also be considered a preventive mechanism if the treatment provided deters future delinquent behavior. Pure prevention

[1]*Juvenile Delinquency Prevention in the United States,* U.S. Department of Health, Education, and Welfare, Children's Bureau, 1965, p. 12.

[2]*Ibid.,* p. 17.

[3]Leslie T. Wilkins, *Evaluation of Penal Measures* (New York: Random House, Inc., 1969), p. 28.

therefore deals primarily with youngsters who have not been adjudicated delinquent, whereas rehabilitative prevention deals with youngsters who have been adjudicated delinquent.

Other typologies have been used to classify programs that attempt to prevent, control, and treat delinquency. Lejins describes the following typology:

> The ambiguity of the concept of prevention is one of the main obstacles to discussing prevention meaningfully to obtain generally significant research data and even to describing existing preventive programs. The term prevention refers to several different types of societal action, so different in fact that in most cases a clarification of the particular type of prevention in question is indispensable to making communication meaningful. Three types of prevention or three distinct meanings of the concept can be differentiated: punitive prevention, corrective prevention, and mechanical prevention.[4]

Punitive prevention is the threat of punishment under the hypothesis that punishment will presumably forestall the criminal act. *Corrective prevention* refers to the attempt to eliminate potential causes, factors, or motivations before the criminal behavior actually takes place. *Mechanical prevention* emphasizes placing obstacles in the way of the potential criminal so that he will find it difficult or impossible to commit an offense. Increased security measures and increased police protection are mechanical efforts at prevention.

Sullivan and Bash use a different type of classification for prevention programs. Like Lejins's classification, theirs includes a three-phase typology:

> 1. Programs that have explicit primary functions and goals involving deliberate intervention in the lives of specifically identified individuals for the expressed purpose of preventing the occurrence of behavior that would label them as antisocial or as delinquent by the laws and rules of general society.
> 2. Programs that have explicit primary goals of planned intervention and participation in the development, employment and organization of interrelationships of various social institutions, groups, and agencies within the community with the intention of preventing formation of patterns of delinquent behavior in specific individuals or groups.
> 3. Programs that have explicit primary goals of deliberate participation in the special processes of reviewing laws, social policies, and public attitudes that have a specific and direct relevance to activities designed to prevent delinquency.[5]

Lejins's typology differentiates prevention programs by their goals and the means utilized to obtain goal achievement. Sullivan and Bash differentiate programs by their service orientation.

---

[4]Peter Lejins, "The Field of Prevention," in *Delinquency Prevention: Theory and Practice*, ed. William Amos and Charles Wellford (Englewood Cliffs, N.J.: Prentice-Hall, Inc., 1967), p. 3.

[5]Clyde Sullivan and Carrie Bash, "Current Programs for Delinquency Prevention," in Amos and Wellford, *op. cit.*, pp. 61-62.

Although the pure prevention and rehabilitation prevention dichotomy was selected to facilitate discussion, it is difficult to pigeonhole prevention efforts into such neat categories because many programs include both adjudicated and non-adjudicated youngsters. Most programs range in the continuum from pure prevention to rehabilitative prevention.

An overview of both pure prevention and rehabilitative prevention programs follows.[6] Many of the programs, however, will be middle-range-type efforts which extend services both to youngsters who have been adjudicated and to those who have not come in contact with the formal criminal justice system. An example of a middle-range program is the Youth Services Bureau concept in the state of Massachusetts:

> The Governor's Public Safety Committee in Massachusetts has developed a Youth Services Bureau emphasizing mental health and special services for referred youth. The Bureau, which serves two communities, has a mental health orientated staff and involves young people in policy decisions and program development. Youth are referred to the Center by schools, police, courts and parents. . . . For each young person referred, the Bureau does a complete diagnostic examination, after which the youth is usually referred to a particular program or agency in the community for specialized treatment. Each young person referred from the Bureau is followed by the community specialists to insure that he or she has received the treatment or services recommended.[7]

The Youth Services Bureau often serves as an alternative to exposing the youngster to the formal court procedures and the stigmatization that often ensues. It can assist almost all children except those who are involved in the serious types of difficulty that endanger both themselves and the community.

> The Youth Services Bureau would provide services ranging from remedial education to psychiatric diagnosis and treatment, either directly through its staff of professional workers and volunteers or by referral to other community agencies whose services should be purchased by the bureau. The Bureau would develop those services lacking in the community, thereby insuring comprehensive services for children rather than becoming a coordinator of existing services. For if the Bureau is viewed as the coordinator of existing services, those services presently lacking in the community will not be provided, and the cooperation of the existing agencies, which seems resistant to the organization of a community 'coordinator' will be more difficult to obtain. The Bureau must be able to offer short-term crisis oriented case work through its full-time professional staff who should have ready access to the services of a psychologist and psychiatrist for assistance in diagnosis and for consultation.[8]

[6]*Annual Report of Federal Activities in Juvenile Delinquency, Youth Development and Related Fields*, U.S. Department of Health, Education, and Welfare, Social and Rehabilitation Service, 1971, pp. 130-32.

[7]*Ibid.*, p. 19-20.

[8]G. David Schiering, "A Proposal for the More Effective Treatment of the 'Unruly' Child in Ohio," in *Diverting Youth from the Correctional System*, U.S. Department of Health, Education, and Welfare, Youth Service Bureau, 1971, p. 77.

The Youth Services Bureau concept is valuable because it can provide services to both adjudicated and nonadjudicated youngsters.

Regardless of the particular type of prevention or treatment program attempted by the community, however, the effort will be meaningless unless the community understands the program, accepts its concepts, and is willing to support it.[9] The efforts of program innovators and initiators will be futile if the community does not understand the seriousness of the problem.

> For example, a community may fail to support and use psychiatric services in a child guidance clinic but may grab at simple solutions such as curfews, banning comics or restricting movie attendance.[10]

There are no simple solutions to delinquency prevention, control, and treatment. Community support is needed so that resources can be provided and well-organized programs based on solid theory and investigation can be initiated. If such programs have community support and built-in methods of evaluation, they will have greater chance of success than piecemeal efforts that do not incorporate these ingredients.

> If the available youth servicing agencies and organizations are to be improved, if needed services not presently available are to be procured, if all resources are to be so articulated that the specialized needs of pre-delinquent and delinquent children are to be met at the strategic time and with the most promising prescription of service, two conditions must prevail: (1) there must be a continuous study of local youth problems and local youth servicing agencies and (2) there must be some community system or body established that will ensure overall organization, planning and coordination of services to all youth.[11]

PURE PREVENTION PROGRAMS

Most pure prevention programs are community endeavors that attempt to identify the conditions and problems that contribute to crime and delinquency. In general, there has been little evaluation of prevention programs. Many of the programs that will be discussed in this section are fairly new, which precludes intensive evaluative comments. Other programs were established under less than optimal conditions, and their planning and implementation did not facilitate meaningful research and evaluation. Wooton mentions that it is difficult to evaluate many delinquency programs because

> they produced insignificant material, because their statistical findings could not be divorced from the tests or were presented in a form which defied

[9]William Kvaraceus, *The Community and the Delinquent* (New York: The World Book Company, 1954), p. 162.

[10]*Ibid.*, p. 162.

[11]*Ibid.*, p. 163.

comparative use or because the samples used were inadequate. Thus, Shaw and McKay's famous ecological study and Lander's Baltimore investigation were excluded on the first grounds, while other studies are excluded because of the latter reason.[12]

The federal government has made vigorous attempts to prevent delinquency and has provided financial support through its various departments. It has also focused on many of the contributing factors to determine methods for successful prevention, control, and treatment. The cross sections of federal government programs that follow are not comprehensive, nor are all government efforts mentioned, but they do present a realistic overview.

Federal Government Efforts

Department of Health, Education, and Welfare. The activities of the Department of Health, Education, and Welfare range from mental health services to educational research and training programs. One of the programs related to delinquency prevention is the Upward Bound Program, which is directly administered by the Office of Education and provides services to the young.

Upward Bound is a precollege preparatory program designed to generate the skills and motivation necessary for success in education among young people from low-income families who do not have adequate secondary school preparation.

> Students must meet income criteria established by the commissioner. Upward Bound consists of a summer program lasting from six to eight weeks and continues through the academic year with programs on Saturdays, tutorial sessions during the week, and periodic cultural enhancement programs.[13]

Youngsters involved in this program are encouraged to complete secondary school training and, if advisable, to pursue a college education. Schools that are involved in the program are given financial support by the federal government.

Because the program focuses on disadvantaged youth and provides them with skills necessary to adapt in their environment and achieve satisfying rewards, many youngsters are given an opportunity fo fulfill these goals who would otherwise not have been able to do so through conventional community services. This program is focused not only on preventing delinquency but also on reducing delinquency. It helps those youngsters who, without the program, often become exposed to the criminal justice system.

Department of Housing and Urban Development. The Model Cities Program is administered by the Department of Housing and Urban Development. Model Cities was established under the Demonstration Cities and Metropolitan Develop-

---

[12]B. Wooten, *Social Science and Social Pathology* (London: George Allen and Unwin Ltd., 1957).

[13]*Annual Report of Federal Activities*, p. 79.

ment Act of 1966 and provides grants to communities to conduct projects in a number of urban areas with high rates of delinquency.

> Typical projects supported include juvenile aftercare centers, group foster homes for pre-delinquents and delinquents, youth councils, recreation-oriented activities, teen centers, vocational training centers, scholarship programs for disadvantaged youths, youth employment placement centers, drop-in centers, service centers for teen-age unwed mothers, youth leadership training activities, programs to reduce the incidence of school drop-outs, new careers programs, youth enterprises programs, legal services to youth, college preparation programs, youth medical careers projects, youth police aid projects, narcotics and substance abuse prevention and rehabilitation activities, and several programs conducted under the auspices of the Big Brother and Upward Bound organizations.[14]

Communities that have effectively utilized the Model Cities Program have developed projects that attempt to determine the causes of crime and social problems as well as define solutions and focus efforts on combating delinquency and crime. Projects that focus on youth can be helpful in reducing crime and delinquency by identifying the causes of social problems and then implementing efforts that relate to problem solving.

Department of Justice. The Law Enforcement Assistance Administration (LEAA) under the Department of Justice created by Title I of the Omnibus Crime Control and Safe Streets Act, has three basic objectives: (1) to encourage state and local governments to prepare plans for comprehensive law enforcement, (2) to improve and strengthen law enforcement through grants to state and local governments, and (3) to encourage research in crime control and prevention.

> Police, courts and corrections are the major concerns of LEAA. The approaches to these areas vary because the states set their own priorities; however, every aspect to the nation's crime problem is being reviewed including the serious juvenile crime problem.[15]

Grants provided by LEAA have been used to facilitate these objectives. Not only are problem areas identified, but youngsters are actively involved in program development and problem solving. Programs such as the control and prevention of gang violence, which was initiated in Philadelphia, have been developed. In this particular project, resources were utilized and the ideas from many academic disciplines incorporated to prevent gang violence and reduce the potential of youngsters' becoming involved in civil disorders. A project in San Antonio, Texas, has as its objective the reducing of juvenile delinquency by offering an educational program for parents and offenders, which includes counseling and job placement services.[16]

[14]*Ibid.,* p. 83.
[15]*Ibid.,* p. 89.
[16]*Ibid.,* p. 90.

The major thrust of the projects developed to reduce juvenile delinquency has been to identify causal factors through research so that solutions to the problems can be given.

Department of Agriculture. Federal extension services under the Department of Agriculture provide programs for youngsters which can often indirectly contribute to reducing juvenile delinquent activities. The 4-H program operated under the Federal Extension Services branch of the Department of Agriculture has become even more involved in preventing delinquency in urban areas:

> Cooperative Extension Service agents work through schools, churches, service clubs, public housing directors, juvenile correctional institutions, neighborhood councils and centers, community action panels, etc., to introduce 4-H programs and methods. Professional Extension staff are assisting in the program through the use of paid program assistance and by volunteer adult and teen-age leaders.[17]

For example, in Providence, Rhode Island, Cooperative Extension Service attempts to reach troubled youngsters in deprived areas through such means as the establishment of storefront offices within the inner city. VISTA workers and volunteers become involved with community residents in problem solving. Hartford, Connecticut, has initiated a program that helps Puerto Rican youths, as well as other community youngsters. An urban 4-H agent is employed and is assigned to the inner city to help youngsters develop socially acceptable behavioral alternatives. In Wilmington, Delaware, Cooperative Extension Service is working with the city to establish and maintain various youth centers. These facilities provide recreational activities for city youngsters who do not have the money or the opportunity to satisfy their needs in a socially acceptable manner.

Federal extension programs under the Department of Agriculture have mainly served rural youths, but because of an increased awareness of the many problems that exist in urban areas an attempt is being made to provide resources to the cities so that many of these problems can be eliminated or alleviated. The resources provided by the government to these communities can be helpful in identifying problems and initiating programs for their solution.

Department of Labor. The United States Department of Labor Manpower Administration operates three types of youth serving activities under the Neighborhood Youth Corps program authorized by the Economic Opportunity Act of 1964.

> The in-school program provides part-time employment, on-the-job training and useful work experience for youths still in school or in need of money to remain in school. The out-of-school program provides work and training and sufficient supportive services to obtain meaningful employment for unemployed or underemployed low-income persons. The summer program is

[17]*Ibid.,* p. 107.

designed to offer training, work experience and income to help disadvantaged students to return to school in the fall.[18]

One of the main programs of the Neighborhood Youth Corps, which was inaugurated in 1965, involves working in the poorest and most disadvantaged areas within inner-city limits. It focuses resources in these areas to help alleviate problems which have often resulted from extreme poverty conditions. In 1968 more than 620,000 youths from disadvantaged areas of the city were enrolled under the auspices of the Neighborhood Youth Corps. Of this number, the Manpower Administration reports that 70 percent have improved themselves after termination of their youth corps projects.[19]

Office of Economic Opportunity. The Office of Economic Opportunity also provides services that either directly or indirectly relate to delinquency prevention. Its Office of Program Development has become involved in several attempts at programs that affect both delinquent juveniles and predelinquent juveniles.

> Through 409 Community Action Agencies, the office administers a youth development program. Despite its emphasis in 1969 on summer recreation, the program is moving toward a year-round project . . . The OEO Office of Health Affairs also funded nine projects dealing with rehabilitation of young addicts in the fiscal year of 1970 . . . These comprehensive drug rehabilitation programs are operated through Community Action Agencies or their delegate organizations.[20]

The programs under OEO, as well as other federal programs previously discussed, are an effort by the government to funnel resources into areas with high rates of crime and delinquency in an attempt at social problem solving. Many of these efforts are relatively new, and therefore it is difficult to generalize about their successes or failures until more meaningful and valid research and program evaluation is available. It should be pointed out, however, that programs of this type can be effective in reducing delinquency and preventing many youngsters from becoming involved in delinquent activities. Resources funneled into areas of high rates of crime and delinquency can be effectively utilized to develop favorable alternatives in behavioral adjustment for youngsters who are not exposed to an adequate opportunity structure. Cooperative endeavors by the federal government and local communities can facilitate the development of pure prevention programs which will improve community conditions and help reduce delinquency and crime.

The next section of the chapter will discuss further efforts at community problem solving. Many of these programs are funded at least partially by the federal government, but like many of the federal activities and programs mentioned, they

[18]*Ibid.,* p. 109.

[19]*The Neighborhood Youth Corps: Hope and Help for Youth,* U.S. Department of Health, Education, and Welfare, Manpower Administration, 1969, p. 6.

[20]*Annual Report of Federal Activities,* p. 111.

have not been subjected to appropriate testing and therefore it is difficult to evaluate them objectively.

Community-Based Programs

The Chicago Area Project. One of the earliest projects to deal with the problem of juvenile delinquency as well as other social problems was the Chicago Area Project. The project operated on the assumption that

> much of the delinquency in the slum areas is to be attributed to lack of neighborhood cohesiveness and to the consequent lack of concern on the part of many residents about the welfare of children. The project strives to counteract this situation through encouraging local self-help enterprises through which a sense of neighborliness and mutual responsibility will develop. It is expected that delinquency will decline as youngsters become better integrated into community life and therefore influenced by the values of conventional society rather than by those of the underworld.[21]

The project concentrated its efforts in areas of high delinquency and crime in an attempt to mobilize the support of the community so that delinquency could be prevented and new opportunity structures provided for area residents. Such programs as the sponsorship of recreation projects, a campaign for community improvement, and other efforts directed at helping youngsters were initiated. Both professional and volunteer workers in the community made contact with those youngsters who were identified as needing assistance. The personalized service and the concentration of resources in the area was felt to contribute to more effective problem solving in the Chicago area. Even though objective research of the success of the program is minimal, this was a very early attempt to mobilize community resources in high crime areas to ensure that the youngsters of the area would be provided with the opportunity to adjust to their environment satisfactorily. It was felt that if legitimate opportunities were provided for youngsters, much of the frustration and strain that exist in the disadvantaged areas of large cities could be reduced and this could have a direct impact on reducing crime and delinquency.

The Midcity Project. The Midcity Project was initiated in a lower-socio-economic class district of Boston in 1954 to reduce the amount of illegal activity engaged in by local adolescents.[22] The focus was somewhat similar to that of the Chicago Area Project because of its thrust in a large inner-city area to reduce and prevent crime and delinquency. This multifaceted program had as one of its major goals the improving of coordination and cooperation between the existing social agencies of the community. In addition, the project attempted to identify and work

[21]Rose Giallombardo, "The Chicago Area Project," in *Juvenile Delinquency: A Book of Readings* (New York: John Wiley & Sons, Inc., 1966).

[22]Walter Miller, "The Impact of a 'Total Community' Delinquency Control Project," in Giallombardo, *op. cit.,* p. 493.

with chronic problem families within the area who had histories of long use of public welfare services and other government programs. Workers were assigned to the area to develop positive relations with juveniles so that solutions to problem solving could be facilitated. Between June 1954 and May 1957 seven project field workers maintained contact with approximately four hundred youngsters between the ages of twelve and twenty-one.

A summary of the findings and an evaluation of the project indicate that there was no significant measurable inhibition of either law violation or unethical behavior as a consequence of project efforts. Even though the statistics and the evaluation of the project were not particularly encouraging, it was felt that the cooperation and communication between residents and agencies had been improved.

South Central Youth Project. The South Central Youth Project was established by the Community Welfare Council of Hennepin County (Minneapolis).[23] The project was directed by a planning committee which included executives of both public and private agencies. Like the Midcity Project, one of its major objectives was to make community agencies more responsive to community residents' needs. In addition, because of many interagency problems, services were not being adequately provided to youngsters and families within this area. The goal of the project was to detect the beginning stages of delinquency and to improve interagency communication and agency cooperation with community residents. Although it was felt that some of the existing agencies within the community were effective, many residents were not receiving the benefit of community resources. These residents lived in the south central area of Hennepin County.

Most of these residents were socially and economically disadvantaged and did not know how to utilize community resources or operate within large bureaucratic structures. Because of these and other factors, they often did not seek the services of their community agencies. Consequently, the project focused on identifying those families that needed help but were not getting it so that resources could be provided. This project, like other programs mentioned, has not undergone rigorous evaluation. One of the conclusions reached as a result of the South Central Youth Project was that agencies established to service community residents are often ineffective. There is a lack of cooperation between the agencies themselves as well as a lack of communication between the agencies and the community residents. New insights were gained as a result of this project in regard to the process of developing linkage between the agencies and the community residents.

The Quincy Community Youth Development Project. The Quincy Community Youth Development Project also attempted to help youngsters in areas with high rates of delinquency.[24] After identification of these youngsters, an experi-

[23]Gisele Konopka, "South Central Youth Project: A Delinquency Control Program (1955-57)," *Annals, American Academy of Political and Social Science,* 322 (1959), 30-37.

[24]Paul H. Bowman, "The Quincy Community Youth Development Project," *Annals, American Academy of Political and Social Science,* 322 (1959), 53-62.

mental and a control group were used in an attempt to evaluate the efforts of the project. The first efforts were directed toward placing children in foster homes as well as utilizing casework and recreation as alternatives for problem solving. The local school system was also involved in the project and two experimental classrooms were established, but the control group was given no special treatment. All the children involved in the project were ninth graders and were below the class average, and they had also done poorly in the eighth grade. The school experiences of these children varied greatly from those of normal ninth graders. Films, tapes, and articles from newspapers and magazines were used as text material. The students in the experimental group did not compete with other ninth grade students. The purpose of this approach was to make the learning process more interesting so that the students would become involved in a learning process and acquire useful skills.

Even though there was apparently only slight improvement in academic skills, personal adjustment, and dropout rates in the experimental group as compared with the control group, the youngsters in the experimental group did have a better job success rate as measured by the number of boys employed and their length of employment. The attendance records also indicated that they had developed a greater interest in school. There was also an indication that the rate of delinquency had dropped in the experimental group while it had increased in the control group.

Although the project attempted to reduce delinquent activity in the area, findings were inconclusive.

The Los Angeles Youth Project. The Los Angeles Youth Project was initiated in 1955 and focused its efforts on youngsters who were difficult to reach and influence.[25] The downtown south end of Los Angeles was used as the target area because of its high rates of delinquency, many health problems, low incomes, and poor housing. Youngsters in the community were contacted, and attempts at communication were initiated. The workers assigned to this area developed a relationship with the members of gangs as well as with other individuals so that the youngsters' needs could be identified and referral to appropriate community agencies could be made. It was difficult for the workers to communicate effectively with the youngsters and develop a positive relationship. Many families in the area were disorganized, and the social control processes both within the family and in the community were ineffective. Many youngsters in these families were hostile and resentful and joined groups within the community in an effort to escape unhealthy family situations. The concentrated effort of the Los Angeles project to identify youngsters and problems attempted, like other programs mentioned, to focus resources in areas of high rates of delinquency. Projects were then started to help the youngsters develop more socially adaptable patterns of adjustment. By focusing resources on families and youngsters who had multiproblems, it was also hoped that the number of unsatisfactory conditions contributing to crime and delinquency could be reduced.

[25]Estelle Aeston, "The Social Welfare Forum Proceedings of the National Conference of Social Work," Atlantic City (New York: Columbia University Press, 1951), pp. 281-94.

The Central Harlem Street Club Project. The Central Harlem Street Club Project was operated under the guidance of the Welfare Council of New York City.[26] The council, a volunteer organization, was created in 1925 to act as a coordinating and planning center for welfare and health services in the boroughs of New York City. Financial support for the project was obtained from such varied sources as individual contributions and foundations. The project began in 1947 and ended in 1950. The target population was four gangs, whose membership ranged from thirty-five to over one hundred. Workers involved in the project contacted about three hundred members and frequent contact was made with about half of this number. The gangs selected were the most antisocial in the area, and they were involved in many delinquent activities within their communities. There was also much intergang conflict and fighting. Many boys joined gangs because of their need for the protection provided by the gang.

Much of the activity in a gang included loitering and was conducive to the development of unproductive and negative personal habits. The workers in the project attempted to influence gang members so that their activities would be more sociably acceptable. Developing a relationship with the youngsters was often difficult because of the conditions that existed in Harlem and the resentment of the youngsters in the area.

This program was limited because of a lack of funds. Lack of resources hindered an intensive evaluation of the program, although the accomplishments listed showed that at least some negative behavior was altered because of the youngsters' relationship with the workers. Also, in some cases, more appropriate alternative modes of environmental adaption were presented to the boys.

The community-based programs that have been presented thus far have some characteristics in common. They were all initiated in areas of high crime and delinquency, and attempts were made to link community resources to area residents. Many variations of programs and alternatives were developed as a result of these projects. More important, however, the focus and emphasis on providing resources in high delinquency and crime areas was seen as the major purpose of these programs. Because these efforts and similar efforts did not run the test of rigorous evaluation, it is difficult to gauge their merits. This is not to belittle the efforts of the communities that were involved in these projects, however. Often projects are not adequately evaluated and researched because of a lack of funds and long-range planning. Future efforts will have to be concerned with sound planning and have methods of evaluation built into the programs so that short- and long-term goals and effectiveness can be determined and the most successful aspects of the programs can be replicated.

The following programs are less ambitious efforts than those community programs already discussed, and their methods of problem solving are more specific.

Louisville Red Shield Boys Club. The Louisville Red Shield Boys Club was established to reduce rates of delinquency in the neighborhood. The club operated

[26]D. Molamun and J. R. Dumpson, "Working with Teenage Gangs" Welfare Council of New York City (New York, 1950).

in an area where the socioeconomic status was low and the housing was substandard. The delinquency rate was high, and the club was the only major youth-serving agency operating within the area.[27]

The program was evaluated by utilizing census data in the area and determining the delinquency rate of youngsters between the ages of five and sixteen. The findings of the research indicated that the delinquency rate decreased rather steadily—from one out of nineteen boys in 1946, when the club opened, to one out of thirty-nine in 1954. The decrease in the delinquency rate in the area served by the club was in contrast to an increase in delinquency for the city overall where delinquency increased from one out of twenty-nine boys in 1946 to one out of eighteen in 1954. The decrease in delinquency in the study area was felt to be at least partly attributable to the activities of the boys' club. There was some skepticism regarding the direct amount of influence the club had had in reducing delinquency, because of some uncontrolled variables. Because the club was the major youth-serving agency in the area and the rates of delinquency were less for that area, it was concluded by the researchers that the club did in fact have an effect on rates of delinquency.

Carson Pirie Scott EE Program. The Carson Pirie Scott EE Program was developed in 1961 in cooperation with the Chicago Board of Education and the Ford Foundation.[28] The EE (Employment Education) program was established by Carson Pirie Scott, a large department store which employs ten thousand persons, after an effort to recruit young men and women for a variety of jobs pointed up a shortage of qualified personnel.

Company officials contacted the local superintendent of schools and were advised that one source of employment might be the large number of youngsters who either had already dropped out of school or had been identified as potential dropouts.

In the spring of 1961 the store began a pilot project in conjunction with the Board of Education and a grant to the school board of sixty thousand dollars from the Ford Foundation. The two major objectives were (1) the training of disadvantaged boys and girls in skills that would ensure their employment in the future and (2) education or study to complement the employment skills that were acquired. A training company was developed, and the trainees spent about forty-eight hours per week in the program, with three days on the job and two days attending classes. Two trainees were assigned to each job to ensure that the position would be filled for the normal work week. They were compensated at an hourly rate and also received raises for satisfactory performance.

The students were also involved in a training program to improve their personal hygiene and grooming and thus increase their employability after the

[27]"The Effectiveness of a Boys Club in Reducing Delinquency," Louisville Red Shield Boys Club, *Annals, American Academy of Political and Social Science*, 322 (1959), pp: 47-52.

[28]William Amos, Raymond Southwell, and Marilyn A. Southwell, "Carson Pirie Scott Double E.E. Program," in *Action Programs for Delinquency Prevention* (Chicago, 1965).

program was completed. They were also given actual experience in retail merchandising by operating their own company, the "Gift Shop," for one month.

The pilot program ended in 1962; the regular program started in the fall of that same year. One hundred twenty-five boys and girls participated in the regular program, and since an evaluation indicated that the program was successful, the project was established on a permanent basis.

The Henry Street Settlement House. An attempt was made at the Henry Street Settlement House in New York City to prevent and treat delinquency through early identification of antisocial behavior. A predelinquent gang project was designed to prevent the development of new gangs in the area. One of the main purposes of the project was to involve parents and youngsters in joint problem solving in the community. It was felt that if children and parents would cooperate and work toward solving both family and community problems, delinquency rates would be reduced—a closer relationship would give parents more control over their children and more influence over their children's activities. The settlement house sponsored, in cooperation with the children and their parents, many activities and programs that could be carried out jointly. Clubs were formed with the guidance of the settlement house and the supervision and interest of the parents. The operation of the club was felt to have influenced delinquency rates in the neighborhood and to have reduced the incidence of negative behavior. As a result of the project, parents seemed to exert more influence over their children and take more interest in their activity.

> It would seem then that when adults, particularly the parents, close ranks and stand together, the very ground that these children travel from home to various parts of the neighborhood becomes more solid.[29]

The Fuld Neighborhood House. The Fuld Neighborhood House of Newark, New Jersey, attempted to identify a target population of boys fourteen to seventeen years of age who had social and emotional problems and had also been involved with the police because of minor offenses.[30] A trained group worker made contact with the neighborhood boys to try to develop a positive relationship with the boys and influence their behavior. The program operated on the premise that the boys viewed their environment as hostile, negative, and manipulative; consequently, they attempted to achieve power and status through negative and devious methods. In the six-week summer program conducted in 1957, the boys became involved in work programs under the supervision of a park commission foreman and a group worker. The organization of the program in its initial stages had some difficulty in that there was not enough structure and coordination within

[29]Ruth S. Tefferteller, "Delinquency Prevention through Revitalizing Parent-Child Relations," *Annals, American Academy of Political and Social Science*, 322, (1959), pp. 69-78.

[30]A. Fried, "The Fuld Neighborhood House of Newark, New Jersey, A Work Program for Potential Delinquents," *Annals, American Academy of Political and Social Science,* 322 (1959), 38-46.

the work program, and many of the boys rebelled and became involved in disruptive behavior. This created additional problems and made it more difficult for the group worker and the staff to communicate satisfactorily with the boys and influence their behavior into positive channels.

Even though the program did not always operate smoothly, it was felt that some positive gains were made and new insights developed. A program of this type, combining work experience and counseling, could undoubtedly be effective if the goals were identified, with sound planning and coordination between the different facets of the program. Sound guidelines and limits would have to be established so that the boys could operate within some structure. In addition, more aggressive leadership by both the group worker and the work foreman was necessary. The boys should also have realistic expectations in regard to the type of work they were expected to do and the quality of their output. Recreation could be a valuable complementary activity, but the boys should be able to choose the form and type of activity. In sum, although the work environment should be structured, the recreational activities should not be. The complementary relationship between recreation and an efficient work program could produce positive results and could have a positive effect on juvenile delinquency if the program was well planned and coordinated.

The preceding four programs described localized neighborhood efforts which attempted to work with socially and economically disadvantaged area residents. Different types of activities and alternatives were initiated, all revolving around the community-based house or center. Upon evaluation it was felt that most of these programs did positively influence the youngsters in the area and did help to reduce rates of delinquency. However, like other programs discussed, the evaluation was not rigorous and many of the variables were not controlled. Therefore it is difficult to realistically evaluate their success and definitely state that they did have a major impact on reducing crime and delinquency.

The next six programs to be described are in some respects present-day counterparts of the Chicago Area Project in that they attempted to mobilize the efforts of community residents in community problem solving. These six programs received support from the Office of Juvenile Delinquency and Youth Development of the Department of Health, Education, and Welfare. They were all based on the assumption that social, structural, and environmental pathology were major causes of youthful deviance.

> The projects varied greatly in size, geography and program—efforts were directed to the evaluating and examining a variety of issues relevant to community organizations represented within the six projects.[31]

Mobilization for Youth. One of the main objectives of the Mobilization for

[31] These six programs are described in Charles Grosser, *Helping Youth, A Study of Six Community Organization Programs,* U.S. Department of Health, Education, and Welfare, Office of Juvenile Delinquency and Youth Development.

Youth project was to overcome the apathy and defeatism of the slum dweller through a system of self-help programs which attempted to organize the unaffiliated residents of the target area.

> The rationale was that youth could not be successfully integrated into socially constructive community life unless their adult role models (parents, etc.) themselves were a part of the community.[32]

The target selected was a sixty-seven-square-block area on the east side of New York, with a population of one hundred thousand persons. The goal of the project was to organize the various groups in this area into an effective source of power. It was felt that the individual in the community was unable to deal with poor housing, poor schools, inadequate police protection, and other issues himself and that in a coordinated group effort many of these problems could be dealt with and solved through pressure exerted by the "people's" organizations. This project met with resistance from one of the city's largest newspapers, as well as from many government officials. There was little cooperation or open acceptance by many governmental units and public officials within the community, and an investigation of the program did turn up irregularities, such as administrative difficulties.

Syracuse Crusade for Opportunity. The Syracuse Crusade for Opportunity was similar to the Mobilization for Youth project in that it attempted to coordinate community resource groups so that action programs could be initiated. The target areas were designated within the Syracuse, New York, area according to the number of problems that existed in various Syracuse neighborhoods. Problems characteristic of the neighborhoods included poverty, transience, and chronic dependency on such governmental services as the welfare system. The particular target area was chosen because of the many pathological conditions that existed. The project's major emphasis was on a community development approach, with the residents themselves becoming responsible for changing the character of their neighborhood.[33]

The crusade began by involving residents in elections to establish neighborhood boards. The boards constituted representation from the various target areas. From time to time these boards would have joint meetings to discuss certain issues and common problems and possible solutions to the problems. Friction did develop between the professional staff and the nonprofessional persons. Because of this conflict there were problems in decision making, with both groups wanting the major voice. Lack of administrative direction and sound decision making did affect the operation of the project, although some of the programs which were established to focus on teen-agers and develop teen-age activities did appear to have a positive impact.

[32]*Ibid.*, p. 7.
[33]*Ibid.*, p. 21.

United Planning Organization. The United Planning Organization project focused on a high delinquency area of Washington, D.C. A strong relationship between juvenile delinquent activity and socioeconomic conditions was thought to exist in this area, which contained many youngsters who had come in contact with the criminal justice system. Because the opportunity structure within this area was obviously not conducive to the youngsters' achieving their goals and satisfying their needs in a socially acceptable manner, it was felt that better community coordination and more efficient delivery of services from community agencies would solve many of the problems.

The development of self-help organizations and the involvement of citizens in community decision making were encouraged. Citizen involvement in problem solving was felt to be one of the answers to developing awareness of the problems and fostering community participation.

Neighborhood centers were developed to filter information about the problems of the community to residents and serve as headquarters for disseminating information. One of the strategies of the project was to change the attitudes of both the residents and the institutions established to serve them. It was estimated that at the peak of the project there were twenty-five block clubs as well as many other organizations working to solve the problems of the area. Better leadership and more active citizen involvement resulted in some projects being more successful than others.

The decentralized approach to decision making and administration was felt to be more conducive to citizen involvement than a centralized orientation. One of the shortcomings of the decentralized approach, however, was that communication channels were often garbled and therefore coordination between different projects and citizen groups was difficult. One of the most interesting aspects of the program was the wide acceptance and use of credit unions owned and operated by community citizens who lived within the target area. Before the United Planning Organization, there was only one credit union for the poor. After the success of the community-operated credit union, similar credit unions emerged in the community and were supported by the residents.

This project also emphasized the solving of practical problems such as housing and unemployment. One of the major efforts was the development of a housing project. United Planning Organization did encounter some administrative difficulties, as did the Syracuse Crusade for Opportunity and the Mobilization for Youth programs.

Houston Action for Youth. The Houston Action for Youth program was similar to the United Planning Organization program in that it was a self-help neighborhood effort that focused on a densely populated target area. The program depended on citizens who had the time and the motivation to devote to community problem solving. Most of those persons involved in the project were from the stable working class in the densely populated areas of Houston, Texas. Self-determination and self-expression were seen as the major goals of the program.[34]

[34]*Ibid.,* p. 30.

Because of the size of the target population and its density, there was a proliferation of community organizations. To combat this problem, many small neighborhood groups were brought together in three area councils. Members from the various groups comprised the board of directors. The thrust of the project was to use low-pressure tactics in solving area problems rather than confront the local government directly. It was felt that confrontation would only create ill will and hinder cooperation. The organization took the position that only through cooperative effort between the community citizens and the community agencies could power be used effectively. Many different types of projects were developed. The success of a project depended on the amount of involvement of the community residents and the degree of cooperation between the agencies and the residents.

Action for Appalachian Youth. The Action for Appalachian Youth program focused on an area near Charleston, West Virginia. The basic premise was that value conflicts between urban and rural society were a source of much tension, strain, and frustration. This supposedly creates a system where there is a lack of "meshing" between persons within the same environment, and this lack of meshing creates conflicts which in turn contribute to social problems like delinquent behavior.[35]

The residents of the target areas were difficult to reach because of such geographical factors as mountains, ridges, and creeks. It took a great deal of physical endurance even to make contact with the residents. Furthermore, because of long years of isolation, the people had developed a life-style much different from that of "conventional persons," which made communication very difficult. Each target "hollow" was assigned a neighborhood worker. The worker's presence was difficult to explain because there was no precedent for such a program. It took a long time to become acquainted with the residents.

Some of the main concerns of the residents were the need for better roads and increased recreational facilities. As a result of assistance provided by the worker, various improvement associations evolved with elected officers, committees, and regular meetings.

Numerous problem issues were raised and discussed at these meetings, and petitions were circulated to elicit public opinion and support.

Each neighborhood improvement association sent delegates to a general council which functioned on a countywide basis. A technique of the neighborhood staff worker was one of nonintervention—a nondirective approach was used with the community. Some workers questioned this role because they felt that a more active, aggressive approach was needed to help solve problems in these isolated backward areas. The project and the contact of the worker with the community facilitated communication, problem delineation, and in some cases problem solving.

The HARYOU ACT. The HARYOU ACT (Harlem Youth Opportunities, Unlimited, Associated Community Teams) was initiated in Harlem, New York, a target area of a quarter million people, 94 percent black, living in a three-and-a-

[35]*Ibid.*, p. 37.

half-square-mile urban area. The program attempted to increase the chances for the youth in the community to lead productive lives and develop socially acceptable types of behavior.[36]

Even though the goal of the program was commendable, it did encounter difficulties in administration and pressures were exerted by various interest groups. There was also competition within the program itself, and "too much was expected too fast."

The massive problems that existed in the Harlem area, along with the administrative and pressure group difficulties, hindered the effective operation of the program.

Unfortunately, many of the potential positive results of the last six programs described were neutralized by inefficient administration, internal problems, and conflict between community interest groups. The actual positive results are also difficult to determine because the areas in which the programs were focused had many massive problems.

Ideally, programs of this kind could do much to solve community ills and help reduce crime and delinquency; however, many of the goals initially established are not achieved. If methods of research and project evaluation were built into all projects dealing with community improvement and crime and delinquency problem solving, the positive and negative aspects could be clearly identified. When program results are not identified, it is difficult to induce community involvement and obtain financial support from the governmental structure. When there are not sound methods of administrative control and a clearly defined goal orientation, many internal difficulties arise and overall sponsorship of the necessary governmental and private units is difficult to obtain. Although one should be skeptical of the operation of some of these projects, this should not detract from the major impetus and idealistic focus of the programs. The goal orientation, and the enthusiasm and motivation, are often commendable.

All the programs discussed thus far can be considered mainly pure prevention efforts, in that their major focus is an attempt to alleviate conditions that breed crime and delinquency by involving community residents in problem solving and decision making. The youngster is assisted before he comes in contact with a formal criminal justice system. The final discussion of pure prevention will identify a few additional efforts at delinquency prevention. These efforts are different from those already examined in that their focus is not as rigorous, nor is the target population as massive and disadvantaged by poverty conditions. The following programs, although they are believed to contribute to delinquency prevention and control, have in many cases not been thoroughly evaluated and researched.

Additional Pure Prevention Programs

Police-School Liaison Programs. The police-school liaison concept is relatively new and has been introduced into various schools throughout the

[36]*Ibid.*, p. 44.

country. Two of the earliest programs originated in Michigan—one in the Flint Police Department and the other in the Michigan Department of State Police. Both departments were concerned with the alienation and hostility that existed between police and youngsters. It was felt that a police-school liaison program could improve communication between the two groups.

A police-school liaison program is initiated when an officer is assigned to a school to act as both a law enforcement officer and a resource person who can also be a counselor. He can listen to student problems, help coordinate efforts to reduce delinquent activities, and foster better understanding between the police and adolescents. The specific duties of the officer will depend on the police department and the school system to which he is assigned.

> The generally stated purpose of such a program is to instill in the pupils a greater appreciation and a better and more positive understanding of the nature of policemen and their work. It is intended that this appreciation of law enforcement and its necessity will help to decrease the number of juvenile delinquencies. It is reportedly a format for building positive police/community relations with that segment of the population just entering an age where attitudes are beginning to crystalize and where a negative attitude toward law enforcement can be most dangerous.[37]

Shepard and James list five objectives of a police-school liaison program: (1) to establish collaboration between the police and the school in preventing crime and delinquency, (2) to encourage understanding between police and young people, (3) to improve police teamwork with teachers in handling problem youth, (4) to improve the attitudes of students toward the police, and (5) to build better police and community relations by improving the police image.[38]

The program in Flint, Michigan, can be considered the forerunner of police-school liaison programs, although the city of Atlanta reports that it had officers assigned to the school more than thirty-six years ago; the duties of these officers, however, were not typical of the duties of present-day school liaison officers.

The Flint program was sponsored by the Mott Foundation, which subsidized the program in its initial stages. Even today the Mott Foundation supports the Flint program, and there is now a liaison officer in each junior and senior high school in the city. Under the Flint concept, the officer is a part of what is called a regional counseling team. This team is comprised of the dean of students, the principals of the elementary schools, and the principal of the high school, as well as the liaison officer. This combined approach is felt to be conducive to solving problems in a coordinated manner and keeping all agency personnel involved in the planning and implementation of programs that serve juveniles within the Flint area. The following quotation describes the Flint approach to police-school liaison:

[37]Charles L. Weirman "A Critical Analysis of a Police-School Liaison Program to Implement Attitudinal Changes in Junior High Students" (Master's thesis, Michigan State University), p. 9.

[38]George H. Shepard and Jessie James, "Police—Do They Belong in the Schools?," *American Education*, September 1967, p. 2.

Let us use the example of the child who steals a lunch. The theft is reported; the accusation is made. The child confesses to the deed. In reviewing the child's background from files kept by each member of the team, the school nurse may discover the child has a history of illness; the dean may discover the fact that the child's grades had been declining. The community school director may be aware of the fact that he is not seeing the child participating in after-school activities as he used to; the principal may recall that the child's family has had minor disturbances in the past. The presence of a police officer with punitive power, although he may not use it in this instance, impresses the child with the seriousness of the wrongdoing. By coordinating their efforts and combining their knowledge of the case, the team can guide the child into safer channels.[39]

Many other programs have been patterned after the Flint program. Police-school liaison programs have been considered effective in preventing juvenile delinquency because of the following reasons:

1. An increase in information and improvement of communication between students and their families.
2. An increase in information and improved communication between the schools and all other groups within the community.
3. Earlier identification of predelinquent children and earlier referrals of such types.
4. Improved communication between the police and the school personnel.[40]

Even though most comments about police-school liaison programs have been positive, there have been some negative reactions. Some of the criticisms have revolved around using students as informers for police, using police as disciplinarians, allowing police to carry weapons on school property, and indiscriminately questioning juveniles even though they have not been charged with an offense. Some persons just generally feel that the school and the police are incompatible.

It appears that fear of the police, which is one of the targets of change in the police-school liaison program, is a primary reason for criticism of the concept. The detractors do not base their opposition upon actual transgressions but rather upon their perceptions of supposed police oppression. That is not to say that their fears could not be based on valid reasons of proven turpitude on the part of the police. There are too many obvious examples of law enforcement's ineptitude in working with juveniles in the past to hold that

[39]The Mott Foundation, "The Police-School Liaison Program" brochure prepared for distribution to interested agencies (Flint, Michigan).

[40]Minneapolis Police Department, "The Police-School Liaison Program," Final Report submitted to the Office of Law Enforcement Assistance regarding their grant 31, mimeographed, November 1968, p. 11.

Courtesy of the Michigan State Police

A Police-School Liaison Officer in Plain Clothes and in Uniform

such views are completely groundless. The fact remains that the literature does not reflect actual reported malfeasance on the part of police-school liaison officers.[41]

There are other approaches that are similar to police-school liaison programs, but they have different names or somewhat different orientations. The "officer friendly" concept in the Chicago Police Department is one example. These programs are aimed at the primary grades and attempt to involve the students in a better understanding of police work and encourage them to be "community helpers."

Various studies have evaluated the police-school liaison concept. Weirman concluded that a police-school liaison program was effective. As a result of comparing a control group (without a liaison officer) with an experimental group (with a liaison officer), he found that whereas negative attitudes of children toward police increased markedly in the control school, negative attitudes of children in the experimental school, with few exceptions, remained relatively constant. Although the attitudes did not show a marked improvement in the experimental school, the officer nevertheless held his ground. As Weirman states:

> Finding that the control school became more negative toward the police while the experimental school remained fairly constant does not indicate that the liaision officer was not successful and positively effective in changing the attitudes of the students of the school he was in. It might rather be interpreted to mean that had the liaison officer not been present attitudes would have become more negative toward the police during that same period of time.[42]

Weirman's study pointed out that negativism toward the police exists in even junior high school students. One method of combating this growing antagonism toward law enforcement and its representatives is the use of a police-school liaison officer. When police-school liaison programs are properly constructed and adequately supervised, they can be effective in changing youthful attitudes toward the police and indirectly influencing the rates of crime and delinquency in the particular school district.

Educational Programs. In communities throughout the United States, programs have been initiated that attempt not only to influence and change youngsters' attitudes toward the police but also to educate youngsters regarding the detrimental effects of using drugs and becoming involved in devious social behavior. Programs developed by some communities are staffed by young persons who attempt to prevent drug abuse by providing counseling services for youngsters who are experimenting with drugs. Educational information and counseling services are also provided for youngsters who may be considering experimenting with drugs, and both professionals and paraprofessionals are used. Psychiatrists, psychologists,

[41] Weirman, *op. cit.,* p. 45.
[42] *Ibid.,* p. 195.

social workers, counselors, teachers, parents, and both high school and college students are often participants in these programs. Assistance is also available from medical doctors, attorneys, and ministers, and funding is provided by governmental, private, and business organizations. The use of drug education centers indicates an awareness by the community that the most effective means of combating illicit nonmedical drug use—and saving youngsters the discomfort and agony related to drug abuse—is having the entire community become involved in drug education.

Communities throughout the United States are also placing an increased emphasis on programs for youngsters who are runaways. The runaway problem has become serious in many communities and specific programs have been established, often operated by youngsters themselves to help the runaway solve his problems. Homes for runaways give the youngster a chance to reflect upon his own situation and with the assistance and guidance of staff members, both professional and para-professional, develop new alternatives to problem solving other than flight. In most of the programs youngsters are encouraged to communicate with their parents or legal guardians to help promote more positive communication. With the assistance, guidance, and counseling of the staff, in conjunction with the cooperation of the parents, problems can often be resolved before they become serious.

Provisions are also made at these houses to allow youngsters to stay overnight if they have permission from parents, legal guardians, or the local detention home. Permission can usually be obtained by telephone. If the youngster stays longer than one night, local laws specify the procedure to be followed and the legal ramifications of extended residence. The administration of such programs will vary depending on the community, the legal limits of the particular jurisdiction, and the orientation of the house staff members. The important concept, however, is that innovative approaches such as homes for runaways can be helpful in reducing delinquency. The youngster can be helped with his problems before they become so severe that formal intervention is necessary.

Many communities have also attempted other educational approaches as well as residential and semiresidential programs to prevent delinquency and assist youngsters in problem solving. Some schools have developed programs that teach youngsters skills through innovative educational approaches while at the same time linking the school experience to the employment world. This provides the youngster with a practical approach to problem solving and increases his chances of being successful in his community.

In Flint, Michigan, a Personality Improvement Program has been initiated. It is sponsored by the Mott Foundation, the Genesee County Board of Education, the Probate Court of Genesee County, and citizen interest groups. The program is designed to help students eleven to fifteen years of age who are having school problems. The goals of the program are as follows:

1. To provide school activity during periods of public school suspension for disruptive students.
2. To remove disruptive students from public school classrooms.
3. To apprise the disruptive student of his potential service to society.

4. To place as many of the students back into the school setting from which they came with as positive an attitude as possible.
5. To provide support services from the Genesee County Probate Court to Flint community schools with incorrigible students.[43]

Some of the problems that the children who are admitted to this program may be encountering in school are generally disruptive-type activities, such as being unable to keep quiet during classroom presentations, not staying in their seats, talking out of turn, not doing homework, or manifesting other aggressive behavioral problems toward their fellow students and teachers.

If it is deemed necessary that the child be referred to the Personality Improvement Program, his school files for written permission to the probate court, requesting that the student be placed in the program. The school then agrees to take the youngster back at the end of a six-week period. If the youngster meets the legal criteria, the court commits him to the Genesee County Children's Facility for a twelve-week period with the recommendation that he be placed in the Personality Improvement Program. The program emphasis is on helping the youngster develop more positive modes of behavioral adaption. The first six weeks involve a day-care program where the child is involved in behavioral modification classes. In the second six weeks the youngster is reintegrated into the public school. A counselor works with him by providing help and guidance to facilitate readjustment to the school situation.

The youngster returns to his home in the evening and commutes during the day. If the youngster happens to be truant, he can be detained in the Children's Facility to assure attendance at class.

Staffing of the Personality Improvement Program consists of a program coordinator and an assistant coordinator, a counseling service supervisor, two instructors certified as public school teachers, two counselors, and a secretary. This type of program is helpful in preventing delinquency by keeping the youngster constructively busy and acquainting him with new skills. It is unlike a detention program where the youngsters are often only held inactive for a period of time. In the Personality Improvement Program the youngster can improve such basic academic skills as reading, English, and mathematics. In addition, an experienced caseworker or counselor works with him on a follow-up basis after the initial six-week day-care program. The immediate goal of the program is to reintegrate the youngster into his public school classroom on a nondisruptive basis. The long-range effects of this program can contribute to the youngster's acquiring new skills so that his behavioral energy will be directed in more socially acceptable channels. The prevention of delinquency is often the result of this program.

The Lansing Police Department has an instructional program, the Community Youth Citizen Project, which attempts to help youngsters formulate new values that will alter negative attitudes and behavior toward authority. Because data

[43]"Personality Improvement Program of Genesee County" (pamphlet, Genesee County Probate Court), p. 1.

reflect that much crime and disruption is caused by youngsters, it was felt that an education program that emphasizes the law, its history and definition, the role and duties of law enforcement, and the citizen's responsibility to his community would be helpful in reducing delinquency. The Community Youth Citizen Project is a joint effort between the Lansing Police Department and the Lansing Board of Education. The objectives of the program are as follows:

1. Prevention of crimes through understanding and communication between law enforcement agencies and the youths of the community.
2. To improve the image and stereotype of the police, family, school personnel and youth by promoting a better understanding of the role each plays in society.
3. To aid in the betterment of society through the understanding of the rights and responsibilities of citizenship.
4. To aid the student in identifying his role and responsibility in the community.
5. To aid the student in making moral decisions.
6. To reveal the intent and purpose of law and interpret its meaning.
7. To clarify the role of the citizen in the procedure and performance of law.
8. To advise the youngster in all phases of law.
9. To present the role and the procedure of law enforcement, encompassing all law enforcement agencies.
10. To clarify the functions of law enforcement in a democratic society.[44]

Five Lansing police officers are involved in the program. The officers are selected from the youth division as well as from the traffic and uniform divisions so that the department will have a well-rounded representation. Many types of educational aids are utilized, such as books, pamphlets, and audiovisual materials. The method of classroom presentation is flexible, depending on the officer and the method he is most comfortable with. Even games are sometimes used to get a particular point across to youngsters. The officer's presentation is made as interesting as possible to insure that the youngsters will pay attention to the speakers.

The topics that the officers discuss in the classroom include the reasons for laws, the way laws pertain to citizens, and the definition of law. There is a discussion of criminal and civil law, as well as a delineation of the consequences of a criminal record. The officer also describes the rights every citizen is guaranteed by the United States Constitution, the various branches of government, and the way they work to protect the citizen and make government an orderly process. Field trips are made to the various court facilities in the community so that the students can observe the different aspects of court administration and processing. Throughout the entire program the youngsters ask questions about the criminal justice process so that many of their misconceptions can be corrected.

One of the secondary benefits of the program is that the participating youngsters learn to relate to the policeman in a much more realistic manner. They learn

[44]"Community Youth Citizenship Project" (pamphlet, Lansing School District and Lansing Police Department), p. 2.

Courtesy of the Michigan State Police

Youth Involvement in Police Work

to look beyond the uniform and to identify with the man who has been their instructor for many weeks. As a result of this closer identification with the officer and the instructional material that he has presented, youngsters have a much better understanding of the law, its function, and the criminal justice process. Programs of this kind can help alter the negative attitudes youngsters have toward policemen. An increased awareness of the processes of law and a more positive concept of authority can indirectly relate to the reduction of juvenile delinquent behavior.

Programs like the Community Youth Citizen Project also give youngsters the opportunity to voice their opinions and make suggestions for improving the process of justice in their community. Such programs have a commendable orientation to problem solving, although there is usually little evaluation or feedback regarding the success of these endeavors.

Many other community programs could either directly or indirectly be considered pure prevention-type efforts. Even when the focus of a program is not on delinquency prevention, one of the secondary results is often the reduction of delinquency. Police athletic leagues, Boy Scouts, youth opportunity centers, youth assistance programs, recreational programs, vocational guidance programs, Alateen (a subsidiary of Alcoholics Anonymous), vocational rehabilitation, and YMCA and YWCA programs can also play a role in preventing and reducing juvenile misbehavior in the community.

The increased emphasis on involving youth in community problem solving and on developing closer relationships between youth and criminal justice agencies, especially police departments, together with a total community effort at delinquency problem solving and a more effective evaluation of programs, will contribute to a more successful delinquency prevention.

All the programs discussed in this section are mainly pure prevention efforts—in other words, they attempt to prevent delinquency before it starts. The next section will emphasize rehabilitative prevention—working with the youngster after he has been exposed to the formal processes of the criminal justice system.

REHABILITATIVE PREVENTION PROGRAMS

Most community and governmental efforts at delinquency and crime prevention emphasize rehabilitative prevention. The reason for the greater emphasis on rehabilitative prevention is not only because of the lack of commitment to, and the lack of resources for, pure prevention programs but also because many of these programs have not had adequate evaluations, nor have they been objectively researched to determine their effectiveness. It is often difficult to convince the community legislators and the funding agencies that pure prevention programs should be initiated and developed, and therefore rehabilitative prevention programs receive most of the attention. Rehabilitative prevention, although at present necessary, would not be needed on a large scale if pure prevention efforts were prevalent and successful. Rehabilitative prevention also suffers from a lack of resources, and community programs are often merely sporadic attempts to deal with the problem once it has occurred. Because the problem has progressed to a very serious point by the time rehabilitative prevention is initiated, it is often difficult to successfully help the youngster.

All the following programs are rehabilitative programs. Some have been evaluated and researched and definite conclusions can be drawn. Others have not been rigorously evaluated, and therefore it is difficult to measure their successes and failures.

Probation

Probation as a tool of rehabilitative prevention was discussed briefly in Chapter 7. According to Haskell and Yablonsky:

> The correctional system provides for the treatment and supervision of offenders in the community by placing them on probation in lieu of confinement in a custodial institution. In most cases probationers serve the sentence of the court under the supervision of the probation officer assigned by the court. The judge has broad powers in this situation and can set the conditions of probation and the length of supervision. He maintains the power to order revocation of probation, usually for a violation of one of the conditions set by him or his agent or for the commission of another offense. The effect of revocation is to send the prisoner to a custodial institution.[45]

The specific administration of the probation program depends upon the state and the jurisdiction. Although in many states probation is a part of the court—a juvenile court, probate court, or some other court jurisdiction, one probation department may be quite different from another, depending upon the jurisdiction. In thirty-two states juvenile courts administer probation services, while in the other states there is a variation.

> More than half the offenders sentenced to correctional treatment in 1965 (684,088 individuals) were placed on probation. It was estimated that by 1975 the number will be over a million. The average caseload assigned a probation officer is usually around 75. The typical probation caseload is usually a random mixture of cases requiring varying amounts of service and surveillance.[46]

The probation officer can use a variety of techniques in counseling the youngster assigned to him—vocational guidance, personal counseling, and in some situations phychotherapy, depending upon the skill of the probation officer (see Chapter 9). It is obviously difficult for the probation officer to adequately serve a case load of seventy-five or more individuals. Much of the time he has to establish a priority list to determine which youngsters are in greatest need of assistance and must be taken care of first. In many jurisdictions the probation officer's major problem is "putting out fires." He has little time for counseling other than on a superficial level. It is, unfortunately, unusual for the probation officer to have sufficient time and resources to adequately serve his case load.

Pilot programs have been initiated which have attempted to provide sufficient resources so that the probation officer can be more effective as a result of a reduced

[45]Martin R. Haskell and Lewis Yablonsky, *Crime and Delinquency* (Chicago: Rand McNally & Co., 1970), p. 432.

[46]*Ibid.*, p. 432.

case load. For example, in Genesee County (Flint, Michigan) two different programs attempt to provide more effective and comprehensive services to probationers. The first program, the Citizens Probation Authority, is a community probation program in which volunteers assist in providing services to the probationer. Probation is used in lieu of full prosecution in the criminal court. Even though this program is mainly for adult law violators, it can also be used with juveniles. The program offers counseling and supportive services for a period of up to one year. Volunteers provide most of the supervision. If the probationer successfully completes the program, the pending prosecution is dismissed and the offender can apply for the removal of the offense from his record. The major purpose of the program is threefold: first, crime prevention; second, volunteer participation in the processes of criminal justice; and third, rehabilitation of first or early stage offenders without the stigma of conviction. Referrals can be made from many sources, but they generally originate from the prosecuting attorney's office or the municipal court.[47]

The second program that assists probationers in the Flint community, Positive Action for Youth, is financed by the Mott Foundation and operated by the board of education and the probate court. This program provides individualized counseling for in-school juvenile probationers on a more intensive basis than could be provided by just the probate court's probation department. The youngster is helped to utilize community resources and mobilize inner strengths and is made aware of the consequences of his behavior and the self-destructiveness of his delinquent orientation.[48]

The Citizens Probation Authority and the Positive Action for Youth programs are examples of how one community is attempting to better serve probationers by providing the necessary resources to deal with the problem. In the Flint programs the use of volunteers is very prevalent. The use of volunteers is also becoming acceptable in other communities throughout the country. This is one method of reducing the pressure on probation officers and involving citizens in the criminal justice system processes. Volunteer programs have been successful in many communities and can be a valuable resource for assisting the youngster, preventing delinquency in the community, and making citizens more aware of the criminal justice system process and their responsibility for helping it operate effectively.

> In 1920 to 1940 court volunteer programs went thoroughly in eclipse; their return in about 1940 was hailed as a fresh discovery of a near-miraculous new problem cureall.[49]

The National Information Center on Volunteers in Courts has provided extensive information relating to the use of volunteers and the methods for proper administration. As the center emphasizes, only skilled leadership can insure the

[47]Citizens Probation Authority (Flint, Michigan).

[48]The Mott Foundation, "Positive Action for Youth" (Flint, Michigan).

[49]Dr. Ivan Scheirer, *Catalog of Volunteer Program Leadership Publications* (National Information Center on Volunteers in Courts, P.O. Box 2150, Boulder, Colo.).

success of volunteer programs. The center provides the latest books, manuals, and films which describe the use of volunteers, the procedures that should be followed when establishing volunteer programs, and the methods for evaluating their success.

Juvenile Institutions

Institutions for juveniles known as training schools or reformatories when originally established were patterned after adult prisons. The major difference over the years has been an increased emphasis on occupational training and rehabilitation. Therapeutic services were introduced during the 1930's and 1940's and these have expanded considerably in the 1950's.[50]

In regard to the function of training schools or juvenile institutions, the Children's Bureau of the Department of Health, Education, and Welfare states that

The prime function of a training school is to re-educate and train the child to become a responsible, well-adjusted citizen—leading figures in the field believe that the main purpose of institutional placement today is treatment and the training schools must be essentially treatment institutions with an integrated professional service wherein the disciplines of education, casework, group work, psychology, psychiatry, medicine, nursing, vocational rehabilitation and religion all play an important role. Through such an integrated program the child is expected to learn self-discipline, to accept more responsibility and act and react in a more socially acceptable manner.[51]

All states have at least one facility for the treatment of youngsters within an institutional setting. Michigan, for example, has a complex of institutional arrangements which are a part of the Office of Youth Services, a division of the Department of Social Services. Institutions are located at various sites in the state, and there are varying degrees of custodial supervision, depending upon the needs of the youngster and the seriousness of his behavior problem. For example, there is a closed facility at Whitmore Lake, Michigan, where youngsters who have severe behavior problems are housed. Another unit of the Office of Youth Services is located in Lansing. This program is a more open facility and serves boys who do not need the intense supervision necessary under the Whitmore Lake program. In addition to these facilities, there are camp programs as well as halfway houses and group homes for those youngsters who do not have to be removed completely from the community but cannot be permitted to stay in the community on probation or some other minimal supervision program. All these facilities attempt to provide the youngster with training and education he can utilize on his release. He also receives counseling to help him conform to the demands of the community and adjust more satisfactorily to his environment.

[50]Haskell and Yablonsky, *op. cit.*, p. 419.

[51]*Institutions Serving Delinquent Children: Guides and Goals,* U.S. Department of Health, Education, and Welfare, Children's Bureau, 1957, p. 3.

As for juvenile institutions, it is far better to find alternatives for the youngster rather than place him in a closed setting. The less the youngster is exposed to the formal processes of the criminal justice system, the greater are his chances of satisfactory adjustment in the community, and the less stigmatization will be a factor in future delinquent behavior. Some youngsters can not tolerate the freedom of the community and need a closed setting like an institution. Institutions, however, often suffer from a lack of resources and trained personnel and should be used only sparingly and when other alternatives are not available.

Additional Rehabilitative Prevention Programs

Probation and juvenile institutions are probably the two most common methods employed in treating youngsters once they have come in contact with the criminal justice system. In addition to the innovative approaches being utilized to serve the youngster who is on probation, new concepts in institutional management are being developed along with more effective procedures for handling youngsters in closed settings. A sampling of innovative programs that have been tried or are at present being used to treat youngsters after they have come in contact with the formal criminal justice system follows. Various types of therapeutic approaches will be discussed.

This section will deal mainly with the rehabilitative prevention program, its goals, and in some cases its effects—rather than provide a description of the therapeutic techniques (see Chapter 9).

The Los Angeles Venture in Treatment. In addition to comprehensive probation and detention services within the Los Angeles County probation department, two special programs have been initiated. The first one is the Family Treatment Program.

> The Family Treatment Program is groups of boys and girls living together at the Juvenile Hall in special units, separate from the other children; like family units sitting down together perhaps for the first time talking about their feelings and thoughts in an attempt to change attitudes and behavior with the probation officer acting as the family therapist.[52]

The Family Treatment Program was developed to cope with the chronic overcrowding in the juvenile halls and to take advantage of a negative situation. Subsidized by the California State Aid to Probation Services Program, the family treatment concept now operates in all three juvenile halls in Los Angeles County. The probation officer acts as the group leader and the catalytic agent to produce change and discussion "within the family." He is not only an authority figure but a parental substitute.

[52]"National Strategy to Prevent Delinquency," U.S. Department of Health, Education, and Welfare, Social and Rehabilitation Service, Youth Development and Delinquency Administration, p. 4.

In family treatment the family is seen as the dysfunctional unit. The goals during the six weeks of intensive counseling are to bring awareness, self-respect, identity, respect of peers, and to help the youth prepare for life as a mature and useful citizen. At the same time by opening up communication within the family and placing emphasis on relationships of all family members, the family as a whole and the therapist can explore and support the positive aspects within the family. The parents of the youngsters also meet in parent group sessions. This enables them to realize that they are not alone in coping with the problems of raising an adolescent in today's society. By interacting they learn of each other's solutions and this often helps them solve their own problems.[53]

The youngsters are allowed to go home on weekends, and after they are released from the program, they can still receive outpatient counseling for a period of up to six weeks. The environment of the Family Treatment Program is constructed to be as similar to the actual family situation as possible. This means that there are many aspects of the program—for example, recreation and educational activities supplement the counseling. All facets of the Family Treatment Program are appropriately coordinated to provide the youngster with a well-rounded experience.

This innovative program utilizes both the internal resources associated with detention and community volunteers to increase programming effectiveness. Los Angeles County reports that 85 to 90 percent of all youngsters sent home following completion of the program are still living at home after six months.[54]

Los Angeles County uses volunteers extensively, and the second program it has initiated is called VISTO (Volunteers In Service To Offenders). The volunteers learn firsthand about the problems of probationers. Many types of workers are involved in the program, including housewives, teachers, college students, businessmen, professionals, and senior citizens.

VISTO seeks to aid the offender who is on probation without removing him from the community. To accomplish this, neighborhood volunteers are trained to work with probationers—both adult and juvenile. Community awareness and concern is created by the use of these volunteers. VISTO volunteers contributed an average of 10,071 hours a month. Out of the total time, 6,646 hours or 66% are utilized to work with probationers on a one-to-one basis and 1,875 hours or 18.6% are spent in working with the probationers in groups. An additional 1,550 hours are contributed to such activities as orientation and training, advisory board meetings, community meetings, and other tasks.[55]

Evidently volunteers have been effectively utilized in the Los Angeles programs and preliminary indications are that the programs have been successful.

[53]*Ibid.*, pp. 4-5.

[54]*Ibid.*, p. 5.

[55]*Ibid.*, p. 6. (For further information regarding these programs write Mrs. Patricia Hunsicker, L.A. County Probation Department, Public Information Office, 320 West Temple, Los Angeles, Calif.)

The Marshall Program. The Marshall Program is a part of the California Youth Authority's short-term institution for the treatment of delinquent boys.[56] The major treatment method is group interaction and counseling. As a result of group interaction and group discussion, it becomes obvious to the delinquent boys that there is a conflict between their behavior and the conventional alternatives provided by society. The program, which deals with boys between fifteen and eighteen years of age, uses a team approach to treatment—involving a variety of specialists.

It is structured to be a model preparole program which bridges the gap between the institutionalization the boy has experienced and the parole supervision he will receive once he is released. The program is similar to the Provo Experiment which will be discussed next. Because many youngsters are susceptible to failure once they are released to the community, it was believed that a more intensive-type approach was needed to prepare the youngster for release. The Marshall Program attempts to provide this.

Some of the conclusions reached as a result of the program were that youngsters involved in such an intensive type of program have to be able to tolerate direct confrontation by their peers in a group counseling session. Much harm can result if a boy cannot tolerate this type of direct approach. It is also important to select boys who can benefit from a direct treatment orientation. The youngsters should be perceptive and fairly intelligent so that they can adequately compare their value systems with those of a larger community. If there is not proper screening, the youngster cannot use the program to its fullest extent and it may even be detrimental to him. It can be another failure which, added to a long list of maladaptive behavior, can contribute to future delinquency.

The Provo Experiment. The Provo Experiment in delinquency rehabilitation was begun in 1956 in Provo, Utah, by a volunteer group of professional and lay people known as the Citizen Advisory Council to the juvenile court.[57] The program was funded by the court, and the research was financed by the Ford Foundation. The program accepted boys from all the major communities around Provo. Only habitual offenders fifteen to seventeen years of age were assigned to the program, and not more than twenty boys were admitted at any one time. The length of stay was specified by the court, and release usually came some time between four and seven months. The boys lived at home and spent only part of each day at Pine Hills, the program center. Otherwise they were free to interact in the community and participate in community activities. The program did not utilize any testing, gathering of case histories, or clinical information. The experiment was initiated because it was concluded that

---

[56]Doug Knight, "The Marshall Program Assessment of a Short-term Institutional Treatment Program," Research Report Nos. 56 and 59, Department of the Youth Authority (Sacramento, Calif., March and August, 1969-70).

[57]Lamar T. Empey and Jerome Rabow, "The Provo Experiment in Delinquency Rehabilitation, *American Sociological Review,* 26 (October 1961), 679-95.

1. The greatest part of delinquent activity takes place in a group—a shared deviation which is a product of differential group experience in a particular subculture.
2. That because most delinquents tend to be concentrated in slums or to be the
   children of lower-class parents their lives are characterized by living situations
   which limit their access to success goals.[58]

The treatment system of the Provo Experiment consisted of two phases. Phase
one, the "intensive treatment phase," was an effort to create a social system
oriented to the task of producing change. Phase two, "the community adjustment
phase," was an effort to maintain reference group support for a boy after the
intensive treatment of phase one. The boy continued to meet with his group
periodically for discussions. Treatment was continued on an intensive basis, unlike
traditional methods such as probation or parole where only periodic visits take
place.

The Provo Experiment was an attempt to treat the youngster in an intensive
manner while allowing him the freedom of the community. It was different from
probation in that the treatment orientation was mainly group counseling and group
interaction. The youngsters assisted each other in problem solving, and they learned
that the gang or group had a great deal of influence on their behavior. When they
formally completed the program, they were aware of the negative influences that
could be exerted by peer pressure. This awareness, it was felt, would help the boys
avoid negative peer group situations. Also, because many of the youngsters who
participated in the Provo program belonged to the same gangs, much of the delinquent activity of these groups would be neutralized. The boys began to use positive
peer pressure to influence each other to become involved in more socially acceptable activities. An evaluation of the program indicated that recidivism rates for boys
in this program appeared to be significantly lower than those for comparable boys
who had been committed to training schools.[59]

The Highfields Project. The Highfields Project was started in New Jersey in
1950 because there was no adequate facility for youngsters on a short-term basis. It
was believed that short-term institutionalization (not to exceed three months)
would be more appropriate for many juveniles. Guided group interaction was the
major treatment method and was supplemented with a work and recreation
program. The program of guided group interaction and exposure to work experience was directed toward providing the boys with increased work skills and
broadening their perspective and alternatives to problem solving.[60]

Two evaluations have been made of the Highfields Project. In the first evaluation, which was made by McCorkle and others, it was determined that although 18

[58]*Ibid.*

[59]*Task Force Report: Corrections,* The President's Commission on Law Enforcement
and the Administration of Justice (Washington, D.C.: Government Printing Office, 1967), p.
39.

[60]Lloyd W. McCorkle, Albert Elias, and F. Lovell Bixby, *The Highfields Story* (New
York: Holt, Rinehart & Winston, Inc., 1958).

Courtesy of Camp Highfields, Onondaga, Michigan

Camp Highfields, a Residential Facility for Boys Located at Onondaga, Michigan

percent of the Highfield boys violated parole, 33 percent of the control group violated parole. The Highfields boys adjusted better over extended periods of time up to five years after release.[61]

In the second evaluation which was made by H. Ashley Weeks, the Highfields boys were also compared with boys who had been sent to the Annandale Reformatory. Whereas 63 percent of the Highfields boys made a good adjustment in the community, only 47 percent of the control groups succeeded on parole.

> The whole Highfields experience is directed toward piercing through the strong defenses against rehabilitation, toward undermining delinquent attitudes and toward developing a self-conception favorable to reformation. The sessions on guided group interaction are especially directed to achieve this directive. Guided group interaction has the merit of combining the psychological and the sociological approaches to the control of human behavior. The psychological approach aims to change the self-concept of the boy from a delinquent to a non-delinquent. This process involves changing the mood of the boy from impulses of lawbreaking to impulses to be law-abiding.[62]

The success of the Highfields Project was one of the major reasons the Provo Experiment was started. An evaluation of the Provo Experiment indicated that 29 percent of the experimental group violated parole after fifteen months, while 48

---

[61]*Ibid.*, p. 143.

[62]*Ibid.*, p. v; also H. Ashley Weeks, *Offenders at Highfields* (Ann Arbor: University of Michigan Press, 1963).

percent of the control group which did not have the benefit of the treatment were parole violators.

The Fremont Experiment. The Fremont Experiment was a short-term residential treatment project operated by the California Youth Authority. Boys randomly selected for the program were exposed to both small-group treatment and a work program. This was supplemented with home visits and other activities. The experimental group of Fremont youngsters was compared with a similar group in a regular institutional program. The control group was not given the same intense exposure to treatment and programming. After a two-year follow-up study, no statistically significant differences emerged between the experimental and the control groups.[63] It was pointed out, however, that

> one bright feature in the report on this experiment is that parole adjustment was better for boys who had gone through the program at a time near its inception than for those who had proceeded through it at a later point. No differences of this sort emerged in the control group. The researcher speculated that this result may have been a reflection of high staff turnover in the Fremont operation in its later stages. If this be so, the results may be more indicative of efficacious treatment tactics than first appearances suggest, in that a stable and continuous program might turn out improved youngsters.[64]

The Fricot Ranch Study. Fricot Ranch is a training school operated by the California Youth Authority. Youngsters at the school were divided into an experimental group and a control group. Those youngsters in the experimental group were exposed to frequent contacts with both their peers and staff members. As a result of comparing boys in the control and experimental groups, there were some interesting findings. Even though the boys who were in the experimental group remained out of trouble for longer periods of time than those in the control group, 80 percent of both the treatment and the control groups experienced difficulties within the three-year follow-up period.[65]

Other studies have also attempted to compare experimental and control groups to determine the effectiveness of the various treatment approaches. In many cases the research findings are confusing, and often specific conclusions cannot be drawn because many variables and extenuating circumstances interfere with effective evaluation. Preliminary indications are that intensive "conventional" treatments, such as casework and psychotherapy (see Chapter 9), are not effective with hard-core delinquents.[66]

[63]Joachim P. Seckel, *The Fremont Experiment, Assessment of Residential Treatment at a Youth Authority Reception Center,* Department of the Youth Authority (Sacramento, Calif., 1967).

[64]Don C. Gibbons, *Society, Crime and Criminal Careers, An Introduction to Criminology* (Englewood Cliffs, N.J.: Prentice-Hall, Inc., 1968), p. 526.

[65]Carl F. Jesness, *The Fricot Ranch Study,* Department of the Youth Authority (Sacramento, Calif., 1965).

[66]Edwin Powers, "An Experiment in the Prevention of Delinquency," *Annals, American Academy of Political and Social Science,* (1949), p. 77; Stuart Adams, "The PICO Project," in

The Need for Evaluation and Research

The importance of adequate evaluative research cannot be overstated. Without proper evaluation and research, new programs cannot be initiated or old programs improved. Many of the programs discussed in this chapter have not been evaluated by vigorous research methods. Only through long-term longitudinal studies can the effects of various prevention efforts be determined and evaluated.

> Development of sound public policy regarding all aspects of delinquency prevention and control requires adequate information upon which to base the decisions. National planning will have to depend on statistical studies of trends in the amounts and types of delinquency. There is need for detailed information on the reasons for referrals to juvenile court and the time spent in detention facilities, on the reasons for the dispositions made by the court, on the personnel who work with juvenile delinquents and on the character of the training schools and other facilities. All these things call for a collection of local, state, and regional data in a national center which can provide statistical analysis and report the results—we are still nearly as deep in ignorance regarding the effects of programs and the conditions producing the effects as we were before the programs were launched. We can only hope that a high priority is given to research in future projects so that we can begin to develop the knowledge base that is essential to the creation of successful programs.[67]

SUMMARY

This chapter has presented a sampling of the various prevention efforts that have been tried and are being used to prevent, control, and treat juvenile delinquency. Many of the programs discussed were *pure* prevention efforts—preventing delinquency before it occurs. Other programs were a combination of pure prevention and rehabilititative prevention—treating both youngsters who have come in contact with the criminal justice system and those who have not. The last programs described were those established mainly for youngsters who have come in contact with the criminal justice system and who need rehabilitation and treatment so that future delinquent behavior will not be manifested in the community.

The next chapter, "Methods of Treatment", will discuss treatment approaches, counseling methods, and other therapeutic strategies. Just as it was pointed out in this chapter that there are many prevention-type programs, the next

Sociology of Punishment and Corrections, ed. Norman Johnston, Leonard Savitz, and Marvin Wolfgang (New York: John Wiley & Sons, Inc., 1962) pp. 213-24; and LeMay Adamson and H. Warren Dunham, "Clinical Treatment of Male Delinquents: A Case Study in Effort and Result," *American Sociological Review,* 21 (June 1956), 312-20.

[67]Stanton Wheeler, Leonard Cottrell, Jr., and Ann Romasco, "Juvenile Delinquency—Its Prevention and Control," in *Task Force Report, Corrections,* p. 424.

chapter will examine a variety of approaches and techniques of treatment that have been tried and are being used with delinquent youngsters.

> The field of delinquency touches a wide variety of social institutions. Its causes are still incompletely understood. There are diverse ways of proceeding with the most important problems and issues. Indeed, the number of proposed solutions is at least as great as the number of occupations, professions, and organizations that have had a stake in delinquency prevention and control programs.[68]

QUESTIONS AND PROJECTS

Essay Questions

1. Differentiate between *pure* and *rehabilitative* prevention.
2. It is recognized that pure prevention is more effective in dealing with delinquency than rehabilitative prevention. Why, then, are there not more pure prevention programs?
3. Compare the advantages and the disadvantages of probation versus institutionalization.
4. What is the difference between punishment and incarceration?
5. Should policemen be placed in schools through police-school liaison programs?

Projects

1. Develop a network of community-based programs for youthful offenders for your community.
2. The child spends more time in school than in any other community institution. Develop a school program that specifically attempts to prevent delinquency.
3. Identify duties and functions within the criminal justice system that can be effectively performed by volunteers.

[68]*Ibid.*, p. 427.

9

METHODS OF TREATMENT

Specific methods of treatment in handling the juvenile are used both in formal prevention, control, and treatment programs and in the agencies that deal with him while he is in the community. Many approaches and methods can be used in treating the delinquent. Most of the methods have a theoretical orientation, and they relate to the theories and assumptions about human behavior that were discussed in previous chapters. For example, the psychoanalytic and psychiatric method of treating the youngster is the outgrowth of research that emphasized the intrapsychic interplay of the dynamics of the individual and the forces that determine his behavior.

The various treatment methods to be described are strategies that attempt to change those conditions thought to be causative factors in juvenile delinquency.[1] Even though an approach can take many forms, it can usually be classified as either an individual approach to treating the offender or a group approach where the offender is treated within the constellation of the group and among his peers. A third category of treatment, punishment, is not as prevalent today as in the past. Although those who prescribe punishment as a method of treatment in itself feel they can justify their position, it will nevertheless not be considered in this chapter as a viable technique of treatment. The rationale underlying the use of punishment

[1]Paul Lerman, *Delinquency and Social Policy* (New York: Frederick A. Praeger, Inc., 1970), p. 37.

is that pain serves as a deterrent to further criminal action. Punishment, as an end in itself, is often used when staff are untrained and when more appropriate methods of treatment are unknown. In the context used in the present discussion, punishment is not to be equated with the setting of limits or the transmission of expectations with resulting enforcement of restrictions or reprimands if reasonable expectations are not adhered to. The setting of limits and restrictions and reprimands are a necessary element in any method of treating and handling the youngster. They can be effective supplements to the major treatment approach utilized. It is when punishment or restriction becomes an end in itself that it cannot be justified or regarded as effective "treatment."

The two basic approaches, then, when dealing with youngsters, are the individual and the group method of treatment. The individual method is generally used by psychiatrists, psychologists, and social workers, while the group method involves school teachers, recreation specialists, and social workers. It is difficult, however, to classify professions by method because psychologists often use the group method, while social workers and even some sociologists use the individual method. There is also a blending of the individual and the group work approach, with the possibility that the same person will be using both the individual and the group method. The method that the therapist or the counselor selects usually fits his professional training, his personality, and his clientele. Even though a combination of approaches will generally be used, one major orientation will be taken, with specific assumptions about human behavior.

Knowledge of the various approaches for treating and rehabilitating the delinquent or the predelinquent is important for the professional within the criminal justice system. Regardless of the phase of criminal justice that he is involved in (police work, social work, courts, probation, parole, corrections, research), an awareness of treatment methods and strategies will familiarize him with the many approaches, the current terminology, and the assumptions about human behavior made by other professionals in the criminal justice system.

Although the policeman, for example, may not use or be trained to use many of these methods and may not even agree with their orientation, knowledge of them will give him greater insight into the reasons why his professional counterparts in other agencies take their particular orientation to delinquent behavior problem solving. Furthermore, exposing all the different professionals within the criminal justice system to the various treatment approaches and strategies may be instrumental in the development of an orientation that will be generally normative and acceptable to all the various professions. A more coordinated and normative orientation to treating the delinquent would be conducive to providing a consistent approach to delinquency problem solving.

Because of the many treatment methods, the professional soon learns that there is no "right way" to treat the youngster and that many approaches have merit. This allows him to select the approach or the parts of many approaches that he feels will be most effective and beneficial for his client.

As pointed out earlier, it is difficult to correlate specific approaches with a particular academic orientation—sociologists usually take a "social engineering" approach to delinquency prevention and treatment, while psychologists treat the individual. In other words, sociologists attempt to determine the conditions of the social structure that breed delinquency, while psychologists emphasize the individual and his interpersonal dynamics. Sociology has typically been regarded as a theoretical discipline researching the causes, rates, and effects of crime and delinquency. The profession of social work is the "practical arm" of the sociologist. The social worker attempts to put into practice the assumptions that have been posited by sociologists. However, social workers base much of their actual treatment of clients on psychological and psychiatric theories and principles. A sociologist, psychologist, or any other professional who specializes in crime and delinquency causation, prevention, control and treatment is a *criminologist.*

The social worker, then, translates the theories and assumptions of both psychological and sociological theory into action. This is one of the main reasons why individual and group approaches to treatment are often blended.

In addition to his theorizing about causes of delinquency, the psychologist, like the social worker, often becomes involved in the specific use of treatment methods. The sociologist usually orients himself to the more massive problem of "social engineering."

The discussion of the functions and orientation of sociologists, psychologists, and social workers can be quite confusing, and because of the blending of approaches, a professional differentiation is often difficult to make because some sociologists are more psychological than some psychologists, and vice versa.

The terminology used for the particular treatment method and the label used for the treater can also be confusing. Some treatment approaches are similar but have different names. Also, the function and the role of the treater can be similar for the various methods, but he may be called a counselor, caseworker, therapist, or psychotherapist.

A discussion of the individual and group methods of treatment follows. Although it is difficult to assign a particular academic discipline or profession to the many approaches, the professionals who utilize the following methods are generally psychologists, psychiatrists, and social workers. There are approaches, however, that such professionals as the police and school counselors can use, and these approaches will also be emphasized.

PSYCHOTHERAPY

Both Kolb[2] and Wolberg[3] define *psychotherapy* as a method of treatment of emotional and personality problems by psychological means. The aim of this method is to remove or retard symptoms or behavior patterns that are contributing

---

[2]Lawrence C. Kolb, *Noyes' Modern Clinical Psychiatry* (Philadelphia: W.B. Saunders Co., 1968), p. 346.

[3]Lewis R. Wolberg, *The Techniques of Psychotherapy* (New York: Grune and Stratton, Inc., 1967),-p. 3.

to dysfunctional behavior. The promotion of personal growth is the end product. Nikelly states that

> any form of psychotherapy involves change in the client's attitude as well as his feelings and such change will ultimately be reflected in the client's value system. The therapist should not hesitate to disclose that he too has values and that his and the client's values may occasionally clash. Such a conflict can actually form a landmark during the process of psychotherapy because the client must examine his own values carefully in order to understand why they fail to help him function effectively as an emotionally healthy and adjusted person.[4]

Psychotherapy is an outgrowth of psychoanalytic and psychiatric assumptions. One of the basic concepts of psychotherapy is the phenomenon of *transference,* the redirecting of feelings from the client to the therapist, which in turn enables the therapist to probe the attitudes, thoughts, and feelings about significant persons in the client's past through his own relationship with the client. Many times the therapist will represent an authoritative figure of the client's early past, and in the case of a delinquent, the therapist often represents a parental figure. Aichhorn felt that transference was one of the most important elements in treating the juvenile delinquent.[5] Through his research, he concluded that all the extremely aggressive boys in his institution had had similar life experiences with their parents, that is, constant quarrels between parents or parental figures. There is much hate between the youngster and his parents because of these early relationships. Since the early relationship of the youngster with his parents was not satisfactory, his emotional development was often retarded, with the effect that a delinquent boy was often impulsive in an attempt to satisfy infantile urges not satisfied in the normal manner within his family. Satisfying these urges and impulses can take the form of antisocial behavior within the community.

One of Aichhorn's methods of handling boys who had grown up in such a situation was to utilize the method of transference and allow the boys to satisfy their impulses while under the guidance of a sympathetic adult (or parental substitute) whom the youngster could trust and rely on.

> If delinquency is to be cured and the asocial youth made fit again for life in society, the training school must provide him with new ties and induce him to attach himself to persons of his environment. We try to bring about such attachments by the kindly manner in which we treat our pupils.[6]

Aichhorn was explaining that the institutionalized child under his direction was allowed to operate in an atmosphere of love and acceptance and therefore did not have to fear severe rejection or physical punishment. The child, under these

[4]Arthur G. Nikelly, "Basic Processes in Psychotherapy," *Techniques for Behavior Change* (Springfield, Ill.: Charles C Thomas, Publisher, 1971), p. 31.

[5]August Aichhorn, *Wayward Youth* (New York: The Viking Press, Inc., 1963).

[6]August Aichhorn, *Delinquency and Child Guidance* (New York: International Universities Press, Inc., 1964), p. 29.

conditions, would learn to develop a satisfactory relationship, trust the adult figure, and satisfy his needs. Aichhorn felt that this trust, as a result of the warm friendly relationship, could be generalized to other adults and institutions in the community. Just as the youngster had generalized his negative experiences from his parents to the community, acquainting him with positive identification models within his treatment environment could effectively help him generalize the positive associations to the community. This would eliminate much of his impulsive necessity to act out against authority substitutes.

Friedlander, whose orientation to human behavior is similar to that of Aichhorn, discovered that there were changes in behavior due to the transference established between boys and the counselor.

> The aggressiveness was not just acted out; the person of the educator [therapist] became an important factor in it. The boys clearly wanted to provoke him to punish them and were therefore specially destructive when in his presence. This punishment would have provided them with an instinctive gratification on the sado-masochistic level which they had been able to obtain in all their former environments. When the punishment did not come, the boys grew dissatisfied. Not only did they not derive sufficient gratification when destroying inanimate things but the unforeseen reaction of their educators put them in a difficult position; there was no longer any justification for their hatred. They still tried to get what they wanted by being more and more aggressive but in the end they had to give in: they began to feel guilty (the first stage of superego development) and they broke down. Behind their aggressiveness and their wish to be punished, which had been transformed to the educators, there now appeared a fierce longing to be loved. This was still very untamed. Their demands for the affection of the leader being insatiable but they now had an emotional relationship to an adult which made education possible.[7]

The above quotation illustrates the transference phenomenon in operation. The boys generalized to the educator or the therapist their early attitudes and feelings toward adults. They expected the therapist to react the way their parents would have reacted. When they found that not all adults reacted the same as their parents, they began to evaluate their attitudes and their behavior and concluded that not all adults were the same and that a discriminating approach to evaluating adults and the environment was most effective. When the youngsters began to evaluate adults on an individual basis, they did not have the generalized hatred to all adults or all adult institutions, and their acting out behavior began to diminish greatly.

Long and Kamada believe that in the initial therapeutic stages, it is essential to develop a basis of trust between the therapist and the youngster.[8] All youngsters, whether in a therapeutic situation or in the family constellation, constantly test to determine the limits of acceptable behavior and the reaction of the adult. Most delinquents come from family situations where there was very little trust in the

---

[7]Kate Friedlander, *The Psycho-Analytical Approach to Juvenile Delinquency* (London: Routledge & Kegan Paul Ltd., 1947), p. 243.

[8]Anna Marie Long and Samuel I. Kamada, "Psychiatric Treatment of Adolescent Girls," *California Youth Authority Quarterly*, 17 (Summer 1964), 23-24.

family and very little predictable emotional security. Sometimes even such basic necessities as food and clothing were not provided. Therefore, they are very skeptical in treatment situations, and it is difficult to build up a trust relationship. If the therapist cannot establish himself as a trusting person who will be unlike the youngster's brutal and insensitive parents, it will be difficult for the youngster to benefit from the treatment.

Szurek stresses the importance of recognizing that the impulsive child needs to receive the experience of love previously denied him and that he needs to receive this love as a person, not merely as a reward for conformity.

> He needs this love for the prolonged period necessary for him to develop an essential sense of security. He also needs frank unyielding firmness coupled with uncompromising fairness and justice. The therapist needs to be able to recognize the many forms which the patient's distressful unmodified egocentricity and revengefulness may take and yet not be swayed from this therapeutic goal. . . . At least an approximation of these conditions may offer a chance that the child will become attached to the adult; if the relationship is continued long enough he will begin to identify with the adult's ideals, to understand the adult wishes for his own welfare and to acquire a new sense of his own worth as a person.[9]

It is important for the therapist to be well adjusted and not have an extensive amount of "hangups" or difficulties with authority himself. Unfortunately, too often the therapist or the counselor does have psychological problems of his own, and these are transferred to his work with youngsters. If the therapist is emotionally unhealthy himself, the therapeutic situation can do more harm than good, and the transference created may perpetuate and even foster negative behavior within the community. Chapter 4 pointed out that the unhealthy and dishonest professional can often perpetuate negative behavior, and it is precisely within the therapeutic situation and often through the transference phenomenon that it is fostered.

Holmes points out that many delinquent youngsters, even though they may be in their late teens, fantasize a great deal and have feelings of omnipotence. Everyone is aware that a very young child, as a result of his fantasizing, can pretend he is anybody he likes, including strong and powerful individuals. Because delinquent youngsters have not had satisfying or emotionally secure environments, they utilize fantasy to increase their feelings of worthfulness, deny unpleasant circumstances, and avoid facing the reality of their environment and its demands and requirements. When the youngster's behavior is dealt with thoroughly and objectively by the therapist, this can be surprising to the youngster and can neutralize many of his fantasies about adult authority figures. Being treated fairly and objectively is often a new experience for a youngster, and when this does occur it is both unexpected and incongruent with his earlier life experiences.

[9]S. A. Szurek, "Some Impressions from Clinical Experience with Delinquents," in *The Antisocial Child: His Family and His Community*. ed. S. A. Szurek and I. N. Berlin (Palo Alto, Calif.: Science and Behavior Books, Inc., 1969), pp. 80-81.

> Although it is often necessary to outsmart the delinquent youngster, it is not necessary to withhold a reasonable expression of critical appreciation for his manipulative virtuosity. Even as he frustrates an attempted swindle, the therapist may use the incident to demonstrate some of the advantages of a direct as opposed to a devious approach to people.[10]

Holmes is emphasizing the importance of directness with the youngster. When the delinquent youngster manipulates and uses devious means to satisfy his needs, he is usually accustomed to the same type of reaction from adults within his environment. When this negative, manipulative, devious cycle is interrupted by the efficient therapist, the youngster becomes aware of his negative cycle of behavior and realizes that some adults do react differently and do not always play dishonest games of manipulation. Holmes is also careful to point out the importance of going beyond merely making interpretations of behavior in psychotherapy. Interpretation in itself does not always alter behavior.

> If an adolescent boy prefers stealing cars to suffering the anxiety he would experience if he did not steal cars, he would probably not be helped by interpretation alone. The general principle is the same as in the treatment of addictions of perversions. It is virtually impossible to treat a chronic alcoholic successfully in a tavern.[11]

The therapist, then, interprets behavior to point out the negative dynamics, and he must also point out the reality of the situation and of the behavior itself. For example, to merely explain to a youngster that he is stealing cars because of an unresolved oedipal conflict will not usually in itself contribute to diminished car stealing. This interpretation, however, along with pointing out the reality of the negative ramifications of car stealing and the long-range problems that will be created by it, can be helpful. The youngster will learn that the negative consequences of stealing cars and possible incarceration are not very pleasurable and that other modes of behavior or other alternatives can be developed to satisfy his desires and impulses. The therapist as the authority person can, in addition to making an interpretation, provide healthy alternatives and guidelines for the youngster. The inefficient therapist may be able to interpret, but he will be unable to provide feasible and positive alternatives that will be compatible with the expectations of the youngster's environment.

In addition to being honest and direct, the therapist has to avoid empty threats of punishment not only because they do not work in most cases but because they may also transmit failure to the youngster and indicate that he is incapable of handling his problems without them. The therapist has to be realistic and point out that if the youngster is involved in uncontrolled deviousness within the community, he cannot expect the same warm humanistic treatment by community agencies whose duty it is to control and interrupt negative behavior. For example:

[10]Donald J. Holmes, *The Adolescent in Psychotherapy* (Boston: Little, Brown and Company, 1964), p. 158.

[11]*Ibid.*, p. 185.

> when a boy runs away from the hospital and steals a car which is a felony we
> would be doing him a serious disservice to withhold the explanation that
> although we are willing to view this as symptomatic it can be examined in
> quite another light under the law and can possibly result in his being removed
> from our relatively benevolent sphere of influence. He has a right to know this
> and we have an obligation to tell him. In some psychiatric settings it is too easy
> for the antisocial adolescent to nourish the delusion that his status as a
> patient automatically exempts him from all other legal, moral and religious
> responsibility.[12]

Jurjevich also believes that the delinquent youngster must be responsible for
his own behavior even when he is in an institution, or on probation, or in another
facility where an attempt is made to provide a benevolent and warm atmosphere.[13]
From the many case histories that Jurjevich reviewed and the clients he worked
with he found that there were many difficulties in the youngsters' backgrounds, but
he felt that these unfortunate circumstances could not be used by the clients as
excuses to act irresponsibly because they would still be evaluated according to the
normative criteria established by society, which its institutions of control would
enforce. Thus his main direction was not focused on past traumas or injuries or on
personal handicaps, but in the direction of providing new alternatives for the
youngster so he could avoid future problems in the community. He assisted his
clients in developing a life process so that they could achieve their goals yet avoid
the deviant behavior that was so much a part of their past.

> The main method of achieving changes in the girls was considered to be
> helping them comply with the reasonable demands of training and discipline
> and accept the stresses of their situation without overreacting—the main
> facilitating factor in changing them appeared to be a warm respectful and
> when necessary frank but not a bluntly disapproving relationship between
> them and the therapist.[14]

Jurjevich never openly forced the girls to change or comply to normative behavior,
but he was always quick to point out what would be more acceptable and more
rewarded in the community and what would be most disapproved of and sanc-
tioned.

The psychotherapeutic method is often ascribed an aura of mysticism. In very
simple terms, psychotherapy is merely a method of conversation between the client
and the therapist to allow them to get to know each other so that they can be
comfortable in exchanging communication. The communication allows the client to
begin to relate personal experiences, perceptions, ideas, and reasons for negative as
well as positive behavior so that solutions will be forthcoming. The effective
therapist will create an atmosphere where the youngster can be comfortable and
can relate his feelings and attitudes but will always be provided a base or reference

---

[12]*Ibid.*, p. 262.

[13]Ratibor-Ray M. Jurjevich, *No Water in My Cup: Experiences and a Controlled Study
of Psychotherapy of Delinquent Girls* (New York: Libra Publishers, 1968).

[14]*Ibid.*, p. 107.

to reality. The emotionally secure and able therapist or counselor will provide these reference points even when they are not popular with his client but in the long run will be most effective for positive behavior.

In conclusion, psychotherapy is the technique utilized by individuals who call themselves therapists, and it emanates from the framework of psychoanalysis and psychiatric theory. The therapist or, in layman's terms, the counselor evaluates the client's feelings, experiences, and inner dynamics. He attempts to point out faulty perceptions and provide positive alternatives to behavior adaption. He facilitates the solving of conflicts and helps the client make a positive adjustment to his environment. The therapist usually represents many adults in the youngster's past. An effective therapist can influence the youngster in a positive manner, facilitating the generalization of the results of this relationship to other adults in the community. The new positive attitude of the youngster which results from his relationship with the therapist can effectively alter his negative behavior in the community and contribute to his satisfactory adjustment.

SOCIAL CASEWORK

Social casework, according to Tappan, is that phase of social work dealing directly with the maladjusted individual to determine the kind of help he needs and to assist him in coping with his problems.[15] Ferguson feels that "when social work is primarily concerned with the fullest possible degree of personality development we call it social casework."[16]

Although similar in many respects, technically social casework should be considered different from psychotherapy, and professionals working in the community are not often able to distinguish between them. In fact, those social workers utilizing social casework often see themselves as therapists and feel that even though they have been trained in social casework, the specific focus of their social casework training has been in the psychotherapeutic area. Regardless of the technical difference between the two, they both rely on developing a positive relationship with the client so that he can be assisted in problem solving. In casework, as in psychotherapy, the client relates on a one-to-one basis with the caseworker (or therapist, counselor, etc.). This type of interaction can result in a joint effort at problem solving and the development of socially acceptable alternatives to community adjustment. The American Correctional Association states that the casework method is very helpful in altering deviant behavior.[17] The casework method is conducive to determining the conditions that contribute to deviant

---

[15]Paul W. Tappan, *Juvenile Delinquency* (New York: McGraw-Hill Book Company, 1949), p. 362.

[16]Elizabeth A. Ferguson, *Social Work: An Introduction* (Philadelphia: J. B. Lippincott Co., 1963), p. 9.

[17]The American Correctional Association, *Manual of Correctional Standards* (Washington, D.C.: The Association, 1966), pp. 422-23.

Courtesy of Camp Highfields, Onondaga, Michigan

Figure 13
One-to-One Counseling Need Not Take Place in an Office

behavior and pinpointing the resources necessary to support the client in his efforts to become a contributing member of society. The caseworker utilizes the social history to explore the client's background, environment, and relationship with his family, friends, and peers. The social history, or case history, affords the case-worker who may be a probation officer, parole officer, prison counselor, mental health worker, or school social worker the opportunity to evaluate the personal strengths and weaknesses of the client as well as his environment so that a treat-ment plan can be devised and carried out. The youngster will be counseled or "treated," and if possible his environment will be altered. In terms of environ-mental manipulation, the youngster may be removed from his environment and placed in a rehabilitative agency or treatment program so that he does not have to experience the severe pressures of his family or peer group who are contributing to his negative behavior.

When working with delinquents it is often difficult to obtain their coopera-tion because they are unwilling to trust the caseworker. The delinquent's family may also be resistant and may become defensive and feel threatened by the caseworker's "probing." Parents often fear that the negative dynamics of their family and their relationship with their youngster will become known and that they will be blamed for their youngster's predicament. Even though social casework, like many other methods, has been successful with neurotics, it has often not been successful with delinquents. Neurotics are usually motivated in the helping rela-tionship, while delinquents are not. The intensity of the one-to-one relationship with the caseworker is also threatening. Some of the assumptions of social casework are not applicable when treating the delinquent. For example, the caseworker often takes a passive approach to treatment under the guise of client self-determination and the need for client involvement and commitment. Delinquents need a more direct and aggressive approach, which accelerates client involvement and joint problem solving. Because passive techniques have generally been unsuccessful with delinquents, the present trend is to use a more aggressive approach.

> The word aggressive ... describes nothing new in casework. It is used to characterize the kinds of adaptions in practice which are necessary when, because children are in trouble, a caseworker goes out to serve families who do not want her.[18]

The caseworker often meets with much resentment and hostility not only from the delinquent who did not ask for help but also from the youngster's parents who are perpetuating the delinquent behavior. Nevertheless, the caseworker, if he is going to be successful, must convince the family that casework intervention and counseling are needed to assist them in problem solving. It is often difficult to convince the parents that they need assistance, and this necessitates a great deal of effort and perseverance by the caseworker. He can explain that it is to the family's advantage to accept assistance and solve the problem before it becomes so unmanageable that the youngster will seriously harm himself or the community.

In some cases the family refuses to become involved in the helping process even when the *aggressive casework* method is utilized; consequently, the caseworker may have to call upon an authoritative agency like the juvenile court to intervene in the problem situation.

> Steps toward the use of aggressive casework arise from the acceptance of a social philosophy that assigns to the community not only the right to protect children but the responsibility of taking vigorous action on their behalf when their behavior reflects a destructive process that the family itself cannot or will not control.[19]

Casework with delinquents can be viewed as a three-phased process. Initially and in less-severe cases, the typical method of passive involvement with the clients can often be utilized. If, however, the youngster is a chronic offender, he has usually been through the passive processes of self-determination and cathartic verbalization. He may be resentful and cynical of not only the process itself but also the adult who is using it. Furthermore, if the parents are contributing to and fostering his delinquent activity, the caseworker's passive methods will not be successful because of their hostility and unresponsiveness. Therefore, the second phase involves the use of aggressive casework in which the worker has to be persistent and direct in his approach to the problem. He confronts the parents and defines the problem, the consequences if the problem is not handled, and the alternatives he sees for its solution. The worker has to provide a great deal of

[18] Alice Overton, "Aggressive Casework," in *Reaching the Unreached*, ed. Sylvan S. Furman (New York: New York City Youth Board, 1952), p. 51.

[19] Harry Manuel Shulman, *Juvenile Delinquency in American Society* (New York: Harper & Row, 1961), p. 642.

support in the early stages of treatment so that the family will become involved in the problem-solving process and will be able to make realistic decisions and accept responsibility.[20] Finally, if the first phase of passive casework and the second phase of aggressive casework are not successful, an authoritative agency such as the juvenile court may have to be presented to the family as the only alternative and may have to intervene to insure that the parents and the youngster will begin to look at their problem realistically and attempt to seek solutions.

Frequently, regardless of whether the technique utilized is the passive approach of the aggressive approach, it is still difficult to work with youngsters and their families because the atmosphere is usually tense and pervaded with hostility and resentment toward the criminal justice system. A new form of casework called "directed friendship" is becoming popular. This approach actively seeks out clients and is described by Powers and Witmer.[21] They point out how paid nonprofessionals can visit homes and schools for the express purpose of giving personal advice and guidance. A relationship with the youngsters is developed so that the "friendship person" can be a readily available source of advice, guidance, and support to the youngster before he becomes involved in more difficulty with the law. This is a much different approach than waiting until the youngster becomes chronically involved in serious difficulty.

After the onset of chronic delinquency, the youngster and his family are often hostile and resentful. The directed friendship technique in seeking out youngsters who may be borderline delinquents, or at least less than chronic, can be effective in not only pinpointing delinquents but in utilizing casework or other techniques before the problem becomes extremely serious for the youngster and the community. Once a serious problem occurs, it is twice as difficult to deal with the problem and develop a positive relationship with the youngster and his family.

REALITY THERAPY

The major basis of the *reality therapy* approach is that all persons have certain basic needs. When they are unable to fulfill these needs, they act in an irresponsible manner. The object of reality therapy is to help the person act in a responsible manner—in the case of a delinquent, to help him refrain from antisocial activity. A premise of this approach is that regardless of what the delinquent youngster has done and the extenuating circumstances—for example, inadequate parents or negative environmental conditions, the youngster is still responsible for his behavior. There are no acceptable excuses, and the irresponsibility that is manifested through delinquent activity and law breaking is not condoned. The reality therapy method is an understandable, commonsense approach which its originator,

[20]Overton, *op. cit.,* p. 54.

[21]Edwin Powers and Helen Witmer, "The Cambridge-Somerville Study," in *The Sociology of Punishment and Correction,* ed. Norman Johnston, Leonard Savitz, and Marvin E. Wolfgang (New York: John Wiley & Sons, Inc., 1970), p. 588.

Dr. William Glasser, holds can be utilized by all members of the criminal justice system ranging from the arresting police officer to the counselor in the training school. Anyone who comes in contact with the delinquent can utilize this approach because it does not emphasize nebulous psychiatric terms, extensive testing, or time-consuming case conferences.

> The only case records needed are occasional notes about what has occurred that shows increased responsibility. If the boy fails, the reason is that we were not able to help him become responsible enough to live in society. We need no detailed record of this failure to explain why.[22]

In sharp contrast to the psychotherapeutic methods, reality therapy emphasizes the present behavior of the youngster and considers it the most important event. What happened in the past is insignificant because regardless of how much is known about the past extenuating circumstances and the relationship of the youngster with his parents, the past cannot be changed. The basis of psychotherapy is that a person cannot change his present behavior unless he can clearly tie it to events in the past. Glasser states that delving into the past is "a fruitless historical journey—which leads to excusing the offender's present actions as an unfortunate culmination of his history."[23] The premise is that since a person's past history cannot be changed or objectively reconstructed, he can never fully understand the reasons why he committed a certain act, and interpretations are often merely guesses as to causative relationships. Furthermore, if present behavior is merely a reflection and the sum total of all past experiences (as traditional psychotherapies propose), then when the present behavior is modified and changed this nullifies all past experiences. In other words, if the child learns to refrain from delinquent activity, the drives, urges, impulses, and experiences that caused the symptomatic delinquent manifestation will be nullified as a result of the new socially acceptable life-style.

If there is too much emphasis on the past and on extenuating circumstances, this can excuse the client's transgressions, contribute to his feeling that he is sick, and thus excuse his present and future delinquent activity within the community.

Glasser believes that many therapists, caseworkers, and counselors feel that the youngster is unhappy because of his past circumstances, and therefore he acts out within the community because of this unhappiness. Efforts to make the youngster happy invariably fail because the unhappiness is the result of irresponsible behavior (delinquent activity) and not the result of past personal and environmental circumstances. Since everyone wants to feel worthwhile and be evaluated positively by his peers, irresponsible delinquent behavior causes negative self-evaluations and hence feelings of worthlessness or unhappiness. The only way a

[22]William Glasser, "Reality Therapy: A Realistic Approach to the Young Offender," in *Readings in Delinquency and Treatment,* ed. Robert Schasre and Jo Wallach (Los Angeles: The Delinquency Prevention Training Project, Youth Studies Center, University of Southern California, 1965), p. 65.

[23]*Ibid.,* p. 57.

person can be made to feel worthwhile and fulfill his basic needs is by acting in a responsible manner, which means avoiding delinquent behavior.

The main objective of reality therapy is to make the individual a responsible person within the community, and this starts with a positive relationship and inter-action between him and the therapist. If the therapist treats the youngster as a responsible person and expects him to respond in a positive manner, this trans-mission will give the child confidence and will be the catalytic agent in his acting positively. If the child is treated as a responsible person and not as an unfortunate youngster, this will transmit strength to the youngster. The therapist should be a warm and honest person who emphasizes the positive rather than the negative and strength rather than weakness, and he should have confidence that the youngster will act responsibly. The youngster is expected to obey rules, but he is not rejected when he breaks one. The reality of the situation and the possible negative conse-quences of his unlawful activity are, however, pointed out to him. The therapist never asks why the youngster became involved in the activity. Only present events are considered. Questions by the therapist concern only the circumstances of the youngster's problems, not their underlying causes.

> Open ended questions such as "Why did you do it?" should be avoided. Too much questioning, too much initial conversation gives him the opportunity to make excuses, to feel antagonistic toward authority, to justify in his mind that what he did was not very wrong or if wrong not really his fault.[24]

In reality therapy, the therapist always gives the client a great deal of support when he acts in a responsible manner. He always transmits to the youngster a certain set of expectations or rules, defines the limits of acceptable behavior, and follows through with any consequences that have been laid down in the "contract."

Reality therapy has been criticized because many feel that it is an oversimpli-fication of human behavior and that in some cases the transmitting of expectations to the youngster can have negative effects if the youngster came from a situation in which there were a great many expectations transmitted to him which he could not live up to and follow. Regardless of the criticism, however, Glasser has proved through research that his method can be effective not only in juvenile courts and in probation settings but also in institutions.

Reality therapy, like other therapies, is only as good as the individual coun-selor or therapist who is using it. Reality therapy is a logical, down-to-earth, and commonsense approach, but if it is not used correctly it can be a punitive technique when treating youngsters. For example, a therapist, in a coldhearted manner after a youngster has been apprehended, can say to him, "I don't want to know why you are involved in a difficulty. You are irresponsible and I will not become involved with you as your counselor until you react in a more responsible manner." This, of course, can be a very hostile attitude transmitted to the youngster under the guise of reality therapy. Any therapy, regardless of its techniques, can be used as a hostile, punitive mechanism by an inefficient therapist.

[24]*Ibid.*, p. 53.

As stated earlier, reality therapy can make an important contribution to the criminal justice system process. One of the major problems in handling and treating juveniles is *consistency*. Because the criminal justice system is composed of professionals from various backgrounds, training, and orientation, consistency is often lacking within the system.

In Chapter 4 we saw how inconsistency in the family can contribute to "acting out" behavior by the youngster. Inconsistent handling of the juvenile in the criminal justice system can also have negative consequences. Reality therapy can be effective in combating inconsistencies in treatment and handling and can provide the base for a more coordinated approach to treating the delinquent. All professionals within the system can use this approach with a minimal amount of training.

TRANSACTIONAL ANALYSIS

Transactional analysis, which can be utilized both individually and in groups, is mainly concerned with evaluating and interpreting interpersonal relationships and dynamic transactions between the client and his environment. According to Berne, transactions between individuals can be viewed as "pastimes and games."[25] In other words, much of the interaction that takes place with individuals can be viewed as games or game playing.

Transactional analysis is based on the following assumptions. (1) Human relationships consist of competitive acts of social maneuvers which serve a defensive function and yield important gratification which can be labeled "games." (2) All persons manifest three different "ego states": the *child,* a relic of the individual's past; the *parent,* whom he has incorporated through identification with his parents; and the *adult,* who is the mature and responsible self. (3) Each of these "ego states" perceives reality differently: the child prelogically, the parent judgmentally, and the adult comprehensively on the basis of past experience. (4) The three states operate constantly in response to the person's needs and the "games" in which he indulges at a given time.[26]

The major purpose of therapy is to point out the various games that the client plays and attempt to strengthen the adult component of the personality, displace the immaturities of the child component, and reduce the subjective judgment of the parental component. Before using transactional analysis, the therapist, through diagnosis of the patient's demeanor, gestures, vocabulary, and voice, attempts to determine the ego state responsible for the patient's symptoms and disturbances. For example, it may be pinpointed that even though the delinquent youngster is an adolescent, much of his behavior is manifested like an impulsive, immature child and this is the reason he gets involved in difficulty. In other words, the game playing that he is involved in is through the dynamic child component, and the

[25]Eric Berne, *Transactional Analysis in Psychotherapy* (New York: Grove Press, 1961).
[26]Wolberg, *op. cit.,* p. 257.

major portion of his time is spent in these childish activities which ultimately result in hedonistic, impulsive behavior within the community. After the initial diagnosis and interpretation, the individual may have sessions with the therapist to further pinpoint his game playing and those components that are most manifest. He may also be placed in a group where his transactions and game playing become more revealing in interaction with others.

Even though this method has primarily been used with adults, Berne feels that it has a special value for adolescents because of their typical resistance to psychotherapy. Not only are adolescents resistant to psychotherapy, delinquent adolescents are even more so:

> Since the majority of teenage patients are sent or brought to treatment, the relationship to the therapist is not an autonomous one so that there is a strong temptation to rebellion, withdrawal, or sabotage. In effect, the therapist becomes a delegate of their parents which under the usual contract puts him in a great disadvantage from the beginning. The sought for "cure" too often resembles a prescription written by the parents, who visualize the therapeutic relationship as a *Parent-Child* one, and the patient tends to do the same. The situation can be decisively altered at the social level by explicitly setting up an *Adult-Adult* contract, whereby the therapist offers to teach the patient transactional analysis, with the provision that the patient can do as he pleases with what he learns.[27]

In this situation the adolescent or the delinquent adolescent does not necessarily take a subservient role but is taught the method of transactional analysis. The major principle learned is how to identify the three dynamic components of the personality. The therapist can point out that he too has components of the *parent* and the *child* as well as of the *adult*. He can also illustrate to the youngster in what cases his own *child* component, or childishness, is manifested. The child then does not have to operate as a subservient, he can learn the method and apply it to his own situation when he is ready and feels it will be helpful. Transactional analysis can be effective by teaching the youngster a method of evaluating his own behavior and categorizing it as adult oriented, parent oriented, or child oriented. In most cases the youngster can make the final determination as to the appropriateness of his behavior and the category into which it falls. If he constantly evaluates his behavior and actions as childish, through his own awareness of the method and "diagnosis," he can alter the impulsive childish component of his personality and emphasize the more acceptable adult characterization.

VOCATIONAL COUNSELING

Vocational counseling is different from the preceding therapeutic methods and does not necessarily attempt to understand the interpersonal dynamics of human behavior or spend a great deal of time on diagnosis. The main purpose of vocational

[27]Berne, *op. cit.*, p. 355.

counseling is to increase the client's knowledge of career choices, job specifications, and qualifications and training needed for successful employment. The vocational counselor can help the young person identify his interests by questioning him about his attitude toward work in general and the specific types of employment that appeal to him. Aptitude and interest testing may also be used. This experience is often a whole new area for the delinquent adolescent because he has never held a job and hence has never experienced the problems that exist or the positive rewards that can result. The positive attitudes, skills, and habits that the youngster develops and refines in the work situation can be carried over to the community and can positively affect his relationships with others.

> Perhaps the most crucial problem to tackle in helping young people prepare for the adult world of work is in positively influencing their attitudes toward work. Many characteristics typical of the delinquent youth militate against a ready adjustment to employment. Typically the delinquent lacks self-confidence. He knows that he will make serious mistakes on the job. He goes forth expecting not to be liked, looking for slights and unfairness. He seeks immediate gratification of his impulses and has difficulty in working toward goals which are as remote as a pay check which comes only once a week. Basic skills are important primarily because they influence a child's attitude toward work and self-confidence. It is upon the development of constructive attitudes toward and reactions to work that emphasis should be placed. This means that an analysis of each child's interest, aptitudes, and capacity to tolerate the demands of the assignment should be made before work and shop assignments are made. His initial work experience should be carefully structured to assure some sense of achievement and to avoid too much frustration.[28]

The work situation can provide a realistic environment where behavior can be evaluated and many of the youngster's problems can be resolved. The astute counselor can utilize problem situations that occur in the work environment to point out interpersonal difficulties that the youngster has, which usually also exist outside the work environment. The personal relationships that exist between youngsters and their work supervisors or work peers can be critical in altering attitudes and behavior and in facilitating solution to problems.

> Whether or not a boy or girl becomes particularly skilled on the work assignment is one factor but more important is the satisfaction he realizes from a working relationship. If he can gain confidence in his supervisor he has made the first step toward placing confidence and trust in other individuals—If the training can reconcile the child's aptitudes and personality needs with the basic rules of society then it has accomplished this rehabilitation and has indeed trained and educated him for life in the community.[29]

A positive identification model can frequently be the most effective means of influencing the youngster to develop positive alternatives to problem solving.

[28]National Conference of Superintendents of Training Schools and Reformatories, *Institutional Rehabilitation of Delinquent Youth: Manual for Training School Personnel* (Albany, N.Y.: Delmar Publishers, Inc., 1962), pp. 106-7.

[29]*Ibid.,* p. 108.

The astute counselor (therapist, caseworker, etc.) is also aware of the resources in his community and the programs available to help train and retrain youngsters so that they can become more effective citizens and successful workers. Helping the youngster adjust to his work environment is as much a part of therapy or counseling as the communication and interpretation of interpersonal dynamics that take place within the context of therapeutic interview.

Vocational Guidance

Vocational guidance programs that involve vocational counseling have often been effective in redirecting the energy of delinquent youngsters into positive channels. Experimental projects have been developed to encourage youngsters to stay in school so that they can acquire a vocational goal and increased skills which will contribute to a more positive self-image and success in the community. Various attempts have been made both with individuals and with groups to encourage youngsters to develop needed skills and discuss their attitudes about work and the problems that they perceive or encounter in the work world. One such project attempted to encourage boys to discuss their perceptions of work. This was accomplished through the group process of discussion meetings.

> The only regulations voiced at the very onset were that the participants must not damage or destroy any of the office property and not do bodily violence to any member of the group. These regulations were accepted and respected throughout the group sessions.[30]

The meetings were set up to discuss various situations that the boys encountered at work and the relationships they had with work supervisors, work peers, and other persons within the environment. In other words, the entire constellation of factors that related to work assignments, work skills, and activities and duties were covered. The open discussions were

> not merely an outpouring of hostility because as the meetings progressed some of the boys interpreted the behavior of others in the group. They began to be critical of themselves. At first their hostility was directed towards school authorities and then to their parents, representatives of the law, and peers. Finally they began to realize that they were also involved.[31]

The main point is that the effective counselor can utilize the group itself to solve problems and increase the awareness of individual members in the group of their involvement in the interpersonal work processes. In addition, new alternatives for behavioral adaption can be developed for the work environment and the community in general.

[30]Frederick Weiner, "Vocational Guidance for Delinquent Boys," *Crime and Delinquency,* 11 (October 1964), 368.

[31]*Ibid.,* p. 369.

Programs like the Neighborhood Youth Corps (see Chapter 8) have been effective in combining work training with vocational and interpersonal counseling.

> It is work focused so that all aspects of the youth's life are dealt with in terms of their relevance for his career. Counseling is concerned primarily with helping the youth examine his desires, feelings, and attitudes, his day-to-day problems and his behavior in the counseling situation itself. The group is used as a reference group and all are expected to help each other.[32]

The New Careers Program concentrates on creating new technical-level jobs by providing counseling, education, skill training, and supervised on-the-job training and experience. Programs such as these have been successful in realistically helping the youngster develop work skills in addition to providing counseling for interpersonal problems. Vocational counseling and vocational guidance programs can play an important part in preventing delinquency and rehabilitating a youngster who has been labeled delinquent.

BEHAVIOR THERAPY

Behavior therapy, or behavior modification, is based on the assumption that delinquent behavior is learned. Maladaptive behavior usually has to be modified through the development of new learning processes. Generally, behavior therapy assumes that behavior will change in direct proportion to the amount of rewards or punishments that exists as reinforcement—negative or unpleasant reinforcement will reduce or eliminate much negative behavior, whereas positive or pleasant reinforcement will tend to maintain or even increase positive behavior. If positive behavior is adequately rewarded, it will be perpetuated. Conversely, if negative behavior is not rewarded, it will eventually subside.

Shah states that according to the behavioral approach the therapist must deal with clear and observable aspects of behavior so that objective conclusions and evaluations can be made.[33] Thorp and Wetzel point out that observable behavior, whether positive or negative, can be reinforced or punished accordingly.[34] The client can be made aware of the sequence of events that culminate in particular types of behavior. Negative behavior like delinquent activity can be pinpointed, and negative reinforcements like restrictions can be implemented. Positive behavior, like success on the job and in school, can be positively reinforced and rewarded.

Dressler points out that if the therapist is going to be effective in accomplishing behavior modification, he must first determine each individual's "reinforcers."

[32]Beryce W. MacLennon and Naomi Felsenfeld, *Group Counseling and Psychotherapy with Adolescents* (New York: Columbia University Press, 1968), p. 148.

[33]Saleem A. Shah, "Treatment of Offenders: Some Behavioral Concepts, Principles and Approaches," *Federal Probation*, 23 (September 1959), 29.

[34]Ronald G. Thorp and Ralph J. Wetzel, *Behavior Modification in the Natural Environment* (New York: Academic Press Inc., 1969), p. 186.

A youngster's reinforcers may be determined by carefully observing his behavior, since each child has his own list of reinforcers which can be ranked for importance. Candy for the quite young and money for those who are older are generally in the category of reinforcers but, aside from these, reinforcers usually cannot be accurately determined without observation of the child and inquiry of him and significant others, such as family, peers, and teachers. The investigator wants to know what people, things, and events motivate the particular individual. What does he want to get out of them?[35]

Reinforcers, then, are those aspects that are deemed important by the youngster, which he will strive to achieve so that he will gain personal satisfaction. Praise, attention, money, food, and privileges can be considered positive reinforcers. Threats, punishment, confinement, and ridicule are negative reinforcers. Even though both types can be employed in modifying behavior, research has shown that positive reinforcements tend to produce more effective and enduring behavioral changes.[36]

The therapist, in an attempt to achieve a desired goal, tries to shape the behavior of the youngster by employing slow and gradual changes beginning with the individual's existing level of performance—the therapist determines the behavioral level of his client. For example, the youngster may be a chronic delinquent who has been involved in much delinquent activity. The "treatment" has to begin at this point. Because the therapist proceeds at a very slow pace and behavior modification is attempted in only small doses, success is a gradual process and the little successes become stepping-stones to larger achievements.

Each appropriate or correct move toward the goal is provided external or extrinsic reinforcements (praise, approval, prizes, candy, good grades, etc.). Such progress may also generate internal or intrinsic reinforcements for the individual.[37]

In other words, as the behavior is modified and as rewards are provided, the delinquent activity is reduced, allowing the individual to develop a self-image of being able to achieve personal satisfaction in a socially acceptable manner. If the youngster is able to stay on the job and receive gratification through the paycheck he receives, this may be a new experience for him, and the satisfaction and the positive reinforcements can affect his internal self-concept and alter his behavior in the community.

Schwitzgebel utilized behavior modification in his research and work in communities with high rates of delinquency.[38] He told youngsters that he was an experimenter who was studying delinquency and needed subjects whom he would

[35]David Dressler, *Practice and Theory of Probation and Parole* (New York: Columbia University Press, 1959), pp. 229-30.

[36]*Ibid.*, p. 230.

[37]Shah, *op. cit.*, p. 32.

[38]Ralph Schwitzgebel, *Steetcorner Research* (Cambridge: Harvard University Press, 1964).

pay to help him. Each subject came to Schwitzgebel's office to talk about anything he wanted to related to juvenile delinquency. The sessions were recorded. At the end of the session Schwitzgebel paid the youngster for the information provided and set up another appointment. Because each subject obviously spoke of delinquency partly in terms of his own involvement, Schwitzgebel hoped that the result would be an extensive self-examination leading to development of insights and, ultimately, the desire to change. Important in his experiment was the aspect of the experimenter being the employer by giving cash or rewards to the youngster *and* the youngster being the employee or the recipient of the cash or rewards. The arrangement was a business relationship, and the youngster was encouraged to believe that he was coming to collect his pay for providing a service and that he was not coming to receive counseling. The payment was used to effect behavioral change. Schwitzgebel discovered that delinquents seemed to be deficient in time sense and attempted to modify their behavior:

> They [delinquents] treated appointments casually, they arrived at the office almost any time except when scheduled. It was not uncommon for them to arrive even on a wrong day. At first Schwitzgebel did not reprimand them, making use of their services no matter when they arrived. Little extra rewards were paid for arriving at all—candy or fruit, for instance. When the youth's adherence to schedule improved even slightly, he was rewarded with praise. If he produced especially good material in the session, he might receive a $.50 or $1.00 bonus on top of his regular pay. With these positive devices, Schwitzgebel was teaching the boys to appreciate and adhere to time schedules.[39]

Thus, in the slow process of paying the boys or rewarding them for the information they were providing as well as rewarding other behaviors, like being on time for appointments, the boys unknowingly began to develop certain positive habits which could be carried over to the work world or to other situations in their community. For example, their new time sense would be helpful in attending school or getting to work on time. The slow process of change through the reward or positive reinforcement system established by Schwitzgebel could have both immediate and long-range positive results, especially if positive behavior continued to be rewarded. If the youngster, however, did not receive encouragement from his family or his reference groups he might relapse into old habits and become further involved in delinquent activity.

The National Training School Project also used behavior modification techniques. Successful performance was reinforced by a point system. Points earned could be used to purchase a variety of items, such as cokes, food, clothing, and access to a comfortable lounge. The boys were not compelled to study, but their performance and motivation did show marked improvement.

> The points could only be *earned* by the individual's satisfactory performance in educational work and a careful record of the points earned by each person

[39] Shah, *op. cit.,* p. 34.

was kept by the project staff. Thus, points could *not* be given away, loaned, borrowed, begged, or stolen—they could only be earned and used by the person working for them. Since behavior upon which the points were continued was rather concise, it could objectively be measured, . . . only the desired educational behaviors were reinforced.[40]

Behavioral modification has been used successfully to alter negative behavior and encourage positive achievements. The family is the first "institution" that either directly or indirectly uses the behavior modification approach. The youngster is rewarded for positive behavior and punished for negative behavior. He soon learns how to respond to his environment. Parents who have been consistent in their reward and punishment system can influence their children to act in a socially acceptable manner. If parents are inconsistent or perverted in their approach to child rearing (as Chapter 4 points out), they will not be successful in positively influencing their children. Ineffective role modeling by parents will often result in their youngsters' becoming involved in delinquent behavior.

Behavior modification is simply a method of establishing or reestablishing an effective reward and punishment system to help the youngster become more compatible with the expectations and demands of his environment.

CRISIS INTERVENTION

Even though *crisis intervention* has not been utilized extensively with youngsters in the past, Villeponteaux believes that it can have great therapeutic value in dealing with acting out adolescents.[41] The basis of the theory is that when a person experiences a crisis, his psychological resources may become overtaxed, making him vulnerable to further breakdown. The resolution of the current crisis may lead to the solution of older problems as well because of the reawakening of fears and repressed problems that reoccur during time of crisis. Redl and Wineman describe it as "emotional first aid on the spot." Vernick states that

> problem situations in the child's day-to-day life have strategic and therapeutic importance when they can be dealt with immediately before or immediately after they occur and even more when the person who deals with them has witnessed the incident.[42]

The delinquent, unlike most typical middle-class persons who use verbalizations to express aggression, usually expresses his aggression by acting out in the community and coming in conflict with the law. If the therapist witnesses or is told how the youngster handles and expresses his aggression and how he reacts to

---

[40]*Ibid.*, p. 36.

[41]Lorenz Villeponteaux, Jr., "Crisis Intervention in a Day School for Delinquents," *Crime and Delinquency*, 16 (July 1970), 318-19.

[42]*Ibid.*, p. 319-20.

frustration and strain, he can use the immediate situation to help the youngster develop new methods of adaption. Villeponteaux provides an example of the techniques used at Horizon House:

> A minor infraction of a rule could be handled in one of several ways. For example, a boy might (and in fact, often did) come late to the program. If he was three or four minutes late, the worker could simply overlook this tardiness, or could reprimand, or warn him, or "make an issue" of it.[43]

If the therapist wanted to "make an issue" of the boy's behavior, he could emphasize the problem by pointing out in an actual and objective manner how the boy was functioning. The immediate problem could then be related to the way the boy functioned in other situations in the past. The present situation or crisis can be used for problem solving because it is probably part of a pattern of behavior that the youngster uses in relating to the environment. This pattern often contributes to a delinquent behavioral adaption. The successful resolution of the crisis in the immediate situation can be generalized to similar situations in the future and can be helpful in acquainting the boy with a new problem-solving process that will contribute to more appropriate behavior in the community.

Handling problems when they are at the crisis stage and when there is a great deal of anxiety can contribute to problem solving. Because youngsters who are involved in chronic delinquent behavior often do not experience anxiety and guilt, it is difficult to rehabilitate them or motivate them enough so that they want to get involved in the change process. The anxiety that exists in the crisis situation can be used as a motivating force for change. Crisis intervention, as a technique for dealing with problems on the spot, can be effective in producing change and helping the delinquent develop new methods for handling strain, frustration, and aggression in crisis situations.

INDIVIDUAL AND GROUP COUNSELING

Counseling can be used with both groups and individuals. Usually, the major goals of counseling are support and reeducation.

> The counseling procedure involves the client's understanding of his immediate situation and the solving of a problem which affects him and others. No attempt is made to affect a fundamental change of the client's personality— when a person needs reorientation to a particular situation, counseling is indicated. If the problem is of a long-standing duration, psychotherapy is recommended.[44]

The American Correctional Association defines the technique as follows:

[43]*Ibid.*, p. 320.
[44]Nikelly, *op. cit.*, p. 28.

> Counseling is a relationship in which one endeavors to help another understand and solve his problems of adjustment. It is distinguished from service or admonition in that it implies *mutual* consent.[45]

These quotations illustrate an important principle. Methods of treatment can be viewed on a continuum. Vocational counseling and individual and group counseling are sometimes considered superficial approaches to interpersonal problem solving. Their main objective is usually to help the client handle immediate practical problems. No major attempt is made to restructure the personality or make extensive diagnostic evaluations. More sophisticated methods, such as social casework and psychotherapy, are needed for intensive personality evaluation and treatment. Approaches like transactional analysis and reality therapy fit somewhere between the more superficial counseling methods and the more intensive psychotherapeutic methods. A youngster could conceivably be receiving assistance simultaneously from professionals using the various methods mentioned. For example, his school counselor or vocational counselor could be helping him handle the day-to-day problems that occur in school and on the job, while his probation officer could be helping him through the use of principles extracted from reality therapy, behavior therapy, or transactional analysis. At the same time the youngster could also be evaluated and even treated by a psychiatrist who used psychotherapeutic techniques. Although this example would not be typical, it would be possible.

The most prevalent group treatment approach in institutional settings and juvenile court programs is called group counseling, which involves the sharing of personal concerns, problems, and day-to-day experiences within the group.[46]

Sharp notes that the group approach often is successful in teaming up with individualized services.[47] Together they provide a complementary orientation to individual and group problem solving.

In the counseling situation, the

> counselor establishes and operates within an atmosphere which is open and accepting. It is only when the child is free from the feeling that he must defend himself that he is also free to explore himself openly with a degree of candor. ... The counselor is an "enabler"—not a judge or an instrument of retribution.[48]

In group counseling, it is important to select those youngsters who can benefit from the group but who will not be scapegoated. Some youngsters, for personality reasons or for other factors such as extreme passiveness and dependency, can be

---

[45]The American Correctional Association, *op. cit.*, p. 422.

[46]Rosemary C. Sarri and Robert D. Vinter, "Group Treatment Strategies in Juvenile Correctional Programs," *Crime and Delinquency*, 11 (October 1965), 330.

[47]E. Preston Sharp, "Group Counseling in a Short-Term Institution," *Federal Probation*, 23 (September 1959), 8.

[48]*Ibid.*, pp. 8-9.

harmed by the group because of the hostility that will be directed toward them and the scapegoat role that they may be forced into.

Role playing may be a highly effective component of group counseling because it enables youngsters to view situations as others do. The participants in the group have to be comfortable enough with one another so that the role playing will come naturally and so that they will not feel self-conscious or inhibited by the role-playing process. The basic concept of role playing is that because behavior of an individual is mainly the result of a reaction to what other people think of him or what he believes they think of him, the assuming of different roles will allow the youngster to test out his perceptions in a nonthreatening situation. The counselor or the group leader can objectively evaluate the role-playing behavior and the responses of the group to it. New insights which can be carried over to real life situations can then be fostered.

> In these processes, the group members are given an opportunity to try on the psychological shoes of others. They are exposed to processes which may give them some idea about how others may feel or think. A lack of awareness or caring about how others think or feel may be one of the major causal factors of delinquent behavior. It has been found that many delinquent children cannot realistically appraise or react to the feelings and thoughts of others.[49]

Many formats can be followed when utilizing the role-playing method. An actual skit can be developed, with participants placed in various roles. The role playing can also be spontaneous as a result of suggestions by either the members of the group or the leader. Sharp relates a case study in which boys were constantly complaining about the staff and their mistreatment of the boys.[50] The boys were asked to reverse roles and play the parts of the supervisors. As a result of this reverse role playing, the boys soon learned how to look at problems through the supervisors' eyes and were able to understand their roles. Likewise, the supervisors were able to understand the boys' position and this mutual understanding contributed a great deal to the formation of increased positive relationships between the boys and the staff.

It often becomes difficult to manage these group sessions because of the very nature of the boy's personality and the hostility that is often directed at the group leader.

> A leader needs to have some concept of what is the therapeutically effective activity on the part of the group and when it is utilizing the time efficiently toward moving in that direction. (This is determined by the degree of expression of feeling, the group interaction, sincere interest in helping each other, the feeling of group intensity, evidence of insight being developed, attitude changes, etc.)[51]

[49]*Ibid.*, p. 10.

[50]*Ibid.*, p. 11.

[51]Glen J. Walker, "Group Counseling in Juvenile Probation," *Federal Probation*, 22 (December 1959), 34.

There does have to be some initial structure from the group leader. He should point out that the major purpose of the group is to solve problems through the understanding of each other's viewpoints and the expression of ideas, feelings, and alternatives. The group leader is mainly an objective observer who can give the group direction. He should not be an authoritarian and should be open to a variety of topics within a broad framework. It is the group's responsibility to initiate subjects that will be worth listening to and of interest to other group members. Even though the group leader will manage the discussion to provide some direction, it is up to the group to keep the discussion going. The two major results of the group discussions will be the expression of feelings and ultimately a concerted effort at problem solving by the entire group.[52]

GROUP THERAPY

Differentiating between *group therapy, group counseling, group psychotherapy, guided group interaction,* and *social group work* can be confusing. Sarri and Vinter, in summarizing juvenile group treatment strategies, include group psychotherapy, guided group interaction, and social group work under *group therapy.*[53] They maintain that these various methods are distinguished only by the type of worker who performs the service. Gazda feels that the terms *group therapy* and *group psychotherapy* are generally used synonymously.[54]

> Parole and probation agencies have been experimenting with group methods in recent years. Rather loose and ambiguous terminology has resulted. The terms group therapy, group counseling, group guidance, and guided group interaction are employed variously and often interchangeably. Almost anything undertaken with more than one individual at a time is likely to be termed group work or group therapy.[55]

Some writers feel that group therapy is a more intense process than social group work and that the emphasis is still on the individual while utilizing the group as a mechanism to better understand the individual and his behavior. Because the delinquent often manifests his behavior as a part of a group or a gang, it is felt that the group therapy situation is the natural vehicle in which to view the way he reacts to the group and the pressures it produces to influence his behavior. Furthermore, the one-to-one relationship with a therapist in social casework or individual psychotherapy can be very threatening to adolescents, since they are more comfortable interacting with their peers and being a part of a group. The adolescent often acts much differently outside the natural environment of the group. In

---

[52]*Ibid.,* p. 35.

[53]Sarri and Vinter, *op. cit.,* p. 332.

[54]George M. Gazda, *Basic Approaches to Group Psychotherapy and Group Counseling* (Springfield, Ill.: Charles C Thomas, Publisher, 1968), p. 4.

[55]Dressler, *op. cit.,* p. 183.

addition, in individual counseling there is a more obvious superior-subordinate relationship. This situation is neutralized in the group where the youngster can receive a great deal of support from his peers. The "naturalness" of the group and the interaction are often conducive to the leader's making more valid judgments about the youngster, his patterns of interaction, and his method of problem solving.

> The mere fact that the group therapist is outnumbered by the adolescent and his peers frequently has a dramatic impact on the over-all attitudes of the client toward the therapist and vice versa. There is a freedom about openly acknowledging and sometimes overtly expressing feelings in the group situation which often appears only during the later phases of individual treatment.[56]

The group can either support or not support the individual in his reactions both positive and negative in the group. The individual group member can find a great deal of reassurance from his peers, thus facilitating the expression of feelings. Even though the group can facilitate problem solving, not all youngsters should be placed in a group. Placement in a group has to be on a voluntary basis, and the group member should be allowed to quit whenever he feels that the situation is too threatening or that he would prefer to continue his counseling or therapy on a one-to-one basis. If the group member cannot be encouraged to talk freely, and if he is extremely threatened by the group, keeping him in the group can do more harm than good.

The group process does not in itself solve all the problems of resistance to treatment. Just as there is resistance to the individual method, there is resistance to the group method. The groups generally pass through various phases with distinguishable characteristics and processes. In the initial stages of the group meetings, some boys will not talk at all, while the more verbal boys will try to monopolize the conversation with trivia. The group manipulators attempt to justify their involvement by making the leader and the group members believe that the group cannot function without them and that they are the leaders. Many times these pseudotherapists attempt to manipulate the group to the point where meaningful and relevant problem situations are never discussed.

> The therapist has to recognize the mood of the group and the correlary role that the con man is playing. He tries to elicit general feelings and tries to open up the hitherto silent members of the group. These sleepers often provide the therapist with a clue as to what is going on at the moment.[57]

Once the "con man," or manipulator can be controlled to the point where more significant group verbalization and discussion can take place and where the other group members are finally able to express their feelings, the group begins to

[56]Harris B. Peck and Virginia Bellsmith, *Treatment of the Delinquent Adolescent* (New York: Family Service Association of America, 1954), pp. 25-26.

[57]Robert S. Shellow, Jack L. Ward, and Seymour Rubenfeld, "Group Therapy and the Institutional Delinquent," *International Journal of Group Psychotherapy,* 8 (1958), 267.

open up and their ideas and gripes begin to be manifested. The youngsters soon find that they can make their ideas known and can express their feelings without the threat of retaliation by other group members or by the group leader. Manipulators in the group constantly try to test the group leader's authority and position. In the early stages of the group meetings, the group members do not want the spotlight focused on them. Hence the reason for the expression of hostility toward the leader and the attempt to divert the group processes into unproductive channels. The astute group leader, however, is not easily manipulated and understands the group process and the phases that the youngsters have to go through before meaningful dialogue, discussion, and problem solving can take place.

Throughout the group sessions and especially in the initial and middle stages, there is also considerable ambivalence toward the authority figure who is the group leader. Although the boys often want to receive the guidance of the leader in problem solving, they are not sure whether the leader can be trusted because of their past negative experiences with adults. The group leader has to recognize this and allow the youngsters to go at their own pace.

Ideally, the group will advance to the point where the expression of honest feelings will become commonplace. Once positive feelings begin to be expressed about the group leader, it is an indication that the group is progressing to the point where they will begin to look at their problems in a realistic manner and assist one another, with the help of the leader, in arriving at successful alternatives and solutions to common problems.

The group method does not always follow the sequence that has been described—the discussion of trivia, the expression of hostility toward the adult authority figure, the phase of acceptance of the authority figure, and then problem solving. There are peaks and valleys, and often when the group seems to be progressing well, there are backward trends or regression to earlier phases. However, the regression does not last long, and if the leader can ride out the storm, the group begins to progress again and can attain new levels of interaction and understanding.

Of the many variations of the group method, Allen describes an approach in which the professional group leader is a "silent observer." Allen feels that this facilitates problem solving.

> The silent observer method is a variation on traditional dual therapy techniques. It is hypothesized that group interaction might be improved by the adoption of a dual therapy technique in which the role of the second therapist was modified to that of a silent observer. Among the potential advantages of the new method was the fact that the observer being less involved with the group than the therapist himself would be in an excellent position to make objective observations about the group.[58]

Even though the observer does not react directly, he can evaluate the dynamic interplay taking place in the group. He is also not placed "on the defense"

[58]James E. Allen, "The Silent Observer: A New Approach to Group Therapy for Delinquents," *Crime and Delinquency*, 16 (July 1970), 325.

or "on the spot" like the primary group leader. After the group meeting, he can provide the primary therapist or the leader with new insights regarding the dynamics of interaction and alternatives for problem solving. Allen feels that the use of the silent observer not only accelerates and enhances the treatment process in the group but also provides a training laboratory for new group leaders. The training aspect of the silent observer role may well be the most important benefit of the method.

Like most other methods discussed, the specific orientation (within a general structure) that the group leader takes and the path he pursues toward his goal of helping youngsters will vary depending on his training, his personality, and his client group. The various group methods, just like the individual methods, do allow for individual variation and experimentation.

SOCIAL GROUP WORK

Ferguson defines *social group work* as social work "focused on the individual in a group setting" which attempts to help him function more effectively in groups and derive greater satisfaction from this participation.[59] According to Dressler, social group work is differentiated from social casework by its additional goal of furthering the group's accomplishment of a social purpose as a group;[60] its similarity to social casework is evident in its goals of improving the individual's relationships and subjective responses to the social environment.[61]

The social group work method operates under many of the same assumptions as social casework, although it is more complex because of the number of group members and the increased interpersonal dynamics. It is possible for an individual to be involved in both social casework and social group work at the same time, but not all clients are capable of this dual involvement. Konopka lists some of the principles of social group work:

1. The worker's main function is helping and this helping is perpetuated to establish purposeful relationships with group members.
2. The worker must be warm, understanding, and spontaneous, but yet be able to maintain and enhance group direction.
3. The worker has to accept group members without accepting their behavior and often "limits" have to be utilized but in a constructive manner.
4. The worker has to manage the group while at the same time not forgetting the uniqueness of the individual.[62]

[59]Ferguson, *op. cit.*, p. 13.

[60]Dressler, *op. cit.*, p. 162.

[61]Tappan, *op. cit.*, p. 366.

[62]Gisela Konopka, "The Social Group Work Method: Its Use in the Correctional Field," *Federal Probation*, 20 (July 1956), 26-27.

In summary, the worker has to be able to not only empathize and understand individual problems but also visualize and conceptualize how the group processes can contribute to problem solving. He must also be both sympathetic and consistent in the way he manages the group so that there will be a structural framework that will facilitate goal achievement.

Pierce visualizes the group as a "social laboratory" in which the individual group member experiments with new patterns of social functioning.[63] The individual can then evaluate his new patterns of behavior by the reactions of the group members. If there is satisfactory response, he may try them in his relationships with peers outside the groups or in institutions in the community.

> As group members develop a sense of the group as something more than a collection of individuals interacting, they are able to use this identification with the group as a force for modifying their own behavior and attitudes. Often one is able to risk change or growth because "the group is behind me."[64]

Of the many different types of group work and group therapy, one particular variation that has been effective with gang members in large cities is what is called the "detached" group work method. Some youngsters do not have the desire to come to an agency to participate in formal group meetings; therefore, the group worker has to extend beyond the confines of his agency and develop relationships with youngsters "on the street."

> Group workers act on a tolerant basis and accept the gang members as individuals while making clear that they do not go along with their delinquent behavior. This gain and acceptance requires time. In time, the group worker hopes to get the gang to modify its role in the community and the priority of the individual's role. The aim is to reduce the individual gang member's role as a delinquent.[65]

The role of a detached group worker is difficult, and McCarthy and Barbaro have summarized his objectives. Basically, he attempts to reduce antisocial behavior within the community, broaden the gang members' social horizons, provide the individual gang member with new alternatives to social behavior both with his peers and with community institutions, and generally improve his personal and social adjustment which, in turn, will improve his relations with the community. It is difficult, however, to achieve these ends if the group worker is not able to interact meaningfully with the gang members, gain their acceptance and trust, and influence their behavior.

The personality of the gang group worker has to be such that he is comfortable interacting in the community and associating with youngsters who

[63]F. J. Peirce, "Social Group Work in a Women's Prison," *Federal Probation,* 27 (December 1963), 37-38.

[64]*Ibid.,* pp. 33-38.

[65]Mabel A. Elliott, "Group Therapy in Dealing with Juvenile and Adult Offenders," *Federal Probation,* 27 (September 1963), 54.

frequently typify a life-style and personal orientation much different from his own. The youngsters will only develop trust and confidence in the worker if he is able to understand their life-style and empathize with them. Youngsters quite naturally in these situations wonder what the worker has in mind and how he is going to benefit from helping them. Gang workers are often considered intelligence agents for the police, thus making it difficult to gain youngsters' trust and confidence. Once the gang worker demonstrates that he is there to help—to look at their situation and help them solve their problems—trust and positive results will be forthcoming. Many of the youngsters whom the gang worker comes in contact with have had few positive life experiences. Once their trust is gained, the gang worker can begin to redirect the gang members' energy into socially acceptable channels through many different means, such as organizing athletic teams or dances.[66] "Inasmuch as many of the intergang conflicts stemmed from a need for status or 'rep' for being the 'baddest gang' [sic], it was assumed that if the gang gained a sufficient status through socially acceptable activities it would not need to maintain their 'rep' through fighting."[67]

Not all social group work takes place within a gang setting, but many of the positive results that have taken place in social group work with delinquent youngsters is the result of gang workers' interacting with youth in their "natural setting."

> The essence of working with street clubs involves the establishment of meaningful relationships between the worker and gang members, so that these relationships can be utilized for the redirection of the anti-social activities of gangs and their members.[68]

The social group work method can be effective, especially in helping delinquent youngsters to understand their deficiencies and developing new and more productive patterns of interaction in the community.

GROUP PSYCHOTHERAPY

Even though there is a blending of the various therapeutic approaches and it is often difficult to differentiate between them, a separate discussion of each is helpful because it illustrates, at least numerically, the descriptive approaches that exist. *Group psychotherapy*, when compared with other group methods, is usually thought of as having more ambitious goals, such as deep insight development and personality restructuring. Many of the techniques utilized, however, are similar to other group methods, and the major difference is in the *degree* of "probing" and the intensity of the relationship.

When working with adolescents, it is often difficult to develop group unity

---

[66]James E. McCarthy and Joseph S. Barbaro, "Redirecting Teenage Gangs," in *Reaching the Unreached*, ed. Sylvan S. Furman (New York: New York City Youth Board, 1952), p. 108.

[67]*Ibid.*, pp. 110-11.

[68]*Ibid.*, p. 111.

Courtesy of Camp Highfields, Onondaga, Michigan

Figure 14
A Group Treatment Experience

and common goals in the group treatment. Often little commonality exists between group members, although this can be somewhat controlled with adequate selection procedures. Even in groups that have many similar characteristics, it is difficult for group members to empathize with one another.

> This may be particularly true of delinquents who are notoriously self-centered. They form groups not out of friendship, but for mutual security against the adult world which is perceived as hostile.[69]

Schulman states that the components necessary for an effective group psychotherapy situation, such as personal interaction, cooperation, and tolerance, are in direct conflict with the dissocial, antagonistic, and exploitive orientation of delinquents.[70] He feels that traditional therapeutic techniques must be modified when working with the delinquent, who is not motivated for psychotherapy and lacks the qualities of group identification and empathy which are necessary for positive group results. To facilitate group identification, it is important to point out the common benefits that can be gained by all group members by their participating in the group. Even though group members will initially be skeptical of the benefits they can receive, once the group is in progress, the secondary benefits of associating with the group and socializing with their peers will contribute to greater cooperation and goal achievement.

One of the major problems that delinquents have in their communities is that

[69]Marvin Hersko, "Group Psychotherapy with Delinquent Adolescent Girls," *American Journal of Orthopsychiatry*, 32 (January 1962), 170-71.

[70]Irving Schulman, "Modifications in Group Psychotherapy with Antisocial Adolescents," *International Journal of Group Psychotherapy*, 7 (1957), 310.

their behavior and demands are not realistic. In other words, they are not very effective at "reality testing." Their personalities, in many cases, have been retarded at early impulsive levels of functioning, and they often do not have adequate reality reference points. Group psychotherapy, as well as some other group methods discussed helps the delinquent to test reality and the attitudes and reactions of the leader and the other group members before extending into the "uncertain waters" of the community.

For increased effectiveness with delinquent youngsters, it is helpful if the parents also receive some type of treatment. It is discouraging to treat the youngster and then release him to a family that will contribute to further delinquent behavior. Parents who tend to subvert the efforts of the therapist with their youngster and who contribute to his acting out behavior in the community often have to be confronted and dealt with on the same therapeutic basis as their youngster. Many examples can be given of how parents can destroy all the positive efforts of the therapist. If the family is not treated along with the youngster, results will be minimal and the youngster will fall back into the same trap that existed before his exposure to treatment.

Through *family therapy*, parents are made aware of the often hidden and distorted negative aspects of their relationship with their youngsters. The therapist can point out these negative dynamics and patterns of behavior so that they will be recognized and altered.

Regardless of whether the therapy involves a group of family members or a group of delinquent youngsters, the techniques are similar in that the group is used as a vehicle to foster expression of feelings, to involve the members in problem solving, and to observe the interaction and interplay of group participants. The positive insights and the behavioral modification that take place in the group can then be transferred on a more permanent basis outside the group to the community.

ACTIVITY THERAPY

Many clients do not have the verbal ability necessary to communicate effectively in a conventional individual or group therapeutic situation. Very young children and resistant subjects such as delinquents and predelinquents are especially suited to the *activity therapy* method. A group of six to eight children are gathered or invited to meet at a specific time and place to engage in play, such as group games or some artistic endeavor like modeling clay. The atmosphere is permissive, and the youngsters can use their time as they wish.

> A moderately neurotic child finds great release in a permissive environment where he can act out his repressed hostility and aggression in creative work, play, mischief, and hilarity. Because his behavior does not call for retaliation, punishment, or disapproval, pent-up emotions find appropriate discharge. Perhaps of even greater value is the fact that he sees other children act freely

without dire or destructive consequences. This has the effect of reducing guilt about hidden impulses of hate and feelings of being bad or worthless. Not only are the blockings to free expression through unrestricted acting out removed by *activity catharsis*, but the individual psychotherapy with these patients is facilitated as a result. The child communicates more freely and is less protective and less suspicious of the caseworker or psychiatrist.[71]

Slavson points out that only certain types of children can effectively utilize activity therapy as a substitute for the more verbal orientation of conventional group therapy or individual psychotherapy.[72] The open aggression and hostility that is permitted within a permissive situation can create anxiety in some neurotic children and overwhelm them to the point where the activity group experience can become devastating. Chapter 3 pointed out the many different diagnostic and classification categories that exist to label delinquents. The typologies range all the way from the accidental or situational offender to the chronic character disorder offender. Each of these diagnostic classifications often necessitates special consideration and specific therapeutic techniques. For example, because the neurotic offender suffers from anxiety and guilt, his delinquent behavior is merely a symptom of his attempt to resolve this inner conflict; whereas the character disorder offender has a minimum amount of anxiety and guilt, and his acting out is a result of a lack of conscience structure, or superego. Thus, methods of treatment will have to vary considerably between the two diagnostic categories. Anxiety and guilt should not be clinically induced in those neurotic children who already suffer from them, but methods that use even the minimal amounts of anxiety felt by the character disorder client can be the motivating force for his seeking inner change and new modes of adaption.

Even though the pure categories of *neurotic* offender or *character disorder* offender may not actually exist, those youngsters whose personality structure can be evaluated as predominantly neurotic can benefit most from such insight-type methods of treatment as psychotherapy and casework. The character disorder offender can benefit most from such methods as reality therapy and behavior modification because he does not have as much motivation, anxiety, or desire to develop deep insight into his problems—the main goal is to interrupt his negative cycle so that he ceases to come in contact with the law. Any insight that he gains into his problem and the reasons for its manifestation is a bonus.

Activity therapy can therefore be useful for some youngsters. But the neurotic child who has difficulty handling his hostile impulses may be extremely threatened by a technique like activity therapy with its permissive open atmosphere where impulses can be easily manifested. It is often difficult for him to control the expression of these impulses once he leaves the confines of the activity therapy room and returns to his home and community. Regardless of the therapeutic technique utilized, a careful evaluation has to be made regarding its appropriateness for the particular client. Not all clients can benefit from the same technique, and in fact a combination of techniques is often required.

[71] S. R. Slavson, quoted in Tappan, *op. cit.,* p. 368.
[72] *Ibid.*

GUIDED GROUP INTERACTION

Guided group interaction is basically similar to group therapy or group psychotherapy in that it is also based on the assumption that through the group and its processes the delinquent can solve his problems. The group is the major vehicle for change.

According to McCorkle, guided group interaction assumes that delinquents will benefit from the freedom to discuss and analyze problems and their own roles and relationships within the group.[73] McCorkle feels that guided group interaction operates most effectively in an informal atmosphere where most of the social controls evolve from the group itself and where meaningful interaction of group members can ultimately produce insight and new patterns of adaption to the community.

> The object is to develop a group culture in which those involved will make themselves responsible for helping and controlling each other. The assumption is that a delinquent is more likely to be influenced by his peers than by professional staff. The individual member is not likely to manipulate others nor will he be able to lie or alibi himself out of uncomfortable situations in front of his peers. They have all been down the same road and they are not easily hoodwinked.[74]

This description of guided group interaction is not much different from the description of group psychotherapy and group therapy. The group can exert a great deal of pressure on its individual members after the group has been stabilized and the leader trusted, and meaningful dialogue has taken place. The peer group has extensive power over the individual members and can impose sanctions if one of the members does not become meaningfully involved. Empey and Rabow relate that at Pine Hills, a facility for delinquent youngsters, the group is permitted to use sanctions, within the confines of the treatment system, on members who do not cooperate. The ultimate sanction is refusal to release a boy from the program.[75]

The process described for guided group interaction in regard to the structure of the group and the means it takes to achieve meaningful dialogue, communication, and expression of feelings is similar to the group processes discussed earlier. The group leader plays an important role in directing and managing significant aspects of the interaction, although he attempts to do this according to a democratic model of group participation, discussion, and ventilation of feelings. The initial stages of the group are used to vent hostility and aggression. Initially the

---

[73]Lloyd W. McCorkle, "Group Therapy with Offenders," in Johnston, Savitz, and Wolfgang, *op. cit.,* p. 518.

[74]Dressler, *op. cit.,* p. 202.

[75]Lamar T. Empey and Jerome Rabow, "The Provo Experiment on Delinquency Rehabilitation," in *Juvenile Delinquency: A Book of Readings,* ed. Rose Giallombardo (New York: John Wiley & Sons, Inc., 1966), p. 541.

group members are self-centered and unable to realistically or meaningfully involve themselves or their peers in the problem-solving process. Later, as the group progresses and the group members see that their group peers have similar problems and backgrounds, empathy and group identification is facilitated.

> Simultaneously, the behavior of the group becomes more orderly and the leader finds increased support for its earlier definitions. If the initial anxieties and resistances have been adequately handled, warmer, friendlier relations replace the earlier aggressive, destructive, hostile responses. With the release of hostile, aggressive feelings and some understanding of the origin of these feelings, deeper levels may be reached.[76]

McCorkle gives the following criteria for selecting a boy for a group and for using when the group is in actual operation: The boy should be able to contribute to group maintenance, and members should be suited to each other. Generally, group members should be of the same age, educational level, and intelligence, and participation should be on a voluntary basis. The group should meet at regular intervals and at specified times and should not exceed twenty in number.[77]

MILIEU THERAPY

Whether the youngster is in an institution, a halfway house, or some other controlled or semicontrolled setting, *milieu therapy* attempts to produce an environment that will facilitate meaningful change, increased growth, and satisfactory adjustment.

Slavson feels that milieu therapy is suitable for persons whose deviant behavior is a reaction to unfavorable life conditions.[78] If the milieu, or environment, is carefully planned so that deviant adaption will not be needed, fostered, or encouraged, delinquent behavior will be modified or eliminated. Kane feels that the milieu consists of everything happening to the child in his therapeutic environment, whether it is the institution, a halfway house, or some other controlled setting.

> It is as subtle as the attitudes of staff and the kinds of controls administered and the purpose of those controls, constructive or punitive. If one is to single out the essence of a therapeutic milieu, I would say that it is found in the quality of relationships between the children and the direct contact staff.[79]

Because their environment is, in fact, the therapeutic setting, daily activities, including both failures and successes, are the topics of discussion between the client

[76]McCorkle, *op. cit.*, p. 522.

[77]*Ibid.*, p. 523.

[78]S. R. Slavson, *Reclaiming the Delinquent* (New York: The Free Press, 1965), p. 17.

[79]Joseph H. Kane, "An Institutional Program for the Seriously Disturbed Delinquent Boy," *Federal Probation*, 30 (September 1966), 42-43.

and those persons who are a part of his milieu. Fenton and others define the correctional milieu and the goals of milieu therapy in this setting:

> The correctional community is a method of social therapy in which staff and inmates make a conscious effort to utilize all the experiences in all areas of the group existence in a therapeutic manner. This program bridges a communication gap between staff and inmates typically found in correctional institutions and also utilizes inmate peer influence—the self-help concept—to help inmates gain self-awareness and a more responsible outlook. Inmates who live and work together meet with the staff regularly with an expressed goal of improving postrelease performance. By employing, under staff direction, open communication, confrontation, as well as other treatment methods, inmate participants can model and adjust their behavior through learning, testing, and fixating newer and more effective modes of perceiving and relating to others.[80]

Milieu therapy takes a more general orientation to treatment than guided group interaction, group therapy, social casework, and the other methods because it focuses on the total environment of the individual and is viewed as the major therapeutic agent. Milieu therapy is generally utilized in controlled or semicontrolled environments where the client's behavior, actions, and experiences can be somewhat regulated. The many other techniques discussed in this chapter, such as casework and group therapy, can be used to supplement the milieu therapy approach.

SUMMARY

This chapter has described some of the specific methods of treatment that are used in handling the juvenile. One or all of these methods could technically be utilized in one large program.

There are additional therapeutic methods that can supplement some of the primary methods discussed. For example, some agencies and programs have a religious orientation or affiliation, and religious or moral reeducation techniques are often used. Moral reeducation emphasizes religious self-contemplation and familiarity with religious history, principle, and doctrine. The Youth for Christ movement is an example of a religious approach aimed at rehabilitating juvenile delinquents. This method has proved successful with some youngsters, especially when supplemented with other methods of treatment.

Medical techniques of treatment, such as the use of tranquilizers, can also affect or supplement one or all of the approaches mentioned in this chapter. The administration of drugs is no substitute for effective treatment, however. They can

---

[80]Norman Fenton, *et. al.,* Explorations in the Use of Group Counseling in the County Correctional Program (Palo Alto: Pacific Books, 1962).

be very useful in helping the client "calm down" so that conventional methods can be used, but they are not a panacea for a complex problem.

In addition, medical assistance such as cosmetic surgery, which is time consuming and expensive, can sometimes be utilized to remove scars and deformities and can alter the client's self-concept and the way he interacts in his community. Negative reactions toward him often change, and this can affect his self-perception and reduce his defensiveness.

Sensitivity training has also been used with social deviants. Its principles are somewhat similar to those of other treatment approaches mentioned, although it is broader in scope. Sensitivity training has often been equated with role playing; however, it is quite different. In role playing the person assumes a specific role, either similar to, or different from, one he has already experienced. In sensitivity training no roles are played, and the major goal is merely interacting as "an honest human being." Sensitivity training has been said to increase the listening power of the participants, develop a better understanding and sensitivity of oneself, and foster a much more considerate attitude toward others.[81]

The sensitivity approach, the medical approach, and the religious orientation are generally only used as supplemental helps in treating the delinquent.

As pointed out in the preceding chapter much more effort has to be made toward more sophisticated evaluation and research procedures if successful programs are to be perpetuated and replicated and unsuccessful ones eliminated or improved. Evaluation and research should be an integral part of any program established to assist the delinquent.

> It is common to hear from social scientists that more research is needed and it is probably not much less common to hear from practitioners that research is usually inconclusive and that it is more important to get underway with action programs. But whatever its implication, long term development of delinquency control measures requires the kind of knowledge that only comes from systematic research efforts. Three specific types of research now seem required. National statistical data are necessary for long term planning and for keeping the public informed. There is a desperate need for description and evaluation of alternative programs of prevention and control and the techniques which will aid in the development of such programs. Finally theoretical research is needed to provide a base for the creation for more meaningful and theoretically sound action programs.[82]

The next chapter will provide an example of a treatment and rehabilitative prevention program and will incorporate the concepts discussed so far.

---

[81] John E. Wilkinson, Donald Muller and Robert P. Morton, "Sensitivity Training for Individual Growth—Team Training for Organization Development," *Training and Development Journal*, Vol. 22, No. 1 (1965) p. 47-53.

[82] Stanton Wheeler, Leonard Cottrell, Jr., and Ann Romasco, *Juvenile Delinquency—Its Prevention and Control*, in Task Force Report, *op. cit.*, p. 424.

QUESTIONS AND PROJECTS

Essay Questions

1. Compare the advantages and the disadvantages of individual treatment versus group treatment.
2. What treatment method do you think is most appropriate for juvenile delinquents?
3. Why have "conventional" treatment approaches not been effective with juvenile delinquents?
4. Why can't all youngsters benefit from a group treatment experience?
5. Why are there so many different methods of treatment?

Projects

1. Attempt to identify the major treatment methods of the various agencies within your community.
2. Develop a list of criteria that will facilitate determining the effectiveness of a particular treatment method.
3. Develop a coordinated educational program for the professionals in the criminal justice system to acquaint them with the various methods of treatment in your community.

10

AN EXAMPLE: COMMUNITY-BASED TREATMENT PROGRAMS

A *community-based prevention and treatment program* can be defined as any program that attempts to mobilize the resources of the community in an effort to prevent and treat delinquency. Resources are based in the community, and most of the youngster's time is spent participating in community activities and utilizing those agencies and institutions that are a part of the community. The program that we will discuss specifically, a halfway house, is an example of both a prevention and a treatment program. A youngster who is in the halfway house has already been in contact with the criminal justice system, and therefore a halfway house is not a *pure* prevention program. If the treatment that takes place is successful and future delinquent behavior ceases, however, then the halfway house can be considered both a treatment and a prevention program.

An example of a halfway house that is a community-based treatment and prevention program will facilitate the tying together of many of the principles that have been discussed thus far. The establishing of a program is not a simple process, and more than a knowledge of delinquency causation is necessary (Chapter 3). We have seen that juvenile delinquency is only a subcategory of the overall general concept of deviancy (Chapter 2) and that it is manifestation of youngsters who are adolescents (Chapter 5). It is necessary to understand both concepts, deviant behavior and adolescent behavior, to understand the theories of causation. It also logically follows that to establish or work in a prevention program (Chapter 8), and to develop treatment therapies (Chapter 9), a knowledge of organizational principles, dynamics, and theory is mandatory, since there are common principles in the operation of all organizations regardless of their complexity or orientation (Chapter 6). All of the above revolves around the handling of juveniles (Chapter 7).

The question could be asked, Why community-based treatment and prevention? This question was probably not asked or answered soon enough because community-based treatment on a large scale is a relatively new concept and could be one of the major breakthroughs that has occurred in the last several years.[1] Community-based treatment and prevention programs have become popular today because, through research and observation, it has been determined that institutions are artificial and do not provide the type of atmosphere where the youngster can learn to work out his problems in a realistic manner. Institutions have been notorious for their irreconcilable philosophies of treatment and intergroup conflict—problems between the custody staff and the treatment staff. Even though institutions are needed for some youngsters, as a last resort and final alternative, they have been utilized too frequently. In 1967 approximately fifty-three thousand children were living in public institutions for delinquents with the average cost per child being approximately thirty-eight hundred dollars.[2] This does not include those children housed in private institutions or children temporarily placed in detention homes. The institution can reinforce the child's negative attitude toward authority and make it difficult for him to work out his problems. This, coupled with the artificial atmosphere of the institution, does not create a situation conducive to personal growth, rehabilitation, or increased social functioning. Finally, as Chapter 9 pointed out, methods of treating the juvenile and his problems have not always been effective.[3]

As early as 1920, when Shaw and McKay studied the Chicago crime situation, research has shown the strong connection between social factors and delinquent behavior.[4] More recent studies have pointed out the effect the environment can have on the individual and his future delinquent behavior. The environment of the community does play an important part, if not the major part, in the formation of the delinquent personality.

There have been piecemeal attempts to utilize community resources and treat the delinquent within the confines of his own environment. Many programs, however, have only been appendages to existing institutional facilities. Independent community programs have only been used for a selective small number of

[1] Oliver J. Keller, Jr., and Benedict S. Alper, *Halfway Houses: Community Centered Corrections and Treatment* (Lexington, Mass.: D.C. Heath & Company, 1970), p. 174.

[2] *Statistics on Public Institutions for Delinquent Children, 1967,* Children's Bureau Statistical Series No. 94 (Washington, D.C.: Government Printing Office, 1969), p. 13.

[3] John M. Martin, *Delinquency Today: A Guide for Community Action,* Office of Juvenile Delinquency and Youth Development (Washington, D.C.: Government Printing Office, 1962).

[4] Clifford Shaw and Henry McKay, *Juvenile Delinquency and Urban Areas* (Chicago: University of Chicago Press, 1942).

delinquents. Community-based programs can facilitate the youngster's identification with positive role models in the community.

Community-based control, treatment, and prevention programs can also be much more effective in integrating the individual into his home community and enabling him to adapt to his environment because treatment personnel will be familiar with the community resources available, such as educational and employment opportunities. Treatment can be based on the utilization of community resources. With help from professionals and volunteers, the offender can become acquainted with community resources and receive support and guidance as he adjusts to his community and faces its pressures and responsibilities. The mobilization of community resources of both private and public agencies as well as the assistance of professionals and nonprofessionals will help integrate the delinquent into the community processes. In the artificial institutional setting, the delinquent more often than not loses touch with his community and the resources available and does not learn the problem-solving process that will contribute to his personal and social adjustment.

In addition to academic and employment facilities, many resources within a community can help the youngster. Innovative approaches have been taken by local, state, and federal governments to help control, prevent, and treat delinquent behavior. For example, vocational rehabilitation provides academic, vocational, and on-the-job training services to persons who are culturally, economically, and socially disadvantaged, including persons convicted of crime or judged delinquent. Another recent program that can have positive effects on preventing delinquency is the Model Cities program, which is a part of the Demonstration Cities and Metropolitan Development Act of 1966 and is administered by the Department of Housing and Urban Development. Model Cities grants provide technical assistance to communities to help them focus on their crime and delinquency problems and develop programs and plans to upgrade areas that produce delinquents. These programs provide unique services so that alternatives other than delinquent behavior can be made available to youngsters within the community.

In sum, community-based treatment centers and other prevention, treatment, and control programs located near population centers permit the flexible use of community resources and enable the delinquent, in cooperation with treatment personnel, to establish new community ties where he will be assisted not only in becoming satisfactorily integrated into the community but also in developing new social, educational, and employment skills.

HALFWAY HOUSES

The use of halfway houses in delinquency prevention and treatment is becoming increasingly popular. The halfway house is a community-based program small enough to facilitate individualized treatment but still large enough to necessitate a knowledge of organizational principles, as well as an understanding of theories of causation, deviant and adolescent behavior, treatment therapies, prevention concepts, and procedures and methods for handling juveniles.

History

Even though halfway houses have only recently been used on a large scale, the halfway house concept is not a new one. As early as 1916 the Hebrew Orphan Asylum in New York established a home for adolescent girls who had been discharged from the asylum but were unable to adjust in their own homes, with foster families, or on their own.[5]

Although there have been exceptions, such as Pioneer House established in Detroit in 1946 and Highfields established in New Jersey in 1950, little actual development of this type of treatment facility took place until after 1960. In comparison with such other methods of treatment as the training school, after care, and probation, the halfway house is still in its infancy.

Halfway houses have been described in various ways. "The trend has been to name these facilities group homes, pre-release guidance centers, transitional homes and the like."[6]

The main idea behind the halfway house concept is that it should help bridge the gap between the confinement of the institution and the total freedom of the community.

Types of Youth Served

According to Carpenter, the youth for whom halfway house programs

appear to be most helpful are those who have no home to return to, those whose parents are sufficiently inadequate or rejecting to give them the necessary guidance and support for successful adjustment, those whose parents may be fostering their delinquent behavior or those whose parents live in neighborhoods in which the youth are unable to cope with the many pressures they would face upon return to their home community.[7]

Use of Structure

Structure is an important aspect of halfway house programming. Rabinow lists some factors that must be considered in the structure of the halfway house program:

[5]Martin Gula, *Agency Operated Group Homes,* U.S. Department of Health, Education, and Welfare (Washington, D.C.: Government Printing Office, 1964), p. 2.

[6]Kenneth Carpenter, "Halfway Houses for Delinquent Youth," in *Children,* U.S. Department of Health, Education, and Welfare, November-December 1963, p. 224.

[7]*Ibid.*

1. A living situation that has limits to which the child can relate.
2. Adults who reflect maturity in their behavior.
3. A peer group that does not have too much extreme in age or behavior.
4. Living quarters that provide some degree of privacy.
5. Community resources such as schools, recreational facilities, and work opportunities that do not make overwhelming demands upon him.
6. Professional assistance to help in dealing with personal problems, family relationships, and peer relationships.
7. The security of knowing that food, clothing, financial aid, medical care, etc., are always provided for him no matter what his behavior.
8. The security of knowing that he will have competent assistance to aid in making plans for the future when he leaves placement.[8]

Personnel

Competent staff personnel are an important aspect of the total halfway house program and structure.

The opportunity to live closely with adults whose behavior can be a model to emulate and from which to take strength is a unique one for most of the adolescents in placement. Immature, undisciplined, and inconsistent behavior by house staff can have a most destructive effect.[9]

Location of the House

The location of a halfway house can have important ramifications and should be given careful consideration. The halfway house should be located in a metropolitan area near the resources of the community. It should also be located in a neighborhood where it will be accepted by the residents and where there will not be animosity between the community and the program.

There should be schools and recreational facilities available and places of employment that are within a reasonable distance. Chapter 3, "Theories of Delinquency Causation," discussed the importance of the environment and institutions like the school in preventing delinquent behavior.

Economic Benefit

The halfway house program is much less costly for the taxpayer than other programs. Even though the cost per resident may be the same as the cost at an institution, or even slightly higher, the halfway house returns the youngster to society sooner, making the cost per individual treated much lower. In New Jersey eight out of ten releasees from the Highfields Program were "successful" for one

[8]Irvine Rabinow, "The Significance of Structure in the Group Release Program," *Journal of Jewish Communal Service,* 38, No. 3 (Spring 1962), 302.

[9]*Ibid.,* p. 301.

year after release as opposed to five out of ten releasees from the training school at Annandale. The costs per inmate per day were approximately equal. "On a strict per capita basis the Highfields Program cost one-third as much as the traditional program for each boy treated."[10] The reason is that the average term of treatment at Highfields was approximately five months, whereas the average term of treatment at Annandale was slightly over a year.

Halfway Houses in Michigan

Because Michigan is one of the leaders in the nation in halfway house development and utilization and also because I was a director of a halfway house in Michigan for a period of time, the example presented will be taken from my experiences in the halfway house program. Halfway houses in Michigan are operated by The Office of Youth Services, a division of the Department of Social Services and serve children between the ages of thirteen and nineteen, with the average term of residence being six months. Although halfway houses have been utilized on a limited basis in the past, there are plans for expansion so that most juveniles who are committed to the department's Office of Youth Services will be able to profit from this community-based treatment method. Only those youngsters who are unable to tolerate the closeness and pressures of the community will be sent to institutions and this will be on a much smaller scale than now.

Administration and Programming

Halfway houses in Michigan are staffed by a caseworker, who is the director, and five child-care workers (boys' supervisors) who work on an eight-hour-shift basis. The houses, which have a capacity of twelve wards each, are programmed to provide both school and work experience. In the *academic program,* those wards who are motivated and capable of further academic training are given an opportunity to continue their education. A ward also has the opportunity to enroll in a joint academic and work program, which allows him to continue his education, obtain some work experience, and achieve some financial independence. In the *work program,* wards who are not capable of, or not interested in, furthering their formal education are given the opportunity to work full time.

PROBLEMS INVOLVED IN OPERATING
A HALFWAY HOUSE PROGRAM

Although the halfway house program that will be described was operated by the Department of Social Services, the development of new techniques and methods

---

[10]H. Weeks, "The Highfields Project," in *Juvenile Delinquency: A Book of Readings,* ed. Rose Giallombardo (New York: John Wiley & Sons, Inc., 1966), p. 530.

Figure 15
Pine Lodge Halfway House, Lansing, Michigan

was highly flexible. The operation of the house was based on the integrated view of organizational theory, and both Classical and Human Relations Organizational principles were used (see Chapter 6).

The Treatment-Custody Dilemma

The major problem that exists in correctional programs employing a wide variety of professionals is a communication breakdown between the college-educated and the non-college-educated staff. This is merely a sympton of the age-old treatment-custody dilemma. This phenomenon occurs in a number of institutional and parainstitutional settings, and a review of the literature in this area reveals that this is a universal problem in the treatment of juvenile offenders regardless of the type of facility.

This dichotomy usually exists because institutional staffs have historically been segregated—first by function, and second by training. On the one hand, the custody staff, who have the function of controlling (guarding) the clientele, usually have no formal training. On the other hand, the treatment staff, whose function it is to "treat" (however this is interpreted), usually have extensive formal training. Also implied in the treatment-custody dilemma is the treatment staff's decision-making power in the institution. The custody individual is typified by his role of "watchdog" and "inhibitor of privileges," while the treatment individual is the "giver of privileges." Animosity can obviously exist in such a situation. This conflict of roles not only affects the relationship between the custody and the treatment personnel but also has implications in their relationship with the clientele. The dilemma affords a natural and opportune situation for the clientele to manipulate the staff and turn them against one another, which can have a decided negative effect on the total administration of the treatment program. Also, because of basic philosophical differences that often exist between occupational groups working in the criminal justice system, the custodial staffs of institutions and even the noncollege educated staffs of smaller programs like group homes and halfway houses are usually oriented both criminologically and organizationally to viewpoints similar to those of policemen. They subscribe to the Classical school of criminology and the Classical view of organization, whereas treatment personnel subscribe to the Postive school of criminology and the Human Relations view of organization.

Several questions can be asked: Is the treatment-custody dilemma inevitable? Will it always exist because of the division of labor by function and training? What can an administrator do organizationally to alleviate this problem? These questions and others will be answered in the next section.

The Type of Clientele

Another problem that exists in correctional facilities is the type of clientele served. Persons adjudicated delinquent do not usually voluntarily seek treatment for their problems; on the contrary, they often attempt to perpetuate their condition. Unlike neurotics and psychotics who are plagued by anxiety and distress, most delinquents are unaware that they have problems. Because of their psychological makeup and learned social behavior, delinquents can be expert manipulators and effective con men, and this is often an integral part of their value system. Manipulation is more than merely a prized and desired asset, it is a tool with which most delinquents "ply their trade." Hence, they have an extraordinary ability to manipulate people, and the treatment-custody dilemma plays right into their hands and perpetuates this pathological process.

This major clinical difference between the delinquent and the neurotic or the psychotic necessitates not only a knowledge of deviant behavior but also an awareness of therapies available for the treatment of the different diagnostic categories.

Generally, neurosis and psychosis are manifestations of an excessive amount of guilt and anxiety. Conversely, the delinquent's pathology is many times directly attributable to a lack of guilt and anxiety. The delinquent, throughout his entire life, has not had positive identification models who could transmit the values of the larger society. The result is that a social and moral void exists in his conscience structure. Hence the attitude "take what you can get" and "it's only wrong or immoral if you get caught."

If, then, the delinquent is different from the neurotic or the psychotic, should the techniques for treatment be different or the personnel performing the treatment be different?

Serving a Human Being

The "commodities" that are being produced and served in correctional settings are not inanimate objects, but human beings, and human beings have the innate ability to affect one another in many ways. For example, an assembly line worker operating under Classical organization theory receives instructions and orders from his supervisor and then performs his task of riveting the right front fender of a new automobile. The fender does not respond in a manner that can cause an emotional reaction in the worker. However, something quite different happens when the worker (the child-care staff member) is dealing with a human being (the delinquent). The worker may get his instructions and advice from his supervisor, but a second element is involved in the process—the worker not only performs an action, but the object on which he performs the action is capable of producing a reaction in the worker. Thus a reciprocal emotional situation evolves. The delinquent can accentuate an emotional reaction in others because of his aggressiveness and antisocial attitude. He often exhibits behavior that is boisterous, aggressive, and cocky to disguise his feelings of worthlessness, fear, and insecurity. In effect, he actively attempts to antagonize society so that he will be rejected, thus reinforcing his self-concept that he is worthless and a social outcast. He has been hurt emotionally and hence does not want to take the chance of being hurt again. The dynamic of rejecting before being rejected is a defense against getting close to people. Because serving human beings is different from producing a material product, organizational assumptions have to be altered to consider the human factor, an important reason why Classical organization theory cannot be easily transposed to situations where the "product" is human and not material.

The questions to be asked are: How can positive communication be facilitated between the staff and the boys? What effect does an emotionally charged situation have on both the boys and the staff? What techniques can be utilized to keep negative reinforcement and reactions at a minimum?

Personnel

Persons attracted to the correctional field can present certain problems. This is not to imply that all persons attracted to this field are negatively motivated, but it is important to mention that some of them are, and it is in reference to these individuals that this section attempts to raise some questions.

The child-care staff, since they are on the "firing line" and in constant contact with the boys, are in a position to exert a great amount of influence as identification and authority models. Whether this influence is positive or negative depends on the individual staff member.

People satisfy their emotional needs in a variety of ways. In most instances, delinquents are vulnerable to displaced hostility and negative reinforcement from persons working in correctional settings. An "energy surplus" exists in the work situation—the worker has more energy left than is needed to perform his job, and much of this energy is psychological and is manifested in the work group. Where the "product" is human, the surplus energy can be focused on the clients as well as on the work group. It is possible that some persons are attracted to this field because they can overassert their authority and direct their energy into negative channels.

Conversely, an individual can mask his intense hostility by being overpermissive and oversolicitous even to the point where he encourages the delinquent to act out. The staff member, if he also has a problem accepting authority, can experience vicarious satisfaction when the delinquent acts out against society and specifically against the correctional administration. Deviant behavior by staff members in such instances can become commonplace.

Some questions to be asked at this point are: How do delinquents affect persons who are negatively motivated and attracted to the correctional field, and in turn how does this affect the treatment-custody dilemma? Do some staff members prefer and even perpetuate the treatment-custody dilemma? What are the ways in which staff members can be used most effectively?

The Treatment Concept

Another problem in correctional administration is the defining of the word *treatment*. Many times treatment personnel are not clear as to what is meant by the concept and what it entails. Treatment usually varies with the treater and the situation. Many different approaches can be used, depending on the orientation of the agency and the academic and personal preferences of the therapist or the counselor (see Chapter 9). Can *treatment* personnel expect *custody* personnel to understand and accept the treatment concept if, in fact, it is not clearly defined and it changes like a chameleon depending on the circumstances? Does treatment mean being extremely permissive? Is treatment dependent on the treater's ability to use superfluous psychological jargon? Is it necessary that treatment be practiced in a clinical setting? Isn't the definition of treatment really a definition of the particular organization's purpose and goals? Isn't it possible to transform theoretical concepts into manageable and practical terms for the line staff?

Training

The area of training can present sizable problems for the administrator. The training concept has implications for the treatment goals. If the goals and purposes of the organization are clearly defined and if the staff understands the criminological and organizational orientation of their organization and the assumptions that its operation is based on, then the treatment techniques and the training methods needed will be a logical consequence.

Just as training will have to fit the goals and purposes of the organization, so will the trainer have to be acquainted with the problems peculiar to that organization. It is one thing for the trainer to impart certain concepts, methods, and techniques on how to react in a certain volatile situation and another thing for the trainer to experience the actual aggressiveness. Can the trainer, who is usually the college-educated treatment person, summarily chastise a staff member for reacting negatively to being called a derogatory name if he has not experienced the situation himself? (This does not mean the trainer has to agree with the negative reaction, but it is mandatory that the potential emotional ramifications be recognized.) Or should the trainer stay away from the firing line so as not to taint his humanitarian image?

The Community

The relationship to the community can also pose certain problems. In the halfway house operated in Michigan, there was often a direct correlation between the amount of aggression exhibited in the house and the amount of negative behavior exhibited in the community. Those boys who would verbalize and rebel in the house would not act out in the community. Therefore, our general philosophy was that it was better for the boys to act out in the house because the problem could be dealt with on the spot, and hence there would be less of a tendency for them to displace their aggression onto the community. This did not mean that the boys were free to express themselves in any manner they desired. They could not, for example, destroy the furniture; they could, however, express verbal anger and discontent to the staff.

Concomitant with this philosophy, our major emphasis was not on regimentation. On various occasions boys would rebel by not making their beds or doing other assigned chores. The house, however, usually never looked any worse than it would have if a normal group of teenagers had been living in it. (Chapter 5, "The Adolescent," provided background on what is considered "normal.")

It was interesting to note that even though visitors to the house seemed to accept our Integrated organizational philosophy of "controls but not regimentation," they usually expected to see the "shiny institution" characteristic of Classical organizational theory. Their disapproval and surprise could often be observed by staff members, who were presented with a role conflict that made them uncomfortable. On the one hand, they were attempting to play their roles according to the norms on which the program had been established, but on the other hand, they were being evaluated according to normative criteria with which the philosophy of the program did not adhere. What effect could this organizational paradox and role conflict have on the operation of the program? How could this situation be alleviated?

SOLUTIONS TO THE PROBLEMS:
DEVELOPING A NEW ORGANIZATIONAL
AND PHILOSOPHICAL (CRIMINOLOGICAL) SYSTEM

In the halfway house operated in Michigan, it was felt that the staff should not have to be dichotomized into treatment and custody. In other words, there did not have to be such strict division of labor and emphasis on specialization, two key principles of the Classical view of organization. The same person could play the role of both "giver" and "taker," "controller" and "liberator." In effect, with adequate staff selection and training, one person could make the decision as to the proper treatment technique at any given time, which is congruent with the Human Relations view of participation in decision making.

Employing staff members who will perform what some people consider a dual function (treatment and custody) implies certain alterations in Classical organizational theory concepts, namely, the decentralization of authority and decision making from the caseworker (administrator) to the line staff.

It was felt that if the new concept of decentralization of authority, which involved participation in decision making by the entire staff, was introduced into the halfway house program, the child-care staff would see their role more favorably and would feel a part of, and identified with, the total treatmen program, which would increase the congruent normative orientation of all concerned. This would specifically result in better communication between the caseworker and the staff, a more effective treatment program, and the solidification of the group—with corresponding social rewards for the group members.

It was also assumed that each staff member would be given authority commensurate with his responsibility and that authority and communication would be a two-way process. Even though the major decisions would be made by the entire staff at the weekly staff meeting (group participation in decision making), day-to-day decisions would still have to be made by the particular staff member who was on duty. His decisions would never be reversed by the caseworker, and if a difference of opinion arose, the problem would be discussed either privately or publicly at the staff meeting. In addition, the staff members were kept informed and were involved in every phase of both the house operation and the boys' status in terms of past, present, and future diagnosis, treatment, and planning. Hence the necessity for all staff to have knowledge of deviant behavior, theories of causation, therapies, and adolescent behavior.

Finally, because the boys had also witnessed the treatment-custody dilemma before coming to the halfway house, it was thought important that some tangible administrative responsibility (a form of division of labor and specialization) be given to each staff member to reinforce the concept that the entire staff was involved in decision making and also to increase the status of the child-care staff. Each staff member was therefore given a major administrative responsibility; for example, one staff member was responsible for all monetary transactions in the house and another staff member was responsible for programming all house activities.

Organization Structure

The organization chart took a new shape. Previously the chart had resembled and had typified the Classical organizational model shown in Figure 16. Under this system the head boys' supervisor did most of the actual staff direction, but the caseworker made most of the decisions. The decisions were meant to be categorized

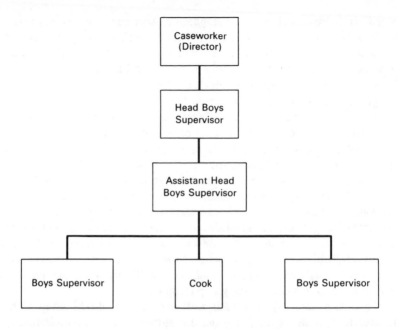

into treatment decisions (made by the caseworker) and house management decisions (made by the child-care staff). This was a very hazy line, however, and conceivably the caseworker could (and sometimes did) reverse a decision made by the child-care staff by rationalizing that it was a treatment decision. For example, if a boy was involved in a drinking escapade within the house and the child-care staff restricted him to the house, the caseworker could reverse the decision on treatment grounds (because he exercised his authority according to the Classical principle) and allow the boy to go on a home visit because "the boy's drinking was the result of an excessive amount of pent-up frustration and anxiety." A situation like this can obviously affect the morale and the motivation of the child-care staff and the treatment of the boy. The staff would undoubtedly feel powerless in their roles, the boys would be able to utilize the situation for manipulating, and most importantly the normative bonds that have to exist for effective functioning would be non-existent.

As seen in Figure 17, the new organizational chart of Pine Lodge was much more decentralized, with a "flattened" hierarchy. In this chart, the caseworker was the director and was responsible for supervising the staff, providing casework for the boys, and administering the total program. However, the total administrative and social structure of the house was considered the major therapeutic agent. This means that house management activities and house controls were considered as much a part of the treatment program as were direct casework services. There was an Integrated approach to both the organizational structure (combining Classical and Human Relations principles) and the treatment structure (combining Positive and Classical principles).

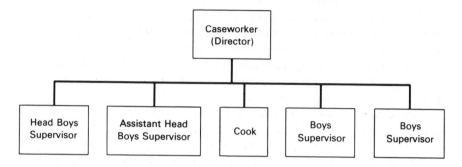

Differences in Treatment. Treatment techniques in correctional settings have to be different because the clients are different. Treatment of the boys in the halfway house was a twenty-four-hour-a-day job. In a typical clinical or psychiatric setting, a client might tell the therapist that he was involved in a "beer blast" at home. The therapist would discuss the situation with the client and would try to determine the etiology of the problem and the psychological dynamics present. In the halfway house, the staff did not have the luxury of merely discussing the problem in a second-hand manner. In addition to being concerned with the psychological dynamics of the client, the staff had to be concerned with controlling the client. Obviously, the boys could not be allowed to have a "beer blast," especially on state property.

Because the treatment program was viewed as involving the boys' total life process within the organization structure, it was not feasible or desirable that the house staff be specialized into treatment areas and house management areas. Hence, decision making could not be dichtomized into decisions made by the caseworker and decisions made by the child-care staff. The entire staff had to participate in all decision making that affected the boy and the operation of the house.

This, however, did not necessarily mean that there was no division of labor or specialization of duties according to the staff members' position as determined by their Civil Service classification. There was still a hierarchy of responsibilities, the head boys' supervisor having more responsibility, and so on. The responsibility, however, related to objective administrative functions, such as making out the staff payroll and being responsible for calling repairmen, not to decisions concerning the boys. The division of labor referred more to differences in responsibility for house management, not to differences in power or authority over the boys.

The more pronounced the hierarchical structure, the more the boys will have the opportunity to manipulate the "boss" against the "staff," and the more they will, in fact, manipulate. A flattened hierarchical structure with equal decision-making power for all eliminates much of this manipulation and thus interrupts one of the boys' major pathological processes.

Even though treatment objectives should be specifically defined, the techniques for attaining these specifically defined goals should be kept flexible to encourage the staff to use their own initiative and personal assets. This would also facilitate decision making because the staff member would not have to be concerned about using the "right" technique. The "right" technique could apply in an industrial organization operation if under Classical principles, but not in a situation where managing and dealing with human behavior was a major variable. Staff members could try innovative techniques, and this would eliminate their need to try new methods through devious means (see Chapter 2).

There were, however, specific guidelines under certain circumstances. For example, if a boy was placed on restriction by the entire staff, a staff member could not make the decision on his shift to allow the boy to go out on "free time." This, however, referred more to the concept of consistency in decision making than it did to flexibility in the particular technique applied. If an individual staff member deviated from the norms established by the rest of the staff, the informal sanctioning process was very effective. Because the size of the staff was small, and the problems the boys presented difficult and frustrating, the individual staff member needed the support of his peers. Hence informal sanctioning by the staff, which many times meant withholding of social rewards (participation in social activities and other forms of socialization), was very effective. Formal sanctioning, like firing and administrative reprimand for deviations that were more serious, although infrequent, nevertheless had to be resorted to on occasion.

Another point should be clarified. Even though each staff member had the authority to make decisions about problems that would arise on his shift, he could always telephone another staff member for advice (usually the caseworker). At first the staff did this constantly, but when they became confident and comfortable with their decision-making ability and the normative orientation of the organization, consultation by telephone decreased.

Staff members were also informed that treatment did not necessarily mean a clinical setting and the use of psychological jargon. Treatment could be taking a boy shopping for clothes, giving him advice on dating, or helping him with his homework. Treatment could take place over a pool table or at the dinner table. In other words, treatment was considered anything that related to the boys' total life process. The importance of understanding all aspects of adolescent behavior was also emphasized. If staff members understood "normal" adolescent behavior, it was felt that they would be less critical of the boys when they manifested normal adolescent "symptoms" like being loud, boisterous, moody, secretive, and defiant.

The Treater: Facilitating Communication

People are attracted to certain types of work and organizations for many reasons, psychological, educational, monetary, social, and so on, and individuals working with juvenile delinquents are no exception.

It was mentioned earlier that since the delinquent was usually clinically different from the neurotic or the psychotic, it followed that the treater did not need the same clinical experience—the clinical difference between the delinquent and the neurotic or the psychotic was that the delinquent lacked an adequate conscience structure as a result of inadequate identification models. (Chapters 3 and 4 illustrated this.) At the halfway house it was felt that because positive identification models were so important, the major treatment device would not be the using of clinical jargon and knowledge to alleviate guilt and anxiety, since the client had a minimal amount of both, but would be the providing of positive identification models. Making this assumption would be a logical conclusion if theories of delinquency causation were understood and made effective by translating them from theory into practice. Because positive identification models could be found in every walk of life, we did not look for persons with a particular educational background—according to our definition and requirements, formal education was not a prerequisite to being an effective therapist. Not emphasizing a particular educational background would facilitate the combining of the Classical and Positive schools of criminology because the person we were looking for had to be cognizant of social and psychological factors that contribute to delinquency (the Positive school) but had to be practical with an emphasis on personal responsibility and free will (the Classical school). In addition to being a positive identification model, it was therefore mandatory that the person be mature and understand his own personal dynamics as well as psychological and social dynamics contributing to human behavior. This would enable him to transmit to the boy that he was honestly concerned and understood extenuating circumstances and variables. If a staff member's actions toward a boy were inappropriate, it was important to determine if he was displacing negative feelings from other persons or situations onto the boy. Staff members therefore had to understand psychological dynamics and be constantly introspective.

We also attempted to find a person who liked children and had the ability to (1) tolerate and understand aggressive and demanding behavior, (2) give of himself emotionally and mentally without expecting or demanding something in return, (3) work with other staff members, and (4) be understanding and flexible yet firm and consistent in the enforcement of house rules.

It was observed that certain boys were attracted to, confided in, and communicated with specific staff members. We encouraged this natural attraction because of the importance of the relationship with a positive identification model in helping the boy to modify his socially deviant behavior. This positive relationship with a particular staff member was beneficial because it not only accelerated the treatment process but also gave the boy someone he could emulate and please through socially acceptable behavior. In effect, we utilized and perpetuated the natural channels of communication, unlike the authority structure in Classical organization theory with communication structured between layers, ranks, and positions. The caseworker would still provide supervision (unity of command principle) to the particular staff member, but the actual casework was being performed by the staff member the boy trusted and had chosen as his friend. The caseworker's supervision mainly involved interpreting the meaning of various behavior patterns and helping the staff member understand what dynamics were present and operating in the boy. Because of the small size of the staff, span of control was not a factor.

Because one specific kind of formal education or one specific kind of personality was not required for work in Pine Lodge, the staff consisted of a variety of personality types. We attempted to utilize a person's positive personality characteristics to the program's best advantage. For example, an athletic staff member would program athletic events for the boys, and this could literally mean altering the organization to fit the employee (engineering psychology). Altering the organization to fit the employee was done by choice in this instance, but it was also sometimes done by necessity. If some staff members had negative personality characteristics, these could also be utilized to the program's advantage. For example, a staff member who had difficulty exerting even minimal controls for fear that he would lose his "nice guy" image could be put on a shift that had the greatest amount of flexibility in regard to controls. He could also be used effectively to perform duties that involved being "nice" to the boys. Conversely, a staff member who was excessively controlling could be used effectively in another phase of the program where, for example, the setting of the controls and limits would be beneficial to the program.

Like other delinquents, the boys at the halfway house had reached adolescence with many of the same likes, dislikes, and pressures as normal adolescents, but they had fewer social, intellectual, and occupational skills. They had experienced little success in life. The staff attempted to intervene in their life process and acquaint them with positive life experiences.

We encouraged the staff members to react spontaneously. If a staff member was angry at something a boy had done, it was much better to express the anger than to suppress it, displace it, and have it come out in a subtle punitive, passive-aggressive manner that the boy could neither accept nor understand. (Chapter 4 pointed out the negative effects of inconsistent discipline and passive hostility in child rearing.)

Staff members involved themselves personally. They took the boys job hunting and on recreational activities, and they gave advice on social amenities. Even when staff members were looking for a new car or shopping for clothes, they often took boys with them.

Because the boys were impulsive, hedonistic, and unable to tolerate much frustration, they needed constant support and encouragement to stay on their jobs, to stay in school, and to refrain from acting out behavior.

Staff members were always willing to give a boy a ride to and from work, advance money from the house fund until he received his first paycheck, and allow him much freedom in purchasing, with his pay, such items as record players, guitars, bicycles, and radios.

This action not only supported the boy while he was experiencing the first few frustrating days on the job, it helped satisfy his need for immediate gratification and showed him that by means of employment it was possible to acquire pleasurable items legitimately. The staff should be aware of the clinical differences in delinquents, such as their impulsiveness and low frustration tolerance level, because this understanding provides a basis for developing a treatment plan and orientation. Our constant support of the boys as they moved out into the environment was predicated on the clinical peculiarities of delinquents.

We were not so naive as to assume that a boy who had already utilized almost every state and local service available would suddenly succeed in the community because of some deep psychological insight into the nature of his behavior. If he refrained, for example, from shoplifting, it was probably because of the money in his pocket earned from a job to purchase the items rather than because of any insight into the nature of his "oedipal problem."

We were very direct in our approach with the boys, always emphasizing the reality of the situation. The method of reality therapy was the basis of treatment (see Chapter 9). Reality therapy emphasizes individual responsibility for actions, which is similar to the Classical school of criminology's concept of free will. We considered psychological and sociological variables, principles of the Positive school of criminology, but we also combined these variables with the concept of free will through our use of reality therapy. We did not attempt to delve into the unconscious, mainly because of the type of boy treated, with his impulsivity and need for immediate gratification. Time was also a factor.

If, for example, a boy had the urge to steal a car, we emphasized the reality of the situation rather than the boy's "unconscious conflict with authority." Stealing the car was the important event. We did not have the time to—nor did the boy want to—look introspectively at the unconscious conflict. We had to deal with the present event and its consequences because otherwise, unlike the neurotic who would have had an anxiety attack, the boy would have acted out in the community and would have been in conflict with the law.

It was also important for the boy to please an adult with whom he had a positive relationship (the identification process) so that if the adult was mainly concerned with obtaining information relating to the psychodynamics of the boy, then the boy would naturally attempt to please the adult by giving him such information. If the adult was too eager to explain to the boy the reason why he went wrong, the boy might too eagerly accept this way of avoiding reality.[11] When we emphasized the reality of the situation, we eliminated many of the boy's attempts to manipulate by means of psychological jargon in the interview. We encouraged him to look at the situation and its consequences, and we did not dissipate the boy's guilt, which could be a motivating factor for change.

We constantly utilized the structure of the house in the treatment of the boys. We did not have many rules, but we enforced the ones we had, consistently and firmly, using as a basis the works of many of the authors who were discussed earlier (see Chapter 4, "The Family and Juvenile Delinquency").

The boys also had the opportunity to go on home visits. This assisted them in experiencing home and community pressures in a less-intensified manner. It gave them the opportunity to test out new skills and attitudes and then return to the halfway house to share their experience with staff members. The staff not only supported them in their responsible home behavior but also assisted them in seeking and implementing alternative socially acceptable solutions to problems. In addition, staff members involved themselves in community activities so that they could

---

[11]William Glasser, *Reality Therapy* (New York: Harper & Row, Publishers, 1965).

influence "social engineering" and help change environmental conditions that contribute to delinquent behavior.

Training

Utilizing the personal assets of the staff also had implications for staff training. Even though staff training was usually geared to impart certain general principles and techniques for the entire staff, training also had to be geared to individual needs and abilities. In the halfway house some staff members had innate, intuitive, and empathic qualities that assisted them in relating positively to the boys and reacting appropriately to emotion-laden situations. Others did not have these innate personal assets and in effect had to be "conditioned" to act in a certain manner even though they did not "feel like it." Of course, it was not merely a matter of either having the qualities or not having them. It should be viewed on a continuum, with some individuals having both more innate assets and a better ability to be introspective. Training can accentuate a person's positive traits and provide him with new skills.

One of the trainers' major responsibilities should be the transforming of theoretical concepts into practical terms to make them more acceptable to the staff. Working with delinquent boys could be frustrating, and the staff might often need something tangible to look at in terms of their accomplishments. The trainer would be much more effective if he pointed out to the staff that a particular boy had improved a great deal because he was staying in school or on the job regularly for the first time in his life, instead of saying that the boy had increased "frustration tolerance" and "impulse control." This would eliminate one of the major criticisms and problems of many theories, namely, that they were impractical and their propositions not easily translated into practical application.

The trainer should also be realistic and able to empathize with the staff. As director, I covered at least one shift a week so as to have an opportunity to observe what took place "on the firing line." After having experienced various situations, it was easier to be more tolerant and less judgmental of a staff member who might have reacted angrily in a particular situation. Such an experience would afford the trainer new insights into the dynamics of human behavior and help eliminate many of the problems inherent in staff-line relationships.

In relation to the caseworker's covering a shift, many persons mistakenly believe that the "treatment person" should not become involved in the areas of disciplining and controlling. If we extend our thesis concerning the staff (including the caseworker) acting as parental substitutes, in how many families is one parent the "good guy" and giver and the other parent the "bad guy" and disciplinarian? The same parent can perform both functions effectively, and the child readily accepts and wants this. Why then can't parental substitutes perform the same dual function? It realistically illustrates to the boys that adults play many roles and perform many functions, some pleasing and some displeasing, and it is an honest approach to child rearing (see Chapter 4).

Extending the analogy between parents and parental substitutes, just as teen-agers in "normal" families "act up" and become aggressive, so do delinquent teenagers in a halfway house setting. The difference is that delinquents act up to a greater degree, and their acting up is much more difficult for the staff (parental substitutes) to tolerate because, even though the staff members are parental substitutes, there is not as great an emotional bond between them and the boys as there is between a parent and a child. Because of the different backgrounds and personalities between the boys and the staff, there is bound to be more of a chance for a personality clash than in a normal family. Different types of behavior by the boys will affect individual staff members differently. Hence the necessity of staff members' understanding their own psychological dynamics and motivation as well as normal adolescent behavior.

If it was felt that a particular boy who had been referred to the house might present a particular problem to a certain staff member, the staff member would be involved in the interview with the boy regarding his being accepted by Pine Lodge. The boy was usually at his best when he was being interviewed, and therefore it was unlikely that he would make a negative impression. The staff member was usually in favor of accepting the boy. After the boy had been accepted and was a resident of the house, he began to "learn the system" and his particular idiosyncrasies began to emerge. At this point the staff member might become very irritated with the boy. Because he had been involved in the acceptance process, however, he would be less likely to insist prematurely that the boy be returned to the Boys Training School. This technique of involving the staff in accepting the boy to the house was a form of manipulation characteristic of the Human Relations approach to organizational functioning.

In effect, involving the staff in the selection of boys encouraged the staff member to work a little harder, be more tolerant, and try to determine why this particular boy caused an exaggerated and inappropriate reaction within him.

Learning the System

After the boys had been in residence for a few weeks, they began to learn the organizational and social system. We attempted to keep some aspects of our system unpredictable (unlike Classical organizations) because otherwise the boys would have spent much of their time trying to "beat the system" and little of their time trying to positively increase their social and personal functioning. The structure of the house, with its consistent enforcement of the rules was an asset, but a system that was completely predictable could eliminate all anxiety and place a premium on conformity and "playing the game" to attain a release.

It is important to point out that the organization and the organization's system should be constantly evaluated in terms of the implications the system might have for the program.

In our case the system was unlike that of the Classical institution because we did not put a premium on rationality, conformity, and regimentation. However, the boys quickly learned what we did emphasize, namely, expression in the house rather than in the community, and some of them began "playing the game" in regard to our system. In other words, they were expressing themselves in the house so as to elicit the response, "Well, at least you must be improving because you are able to express yourself directly (in lieu of displacement) in the house." These same boys might also be "expressing" themselves in the community, however, and much of their energy might be expended in playing "our game." Thus the need for constant organizational evaluation, updating, and innovation.

Relation to the Community

It was mentioned that there were many community visitors to the halfway house. This in itself was not a problem. The problem arose when the visitors transmitted to the staff surprise and disappointment that there was not more uniformity and regimentation, which typifies most institutions that operate under the Classical philosophy.

Quite naturally the staff wanted to operate within the philosophy of the program, but they were also concerned that the visitors would interpret the lived-in look as being a symptom of poor functioning. There was a role conflict.

Even though much of the negative communication from the visitors could not be dispelled, the problem took care of itself. As the staff became more identified with the treatment program and more committed to the philosophy of the program, they became less concerned with negative comments and more enthusiastic about the program and the special techniques we used in the treatment of the boys. This increased enthusiasm, and *esprit de corps* and normative transmission made a positive impact on the visitors, with the result that fewer negative comments were made about the lack of uniformity and regimentation. In other words, the visitors, because of good public relations work and commitment by the staff, began evaluating the program in terms of content rather than in terms of what could be seen (shiny floors, regimentation, and so on). This is not to imply, however, that we did not attempt to "tidy up" the house when a particular influential person who was "institution oriented" visited. This is merely astute organizational management and perception of the reality of the need for public support if the program is going to succeed.

Conclusion

Throughout the chapter, involvement of the entire staff in the total program, and especially in decision making, has been emphasized. This does not mean, however, that there was not a central figure to give guidance and direction. The caseworker (administrator) was responsible for directing and supervising the staff. To be effective, the caseworker must be the "boss" in that he provides direction, guidance, and support, but he must not be so "bossy" that he squelches individual initiative and thinking. A combination of Classical principles to provide structure for the orderly transaction of "business" and Human Relations principles to allow for individual differences and expression is most effective for insuring positive and effective staff functioning.

EVALUATION OF THE PROGRAM

Although some of the boys may not have developed any additional insight into the etiology of their behavior, they have experienced some success and gratification in the areas of employment, education, and recreation. They have been able, with the support of the staff, to delay immediate gratification and tolerate unpleasant situations even though the temptation to become involved in deviant behavior is always present.

In effect, the boys have demonstrated to themselves that it is, for example, possible to go downtown without shoplifting because there are other means, namely, through employment, to acquire pleasurable items. Also, it is possible to get "chewed out" by the boss without quitting the job because the boys realize from previous experience that the paycheck received will be a source of much gratification.

From June 1965 to June 1969, eighty boys were accepted by Pine Lodge. Eleven boys were returned directly to the Boys Training School after a short stay, twelve were residents at the time of the evaluation, and the remaining fifty-seven were released to the community.

Of the fifty-seven boys released from Pine Lodge to their home communities after an average stay of seven and one-half months, eleven (19.3 percent) were released to independent living arrangements, three (5.3 percent) enlisted in the armed forces, twenty-seven (47.4 percent) were released home, and sixteen (28 percent) went to live with relatives or at a foster home.

Eleven of the fifty-seven (19.3 percent) had contact with law enforcement officials, necessitating a return to the Boys Training School or some other form of incarceration (an adult institution, a jail, etc.). The remaining forty-six boys (80.7 percent) did not become involved in future negative behavior in the community. At the time of the evaluation some of the boys had been released for up to three and one-half years.

The question will arise, and rightfully so, as to whether the positive results have taken place in spite of the program rather than because of it. This is possible, but it should be remembered that these boys had previously utilized almost every available state and local service, but to no avail. It must, however, be mentioned in all fairness to the various state and local facilities that a halfway house program has the advantage of being community based and able to maintain control over the boy while providing him extensive support and guidance as he moves into the community to face its pressures and responsibilities. Furthermore, the program was established and operated on a sound framework and a knowledge of deviant behavior, delinquency causation theory, organizational theory, adolescent behavior, clinical therapies, and prevention programs.

GUIDING PRINCIPLES FOR
OPERATING A HALFWAY HOUSE

1. A competent staff dedicated to the philosophy that delinquents are persons worth helping.
2. Active involvement of the entire staff in the treatment process.
3. A sound administrative structure with clear lines of communication.
4. A minimum of rules and regulations, but the firm and consistent enforcement of the existing ones.
5. A refined selection process for accepting wards to the program. Each ward's individual needs as well as the group interaction and the problems that can result from either overplacement or underplacement should be considered.
6. Adequate programming and good working relationships with such agencies as the police and the schools.

SUMMARY

Halfway houses are no panacea for the treatment of the delinquent. They cannot serve all children, especially those who need a good institutional treatment program with more stringent controls and at least partial separation from community pressures, but the halfway house does introduce a new resource that seems to be a better answer for certain children.[12]

There are some problems, however, in operating community-based programs, such as a lack of coordination both intraorganizationally and interorganizationally. Negative public attitudes can affect the operation of the program, and jurisdictional disputes between community agencies can hinder and even destroy the program. The next chapter will describe a process whereby these problems can be minimized and even alleviated.

QUESTIONS AND PROJECTS

Essay Questions

1. How can the treatment-custody dilemma be mitigated?
2. Why is proper personnel selection so important for agencies working with juvenile delinquents?
3. Why are programs for delinquents often very regimented?
4. Is a halfway house suitable for all youngsters?
5. Why do you think halfway houses were not utilized more in the past?

[12]Martin Gula, "Agency Operated Group Homes," U.S. Department of Health, Education, and Welfare, Welfare Administration, Children's Bureau, 1964, p. 29.

Projects

1. Develop an approach for convincing community residents that a program like a halfway house will not "contaminate" them.
2. Develop a set of rules and regulations that could be implemented in a halfway house in your community.
3. Describe how you would go about financing a halfway house.

11

A RESOLUTION TO JUVENILE DELINQUENCY PREVENTION THROUGH NORMATIVE SPONSORSHIP

Juvenile delinquency prevention is one of the least refined areas of criminology. The juvenile delinquency phenomenon is extremely complex not only in itself but in the profusion of information available on theories of causation, the allocation of resources to combat it, and the number of assumptions of how to treat it.

Most of the programs established under the guise of prevention are often "after the fact." They attempt to work with the youngster after he has made contact with the formal processes of the criminal justice system. Many different programs exist, ranging all of the way from informal probation to institutionalization. There are also programs such as Project Headstart, Job Corps, and Employment and Manpower projects, which work with youngsters who have not been adjudicated delinquent. Most of these programs have as their major objective the providing of opportunities for youngsters of the community, not necessarily the prevention of delinquency. The prevention of delinquency is often a secondary objective and result.

In addition to the many attempts at prevention through the establishment of specific programs, there are also many psychologically oriented treatment approaches, therapies, and strategies as well as sociologically oriented "social engineering" projects like Model Cities.

The question might be asked, Why with all the resources available and the theories from the many different disciplines have attempts at delinquency prevention been for the most part unsuccessful?

The answer to this question is not a simple one. The conditions that contribute to crime and delinquency are complex, and long-range solutions to such problems as unemployment, inadequate housing, and unequal opportunity will not take place overnight. A massive amount of "social engineering" will be necessary, as well as a commitment by the total community to alleviate these social problems.

Furthermore, it has been naively assumed that theories, manpower, and resources are automatically translated into action programs. For any program, organization, or group of organizations to operate effectively, there has to be more than theories, resources, manpower, and good intentions. There has to be an adequate *structure* to the program or organization as well as a *process* that facilitates cooperation, integration of functions, and orderly procedure for goal achievement.

Developing an organizational structure or even a process, is not difficult if the organization has a well-defined orientation toward a specific goal. Establishing a *structure* and a *process* is not so simple, however, if goal achievement is dependent on a complex system of organizations.

Even though one of the stated goals of the organizations and agencies of the criminal justice system is delinquency prevention, the structures and processes of the individual agencies are often not conducive to interagency cooperation and goal achievement. The philosophical and operating ideologies of the various agencies often conflict with one another, and this leads to interagency bickering, attempts at boundary maintenance, and perpetuation of individualized approaches to delinquency prevention problem solving. The expertise of the numerous disciplines represented in the various agencies is not coordinated or integrated for the common good and welfare of the community.

The core of the problem is developing a *process* that will coordinate and involve the many agencies and community residents so that there will be a normative goal orientation to problem solving and a blending of ideas, expertise, and cooperative effort. The issue of developing and presenting a process that contributes to this end will be discussed shortly. First, however, some of the factors that have contributed to the need for a calculated and formal problem-solving process will be mentioned.

THE PRESENT INEFFECTIVENESS
OF INFORMAL SOCIAL CONTROL

The importance of the family as an institution for transmiting the positive norms of the community is readily acknowledged. Either directly or indirectly, the family influences the behavior of its members and can have a great impact on controlling their behavior. When many families are blended together to form a cohesive community, the impact of influencing the behavior of community members becomes even greater. Ideally, then, the community, through its natural interdependent processes which satisfy individual and group needs, is the most potent force for influencing behavior and preventing deviance.

Because of urbanization, mobility, and many other factors, present-day communities are not as cohesive as they were in the past. Hence they no longer exert the degree of influence over individuals that they did in the past. Before the growth of our complex urban communities, much crime and delinquency was effectively prevented through informal normative influence. Even if the youngster did come in contact with a formal community agency such as the police, the matter was often handled informally because the policeman on the beat knew his community and its residents.

The complexity of present-day communities has reduced the impact and the effectiveness of the policeman on the beat. The informal communication process between the policeman and the community no longer exists, and because of this lack of face-to-face contact, the policeman is no longer as able to empathize with the community, understand the life-styles of its members, or exert informal influence.

In the past, most of the activities of the community residents revolved around community institutions like the family, the church, and the school. Most of the primary relationships and friendships were within the immediate boundaries of the community or neighborhood. The local businessmen knew their customers and community members knew their neighbors, and public and private agency personnel lived in the community.

The interdependence and informal network of relationships that existed effectively complemented the formal institutions. Because of this network of interdependent relationships, if a youngster did happen to become involved in some form of delinquent activity, he could easily be identified as a community resident. His actions would be made known to his parents, most of the time through informal channels, by the policeman or someone in the community.

The policeman, or even a private citizen, knew that the youngster would usually be reprimanded by his parents. The community could also affect the youngster's future behavior through the influence it could transmit through its various institutions, of which the youngster was usually a member.

The preceding description of the community's power over the actions of its members does not mean to imply that crime and delinquency did not occur or that the social environment was devoid of unemployment, poverty, and unequal opportunity. Crime, delinquency, and negative social conditions did exist, but these factors were often counterbalanced by the positive influence exerted by a strong cohesive community and the effectiveness of its institutions of control.

Today the same negative social conditions exist, but without the strong normative community bonds to counteract unpleasant social conditions. Furthermore, increased mobility and urbanization have contributed to the impersonality of both private and public service organizations. Community residents no longer feel that they can effectively exert influence through their community organizations and institutions. The present process of citizen influence usually has to be formal, impersonal and time consuming, often with little assurance of success. This contributes to apathy and to an unwillingness of citizens to become involved in the community problem-solving process.

Contemporary communities are not conducive to encouraging citizen involvement in problem solving or coordinating the efforts of the many community organizations for a common purpose or toward a common goal. The intra-community and interorganization ties are no longer as binding. This contributes to independent and individualized action by both the community residents and the community organizations and agencies.

The question is how to foster cooperation between all the various community interest groups so that the many benefits of an urban society can be realized, but not at the expense of losing complete control and influence over community residents. Without control and influence, delinquency or some other form of deviant behavior can become a common adaptive behavioral response.

MOBILIZING COMMUNITY RESOURCES

Mobilizing community resources in a cooperative, interdependent effort to combat both the symptoms (crime and delinquency) and the causes (unequal opportunity, unemployment, inadequate housing, etc.) will help to solve the problem.

The present theoretical knowledge as well as resources, both human and material, have to be coordinated and blended if action programs are to be initiated and crime and delinquency prevented.

This will necessitate the involvement of all interest groups within the community, including public and private agencies, businesses, and community residents, which includes the youth. Many persons mistakenly assume that if a program is established to help young people, these good intentions will eliminate the need for youth involvement in the planning, initiating, and perpetuating of the program. If the youth are not involved, just as if community residents in general are not involved, community problem-solving programs will not receive their support and will be doomed to failure like so many programs in the past.

In sum, then, the resources, the theories, and often the motivation exist to prevent crime and delinquency. The missing ingredient has been a failure to actively involve all interest groups, especially community residents, in the problem-solving process. Unfortunately, little has been done to replace the informal interdependent relationships that were so successful in the past in influencing citizen behavior.

The following section will describe a process that will facilitate the coordination of the maze of agencies within the community (especially the agencies of the criminal justice system) and involve community residents as well as other interest groups in achieving the goal of preventing crime and delinquency. When there is not reciprocal involvement and cooperation of both the community residents and the agencies that are established to serve them, programs will fail and the processes of social control will not be effective.

A MODEL FOR ACTION:
NORMATIVE SPONSORSHIP THEORY

The *normative sponsorship theory* approach to community problem solving has been used to assist communities in developing programs for the prevention and control of crime and delinquency. The theory was originated and developed by Dr. Christopher Sower, professor of sociology at Michigan State University.

Simply stated, normative sponsorship theory proposes that a community program will only be sponsored if it is normative (within the limits of established standards) to all persons and interest groups involved.

One of the major considerations when attempting to initiate community development and prevention programs is to understand how two or more interest groups can have sufficient convergence of interest or consensus on common goals to bring about program implementation.

Each group involved and interested in program implementation must be able to justify and, hence, legitimize the common group goal within its own patterns of values, norms, and goals. The more congruent the values, beliefs, and goals of all participating groups, the easier it will be for them to agree on common goals. The participating groups, however, do not necessarily have to justify their involvement or acceptance of a group goal for the same reasons.[1]

Whenever areas of consensus are being identified between groups with a different normative orientation, it is important not to deny the concept of self-interest because it cannot be expected that all groups will have common or similar motivations for desiring program development. Self-interest is not dysfunctional unless it contributes to intergroup contest or opposition and diverts energy that should more appropriately be directed at problem solving.

Programs that follow the tenets of normative sponsorship will undoubtedly be more likely to succeed than those that do not. Violation of the normative sponsorship process usually results in apathy or even concerted subversion and resistance to program development.

An example of a community that has been successful in utilizing this approach will be given, and the normative sponsorship process will be explained. This method has been most successful in communities where there are several interest groups and a diverse orientation to problem solving and the expression of needs. For example, in describing a riot in Detroit, the Kerner report states that

> as the riot alternately waxed and waned, one area of the ghetto remained insulated. On the northeast side the residents of some 150 square blocks inhabited by 21,000 persons had in 1966 banded together in the Positive Neighborhood Action Committee (PNAC). With the professional help from the Institute of Urban Dynamics, they had organized block clubs and made plans for improvement of the neighborhood. In order to meet the need for recreational facilities, which the city was not providing, they had raised

[1]Christopher Sower *et al.,Community Involvement* (Glencoe, Ill.: The Free Press, 1957).

$3000 to purchase empty lots for playgrounds [challenge instead of conflict].

When the riot broke out, the residents, through the block clubs, were able to organize quickly. Youngsters agreeing to stay in the neighborhood participated in detouring traffic. While many persons reportedly sympathized with the idea of rebellion against the "system," only two small fires were set—one in an empty building.[2]

The PNAC neighborhood was organized and its positive programs developed by using the concepts of normative sponsorship theory. The above quotation illustrates that when people are actively involved in the community problem-solving process and have some control over their own destiny, they will respond positively and effectively to the implementation of community development programs.

The quotation also illustrates two other important concepts of normative sponsorship orientation to community development.[3] First, the role of the Institute of Urban Dynamics was one of providing technical assistance. The technical assistance concept is different from many contemporary assistance roles. Too often assistance means (either directly or indirectly) paternalism or co-optation of community problem solving.

Effective technical assistance recognizes the vast amount of human resources within the community and the residents' willingness to develop positive community programs if their efforts are appreciated and if they are meaningfully involved in the problem-solving process.

Technical assistance, according to our definition, does not mean co-optation. It means making assistance readily available so that the community can "plug in" to available and appropriate resources. Technical assistance is provided only upon community request. After the specific assistance is rendered, the technical assistance unit withdraws until further requests are made. It is interesting to note that as the community becomes aware of available resources and learns the problem-solving process (which many of us take for granted), their requests for assistance decrease. It takes a special type of professional to operate effectively in a technical assistance role. He must be competent and knowledgeable in the areas of resource identification and problem solving, yet he must avoid a do-gooder or a paternalistic approach. He is not expected to save the world, but only to help make it run more smoothly.

The second important concept that the quotation illustrates is that challenge is a more effective means of program development than is conflict. Normative sponsorship theory postulates that programs that challenge the skeptics through involvement, participation, and cooperative action will be more effective than programs that are conflict oriented. Not only do the skeptics and cynics gain support when there is conflict, interest groups polarize their positions. For example, the community may make unreasonable demands, while the community

[2]*Report of the National Advisory Commission on Civil Disorders* (New York: Bantam Books, Inc., 1968), p. 96.

[3]Also see Robert C. Trojanowicz, "Police Community Relations: Problems and Process," *Criminology*, February 1972.

agencies react by overjustifying their position and actions. The longer and more intense the conflict, the less chance there is to identify and develop consensus points from which viable programs can be implemented.

In sum, the technical assistance role is undoubtedly more conducive to community involvement and participation than are contemporary approaches. Many contemporary "experts" who have attempted to provide "expertise" to community problem solving have "come under fire" from both the community and such community professionals as the police. The community feels that external "experts" often expect the community to act as a human laboratory. The "experts," however, do not have a stake in the community and are frequently unconcerned about the frustration and disruption they create when they fail to keep promises.

The police often feel that the outside "expert," although teaching communication and stressing empathy, is unwilling himself to empathize with the police and understand that the police are merely a reflection of the larger power structure of which the "expert" is also a part. The police, as well as other agency professionals, believe that if the "expert" would provide them with alternatives for action rather than merely castigate them, they would be more receptive to constructive criticism and to "new and radical" ideas. A technical assistance unit should assume a *neutral* position in problem solving, emphasizing cooperative action, not disruptive verbalizations. Cooperation can also be an elusive concept if normative sponsorship theory is not utilized as a model.

Relevant Systems

Before programs that necessitate cooperation of more than one group can be implemented, it is necessary to identify the relevant interest groups—the *relevant systems*. The relevant systems concerned with delinquency prevention would be the community, the police, the court, the social work agencies, the legislature, and the other private and public agencies and business organizations in the community.

The technical assistance unit whose services are secured by the relevant systems is not a relevant system itself because it is usually not an integral part of the community. It is rather, a *neutral external resource*.

The discussion of relevant systems can be somewhat general and abstract. The logical question to be asked is, How can these relevant systems be made manageable so that perceptions and areas of consensus can be identified and viable programs initiated? This is the beginning of the normative sponsorship process.

Step 1: The Identification
of Leadership

To make each relevant system manageable, the leadership interested in and concerned with solving the problem of juvenile delinquency and crime will have to be identified. Some persons within any relevant system are able to reflect the system's norms, values, and goals and are knowledgeable about how it functions. They also exert considerable influence, and their opinions and suggestions are respected and implemented.

They may hold a position in the formal structure of a community organization, such as officer in a block club, or they may hold a command rank in the police department or an administrative position in a social work agency. However, they may not have a formal position in either a community organization or a community agency, yet exert influence through the informal structure.

Identification of these leaders is accomplished through a process of sampling members of the relevant organizations and asking such questions as "Whom do you or most of the people in the organization go to for advice on problem solving?" and "Who in the organization is respected, has power and influence, and has the reputation for getting things done?"

After the sampling process is completed, it is possible to construct a list of those individuals whose names have been mentioned most often as leaders. The sampling process is important for leadership identification. It should not be assumed that sampling is not necessary because leaders are already known. Leadership is not static, and those persons *assumed* to be leaders because of their formal or informal position are not necessarily the major source of power or influence. The identification of true leadership is mandatory if the process of program development and implementation is to be successful.

Step 2: Bringing Leaders of Relevant Systems Together

After leaders have been identified in each relevant system, the next step is to bring the leaders together for a meeting. They should be told that they have been identified by their peers as influential leaders interested in the prevention of delinquency and crime. The initial meetings (the meetings are chaired by a technical assistance adviser) will be somewhat unstructured. The major objectives of the initial meetings will be to—

1. Facilitate the expression of feelings about the apparent problem.
2. Encourage relevant systems to exchange perceptions about each other. (There is often much suspiciousness between the agencies and between the citizens and the agencies.)
3. Produce an atmosphere conducive to meaningful dialogue so that the misperceptions can be identified and the constellation of factors contributing to the causation of the problem can be discussed.
4. Identify self-interest, pointing out that from the self-interest standpoint of all systems, cooperative problem solving to prevent crime and delinquency will benefit everyone. The community agencies will have smaller case loads and more time to provide services, while the citizens will be better protected from threats and offenses against life and property.

It is not the purpose of the initial meetings to produce attitude changes or develop a "love relationship" between the relevant systems. Negative attitudes will change when positive perceptions between the relevant systems increase and when meaningful involvement and positive behavioral action is initiated and carried out through program development and implementation.

Whenever diverse interest groups assemble, they will often have biased opinions, misinformation, and negative perceptions toward one another. If there is extensive defensiveness by the relevant systems and if an atmosphere of freedom of expression does not prevail, the initial stages of the process will be hindered which can have unfavorable implications for future cooperation and program implementation.

In my experience with groups that have assembled to discuss delinquency prevention problems, initially many mutual accusations are made by the various relevant systems. The police, for example, are accused of authoritarianism and aloofness, while the community is accused of complacency and lack of cooperation. Agency professionals also exhibit intergroup hostility and negative perceptions. The social workers may call the police "hard-headed disciplinarians," and the police may retaliate by calling the social workers "permissive do-gooders." If there is a too hasty denial of the accusation, if elements of truth in the accusations are not handled in an honest manner, if the constellation of factors that contributed to the perceptions are not identified and if these perceptions are not discussed, then the communication process will be shallow and the total problem will not be understood.

The technical assistance adviser can play an important role in these early stages. He can help control the meetings so that they are not monopolized by one interest group or so that expression of feelings does not become inappropriate and offensive to the point of disruption and ultimate disbandment of the group. He can also help clarify the issues and provide insight into the problem and the reasons for its existence.

The admission of the obvious truth of some of the accusations by the relevant systems will be helpful in establishing an atmosphere of trust and credibility. This will facilitate understanding and cooperation.

The communication process between the relevant systems should be more than merely the denial or the admission of fact. It should include a discussion of the constellation of factors that can contribute to misperceptions. For example, the citizens could be informed of the policies of the various agencies and the effect these policies have on the delivering of services to the community. Insight in this area may be helpful in explaining that certain administrative considerations have to be weighed and certain priorities have to be established. Citizens could also share with the agencies the reasons why they become frustrated with the apparent lack of concern and impersonality of large agency structures. This will facilitate the agency personnel's empathizing with the citizens, and vice versa. Interagency misperceptions can also be neutralized through the process of sharing problem-solving approaches and reasons why an agency takes a particular orientation.

The increased empathy between relevant systems will help destroy misperceptions and provide the relevant systems with new insights into individual and organizational behavior. This will establish a basis for future understanding and cooperation.

The first few meetings are usually typified by (1) the unstructured expression of feelings and perceptions, (2) the admission of "reality facts," (3) the discussion of the constellation of contributing factors, (4) the facilitation of understanding, and (5) the increased number of positive perceptions. The sessions then begin to take a more focused and less emotional orientation. If the initial meetings have achieved their objectives, the stage is set for the next phase of the process, the identification of areas of consensus and dissensus in the prevention of crime and delinquency.

Step 3: The Identification of Areas of Consensus and Dissensus

In the third stage of the process, the matrix method is utilized for the identification of areas of consensus and dissensus. In dealing with this kind of methodology, Ladd has made an important contribution.[4] He obtained the following kinds of information for each of the major positions of the small society that he studied. This same information will be helpful in understanding the relevant systems involved in crime and delinquency prevention.

1. What are the prescriptions of expected behavior?
2. Who makes these prescriptions?
3. To what extent is there consensus about the prescriptions?
4. Who enforces them?
5. What are the rewards for compliance?
6. What are the punishments for deviance?

As illustrated in Table 3, this kind of information as well as additional information can be assembled into a matrix pattern for the analysis of any system or set of systems.

This method serves as a vehicle for visually and objectively comparing the perceptions among and between relevant systems. For example, the perception the police have of their role can be compared with the perception the community has of the police role, and vice versa. This comparison can also be made with the other relevant systems—police with social workers and vice versa, social workers with the community, and so on.

The perceived roles of the systems can also be compared with the actual behavior of both systems, and then an evaluation can be made regarding whether the behavior is deviant or normative, functional or nonfunctional. Finally, the statement of alternatives for problem solving of each system can be compared with the perceived expected alternatives. It may be learned, for example, that the

[4]John Ladd, *The Structure of a Moral Code* (Cambridge: Harvard University Press, 1957).

TABLE 3

Diagram of the Matrix Method of Identifying Areas of Consensus and Dissensus

NORMS AND BEHAVIOR Perceptions Held by:	NORMS AND BEHAVIOR PERCEPTIONS HELD ABOUT:					
	The Police	The Community	Social Workers	Businessmen	Legislators	Other Agencies and Organizations

The police	Self-Concept
	1. Perceived norms and expected behavior as it relates to delinquency prevention
	2. Description of actual behavior
	3. Defined as:
	   a. Normative
	   b. Deviant
	4. Statement of alternatives for problem solving
		1. Perceived norms and expected behavior as it relates to delinquency prevention
		2. Description of actual behavior
		3. Defined as:
		   a. Normative
		   b. Deviant
		4. Perception as to what alternatives the other systems will select for problem solving
			*	*	*	*

	The community (including youth groups)					

	1. Perceived norms and expected behavior as it relates to delinquency prevention
	2. Description of actual behavior
	3. Defined as:
	  a. Normative
	  b. Deviant
	4. Perception as to what alternatives the other system will select for problem solving
		Self-Concept
		1. Perceived norms and expected behavior as it relates to delinquency prevention
		2. Description of actual behavior
		3. Defined as:
		  a. Normative
		  b. Deviant
		4. Statement of alternatives for problem solving
			*	*	*	*

Social workers	*	*	Self-Concept	*	*	*
Businessmen	*	*	*	Self-Concept	*	*
Legislators	*	*	*	*	Self-Concept	*
Other agencies and organizations	*	*	*	*	*	Self-Concept

*Use the same criteria that are presented in the cell showing the Police Department's perception of the community.

alternatives contemplated by each system are not incompatible or as different from each other as originally perceived.

As a result of the intrasystem and intersystem comparisons, it is easy to compile the information about how each system expects and perceives both its own members and members of the other systems to behave. From this it is not a difficult research task to classify the categories of information as either normative (as they should be) or deviant (different than they should be) to the relevant systems.

A special usefulness of the matrix method of arranging the findings is that it provides a means for detecting the chief nexus points of normative consensus and dissensus among and between the systems.

Step 4: Program Implementation

After areas of consensus and dissensus have been identified, a program can be developed that will incorporate the areas of consensus so that the program will be normative to *all* systems. The systems will not necessarily agree in all areas, but there will usually be enough common areas of agreement so that cooperation and sponsorship will be predictable.

It will be surprising and enlightening to the relevant systems, after using the matrix method, to learn how many areas of consensus are present, which at first glance, after a subjective evaluation, may not be apparent. There generally will be consensus on major goals, such as the need for delinquency prevention programs, for more positive and effective communication, and for cooperation between the systems. Areas of consensus may decrease as specific techniques for problem solving are identified and alternatives for program implementation are suggested by each system. This will be a minor problem, however, because if the normative sponsorship process has been followed, an atmosphere of cooperation will prevail and compromise will be facilitated.

Step 5: Quality Control and Continuous Program Development and Updating

As with any viable program, there is a constant need for quality control and continuous program development and updating. There should be meaningful feedback, the testing of new theories, and reciprocal involvement and program evaluation by the relevant systems as well as individual and system introspection.

Conclusion

The normative sponsorship theory method has been used in many situations to assist communities in problem solving. At present the method is being used at Michigan State University to link the university to the community through extension courses. The extension course can serve the same general purpose as the community meeting if the course has a wide variety of participants. The same type of problem-solving process, as it relates to delinquency prevention that was described earlier, can be facilitated in the classroom. The classroom is conducive to meaningful communication and the transmission of ideas and feelings because the organizational constraints and pressures that often inhibit the communication process in an interorganizational meeting are nonexistent. The instructor can function in the same technical assistance role described earlier. Community improvement projects such as crime and delinquency prevention can be initiated in the community through a cooperative team effort. The team (which is composed of representatives of all relevant systems) can return to the classroom periodically to provide feedback and receive inputs and an objective evaluation of their project by the instructor and class peers.

An effective prevention program results only through a cooperative first-hand experience of all relevant systems in the problem-solving process. A maximum of active involvement and a minimum of shallow verbalization will facilitate cooperation and mutual understanding between the relevant systems.

The most effective means of motivating people is to transmit to them that their opinions will be valued, that they will have a voice in decision making, and that they will be involved in the problem-solving process. Programs will be sponsored and perpetuated if these criteria are adhered to because the parties who comprise the relevant systems have a personal investment in the process. Involved action by the relevant systems will be mutually beneficial and will increase understanding and cooperation between them. "The nature of the group (and group goal) serves to fulfill certain needs of its members, and the satisfaction of these needs is its function. Through the symbolic system of the group, its roles, role-systems, and norms, individual behavior is differentiated and at the same time integrated for the satisfaction of needs, and the fulfillment of its functions."[5]

SUMMARY

Effective prevention includes more than a knowledge of theory, extensive resources, and good intentions. All of these are necessary, but they only become translated into action when there is cooperative involvement in the problem-solving process by the community residents and the maze of agencies and organizations both internal and external to the criminal justice system. This chapter has presented a process that can facilitate the translation of theory, resources, and good intentions into action programs.

Action programs that help prevent juvenile delinquency and involve all community interest groups will be successful because the interest groups will have a stake in both the process and the "product." Although this action involvement by community interest groups to prevent delinquency will not be the same as the informal community processes that were so effective in influencing human behavior in the past, it will be a step in the right direction.

[5]Scott A. Greer, *Social Organizations* (New York: Random House, 1955), p. 24.

The following chapter will present a concluding statement and a look to the future.

QUESTIONS AND PROJECTS

Essay Questions

1. Why is it difficult to mobilize the efforts of community residents to prevent delinquency and crime?
2. Why is informal social control not as effective today as it was in the past?
3. Is the *normative sponsorship* approach realistic for very large cities?
4. Why are resources, theories, and "good intentions" not enough to effectively prevent and reduce juvenile delinquency?
5. Why is it mandatory that the entire community be involved in crime control and delinquency prevention?

Projects

1. Identify all the interest groups in your community that would have to cooperate for effective juvenile delinquency prevention, control, and treatment.
2. Develop a present-day alternative to the policeman-on-the-beat concept.
3. Develop a rationale for convincing adults that youngsters in the community should be actively involved in problem solving and decision making.

CONCLUSION

The purpose of this book has been to discuss the constellation of factors that relate to juvenile delinquency causation, prevention, control, and treatment. Many principles and assumptions were integrated to demonstrate the complexity of the delinquency phenomenon and the many variables that need to be considered for effective problem solving.

To insure that the problem of juvenile delinquency be adequately understood and effectively handled, a number of issues have to be resolved. The conclusion of the book will address some of these issues.

A report of federal government activities in delinquency prevention, treatment, and control listed recommendations made at a conference attended by state governors. The development of new public policies for dealing with youthful offenders was emphasized, in addition to the following:

1. Commitment to long-term research and development adequate to cope with the complexity of the delinquency problem.
2. The conscious broadening of the framework within which problems are analyzed or ultimately solved. There must be a willingness to examine and challenge all traditional operations.
3. The significant involvement of youth in any community effort to understand and prevent juvenile delinquency.
4. Coordination of private and public services to youth, including character-building efforts and those geared to correction and rehabilitation.

5. Focusing attention and effort on youth at an earlier age than we are doing presently and have done previously.

6. A careful reevaluation of the unique role of the family in American society.

7. Realism about the cost of long-range preventive efforts.

8. Establishment of vocational schools without severe standards and criteria to give every boy and every girl an equal education.[1]

Specifically, effective delinquency prevention, control, and treatment involves *research, planning, coordination, processing, personnel,* and *programming.* These issues will now be discussed.

RESEARCH

Vigorous research is necessary to identify the many variables related to the phenomenon of juvenile delinquency. Meaningful research will contribute to the establishment of theoretically sound treatment, prevention, and control programs. Research can provide a sound basis so that successful programs can be replicated in different environments and communities.

At present no adequate data base exists that can provide the necessary information about the relative merits of the many available programs or the alternatives most applicable to the many different types of delinquent behavior syndromes.

Research efforts have to be directed in areas that have heretofore been neglected. In addition, scientists from many different disciplines should participate in delinquency research to make it complete. Empey and Lubeck provide some helpful suggestions, and list the following steps for an effective delinquency research process:

1. Define the target population. Decide whether it is to include young children, a middle-range group, or older, convicted offenders.

2. Conduct a pilot study by which to identify and describe the particular children who fit the general characteristics of the target population.

3. Define objectives for the program. Include administrators, practitioners, and research people in the defining process.

4. Write a contract specifying the obligations and roles of each of these three sets of people.

5. Derive an intervention strategy based upon the general leads provided by the theory and the findings of the pilot study.

6. Establish a research strategy based on the same principles and guidelines and concerned with studying the characteristics of the subject population, program itself, and its outcome.[2]

[1] *Annual Report of 1971 Federal Activities in Juvenile Delinquency Youth Development and Related Fields* (Washington, D.C.: Government Printing Office, 1971, p. 137.

[2] Lamar T. Empey and Steven G. Lubeck, *Delinquency Prevention Strategies,* U.S. Department of Health, Education, and Welfare, Social and Rehabilitation Service, Youth Development and Delinquency Prevention Administration, 1970.

Because of the importance of adequate information, every organization that deals with the juvenile delinquent should allocate a portion of its budget to research. The information derived from research is invaluable because it provides a data base and an orientation to problem solving that are theoretically sound. Research also provides data, which facilitates sound *planning.*

PLANNING

Too often, delinquency prevention, control, and treatment efforts are haphazard. There is neither vigorous research nor sound planning—both essential elements for problem solving. One of the major purposes of the Juvenile Delinquency Prevention and Control Act of 1968 was to provide the necessary resources so that communities could more systematically identify their needs through research and develop plans for delinquency prevention, control, and treatment programs.[3]

Sound planning includes an evaluation of existing programs as well as the identification of problem areas not considered by existing programs. Both the agencies that dispense the resources and the clients who will utilize the services need to be involved in the planning process.[4]

Sound planning is only as effective as the data that are available. As pointed out earlier, these data are acquired through vigorous research.[5] Comprehensive planning is necessary for:

1. Establishing realistic goals and objectives.
2. Measuring accomplishments.
3. Meeting goals and objectives on schedule.
4. Justifying programs to the resource providers.
5. Matching goals and resources and applying acquired resources.
6. Defining and improving continued and subsequent programs.
7. Communicating to all concerned.
8. Motivating all concerned to the achievement of stated goals.[6]

Research and planning go hand in hand. The competent planner benefits from data gathered through research. The research data are necessary as a basis for developing plans that will contribute to the success of the particular program. Research data and sound planning provide reference points with which to evaluate programs and increase the quality of service. Research and planning, however, will be futile if there is not effective program coordination once the research data have been gathered and the planning completed.

[3]Section 2, Public Law 90-445, House Report No. 12120, 90th Cong. July 31, 1968.

[4]*Juvenile Delinquency Planning,* a joint publication of the U.S. Department of Health, Education, and Welfare, Social and Rehabilitation Service, Youth Development and Delinquency Prevention Administration, and the U.S. Department of Justice, Law Enforcement Assistance Administration, p. 3.

[5]*Ibid.,* p. 5.

[6]*Ibid.,* p. 13.

COORDINATION

The agencies that handle the juvenile are often referred to as *components* of a system. Because the process is referred to as a *system,* it is often assumed that coordination is an integral part of the operation. Coordination and even cooperation do not always exist. Mason P. Thomas succinctly points out that

> legislatures have passed laws to establish a separate court system for children under certain ages because youth should not be held accountable under the same standards as adults and because there may be a better chance of reform and rehabilitation with young people. While these concepts contain assumptions that might be questioned, the separate system idea has never been tried with adequate resources and personnel. Separate police services or detention homes are often unavailable. The juvenile court is increasingly absorbed in consolidated court systems, thus becoming less separate and specialized. Juvenile probation may exist more on paper than in actual services to children and parents. Juvenile institutions, while usually separate, are little more than junior prisons that offer little in the way of treatment services. They rarely prepare a child for life in the free community. After-care services are often nonexistent . . . Thus, while our separate juvenile corrections system may be more myth than fact, it seems clear that the professionals involved must develop new strategies to work cooperatively as management teams. In the past, the judge has been the star, with administrative control and other powers over the rest of the system. The challenge for today is whether the separate parts of the system—when available—can develop a team concept to help juvenile corrections to function as a system in a positive way upon the lives of those children who have no choice about being pushed through the various parts of the system.[7]

Coordination will be facilitated if there is a system of *management,* a method of *accountability,* and increased *understanding* between the system's components.

Both personnel engineering (fitting the job to the man) and personnel management (fitting the man to the job) have to be utilized to insure program effectiveness. The *management* approach should be flexible but oriented to goal achievement and problem solving. All the professionals within the criminal justice system will obviously not have the same behavioral style orientation to problem solving. Not all policemen make good juvenile officers, not all social workers are effective with delinquents, and not all judges are adept at handling juvenile cases. An efficient and innovative management system can identify those professionals in each component who will be most successful with the juvenile. When these individuals are placed in key positions, the youngster will be better served, cooperation will increase, and coordination will be facilitated.

[7]Mason P. Thomas, Jr., *Juvenile Corrections—Five Issues to Be Faced,* U.S. Department of Health, Education, and Welfare, Social and Rehabilitation Service, Youth Development and Delinquency Prevention Administration. Reprinted with permission from *Popular Government,* May 1971. Institute of Government, The University of North Carolina at Chapel Hill.

It is also important that a system of *accountability* be developed for the components of the criminal justice system. Accountability will minimize buck-passing and increase coordination. The duties, responsibilities, services, and functions of each component need to be identified so that the accountability can be determined. A sound method of accountability will contribute to more effective processing of youngsters and will ensure that services will be dispensed rationally and equally.

Finally, there should be greater *understanding* between the professionals of the various components of the system. Joint conferences and seminars of the interagency professionals will contribute to this end. The various professional groups can identify their problem areas and make known the alternatives that they feel are available and appropriate for problem solving. As a result of an exchange of ideas, the various professional groups will begin to understand the problems faced by their professional counterparts and the alternatives available or perceived to be available to each component.

Innovative approaches to increasing understanding between components should also be developed. For example, role playing can be useful in increasing empathy. By exchanging roles, the various professionals can put themselves "in the other guy's shoes." This will increase understanding of the problems faced by professional counterparts and reveal the types of alternatives available to each component. Role playing can be helpful in both increasing the professional's ability to empathize with his counterpart and giving him the opportunity to suggest new alternatives to problem solving.

In addition to the issues of research, planning, and coordination, the criminal justice process itself has to be improved to guarantee equality and the provision of services to all youngsters.

PROCESSING

Whether a youngster is formally processed in the criminal justice system or not depends more upon his background and the financial standing of his parents than upon such objective criteria as the type and the seriousness of the offense. Too often the affluent youngster is provided with more acceptable and nonstigmatizing alternatives than his less-fortunate peer. Economically disadvantaged youngsters run a much greater risk of not only coming in contact with the formal system but also having to resort to less-desirable alternatives, such as institutionalization.[8]

The reason for this is that the disadvantaged youngster usually has little influence or power in his community.

The power of a group determines its ability to keep its people out of trouble with the law, even in instances where they have actually violated it. The

[8]*Delinquency Today, A Guide for Community Action,* U.S. Department of Health, Education, and Welfare, 1971.

powerful enjoy a series of formal and informal liaisons or links into the political system, ranging from the ability to put in 'the fix', to finding a friend in court, to getting its own members on the bench. Such groups are able to influence political and related structures because of their own numerical and organizational strength, brought to bear directly through political mechanisms and indirectly through a nexus of institutions created by them which afford them contact with the system. . . . Aside from the straight political power of the vote, especially when used on a block basis by well-organized interest groups, other areas of institutional power which are partially significant for delinquency are those of education, economics, and welfare. When an interest group's capacities to influence are high in any one of these three areas, these capacities tend to be high in all of the areas. When a group's general capacities to influence are high, the official delinquency rates of its children and youth tend to be low. Other institutions, of course, could easily be added to the list—for example, organized religion and the mass media.[9]

Affluence and influence should not be the determining factors in dispensing resources and providing services to delinquent youngsters. Fairness and equality are essential ingredients in any viable system of justice. Eliminating injustice is not a simple process and can be accomplished only by understanding the many variables that contribute to it and the available resources that can help eliminate it. One of the most effective methods of increasing equality in processing and serving juveniles is the selection and training of competent personnel.

PERSONNEL

Adequate services cannot be provided or programs developed and operated without competent personnel. Both the quantity and the quality of personnel have to be considered if the massive problems in our communities are to be solved. A review of existing staff needs and staffing patterns is mandatory in order to reduce overlapping and increase the quality of service. Specialists in all phases of delinquency prevention, control, and treatment will have to be used more efficiently, and the number of paraprofessionals will have to be increased. The volunteer also has a place in the criminal justice system. A sound management system can coordinate the specialists, paraprofessionals, and volunteers in an efficient manner.[10]

A systematic approach needs to be developed to identify those individuals who can be most effective in working with the youngster. Not all professionals in the criminal justice system are adept at assisting juveniles.

Personnel selection and training is a complex process and an important one for problem solving within the criminal justice system. Local communities often

[9]John M. Martin, *Toward a Political Definition of Delinquency,* U. S. Department of Health, Education, and Welfare, Social and Rehabilitation Services, Youth Development and Delinquency Prevention Administration. (Washington, D.C.: Government Printing Office, 1970), p. 9.

[10]*Delinquency Today,* p. 17.

cannot adequately deal with this problem. The National Council of Crime and Delinquency specifically states that federal support is urgently needed for the following:

1. Scholarship and stipend programs to help meet manpower needs with a variety of professional and subprofessional tasks.
2. Grants to help state agencies develop pre- and postemployment training for both state and local correctional agencies.
3. Grants to help appropriate state agencies assume leadership roles in developing a system for balanced planning and assessment of priority needs between state and local correctional services.
4. A standard setting program that would involve leaders from national, state, and local correctional programs in the actual development of standards, the attainment of which would be aided by grant and subsidy programs.
5. Technical consultation services to aid the states in planning and implementing standards for the end that appropriate state agencies would develop similar standards, grants, and subsidies, and technical assistance programs for local services.[11]

Competent personnel and sufficient resources will increase the chances of the successful handling of the juvenile as well as the development of innovative approaches to problem solving.

PROGRAMMING

The successful handling of the juvenile will greatly depend upon the resourceful development of innovative approaches to problem solving. This book has identified many approaches to delinquency prevention, control, and treatment problem solving. One of the most popular new approaches is the use of the Youth Service Bureau.

> These bureaus would act as an important added resource for dealing with difficult youth within the local community, handling referrals from the police, schools, and other agencies. Situated directly in high delinquency neighborhoods, such bureaus would be privately run but largely publicly financed. Referrals would be made in cases involving less serious offenses or to youth involved in nondelinquent difficulties, while criminal behavior in cases involving repeated misdemeanors would continue to be referred to the juvenile court. Drawing upon existing services and creating new ones where needed, the bureaus would provide individualized treatment programs for troubled youth. Not only would such local agencies better meet the needs of youth by offering specially tailored services, but they would also function as an alternative to official court referrals, thereby avoiding the stigma attached

[11]Stanton Wheeler, Leonard S. Cottrell, and Anne Ramasco, *Juvenile Delinquency— Its Prevention and Control*, Task Force Report: Juvenile Delinquency and Youth Crime, The Presidents Commission on Law Enforcement and the Administration of Justice, U.S. Government Printing Office, Washington: 1967, p. 426.

to a judicial proceeding. In effect then, the establishment of youth service bureaus would result in the narrowing of the jurisdiction of the juvenile court—a goal advocated today by many experts. Moreover, these bureaus would enable many communities to gain a better insight into the problems of youth and a clearer understanding of the programs needed to deal with them.[12]

In addition to the Youth Service Bureau concept and other approaches discussed in the preceding chapters, the following methods can be considered in dealing with the juvenile delinquency problem.

Juvenile Information System

A specific system can be established to provide the community, and especially youngsters, with information about the operation of the criminal justice system, the legal rights of citizens, the programs available to community residents, and the referral systems to appropriate agencies.

Regional Centers for Juveniles

Regional centers would provide the gamut of services for youngsters. Some of the services would include diagnosis, treatment, evaluation, and temporary and semipermanent residential care. These facilities would be located in the community so that the youngster would have the benefit of community services. Location in the community would facilitate the youngster's reintegration into the community after a more permanent alternative had been selected and a disposition made.

Information System

A method of collecting, analyzing, and distributing data relating to delinquency prevention, control, and treatment is needed. This information can be used and assimilated at all levels of government.

Cooperative Interagency Programs

Cooperative delinquency prevention, control, and treatment efforts are needed to increase cooperation and coordination between the various components of the criminal justice system. Through cooperative efforts a more consistent orientation to problem solving and goal achievement can be developed.

Community Drop-in Centers

Community-based facilities that afford youngsters the opportunity to expend their energy in a socially acceptable manner need to be developed on a more

[12]*Delinquency Today*, p. 15.

systematic basis. The centers could serve many functions, such as providing recreational activities, counseling, and employment referral services.

High School Dropout Programs

Innovative approaches are needed that focus on high school dropouts to provide them with necessary skills to insure their successful participation in the community.

Police-Juvenile Programs

Programs need to be developed that foster closer cooperation and understanding between police and youth—especially minority youth.

Intensive Treatment for High-Risk Juveniles

Programs should be developed for youngsters who have unsuccessfully utilized many community services. Intensive efforts are needed to interrupt the negative cycle of delinquent behavior of these youngsters so that new modes of behavioral adaption can be initiated. Many other approaches are needed if the problem of juvenile delinquency is to be reduced and the juvenile effectively handled. The aforementioned approaches are only a sampling of possible alternatives to delinquency problem solving.

SUMMARY

This book has attempted to point out the many facets of juvenile delinquency and the many variables that relate to its prevention, treatment, and control. The concluding statements identified some of the requirements that have to be met if the problem is going to be adequately handled—vigorous *research,* sound *planning,* effective *coordination,* equality in *processing,* competent *personnel,* and innovative *programming.*

General services to youngsters have to be increased in number and improved in quality so that long-range delinquency and crime can be interrupted and prevented. Existing methods and procedures have to be renewed and reevaluated, and when they are inappropriate or outdated, they have to be eliminated. Care has to be taken not to expose the youngster to the formal processes of the criminal justice system when other more appropriate alternatives are available.

Ongoing training programs are necessary to keep the professionals of the criminal justice system up to date so that new approaches can be developed. Ongoing research is also mandatory to provide a basis for the development of programs and to evaluate programs, improve them, and alter them when necessary. Without adequate research there will be a great deal of overlapping, misuse of resources, and irrational decision making.

Finally, there needs to be cooperation between the components of the criminal justice system as well as a commitment by the community to the belief that youngsters are persons worth helping. Both the private and the public sectors of the community have to become involved in juvenile delinquency problem solving. The *Task Force Report on Juvenile Delinquency and Youth Crime* made many recommendations relative to community involvement in the delinquency problem-solving process. Some of the recommendations follow:

—Reduce unemployment and devise methods of providing minimum family income.
—Reexamine and revise welfare regulations so that they contribute to keeping the family together.
—Improve housing and recreational facilities.
—Provide help in problems of domestic management and child care.
—Make counseling and therapy easily obtainable.
—Develop activities that involve the whole family together.
—Train unemployed youth as subprofessional aides.
—Increase involvement of religious insitutions, private social agencies, fraternal groups and other community organizations in youth programs.

Other recommendations made by the *Task Force Report* emphasize the importance of education and the school in helping to solve many of the problems that exist in our communities:

—Improve the quality and quantity of teachers and facilities in the slum school.
—Combat racial and economic school segregation.
—Help slum children make up for inadequate preschool preparation.
—Deal better with behavior problems.
—Relate instructional material to conditions of life in the slums.
—Raise the aspirations and expectations of students capable of higher education.
—Review and revise present programs for students not going to college.
—Further develop job placement services in schools.
—Prepare youth for employment.
—Provide youth with information about employment opportunities.
—Reduce barriers to employment posed by discrimination, the misuse of criminal records and maintenance of rigid job qualifications.
—Create new employment opportunities.[13]

It is also important to involve the youth of our communities in the process of justice. It has been suggested that because there is not a federal, state, or local government structure that claims a wide youth constituency, one should be developed. Most other interest groups, such as labor, business, agriculture, and special interest groups, are represented.

[13]*Task Force Report: Juvenile Delinquency and Youth Crime, Report on Juvenile Justice and Consultants' Papers,* Task Force on Juvenile Delinquency, The President's Commission on Law Enforcement and Administration of Justice, pp. 47-57.

Shifts in relationships among social classes, ethnic groups, and interest groups and age groups, all consequent to ongoing social change in American society, have produced in the past innovations in the structure and functions of government agencies. At the present juncture, one possibility may be to provide youth groups with an established channel of access to government and other bureaucratic decision making. Such a move may serve to reduce the hostility and suspicion that some of the most problem-prone segments of the youth groups now direct toward the government, colleges, and industry, and serve to restore the credibility of these institutions in the eyes of youth.[14]

The involvement of the entire community, including the youth, in the juvenile delinquency problem-solving process will be a step in the right direction to solving one of the most pressing and serious problems that exists today. Only a concerted effort by the entire community will be successful in combating delinquency and developing programs for its prevention, control, and treatment.

[14]*Delinquency Prevention Reporter,* U.S. Department of Health, Education, and Welfare, March 1971, p. 4.

BIBLIOGRAPHY

BOOKS

Abrahamsen, David. *The Psychology of Crime.* New York: Columbia University Press, 1960.

Ackerman, Nathan W. *The Psychodynamics of Family Life.* New York: Basic Books, Inc., 1958.

Ackerman, Nathan W., Frances L. Beatman, and Stanford N. Sherman, eds. *Exploring the Base for Family Therapy.* Family Service Association, 1961.

Adorno, T. W., E. Frenkel-Brunswick, D. S. Levinson, and R. N. Sanford. *The Authoritarian Personality.* New York: Harper, 1950.

Aeston, Estelle. *The Social Welfare Forum Proceedings of the National Conference of Social Work.* New York: Columbia University Press, 1951.

Aichhorn, August. *Wayward Youth.* New York: Viking Press, 1963.

———. *Delinquency and Child Guidance.* New York: International Universities Press, 1964.

American Correctional Association. *Manual of Correctional Standards.* Washington, D.C.: The Association, 1966.

Amos, William E., and Raymond L. Manella. *Readings in the Administration of Institutions for Delinquent Youth.* Springfield, Ill.: Charles C Thomas, 1965.

Amos, William E., Raymond L. Manella, and Marilyn A. Southwell. *Action Programs for Delinquency Prevention.* Springfield, Ill.: Charles C. Thomas, 1965.

Amos, William E., and Charles Wellford. *Prevention: Theory and Practice.* Englewood Cliffs, N. J.: Prentice-Hall, 1969.

Andry, Robert G. *Delinquency and Parental Pathology.* Springfield, Ill.: Charles C. Thomas, 1960.

Ansbacher, Heinz L., and Rowena L. Ansbacher, eds. *The Individual Psychology of Alfred Adler.* New York: Basic Books, Inc., 1956.

Ard, Ben N., Jr., ed. *Counseling and Psychotherapy.* Palo Alto, Cal.: Science and Behavior Books, Inc., 1966.

Arieti, Silvano, ed. *American Handbook of Psychiatry.* New York: Basic Books, 1966.

Ball, John C. *Social Deviancy and Adolescent Personality (Analysis with MMPI).* Lexington: University of Kentucky Press, 1962.

Bandura, Albert, and Richard H. Walters. *Adolescent Aggression.* New York: Ronald Press, 1959.

Beard, Belle B. *Juvenile Probation (500 Case Records)* Montclair, N.J.: Patterson-Smith, 1969.

Becker, Howard S. *The Outsiders.* New York: The Free Press, 1963.

Bell, Daniel, and Irving Kristil, eds. *Confrontation.* New York: Basic Books, 1968.

Bell, J. E. *Family Group Therapy.* Public Health Monograph No. 64, U.S. Public Health Service, Washington, D. C.: Government Printing Office, 1961.

Bell, N., and E. Vogel, eds. *The Family.* New York: The Free Press, 1960.

Bennett, Ivy. *Delinquent and Neurotic Children.* London: Tavistock: 1961.

Berne, Eric, *Principles of Group Treatment.* New York: Oxford University Press, 1966.

———. *Transactional Analysis in Psychotherapy.* New York: Grove Press, 1961.

Bernstein, Saul. *Youth on the Streets—Work with Alienated Youth Groups.* New York: Association Press, 1964.

Bier, William C. *The Adolescent: His Search for Understanding.* New York: Fordham University Press, 1963.

Bloch, Herbert A., and Frank T. Flynn. *Delinquency.* Random House, 1956.

Bloch, Herbert A., and A. Niederhoffer. *The Gang.* New York: Philosophical Library, 1958.

Bredemeier, Harry C., and Jackson Toby, *Social Problems In America—Costs and Casualties in the Acquisitive Society.* New York: John Wiley and Sons, 1965.

Brennan, James J., and Donald W. Olmsted. *Training Police in Delinquency Prevention and Control.* East Lansing: Michigan State University Press, 1965.

Caplan, Gerald, and Serge Lebovici, eds. *Adolescence: Psychosocial Perspectives.* New York: Basic Books, 1969.

Cavan, Ruth S. *Juvenile Delinquency.* Philadelphia: J. B. Lippincott, 1962.

———, *Delinquency and Crime.* Philadelphia: J. B. Lippincott, 1968.

Cavan, Ruth S., and Jordon T. Cavan. *Delinquency and Crime: Cross Cultural Perspectives.* Philadelphia: J. B. Lippincott, 1966.

Chess, Stella. *An Introduction to Child Psychiatry.* New York: Grune & Stratton, 1969.

Cicourel, Aaron V. *The Social Organization of Juvenile Justice.* New York: John Wiley, 1968.

Clinard, Marshall B. *Sociology of Deviant Behavior.* New York: Holt, Rinehart and Winston, 1963.

Cloward, Richard A., and Ohlin, Lloyd E. *Delinquency and Opportunity.* New York: The Free Press, 1960.

Cohen, Albert K. *Delinquent Boys.* New York: The Free Press, 1955.

——. *Deviance and Control.* Englewood Cliffs, N. J.: Prentice-Hall, 1969.

Cohen, Sidney. *The Beyond Within—The LSD Story.* New York: Atheneum, 1967.

Cole, Jonathon, and Wittenborn, J. R. *Drug Abuse.* Springfield, Ill.: Charles C. Thomas, 1969.

Coleman, James S. *The Adolescent Society.* New York: The Free Press, 1961.

Coleman, James Samuel; James Johnstone; and Kurt Jonassohn. *Adolescent Society.* New York: The Free Press, 1961.

Conant, James B. *Slums and Suburbs.* New York: McGraw-Hill, 1961.

Cowie, John. *Delinquency in Girls.* New York: Humanities Press, 1968.

Cressey, Donald R. *Delinquency, Crime and Differential Association.* The Hague: M. Nijhoff, 1964.

Crow, Lester D., and Alice Crow. *Adolescent Development and Adjustment.* New York: McGraw-Hill, 1956.

Dale, E. *Planning and Developing the Company Organization Structure.* New York: American Management Association, 1952.

Davidoff, Eugene, and Elinor S. Noetzel, *The Child Guidance Approach to Juvenile Delinquency.* New York: Child Care Publications, 1951.

Dinitz, Simon, Russell R. Dynes, and Alfred D. Clarke. *Deviance—Studies on the Process of Stigmatization and Societal Reaction.* New York: Oxford University Press, 1969.

Douglas, Jack D. *Youth in Turmoil.* Chevy Chase, Md.: National Institute of Mental Health, Center for Studies of Crime and Delinquency, 1970.

Downes, David M. *The Delinquency Solution.* London: Routledge and Paul, 1966.

Dressler, David. *Practice and Theory of Probation and Parole.* New York: Columbia University Press, 1969.

Durkheim, Emile. *Suicide: A Study in Sociology.* Translated by John A. Spaulding and George Simpson. New York: The Free Press, 1951.

Eaton, Joseph W., and Kenneth Polk. *Measuring Delinquency.* Pittsburgh: University of Pittsburgh Press, 1961.

Edelson, M. *Ego Psychology, Group Dynamics and the Therapeutic Community.* New York: Grune & Stratton, 1964.

——. *Sociotherapy and Psychotherapy.* Chicago: University of Chicago Press, 1970.

Eisenberg, Leon. "A Developmental Approach to Adolescence," in *Issues in Adolescent Psychology,* Dorothy Rogers, ed. New York: Appleton-Century-Crofts, 1969.

Eisner, Victor. *The Delinquency Label: The Epidemiology of Delinquency.* New York: Random House, 1969.

Empey, Lamar T., and Jerome Rabow. "The Provo Experiment in Delinquency Prevention," in *Juvenile Delinquency: A Book of Readings,* Rose Giallombardo, ed. New York: Wiley, 1966.

Etzioni, Amitai. *Complex Organizations.* New York: The Free Press, 1961.

——. *Modern Organizations.* Englewood Cliffs, N. J.: Prentice-Hall, 1968.

Fenton, Norman. *A Handbook on the Use of Group Counseling in Youth Correctional Institutions.* Sacramento, Cal.: Institute for the Study of Crime and Delinquency, 1965.

Fenton, Norman, Ernest G. Reimer, and Harry A. Wilmer, eds. *The Correctional Community: An Introduction and Guide.* Berkeley: University of California Press, 1967.

Ferdinand, Theodore. *Typologies of Delinquency.* New York: Random House, 1966.

Ferguson, Elizabeth A. *Social Work: An Introduction.* Philadelphia: J.B. Lippincott, 1963.

Fleisher, Belton M. *The Economics of Delinquency.* Chicago: Quadrangle Books, 1966.

Freedman, Jonathan L., and Anthony N. Doob. *Deviancy—The Psychology of Being Different.* New York: Academic Press, 1968.

Friedlander, Kate. *The Psychoanalytical Approach to Juvenile Delinquency.* London: Routledge and Paul, 1961.

Furman, Sylvan S. *Reaching and Unreached.* New York: New York City Youth Board, 1952.

Gallagher, J. Roswell, and Herbert I. Harris. *Emotional Problems of Adolescents.* New York: Oxford University Press, 1964.

Garabedian, Peter G., and Gibbons, Don C., *Becoming Delinquent: Young Offenders and the Correctional Process.* Chicago: Aldine 1970.

Gazda, George M., ed. *Basic Approaches to Group Psychotherapy and Group Counseling.* Springfield, Ill.: Charles C Thomas, 1968.

Giallombardo, Rose, ed. *Juvenile Delinquency: A Book of Readings.* New York: Wiley, 1966.

Gibbens, T. C. N., and R. H. Ahrenfeldt. *Cultural Factors in Delinquency.* London: J. B. Lippincott, 1966.

Gibbons, Don C. *Delinquent Behavior.* Englewood Cliffs, N.J.: Prentice-Hall, 1970.

——. *Society, Crime and Criminal Careers.* Englewood Cliffs, N. J.: Prentice-Hall, 1964.

——. *Changing the Law Breaker.* Englewood Cliffs, N.J.: Prentice-Hall, 1965.

Glaser, Daniel. *The Effectiveness of a Prison and Parole System.* Indianapolis: Bobbs-Merrill, 1969.

Glasser, William. *Reality Therapy.* New York: Harper & Row, 1965.

Glasser, William, and Norman Iverson. *Reality Therapy in Large Group Counseling.* Los Angeles: Reality Press, 1966.

Glueck, Bernard. *Studies in Forensic Psychiatry.* Boston: Little, Brown, 1916.

Glueck, Sheldon, and Eleanor Glueck. *Ventures in Criminology.* Cambridge, Mass.: Harvard University Press, 1967.

——. *Unraveling Juvenile Delinquency.* Cambridge, Mass.: Harvard University Press, 1957.

——. *Delinquents and Nondelinquents in Perspective.* Cambridge, Mass.: Harvard University Press, 1968.

——. *Family Environment and Delinquency.* New York: Houghton, Mifflin, 1962.

Gockel, G. *Silk Stockings and Blue Collar: Social Work as a Career Choice of America's 1961 College Graduates.* Chicago: University of Chicago, National Opinion Research Center, 1966.

Gold, Martin. *Status Forces in Delinquent Boys.* Ann Arbor: University of Michigan Press, 1963.

Gottlieb, David. *The American Adolescent.* Homewood, Ill.: Dorsey Press, 1964.

Grant, J. Douglas, *et. al. The Offender as a Correctional Manpower Resource: Its Implementation.* Asilomar, California: Institute for the Study of Crime and Delinquency, NIMH, 1966.

Greer, Scott A. *Social Organization.* New York: Random House, 1955.

Gregory, Ian. *Fundamentals of Psychiatry.* Philadelphia: W. B. Saunders, 1968.

Grosser, Charles. *Helping Youth: A Study of Six Community Organization Programs.* U. S. Department of H.E.W. Washington: Government Printing Office, 1969.

Group for the Advancement of Psychiatry. *Normal Adolescense: Its Dynamics and Impact.* New York: Scribner's, 1968.

Gulick, Luther, and Urwick, Lyndall, eds. *Papers on the Science of Administration.* New York: Columbia University, Institute of Public Administration, 1937.

Harper Robert A. *Psychoanalysis and Psychotherapy.* Englewood Cliffs, N.J.: Prentice-Hall, 1959.

Haskell, Martin R., and Lewis Yablonsky, *Crime and Delinquency.* Chicago: Rand McNally, 1970.

——. *Crime and Delinquency.* Chicago: Rand McNally, 1970.

Hathaway, Starke R., and Elio D. Monachesi. *Analyzing and Predicting Juvenile Delinquency with the MMPI.* Minneapolis: University of Minnesota Press, 1953.

Hatt, P. K., and C. C. North, "Prestige Ratings of Occupations," in *Man, Work and Society,* S. Nasow and W. Form, eds. New York: Basic Books, 1962.

Healy, William. *The Individual Delinquent.* Boston: Little, Brown, 1913.

Healy, William and Augusta Fox Bronner. *New Light on Delinquency and Its Treatment.* New Haven: Yale University Press, 1936.

Herbert, W. L., and F. V. Jarvis. *Dealing with Delinquents.* New York: Emerson Books, 1962.

Hewitt, John P. *Social Stratification and Deviant Behavior.* New York: Random House, 1970.

Hewitt, Lester, and Richard Jenkins, *Fundamental Patterns of Maladjustment: The Dynamics of Their Origin.* Springfield, Ill.: State Printer, 1946.

Hirsch, Nathaniel D. M. *Dynamic Causes of Juvenile Crime.* Cambridge, Mass.: Sci-Art, 1937.

Hirschi, Travis, *Causes of Delinquency.* Berkeley: University of California Press, 1969.

Hirschi, Travis, and Hanan C. Selvin. *Delinquency Research.* New York: The Free Press, 1967.

Holmes, Donald J. *The Adolescent in Psychotherapy.* Boston: Little, Brown, 1964.

Hooton, Earnest Albert. *Crime and the Man.* Cambridge, Mass.: Harvard University Press, 1939.

Jacobs, Jane. *Death and Life of Great American Cities.* New York: Random House, 1961.

James, Howard. *Children in Trouble.* New York: David McKay, 1969.

Johnston, Norman, L. Savitz, and M. Wolfgang, eds. *The Sociology of Punishment and Correction.* New York: Wiley, 1962.

Joseph S., ed. *The Difficult Child.* New York: The Philosophical Library, 1964.

Josselyn, Irene M. *The Adolescent and His World.* New York: The Family Service Association of America, 1952.

Joyles, J. Arthur. *The Treatment of the Young Delinquent.* New York: Philosophical Library, 1952.

Jurjevich, Ratibor M. *No Water in My Cup: Experiences and a Controlled Study of Psychotherapy of Delinquent Girls.* New York: Libra Publishers, 1968.

Keller, Oliver J., Jr., and Benedict S. Alper. *Halfway Houses: Community Centered Corrections and Treatment.* Lexington, Mass.: Heath Lexington Books, 1970.

Keve, Paul W. *Imaginative Programming in Probation and Parole.* Minneapolis: University of Minnesota Press, 1967.

King, John F. S. *The Probation Service.* London: Butterworth, 1964.

Klein, Alexander, ed. *Natural Enemies???* Philadelphia: J. B. Lippincott, 1969.

Knulten, Richard, and Stephen Schafer, *Juvenile Delinquency: An Introduction.* New York: Random House, 1970.

Kolb, Lawrence C. *Noyes' Modern Clinical Psychiatry.* Philadelphia: W. B. Saunders, 1968.

Konopka, Gisela. *The Adolescent Girl in Conflict.* Englewood Cliffs, N.J.: Prentice-Hall, 1966.

——. *Therapeutic Group Work with Children.* Minneapolis: University of Minnesota Press, 1949.

Korn, Richard R., and Lloyd W. McCorkle, *Criminology and Penology.* New York: Holt, Rinehart and Winston, 1966.

Kvaraceus, William C. *The Community and the Delinquent.* New York: World Book, 1954.

Kvaraceus, William C., and Miller, Walter B. *Delinquent Behavior.* Washington, D.C.: National Education Association, 1959.

Ladd, John. *The Structure of a Moral Code.* Cambridge, Mass.: Harvard University Press, 1957.

Lander, Bernard. *Towards an Understanding of Juvenile Delinquency.* New York: Columbia University Press, 1954.

Lee, Alfred McClung. *Multivalent Man.* New York: George Braziller, 1966.

Leonard, V. A. *Police Organization and Management.* Brooklyn: The Foundation Press, 1951.

Lerman, Paul. *Delinquency and Social Policy.* New York: Praeger, 1970.

Lewin, Kurt. "Group Decision and Social Change," in *Readings in Social Psychology,* G. E. Swanson, T. M. Newcomb and E. L. Hartley, eds. New York: Holt, 1952.

Lindgren, Henry Clay. *Educational Psychology in the Classroom.* New York: Wiley, 1967.

Lofland, John. *Deviance and Identity.* Englewood Cliffs, N. J.: Prentice-Hall, 1969.

Lombroso, Cesare. *Criminal Man.* New York: G. P. Putnam's, 1911.

Loth, David. *Crime in the Suburbs.* New York: William Morrow, 1967.

Luchins, Abraham S. *Group Therapy: A Guide.* New York: Random House, 1964.

McCord, William Maxwell and Joan McCord. *Psychopathy and Delinquency.* New York: Grune and Stratton, 1956.

McCord, William Maxwell, Joan McCord, and Irving Zola. *Origins of Crime: A New Evaluation of the Cambridge-Somerville Youth Study.* New York: Columbia University Press, 1959.

MacIver, Robert M. *The Prevention and Control of Delinquency.* New York: Atherton Press, 1966.

MacLennon, Beryce W., and Naomi Felsenfeld. *Group Counseling and Psychotherapy with Adolescents.* New York: Columbia University Press, 1968.

March, James G., ed. *Handbook of Organization.* Chicago: Rand McNally, 1965.

Masserman, Jules H. *Current Psychiatric Therapies.* New York: Grune & Stratton, 1969.

Massie, Joseph L. "Management Theory" in *Handbook of Organizations,* James G. March, ed. Chicago: Rand McNally, 1965.

Matza, David. *Becoming Deviant.* Englewood Cliffs, N. J.: Prentice-Hall, 1969.

———. *Delinquency and Drift.* New York: Wiley, 1964.

Mayo, Patricia E. *The Making of a Criminal.* London: Weidenfeld and Nicolson, 1969.

Merton, Robert K., and Robert A. Nisbet. *Contemporary Social Problems.* New York: Harcourt, Brace and World, 1966.

Michaels, J. J. *Disorders of Character.* Springfield, Ill.: Charles C Thomas, 1955.

Miller, Walter B. "The Impact of a 'Total Community' Delinquency Control Project, in *Juvenile Delinquency: A Book of Readings,* Rose Giallombardo, ed. New York: Wiley, 1966.

Mobilization for Youth, Inc. *A Proposal for the Prevention and Control of Delinquency by Expanding Opportunities.* New York: Mobilization for Youth, Inc., 1962.

Mohr, George J., and Marian A. Despres. *The Stormy Decade: Adolescence.* New York: Random House, 1958.

Monger, Mark. *Casework in Aftercare.* London: Butterworth, 1967.

——. *Casework in Probation.* London: Butterworth, 1964.

Morse, Mary. *The Unattached.* Baltimore: Penguin Books, 1965.

Muuss, Rolf E. *Theories of Adolescence.* New York: Random House, 1962.

National Conference of Superintendents of Training Schools and Reformatories. *Institutional Rehabilitation of Delinquent Youth: Manual for Training School Personnel.* Albany, N. Y.: Delmar Publishers, 1962.

Neumeyer, Martin Henry. *Juvenile Delinquency in Modern Society.* New York: Van Nostrand, 1961.

Newman, Charles L. *Sourcebook on Probation, Parole and Pardons.* Springfield, Ill.: Charles C. Thomas, 1964.

Niederhoffer, A. *Behind the Shield.* New York: Doubleday, 1967.

Nikelly, Arthur G., ed. *Techniques for Behavior Change.* Springfield, Ill.: Charles C Thomas, 1971.

Nye, Francis Ivan. *Family Relationships and Delinquent Behavior.* New York: Wiley, 1958.

O'Connor, George W., and Nelson Watson. *Juvenile Delinquency and Youth Crime.* Washington, D.C.: International Association of Chiefs of Police, 1965.

Overton, Alice. "Aggressive Casework," in *Reaching the Unreached,* Sylvan S. Furman, ed. New York: New York City Youth Board, 1952.

Papanek, Ernst, "Delinquency," in *Techniques for Behavior Change,* Arthur G. Nikelly, ed. Springfield, Ill.: Charles C. Thomas, 1971.

Peck, Harris B., and Virginia Bellsmith. *Treatment of the Delinquent Adolescent.* New York: Family Service Association of America, 1954.

Perlman, Helen Harris. *Social Casework.* Chicago: University of Chicago Press, 1957.

——. *So You Want to Be A Social Worker.* New York: Harper, 1962.

Petersen, E., E. G. Plowman, and J. M. Trickett. *Business Organization and Management.* Homewood, Ill.: Irwin, 1962.

Pfiffner, John M., and Frank P. Sherwood. *Administrative Organization.* Englewood Cliffs, N. J.: Prentice-Hall, 1960.

Pins, A. M. *Who Chooses Social Work, When and Why? An Exploratory Study of Factors Influencing Career Choices in Social Work.* New York: Council on Social Work Education, 1963.

Polsky, Howard W. *Cottage Six.* New York: Russell Sage Foundation, 1962.

Powers, Edwin, and Helen Witmer. *Prevention of Delinquency (The Cambridge-Somerville Youth Study).* New York: Columbia University Press, 1951.

Presidents Commission on Law Enforcement and Administration of Justice. *Task Force Report: Juvenile Delinquency and Youth Crime.* Report on Juvenile Justice and Consultants' Papers. Washington, D.C.: Government Printing Office, 1967.

Ramsey, Charles E. *Problems of Youth.* Belmont, Cal.: Dickenson, 1967.

Reckless, Walter C. *The Crime Problem.* New York: Appleton-Century-Crofts, 1961.

Redl, Fritz and David Wineman. *Children Who Hate.* New York: The Free Press, 1951.

——. *Controls from Within.* New York: The Free Press, 1952.

——. *The Aggressive Child.* New York: The Free Press, 1957.

Reiner, Beatrice S., and Irvin Kaufman. *Character Disorders in Parents of Delinquents.* New York: Family Service Association, 1959.

Report of the National Advisory Commission on Civil Disorders, New York: Bantam Books, 1968.

Robins, Lee. *Deviant Children Grown Up.* Baltimore: Williams & Wilkins, 1966.

Robinson, Sophia M. *Juvenile Delinquency.* Holt, Rinehart, and Winston, 1961.

Rogers, Dorothy, ed. *Issues in Adolescent Psychology.* New York: Appleton-Century-Crofts, 1969.

Rosenberg, M. *Occupations and Values.* New York: The Free Press, 1957.

Rosenquist, Carl L., and Edwin I. Megargee. *Delinquency in Three Cultures.* Austin: University of Texas Press, 1966.

Rubin, Sol. *Crime and Juvenile Delinquency.* Dobbs Ferry, N.Y : Oceana, 1961.

Rubington, Earl and Martin S. Weinberg. *Deviance–The Interactionist Perspective.* New York: Macmillan, 1968.

Sagarin, Edward. *Odd Man In.* Chicago: Quadrangle Books, 1969.

Schafer, Stephen, and Richard D. Knudten. *Juvenile Delinquency: An Introduction.* New York: Random House, 1970.

Schasre, Robert., and Jo Wallach, eds. *Readings in Delinquency and Treatment.* Los Angeles: The Delinquency Prevention Training Project, Youth Studies Center, University of Southern California, 1965.

Schein, Edgar H. *Organizational Psychology.* Englewood Cliffs, N. J.: Prentice-Hall, 1965.

Schneiders, Alexander A. *The Psychology of Adolescence.* Milwaukee: Bruce, 1951.

Schwarz, Berthold, and Bartholomew Ruggieri. *Parent-Child Tensions.* Philadelphia: J.B. Lippincott, 1958.

Schwitzgebel, Ralph, *Streetcorner Research.* Cambridge, Mass.: Harvard University Press, 1965.

Sebald, Hans. *Adolescence: A Sociological Analysis.* New York: Appleton-Century-Crofts, 1968.

Seidman, Jerome F. *Adolescent.* New York: The Dryden Press, 1953.

Sellin, Johan T., and Wolfgang, Marvin E. *The Measurement of Delinquency.* New York: Wiley, 1964.

Shaw, Clifford R., and Henry D. McKay. *Juvenile Delinquency and Urban Areas.* Chicago: University of Chicago Press, 1942.

Sheldon, William H. *Varieties of Delinquent Youth.* New York: Harper, 1949.

——. *The Varieties of Temperament: A Psychology of Constitutional Differences.* New York: Harper, 1942.

Sherif, Muzafer, and Carolyn W. Sherif, eds. *Problems of Youth.* Chicago: Aldine, 1954.

Short, James F., and Fred L. Strodtbeck. *Group Process and Gang Delinquency.* Chicago: University of Chicago Press, 1965.

Shulman, Harry Manuel. *Juvenile Delinquency in American Society*. New York: Harper & Row, 1961.

Skolnick, S. H. *Justice Without Trial*. New York: Wiley, 1966.

Slavson, S. R. *Reclaiming the Delinquent*. New York: The Free Press, 1965.

Sower, Christopher, *et. al. Community Involvement*. New York: The Free Press, 1957.

Spergel, Irving A. *Community Problem Solving: The Delinquency Example*. Chicago: University of Chicago Press, 1969.

Stein, Joseph. *Neurosis in Contemporary Society: Process and Treatment*. Belmont, Cal.: Brooks/Cole, 1970.

Steiner, Lee R. *Understanding Juvenile Delinquency*. Philadelphia: Chilton Co., Book Division, 1960.

Sterne, Richard S. *Delinquent Conduct and Broken Homes*. New Haven, Conn.: College and University Press, 1964.

Stone, L. Joseph, and Joseph Church. *Childhood and Adolescence*. New York: Random House, 1957.

Street, David, Robert D. Vinter, and Charles Perrow. *Organization for Treatment*. New York: The Free Press, 1966.

Strong, E.K. *Vocational Interests 18 Years After College*. Minneapolis: University of Minnesota Press, 1955.

Sutherland, Edwin. *The Sutherland Papers,* Albert K. Cohen, Alfred R. Cohen, Alfred R. Lindesmith and Karl F. Schuessler, eds. Bloomington: University of Indiana Press, 1956.

Sutherland, Edwin, and Donald R. Cressey. *Principles of Criminology*. Philadelphia: J. B. Lippincott Company, 1966.

Szurek, S. A., and I. N. Berlin, eds. *The Antisocial Child: His Family and His Community*. Palo Alto, Cal.: Science and Behavior Books, 1969.

Taft, Donald R. *Criminology*. New York: Macmillan, 1956.

Tait, Columbus Downing. *Delinquents, Their Families, and the Community*. Springfield, Ill.: Charles C Thomas, 1962.

Tappan, Paul W. *Juvenile Delinquency*. New York: McGraw-Hill, 1949.

Taylor, Frederick W. *Scientific Management*. New York: Harper, 1911.

Thomas, Edwin J., ed. *Behavioral Approach Applications to Social Work*. New York: Council on Social Work Education, 1967.

Thorp, Roland G., and Ralph J. Wetzel. *Behavior Modification in the Natural Environment*. New York: Academic Press, 1969.

Thrasher, Frederick Milton. *The Gang (1313 Chicago Gangs)*. Chicago: University of Chicago Press, 1936.

Trecker, Harleigh B., ed. *Group Work in the Psychiatric Setting*. New York: Whiteside Inc., and William Morrow, 1956.

Vaz, Edmund. *Middle-Class Juvenile Delinquency*. New York: Harper and Row, 1967.

Walther, R. H. *Job Analysis and Interest Measurement*. Princeton, N. J.: Educational Testing Service, 1964.

——. *The Psychological Dimensions of Work: An Experimental Taxonomy of Occupation.* Washington, D.C.: George Washington University, 1964.

Walther, R. H., S. D. McCune, and R. C. Trojanowicz, *The Contrasting Occupational Cultures of Policemen and Social Workers.* Experimental Publications Systems, Washington, D. C.: American Psychological Association, 1970.

Wattenberg, William W. *The Adolescent Years.* New York: Harcourt, Brace, 1955.

Weaver, Anthony. *They Steal for Love.* New York: International Universities Press, 1959.

Weeks, H. Ashley. *Youthful Offenders at Highfields.* Ann Arbor, Mich.: University of Michigan Press, 1963.

West, Donald. *The Young Offender.* London: Duckworth, 1967.

Whyte, William F. *Street Corner Society.* Chicago: University of Chicago Press, 1955.

Wilensky, H., and C. Lebeaux. *Industrial Society and Social Welfare.* New York: Russell Sage Foundation, 1958.

Wilkerson, David R., with Claire Cox. *Parents on Trial.* New York: Hawthorn Books, 1967.

Wilkins, Leslie T. *Social Deviance—Social Policy, Action and Research.* London: Tavistock, 1959.

Wilson, Harriett. *Delinquency and Child Guidance.* London: George Allen and Unwin, 1962.

Wittenberg, Rudolph M. *The Troubled Generation.* New York: Association Press, 1967.

Wolberg, Lewis R. *The Techniques of Psychotherapy.* New York: Grune and Stratton, 1967.

Wolfgang, Marvin E., Leonard Savitz, and Norman Johnston, eds. *The Sociology of Crime and Delinquency.* New York: Wiley, 1962.

Yalom, Irwin D. *The Theory and Practice of Group Psychotherapy.* New York: Basic Books, 1970.

ARTICLES

Abrahams, Doris Y. "Observations on Transference in a Group of Teen-Age 'Delinquents,'" *International Journal of Group Psychotherapy* 6 (1956).

Abrams, Gene M. "Defining Milieu Therapy," *Archives of General Psychiatry* 21 (1969).

Ackley, Ethel G., and Beverly R. Fliegal. "A Social Work Approach to Street-Corner Girls," *Social Work* 5 (1960).

Adams, Stuart. "Youth Rehabilitation: New Approaches Through Research," *California Youth Authority Quarterly* 3 (1960).

Adamson, LeMay, and H. Warren Dunham, "Clinical Treatment of Male Delinquents: A Case Study in Effort and Result," *American Sociological Review* 21 (1956).

Adler, Jack, and Irwin R. Berman. "Multiple Leadership in Group Treatment of Delinquent Adolescents," *International Journal of Group Psychotherapy* 10 (1960).

Adler, Seymour J. "Effecting Change in Youthful Offenders: Three Case Illustrations," *Federal Probation* 26 (1962).

Aldrich, C. Knight. "Thief," *Psychology Today*, March, 1971.

Allen, James E. "The Silent Observer: A New Approach to Group Therapy for Delinquents," *Crime and Delinquency* 16 (1970).

Allen, Thomas E. "An Innovation in Treatment at a Youth Institution," *Federal Probation* 33 (1969).

Almond, Richard, Kenneth Keniston, and Sandra Boltax. "Milieu Therapeutic Process," *Archives of General Psychiatry* 21 (1969).

Barker, Gordon H., and Adams, W. Thomas. "Glue Sniffers," *Sociology and Social Research* 47 (1963).

Beatie, R. H. "Problems of Criminal Statistics in the United States," *The Journal of Criminal Law, Criminology and Police Science* 46 (1955).

Becker, W. C., D. R. Peterson, L. A. Hellmer, D. J. Shoemaker, and H. C. Quay. "Factors in Parental Behavior and Personality as Related to Problem Behavior in Children," *Journal of Consulting Psychology* 23 (1959).

Berman, Nathan, Jack Purves, and Dorothy Cole. "Casework with Law Violators," *Crime and Delinquency* 7 (1961).

Berne, Eric. "Transactional Analysis: A New and Effective Method of Group Therapy," *American Journal of Psychotherapy* 12 (1958).

Bettelheim, Bruno, and Emmy Sylvester. "The Therapeutic Milieu," *American Journal of Orthopsychiatry* 18 (1948).

Beuhler, R. E., G. R. Patterson, and J. Furniss. "The Reinforcement of Behavior in Institutional Settings," *Behavior Research and Therapy* 4 (1966).

Bilmes, M. "The Delinquent's Escape from Conscience," *American Journal of Psychotherapy* 19 (1965).

Birch, Alison Wryley. "Where Addicts Become Adults," *The Readers Digest*, December, 1970.

Bowman, Paul H. "The Quincy Community Youth Development Project," *Annals of the American Academy of Political and Social Science* 322 (1959).

Brady, John Paul. "Psychotherapy by a Combined Behavioral and Dynamic Approach," *Comprehensive Psychiatry* 9 (1968).

Breidenthal, Don. "The Therapeutic Community, Teamwork, and the Teacher," *California Youth Authority Quarterly* 18 (1965).

Bronfenbrenner, Urie. "Parents Bring Up Your Children!," *Look*, January 26, 1971.

Browning, Charles J. "Differential Impact of Family Disorganization on Male Adolescents," *Social Problems* 8 (1960).

Burchard, J., and V. Tyler. "The Modification of Delinquent Behavior Through Operant Conditioning," *Behavior Research and Therapy* 2 (1965).

Carpenter, Kenneth. "Halfway Houses for Delinquent Youth." Reprinted from United States Department of Health, Education and Welfare, *Children,* November-December, 1963.

Choras, Peter, and Alan A. Stone. "A Strategy for the Initial Stage of Psychotherapy with Adolescents," *American Journal of Psychotherapy,* 24 (1970).

Coleman, Benjamin I. "Reality Therapy with Offenders: II. Practice," *International Journal of Offender Therapy* 14 (1970).

Cressey, Donald, and Rita Volkman. "Differential Association and Rehabilitation of Drug Addicts," *American Journal of Sociology* 69 (1963).

Dalton, Robert H. "Value and Use of Counseling Techniques in the Work of Probation Officers," *Federal Probation* 16 (1952).

Denton, Clifford "The Growing Drug Menace," *Pennsylvania Education* 2 (1970).

———. "Crusade in the Classroom," *Pennsylvania Education* 2 (1970).

Dinitz, Simon, Walter Reckless, and Ellen Murray. "Self-Concept as an Insulator Against Delinquency," *Human Organization* 17 (1958).

Dubin, Robert. "Industrial Workers' Worlds: A Study of the 'Central Life Interests' of Industrial Workers," *Social Problems* 4 (1956).

Elias, Albert. "Innovations in Correctional Programs for Juvenile Delinquents," *Federal Probation* 32 (1968).

Elkin, Frederick, and William A. Westley. "The Myth of Adolescent Culture," *American Sociological Review* 20 (1955).

Elliott, Mabel A. "Group Therapy in Dealing with Juvenile and Adult Offenders," *Federal Probation* 27 (1963).

Epstein, Norman. "III. Activity Group Therapy," *International Journal of Group Psychotherapy* 10 (1960).

Evans, John. "Analytic Group Therapy with Delinquents," *Adolescence* 1 (1966).

Feder, Bud. "Limited Goals in Short-Term Group Psychotherapy with Institutionalized Delinquent Adolescent Boys," *International Journal of Group Psychotherapy* 12 (1962).

Fenton, Norman. "The Prison as a Therapeutic Community," *Federal Probation* 20 (1956).

Ferdinand, Theodore N., "The Offense Patterns and Family Structures of Urban, Village and Rural Delinquents," *Journal oj Criminal Law, Criminology, and Police Science* 55 (1964).

Field, Lewis W. "An Ego-Programmed Group Treatment Approach with Emotionally Disturbed Boys," *Psychological Reports* 18 (1966).

Fike, David F. "Family-Focused Counseling: A New Dimension in Probation," *Crime and Delinquency* 14 (1968).

Franklin, Girard H. "Group Psychotherapy with Delinquent Boys in a Training School Setting," *International Journal of Group Psychotherapy,* IX (1959).

Fried, A. "The Fuld Neighborhood House of Newark, New Jersey, A Work Program for Potential Delinquents," *Annals of the American Academy of Political and Social Science* 322 (1959).

Gadpaille, Warren J. "Observations on the Sequence of Resistances in Groups of Adolescent Delinquents," *International Journal of Group Psychotherapy* 9 (1959).

Gazan, Harold S. "The Informal System—An Agent of Change in Juvenile Rehabilitation," *Crime and Delinquency* 14 (1968).

Ghislane, D. Godenne. "Outpatient Adolescent Group Therapy," *American Journal of Psychotherapy* 19 (1965).

Golombek, Harvey. "The Therapeutic Contact with Adolescents," *Canadian Psychiatric Association Journal* 14 (1969).

Gorlich, Elizabeth H. "Group Methods in Institutional Programming," *Federal Probation* 32 (1968).

Gottesfeld, H. "Professionals and Delinquents Evaluate Professional Methods with Delinquents," *Social Problems* 13 (1965).

Hakeem, Michael. "A Critique of the Psychiatric Approach to Crime and Correction," *Law and Contemporary Problems* 23 (1958).

Harris, Robert L. "Vocational Education as Training and Treatment," *California Youth Authority Quarterly* 18 (1965).

Hartung, Frank E., "A Critique of the Sociological Approach to Crime and Correction," *Law and Contemporary Problems* 23 (1958).

Heacick, Don R. "Modifications of Standard Techniques for Outpatient Group Psychotherapy with Delinquent Boys," *American Journal of Orthopsychiatry* 35 (1965).

Head, Wilson A. "Sociodrama and Group Discussion with Institutionalized Delinquent Adolescents," *Insights* 1 (1966).

Hersko, Marvin. "Group Psychotherapy with Delinquent Adolescent Girls," *American Journal of Orthopsychiatry* 32 (1962).

Hodge, R. W., P. M. Siegel and P. H. Rossi. "Occupational Prestige in the United States, 1925-1963," *American Journal of Sociology* 70 (1964).

Hurlock, Elizabeth B. "American Adolescents of Today—A New Species," *Adolescence* 1 (1966).

Jenkins, Kendall J. "Group Therapy with Wards in the Community," *California Youth Authority Quarterly* 17 (1964).

Jenkins, Richard L. "Motivation and Frustration in Delinquency," *American Journal of Orthopsychiatry* 27 (1957).

——. "Problems of Treating Delinquents," *Federal Probation* 22 (1958).

Kane, Joseph H. "An Institutional Program for the Seriously Disturbed Delinquent Boy," *Federal Probation* 30 (1966).

Kaufman, Irving. "The Psychiatrist in the Institution—Introduction of Mental Health Services into Juvenile Detention Centers and Training Schools," *Crime and Delinquency* 12 (1966).

Kelly, E. L. and L. R. Goldberg. "Correlates of Later Performance and Specializations in Psychology," *Psychological Monographs* 73 (1959).

Kidneigh, J. and H. W. Lundberg. "Are Social Work Students Different?," *Social Work* 3 (1958).

King, C. "Group Therapy with Delinquents in and Out of Institutional Settings," *American Journal of Orthopsychiatry* 35 (1965).

Konopka, Gisela. "Adolescent Delinquent Girls," *Children* 11 (1964).

———. "South Central Youth Project: A Delinquency Control Program," *Annals, American Political, Social Science* 322 (1959).

———. "The Social Group Work Method: Its Use in the Correctional Field," *Federal Probation* 20 (1956).

Larimer, George A., Alvin H. Tucker, and Ellen F. Brown. "Drugs and Youth," *Pennsylvania Health* 31 (1970).

Levinson, Robert B., Gilbert L. Ingram, and Eduardo Azcarte. "'Aversive' Group Therapy— Sometimes Good Medicine Tastes Bad," *Crime and Delinquency* 14 (1968).

Long, Anna Marie, and Samuel I. Kamada. "Psychiatric Treatment of Adolescent Girls," *California Youth Authority Quarterly* 17 (1964).

Lucas, James A. "Therapeutic Use of Limits in Dealing with Institutionalized Delinquent Boys," *Federal Probation* 28 (1964).

Lytle, Milford B. "The Unpromising Client," *Crime and Delinquency* 10 (1964).

McCorkle, Lloyd W. "Guided Group Interaction in a Correctional Setting," *International Journal of Group Psychotherapy* 4 (1954).

McCormack, R. and J. Kidneigh, "The Vocational Interest Patterns of Social Workers," *Social Work Journal* 35 (1959).

Mann J. W. "Adolescent Marginality," *Journal of Genetic Psychology* 106 (1965).

Marohn, Richard C. "The Therapeutic Milieu as an Open System," *Archives of General Psychiatry* 22 (1970).

Massimo, Joseph L., and Milton F. Shore. "A Comprehensive, Vocationally Oriented Psychotherapeutic Program for Delinquent Boys," *American Journal of Orthopsychiatry* 33 (1963).

Mead, George H. "The Psychology of Punitive Justice," *American Journal of Sociology* 23 (1918).

Merton, Robert. "Social Structure and Anomie," *Sociological Review* 3 (1938).

Miller, Walter. "Lower Class Culture as Generating Milieu of Gang Delinquency," *Journal of Social Issues* 14 (1958).

———. "Inter-Institutional Conflict as a Major Impediment to Delinquency Prevention," *Human Organization* 17 (1958).

Monahan Thomas P. "Family Status and the Delinquent Child," *Social Forces* 35 (1957).

Mowrer, O. W. "The Behavior Therapies, with Special Reference to Modeling and Imitation," *American Journal of Psychotherapy* 20 (1966).

Newman, Edward S. "An Experiment in Intensive Probation with Boys," *Crime and Delinquency* 8 (1962).

Nixon, Robert E. "Psychological Normality in Adolescence," *Adolescence* 1 (1966).

Nye, F. Ivan, "The Rejected Parent and Delinquency," *Marriage and Family Living* 18 (1956).

Ordway, John A. "Use of the Offender's Strengths in Psychotherapy," *Crime and Delinquency* 14 (1968).

Papanek, Ernst *"Management of the Acting-Out Adolescent,"* American Journal of *Psychotherapy* 18 (1964).

——. "Re-education and Treatment of Juvenile Delinquents," *American Journal of Psychotherapy* 12 (1958).

Parsons, R. "Relationship Between Psychotherapy with Institutionalized Boys and Subsequent Community Adjustment," *Journal of Consulting Psychology* 31 (1967).

Perl, William R. "Benefits from Including One Psychopath in a Group of Mildly Delinquent Patients," *International Journal of Group Psychotherapy* 6 (1956).

Perlmutter, Felice, and Dorothy Durham. "Using Teen-Agers to Supplement Casework Service," *Social Work* 10 (1965).

Persons, Roy W. "Psychological and Behavioral Changes in Delinquents Following Psychotherapy," *Journal of Clinical Psychology* 20 (1966).

Pierce, F. J. "Social Group Work in a Women's Prison," *Federal Probation* 27 (1963).

Pilnick, Saul, Albert Elias, and Neal W. Clapp. "The Essex-Fields Concept: A New Approach to the Social Treatment of Juvenile Delinquents," *The Journal of Applied Behavioral Science* 2 (1966).

Polsky, Howard W. "Changing Delinquent Subcultures: A Social Psychological Approach," *Social Work* 4 (1959).

Powers, Edwin, "An Experiment in Prevention of Delinquency," *The Annals, The American Academy of Political and Social Science* 261 (1949).

Price, Joseph. "Guided Group Interaction: A Peer Group Approach," *California Youth Authority Quarterly* 10 (1969).

Prigmore, Charles S. "Correction and Social Work," *Crime and Delinquency* 9 (1963).

Rabinow, Irvine. "The Significance of Structure in the Group Release Program." *Journal of Jewish Communal Service* 38 (1962).

Rachman, Arnold W. "Talking It Out Rather than Fighting It Out: Prevention of a Delinquent Gang War by Group Therapy Intervention," *International Journal of Group Psychotherapy* 19 (1969).

Reasons, C. E. "Gault," "Procedural Change and Substantive Effect," *Crime and Delinquency* 16 (1970).

Reckless, Walter, Simon Dinitz, and Barbara Kay. "The Self Component in Potential Delinquency and Non-delinquency," *American Sociological Review* 22 (1957).

Reiss, Albert J., Jr., "Delinquency as the Failure of Personal and Social Controls," *American Sociological Review* 16 (1951).

Reissman, Frank. "The 'Helper' Therapy Principle," *Social Work* 20 (1965).

Rioch, David McK., and Alfred H. Stanton. "Milieu Therapy," *Psychiatry* 16 (1953).

Riscalla, Louise Mead. "Crisis Therapy with Adolescents," *International Journal of Offender Therapy* 14 (1970).

Sarri, Rosemary C., and Robert D. Vinter. "Group Treatment Strategies in Juvenile Correctional Programs." *Crime and Delinquency* 11 (1965).

Scarpitti, Frank R., and Richard M. Stephenson, "The Use of the Small Group in the Rehabilitation of Delinquents," *Federal Probation* 30 (1966).

Schmideberg, Melitta. "Reality Therapy with Offenders: I. Principles," *International Journal of Offender Therapy* 14 (1970).

Schuessler, Karl F., and Donald R. Cressey, "Personality Characteristics of Criminals," *American Journal of Sociology* 55 (1950).

Schulman, Irving. "Modifications in Group Therapy with Anti-Social Adolescents," *International Journal of Group Psychotherapy* 7 (1957).

Schwartz, Martin. "IV. Analytic Group Psychotherapy," *International Journal of Group Psychotherapy* 10 (1960).

Schwitzgebel, R., and D. A. Kolb. "Inducing Change in Adolescent Delinquents," *Behavior Research and Therapy*, 1 (1964).

Schwitzgebel, Ralph R. "Delinquents with Tape Recorders," *New Society*, London, January 31, 1963.

Shah, Saleem A. "Treatment of Offenders: Some Behavioral Concepts, Principles and Approaches," *Federal Probation* 30 (1966).

Sharp, E. Preston. "Group Counseling in a Short-Term Institution," *Federal Probation* 23 (1959).

Shelley, E. L. V., and W. F. Johnson. "Evaluation as Organized Counseling Service for Youthful Offenders," *Journal of Counseling Psychology* 8 (1961).

Shellow, Robert S., Jack L. Ward, and Seymour Rubenfeld. "Group Therapy and the Institutionalized Delinquent," *International Journal of Group Psychotherapy* 8 (1958).

Shepard, George H., and Jessie James, "Police—Do They Belong in the Schools?," *American Education* 3 (1967).

Shoor, Mervin, and Mary H. Speed. "Seven Years of Psychiatric Consultation in a Juvenile Probation Department," *Psychiatric Quarterly* 43 (1969).

Slocum, Walter, and Stone, Carol L., "Family Culture Patterns and Delinquent-Type Behavior," *Marriage and Family Living* 25 (1963).

Sowles, Richard C., and John H. Gill. "Institutional and Community Adjustment of Delinquents following Counseling," *Journal of Counseling and Clinical Psychology* 34 (1970).

Spergel, I. "Selecting Groups for Street Work Service," *Social Work* 10 (1965).

Stranahan, Marion, Cecile Schwartzman, and Edith Atkin. "Activity Group Therapy with Emotionally Disturbed and Delinquent Adolescents," *International Journal of Group Psychotherapy* 7 (1957).

Talor, Alexander. "The Effectiveness of Various Therapeutic Approaches: A Study of Subprofessional Therapists," *International Journal of Group Psychotherapy* 20 (1970).

Taylor, A. J. W. "A Therapeutic Group in Prison," *International Journal of Group Psychotherapy* 11 (1961).

Taylor, Charles W. "An Experiment in Group Counseling with Juvenile Parolees," *Crime and Delinquency* 7 (1961).

Tefferteller, Ruth S. "Delinquency Prevention through Revitalizing Parent-Child Relations," *The Annals of the American Academy of Political and Social Science* 322, (1959).

Terman, L. M., "Scientists and Non-Scientists in a Group of 800 Gifted Men," *Psychology Monographs* 68 (1954).

Tracey, Gerald A. "A Social Worker's Perspective on Social Work in Probation," *Crime and Delinquency* 7 (1961).

Traux, C. B. "Effects of Group Therapy with High Accurate Empathy and Non-possessive Warmth upon Female Institutionalized Delinquents," *Journal of Abnormal Psychology* 71 (1966).

Trojanowicz, John M., and Robert C. Trojanowicz. "The Role of a College Education in Decision Making," *Public Personnel Review* 33 (1972).

Trojanowicz, Robert C. "Factors that Affect the Functioning of Delinquency Prevention Programs," *The Police Chief* 38 (1971).

——. "Inherent Treatment Characteristics in a Halfway House for Delinquent Boys" *Federal Probation* 35 (1971).

——. "Juvenile Delinquency and the Middle Class Parent," *Police* 15 (1971).

——. "Police Community Relations: Problems and Process," *Criminology* 9 (1972).

——. "The Policeman's Working Personality," *The Journal of Criminal Law, Criminology and Police Science* 62 (1971).

——. "The Contrasting Behavior Styles of Policemen and Social Workers," *Public Personnel Review* 32 (1971).

Villeponteaux, Lorenz, Jr. "Crisis Intervention in a Day School for Delinquents," *Crime and Delinquency* 16 (1970).

Vogt, H. "Group Counseling in Probation," *Federal Probation* 25 (1961).

Walker, Glen J. "Group Counseling in Juvenile Probation," *Federal Probation* 22 (1959).

Webb, A. P., and J. Eikenberry, "A Group Counseling Approach to the Acting-Out Pre-Adolescent," *Psychology in the Schools* 1 (1964).

Weiner, Frederick. "Vocational Guidance for Delinquent Boys," *Crime and Delinquency* 11 (1965).

Westman, Jack C. "Group Psychotherapy with Hospitalized Adolescents," *International Journal of Group Psychotherapy* 11 (1961).

Wilkinson, John E., Donald Mullen, and Robert P. Morton. "Sensitivity Training for Individual Growth—Team Training for Organisation Development," *Training and Development Journal* 22 (1968).

Wills, W. David. "The Hawkspur Experiment," *University of Colorado Law Review,* 40 (1968).

Wolk, R. L., and R. Reid. "A Study of Group Psychotherapy Results with Youthful Offenders in Detention," *Group Psychotherapy* 17 (1964).

Zald, Mayer N., and David Street. "Custody and Treatment in Juvenile Institutions," *Crime and Delinquency* 10 (1964).

PAMPHLETS

Adams, S. *Effectiveness of Interview Therapy with Older Youth Authority Wards: An Interim Assessment of the PICO Project.* Research Report No. 20, California Youth Authority, Division of Research, 1961.

Annual Report of Federal Activities in Juvenile Delinquency, Youth Development and Related Fields. Department of Health, Education and Welfare, Social and Rehabilitation Service. Washington, D.C.: U.S. Government Printing Office, 1971.

California Board of Corrections. *Inquiries Concerning Kinds of Treatment for Kinds of Delinquents.* Monograph No. 2, Sacramento, California: Document Section, Printing Division, July, 1961.

Center for Youth and Community Studies. *Training for New Careers.* Washington, D.C.: Office of Juvenile Delinquency and Youth Development, HEW. Washington, D.C.: U.S. Government Printing Office, 1965.

Children's Bureau, U. S. Department of Health, Education and Welfare. *Institutions Serving Delinquent Children: Guides and Goals.* Washington, D. C.: U. S. Government Printing Office, 1957.

Cressey, Donald. *Social Psychological Theory for Using Delinquents to Rehabilitate Delinquents.* Fifth International Criminological Congress, Montreal, 1965.

Delinquency Prevention Reporter. United States Department of Health, Education and Welfare. Washington, D.C.: U.S. Government Printing Office, 1971.

Delinquency Today, A Guide for Community Action. United States Department of Health, Education and Welfare. Washington, D.C.: U.S. Government Printing Office, 1971.

Empey, Lamar T. and Steven G. Lubeck. "Delinquency Prevention Strategies," U.S. Department of Health, Education and Welfare, Social and Rehabilitation Service, Youth Development and Delinquency Prevention Administration. Washington, D.C.: U.S. Government Printing Office, 1970.

Gula, Martin. *Agency Operated Group Homes,* U.S. Department of Health, Education and Welfare, Washington, D.C.: Government Printing Office, 1964.

Juvenile Delinquency Planning. A joint publication of the United States Department of Health, Education and Welfare, Social and Rehabilitation Service, Youth Development and Delinquency Prevention Administration; and the United States Department of Justice, Law Enforcement Assistance Administration. Washington, D.C.: U.S. Government Printing Office, 1971.

Juvenile Delinquency Prevention in the United States. U. S. Department of Health, Education and Welfare, Children's Bureau. Washington, D.C.: U.S. Government Printing Office, 1965.

Knight, Doug, *The Marshall Program" Assessment of a Short-Term Institutional Treatment Program.* Research Report #'s 56 and 59. State of California: Department of the Youth Authority, 1969-1970.

MacLennan, Beryce W. *Children's Groups as Socializing and Rehabilitating Agents.* Washington, D. C.: Center for Youth and Community Studies, Howard University, 1965.

Martin, John J. *Delinquency Today: A Guide for Community Action.* Office of Juvenile Delinquency and Youth Development. Washington, D.C.: U.S. Government Printing Office, 1962.

Martin John J. *Toward a Political Definition of Delinquency.* United States Department of Health, Education and Welfare, Social and Rehabilitation Service, Youth Development and Delinquency Prevention Administration. Washington, D.C.: U.S. Government Printing Office, 1970.

Minneapolis Police Department, *The Police-School Liaison Program.* A Final Report Submitted to the Office of Law Enforcement Assistance Regarding Their Grant #31. Minneapolis, Minn.: November, 1968.

Molamud, D. and J. R. Dumpson. *Working with Teenage Gangs.* Welfare Council of New York City, 1950.

The Mott Foundation. *The Police-School Liaison Program.* Brochure prepared for distribution to interested agencies. Flint, Mich.: The Mott Foundation, 1971.

——. *Positive Action for Youth.* Flint, Mich.: The Mott Foundation.

National Strategy to Prevent Delinquency, U. S. Dept. of H.E.W., Social and Rehabilitation Service, Youth Development and Delinquency Prevention Administration. Washington, D. C.: U. S. Government Printing Office, 1971.

The Neighborhood Youth Corps: Hope and Help for Youth. U. S. Department of Health, Education and Welfare, Manpower Administration. Washington, D.C.: U.S. Government Printing Office, 1969.

New York City Youth Board. *Reaching Adolescents.* Monograph No. 3. New York: New York City Youth Board, 1955.

Personality Improvement Program of Genesee County. Distributed by the Genesee County Probate Court, Flint, Michigan.

Scheirer, Ivan, Dr., Director, National Information Center on Volunteers in Courts, *Catalog of Volunteer Program Leadership Publications.* Boulder, Colorado, P. O. Box 2150.

Seckel, Joachim P. *The Fremont Experiment: Assessment of Residential Treatment at a Youth Authority Reception Center.* Sacramento: State of California Department of Youth Authority, 1967.

Statistics on Public Institutions for Delinquent Children, 1967. Children's Bureau Statistical Series, No. 94. Washington, D.C.: U.S. Government Printing Office, 1969.

Thomas, Mason P. Jr. "Juvenile Corrections—Five Issues to be Faced". U.S. Department of H.E.W., Social and Rehabilitation Service, Youth Development and Delinquency Prevention Administration. Washington, D.C.: U.S. Government Printing Office, 1971.

INDEX

A

Abrahamson, David, 68
Academic resources in community, use of, in treating delinquents, 268
Ackerman, Nathan W., 99
"Acting out," 74
Action for Appalachian Youth, 205
Activity therapy, 259-60
Adaptive behavior (*See* Behavior, adaptive)
Addiction, human, 57
Adjudication, formal, undesirability of, for juveniles, 164-65
Administrative management theory, 130-43 (*See also* Organization, Classical view of)
Adolescence
  cultural perspective of, 90-94
    erratic and hostile behavior in, 95-96
  in industrialized and technologically advanced countries, 91

Adolescence (*contd.*)
  physical changes of, 89
  in primitive societies, 91
  problems in early stages of, 94-95
  problems in transition from early stages of, 95
  psychological changes of, 89-90
  in United States, 91
  vacillation of behavior during, 98
Adolescent, the
  American, 90
  general status of, in society, 101
  lack of outside resources on guidance of, 82-83
  normal, 94-97
  working with, 104-106
  requirements for success in, 105
Adolescent gang, rites of passage of, 92
Adolescent period, as transition from pleasure to reality, 99
Adult behavior codes, adolescent submission to, 96
Adult values, adolescent questioning of, 79-80